D1191616

SERENITY

ROLE PLAYING GAME

WRITTEN AND DESIGNED BY
Jamie Chambers

BASED ON THE MOTION PICTURE SCREENPLAY WRITTEN BY
Joss Whedon

Additional Design: James Davenport, Tracy Hickman, Tony Lee, Andrew Peregrine, Nathaniel C.J.S. Rockwood, Lester Smith, Christopher Thrash, James M. Ward, Margaret Weis
Chapter Fiction: Margaret Weis • Editing: Christoffer Trossen
Chinese Translation: Tony Lee • Cover Art & Interior Graphic Design: 11th Hour (Susan Renée Tomb)
Layout & Typesetting: Jamie Chambers • Art Direction: Renae Chambers
Illustrations: Lindsay Archer, Dan Bryce, Ryan Wolfe

Playtesting: Dylon Abend, Eben P. Alguire, Cam Banks, Kelly Barron, Damon Black, Carl "Browncoat 1" Boothe, Peter F. Daigle, David Dankel, Steve Darlington, Jason Giardino, Chris Goodwin, Digger Hayes, Stephen Herron, Jason "Padre" Driver, Jack Kessler, Tobin Melroy, Jason Mical, Andrew Morris, Mike Nudd, Angela Rienstra, David Ross, Matthew W. Somers, Richard W. Spangle, Jennifer L. Stevens, Kevin Stoner, Clark Valentine, Jeffrey A. Webb, Floyd C. Wesel, Trampas Whiteman, Richard E. Wilhite III, Mitch A. Williams, John Wolf, Yuri Zahn

Special Thanks: Veronika Beltran, Christi Cardenas, Cindy Chang, Joss Whedon

Dedication: Jamie would like to thank Jimmie Chambers, Jim McClure, Don Lewis, and the rest of the "Space Dungeon" game group. Somewhere out there, the *Blackhawk* is still flyin'.

© 2005 Universal Studios Licensing LLLP. Serenity © Universal Studios. All Rights Reserved. Margaret Weis Productions and the MW Logo are trademarks owned by Margaret Weis Productions, Ltd. All Rights Reserved.

Published by
Margaret Weis Productions, Ltd.
253 Center St #126
Lake Geneva, WI 53147

Fourth Printing—2006
Printed in the USA

margaret weis
productions, ltd.

CONTENTS

INTRODUCTION

HERE'S HOW IT IS

SERENITY

Serenity—a beautiful word that conjures images of peace. *Serenity*—a state of being. No anxiety, no cares in this world. *Serenity*—a place not easily reached. Leastways not without eating a bullet or diving out an airlock. Everyone strives for Serenity in this life. Few find it in this life.

Serenity is also a motion picture from Universal Pictures, a science-fiction adventure from the mind of Joss Whedon (a fellow who has earned himself both Emmy and Academy Award nominations). The film combines action, drama, comedy, and a unique perspective on a new kind of science fiction universe.

Inside the film's universe (usually called the 'Verse), Serenity is a valley on the planet Hera. Nothing special in its own right, this valley was the site of the bloodiest fighting during the Unification War. In Serenity Valley, the Alliance Government delivered a crushing defeat to the Independent Faction, sealing the ultimate course of the war. Countless thousands perished in Serenity Valley, and with them died the hope for freedom. Among the rebel Browncoats—so-called for the long dusters they wore—who were defeated that day in Serenity Valley was a young sergeant name of Malcolm Reynolds.

Serenity is also a spaceship, a Firefly Class transport owned by Captain Malcolm Reynolds, a man not yet ready to forget why he fought in the war. Determined to live by their own rules, Mal and his crew sail the black, taking on odd jobs as they come. *Serenity* is home to a group of disparate people: a cheerful mechanic, a hard-bitten mercenary, two professional soldiers, a wise-cracking pilot, a beautiful and seductive Companion, a "Shepherd," a mentally scarred young girl and her brilliant doctor brother. This group, brought together by accident or fate, has become *Serenity's* family.

Together or apart, they work to keep flyin'.

ROLE PLAYING GAME?

You probably picked up this book knowing a little something about the 'Verse, but maybe you haven't the slightest notion of what a role playing game is. After a quick flip through the book, you might even think the game is strange and all manner of intimidatin'. Don't fret—this game really is simple. Child's play, as a matter of fact.

Kids play role playing games every day without ever thinking about it. Cowboys and Indians is good clean fun. Everyone has a part to play—good or bad—and the guns and tomahawks are all imaginary. No one ever "wins" because the goal is simply to

have a good time. A tabletop role playing game (such as the *Serenity Role Playing Game*) is pretty much the same, only it happens to have a few rules to help you figure out things like what happens when a bullet hits you and just how bad it'll hurt. After all, every game has to have some rules to keep things fair. Games also need a bit of unpredictability. In card games that means shuffling the deck. In our role playing game, we use funny looking dice. Above all, remember the most important rule: it's all about the fun.

THE SERENITY ROLE PLAYING GAME

Think of this book as a set of tools—papery, wordified tools that aren't so good for hammering in nails, but will help you recreate all of the adventure, drama, danger, and humor in the movie, *Serenity*. Think of the game as a form of group storytelling, where the only limits are those set by the players. All you need are a few friends, some of those "funny looking" dice, and your imagination.

Everyone has a role to play in this game. One of the players takes the role of Game Master ("GM"), a person who is part referee and part storyteller. The rest play the parts of the main characters in the story, whose fortunes are determined by the choices they make during the course of play and by the luck of the dice. Do you and your group want to play the crew of *Serenity*? Shiny! The ship and its crew are fully detailed and ready to use. We have provided additional sample characters for you to play, but you can always create an all-new crew with their own ship.

If you're new to role playing and don't have an experienced player on-hand to show you the ropes, we recommend you visit the resources we've made available as well as fan-generated material linked to from our website at **www.serenityrpg.com**. Or maybe your group of players wants to find a ship, find a crew, and start flyin'. No matter how you want to play, the rules in this book will get you started and help you and your friends find adventure and action, fame and fortune in the 'Verse.

The style of your game is entirely up to you and your group. You might want to try some "one-shot" adventures, where you play through one self-contained story. The next time you play you start with a whole new story, and maybe even with whole new characters. Most role players prefer "campaign-style" play, which is a lot like a television series or movie franchise. Each player plays the same character every game session with each "adventure" building upon the story that has gone before, just like the next episode in a series.

Along the way, each character will discover things about himself and his fellow crew members. He'll make friends and enemies, learn new skills, and improve old ones. The 'Verse is a dangerous place. If you're clever and more than a bit lucky, your character will survive. If not... Well, you can always "roll up" a new character.

Before you go jumping ahead with the adventure, take some time and read over a few basics of the *Serenity Role Playing Game*.

CREW

The most important characters are the crew, the "stars" of the game. These are the Player Characters (PCs) you and your fellow players create (minus the Game Master, whose role is different). In the film, the crew consists of Captain Malcolm Reynolds and the rest of *Serenity's* family. Supporting roles are played by the GM. These are called Non-Player Characters (NPCs). In the film, the NPCs are The Operative, Alliance soldiers, Feds, and the Reavers, as well as bit parts like the bank tellers on Lilac.

Each player creates one crew character and controls what that character does and says during the game. The amount of detail you put into your character's personality and background is entirely up to you. Of course, the more detail you provide at the beginning, the easier it will be to figure how your character will react during the game.

When you're creating your character, you have a lot of options open to you. You don't have to play yourself. In fact, you could (and many would say should) distinguish yourself from your character. Your character can be as physically, emotionally, and mentally different from you as you want. Crew can even be of entirely different genders—a guy can play Zoe, a gal can play Jayne, and so on.

Some characters like Jayne and Simon may not get along inside the story of the game, but everyone should be friends when they are not in character. Keep arguments and such nonsense inside the game. Remember—it's all about having fun and telling exciting stories.

GAME MASTER

One player needs to take charge of the game, and take on extra responsibilities. That's the Game Master. The GM creates the basic outline of the story that the crew will follow and plays the part of all the NPCs—all those people the crew meets during their adventures. The GM is the players' window into the 'Verse. The GM tells the players what they see and hear (and smell and taste and feel). But the GM needs to remember that the crew are the stars of this tale. The players have to make

their own choices in the story—meaning they'll get themselves into trouble all by their lonesomes! The GM has to think on his feet and adjust the story when the unexpected happens. (And it will happen!)

Another role the GM plays is that of arbiter. The GM will be the only person who knows all the facts in the game. As there will probably be some disagreements, the GM settles any arguments over the game rules or questions about character creation or how the story develops. Final decisions rest with the GM, but he should remember that his chief job is to help everyone have fun. Fair play is a part of that notion. After all, with power and authority comes responsibility. (If you're the GM, you'd much rather be like Mal than an Alliance stooge, right?) The GM needs to be fair, while still keeping things fun for everyone.

SESSIONS, ADVENTURES, AND CAMPAIGNS

If you're not familiar with role playing games, you probably don't know the difference between "sessions," "adventures" and "campaigns". We'll fix that in a jiffy.

A "session" is whenever you and your group sit down to play one installment of the game. A session can last a whole day or just a few hours. Depending on what happens, you might be able to play through an entire story or just a small bit. Since most of you have jobs or school or families to eat up your time, you should probably schedule your game sessions in advance (including how long the session will last). Some people like to play once (or more) every week, while others get together less frequently. How often and how long you play is up to you and your group. Plan ahead and be considerate of everyone's schedule.

An "adventure" is a single story that is generally played out over several sessions. An adventure has a beginning, a middle, and an end, just like an episode of a television show. Some adventures can last a single session, but only if the adventure is very short. Normally, it will take a crew a few sessions to complete a single adventure.

A "campaign" is a series of adventures that ties the characters and stories together into a larger story, much like an entire television series. The campaign can be "episodic," where the adventures don't share many common threads. Or it might have an arc that ties several adventures together into an interweaving storyline. Most groups usually prefer campaign play because it gives them more chances for character development and allows them to be part of a much larger drama.

THE DICE

The *Serenity Role Playing Game* uses six different types of polyhedral (multi-sided) dice. That's not quite as scary as it sounds. You roll the die type called for by the game and use the result rolled.

d2 • d4 • d6 • d8 • d10 • d12

The dice are mostly self-explanatory (a d4 has four sides, a d6 has six sides, and so on), except for the d2. While you might be able to purchase six-sided dice with only 1s and 2s on the faces, it's just as easy to use a normal d6. A roll of 1–3 indicates a 1, while 4–6 means a 2. You can also be able to purchase a blank die and mark it with 1s and 2s yourself.

You can purchase gaming dice at almost any hobby or book store that sells role playing games. Beginners find it helpful to have dice of different colors so to tell them apart, while others pride themselves on matching sets of dice.

One thing to note is that in our game, larger (with a better range of numbers) dice are always better than small, and it is always better to roll high than low.

GAME BASICS

Here are a few basic concepts so you can understand how the *Serenity Role Playing Game* works. The game rules cover a lot of ground, but the fundamentals are not hard to grasp.

Attributes: Characters in the 'Verse have six Attributes to represent their most basic abilities. Half the Attributes are mental, half are physical. The six Attributes are Agility, Strength, Vitality, Alertness, Intelligence, and Willpower. Each Attribute has a die type.

Skills: These reflect a character's training and education, even things that are self-taught. Each Skill has a die type.

The Core Mechanic: Almost every time a character does something, he rolls an Attribute and a Skill die and adds the results together. If the combined roll is high enough, he succeeds at his action!

Steps: Some circumstances make an action easier or harder. The dice can change in "steps," changing the die type to a higher or lower value.

For more information about running *Serenity* adventures and campaigns, see Chapter Six: *Out in the Black*.

GEAR

The good news is that you don't need tons of equipment to play the game. Each group needs a copy of the rulebook, pencils and paper, and a set of gaming dice. (You also need friends and imagination, but we figure you've already got those covered!) No boards, computer parts, upgrade cards, duct tape, or additional cabling are required.

You'll want a quiet area where your game won't disturb anyone, and where your group won't be distracted by noise and activity. Sometimes the GM is the host, but any place that suits your needs and everyone can agree upon will do. Usually, groups like to play around a table, but that isn't necessary. As long as everyone has a comfy chair and a level place to roll their dice, just about anywhere will do.

Optional items include pizza, chips, and soda—though eating something healthy once in a while is recommended. Alliance hospitals are expensive and far away.

THE 'VERSE

You might be a *Serenity* fan ready to jump into gaming for the first time or you might be an experienced gamer ready to try a new system and find out just what the 'Verse is all about.

If you listened in school, you already know that the 'Verse is a huge planetary system with a whole heap of inhabited planets and moons. Much of the real estate has been terraformed—a long and hazardous process—to support human life. Spaceships of every size sail the black in between.

The central Core planets—them as formed the Alliance—decided to unite all the outer worlds under their rule. Some people didn't take kindly to that notion and fought hard to maintain their independence. The Unification War ended some seven years ago, after the Independents suffered a crushing defeat at Serenity Valley on the planet Hera. Since the war, many rebels drifted to the edges of the system. Here they take on work as they can find it, determined to live as free as they can in a 'Verse strictly controlled by the Alliance government. Memories of the war still claim a powerful hold on those who fought in it—on both sides.

On the central (or "Core") planets, life is good, flush with technology. The rich and prosperous have laser guns, holo-scanners, and flying cars. Food, shelter, and health care are readily available—which gives folk time to think on more than the basics.

On the outer worlds, known as the Rim, folks have to make do with the most basic technologies. Newly terraformed worlds are raw and primitive. Lacking paved roads, people ride horses. Lacking lasers, they make do with bullets. Survival takes precedence over good manners and education, which is why some Core world folk consider those on the Rim to be a bunch of ignorant hicks. And while the Alliance rules over the Border planets in theory, enforcement is a mite spotty, so most folks go armed for their own security.

Strung between the Rim and the Core is the Cortex—a system-wide information network that can be accessed on ships or groundside with a terminal or dedicated sourcebox. News, communication, law enforcement bulletins, and online shopping are all available. Nodes are placed throughout the system, allowing for unrestricted information to be accessed just about anywhere by just about anyone.

OUT TO THE BLACK...

How your crew fits into the greater scheme is up to you. Most likely your crew aren't important military types off to discover strange new worlds, but rather working class folk who simply want to keep flyin'. You might have a ship, but it's probably an older, refurbished model that flies only with equal helpings of love and luck and a whole heap of duct tape. The ship is freedom—from your enemies and the ghosts of your past. The 'Verse is a harsh place, and if you ain't workin', you ain't earnin'.

The 'Verse is big. There are plenty of places to find work and just as many places to hide if the Alliance gets wind of your doings. Keep true to your integrity, do right by people, and work may come find you.

Freedom is out there, waiting.

Find a ship. Find a crew. Keep Flyin'.

MAL
CAPTAIN OF SERENITY

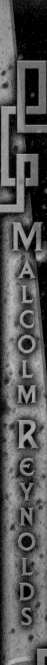
MALCOLM REYNOLDS

ATTRIBUTES

Agility d6

Strength d8

Vitality d10

Alertness d6

Intelligence d8

Willpower . . . d10

Life Points 22

Initiative . . . . d6 + d6

Skills

Skill	Rating
Animal Handling	d6
Athletics	d6
- Dodge	d8
Covert	d6
Discipline	d6
- Leadership	d8
Guns	d6
- Pistol	d12
- Rifle	d8
Heavy Weapons	d6
Influence	d4
Medical Expertise	d2
Perception	d4
Pilot	d4
Planetary Vehicles	d2
Survival	d6
Unarmed Combat	d6
- Brawling	d10

W

LIFE POINTS

S

WEAPONS & EQUIPMENT

Pistol - Mal has carried his service pistol since the Unification War and wears it on his hip whenever the situation warrants. The gun holds 8 rounds per clip, and can fire up to 3 times per turn. Damage d6W. Range Increment 100 ft.

Mal usually wears the long "Browncoat" that instantly identifies him as a former Independent soldier to any war veteran.

TRAITS

Fightin' Type (Major Asset) - Mal is always ready for a tussle and can handle himself in a fight.

Friends in Low Places (Minor Asset) - As someone who engages in clandestine dealings, Mal knows lots of smugglers, thieves, and low-lives.

Leadership (Major Asset) - Mal has a tendency to inspire loyalty in those who serve under him.

Military Rank (Minor Asset) - Mal is a war veteran, having fought with the Independents through the war and survived the Battle of Serenity Valley.

Tough as Nails (Minor Asset) - Mal can take more punishment than most folks, leading some to underestimate him.

Deadly Enemy (Minor Complication) - A psychotic crime lord with a penchant for robbing trains is hunting Mal down, seeking revenge.

Credo (Major Complication) - Mal has a strong personal code of honor that he will not violate, which includes honoring his side of an agreement whenever possible.

Loyal (Minor Complication) - Mal is devoted to his crew and former Browncoats he served with in the war.

Prejudice (Minor Complication) - As a former Independent soldier, Mal takes an irrational dislike to Alliance feds and military officers.

Things Don't Go Smooth (Major Complication) - Mal has absolutely terrible luck, with even the simplest plans somehow going awry.

ROLE PLAYING NOTES

"Find a ship. Find a crew. Keep flyin'. I found a ship, name of *Serenity*. I found a crew. Some I didn't go looking for, but they're here and so long as they work to keep us flyin', they'll stay.

"Name's Malcolm Reynolds. I'm captain of *Serenity*. Some call me 'Mal.' Others call me 'Captain.' I answer to both, so long as it's understood who's in command. Which would be me.

"I was born on Shadow. Family owned a ranch there. Mother raised me, along with a few dozen hired hands. She saw to it that I had a goodly amount of schooling, though that's nothing I brag on. Our hired hands saw to it I had a good amount of schooling, too, though not of the same sort. My mother taught me to play the gentleman's part at a fancy dress ball. The ranch foreman taught me how to shoot my way out of that fancy dress ball, if I had to.

"Mother raised me to be a man of faith. I lost that faith in Serenity Valley. Found something else there, though. More on that to come.

"The central planets' government—the Alliance—was always trying to meddle in our affairs. Their meddling got worse and worse and finally some of us lost our stomach for it. When the Unification War broke out, I volunteered for the side that believed a man should be able to live his life pretty much as he wants, so long as he doesn't take to harming others, with no one havin' the right to tell him what to think or how to think it. Our side was called many things, 'Independents,' 'Browncoats.' Our side lost.

"I was Sergeant Malcolm Reynolds then, of the 57th Overlanders. We were stationed on Hera, in Serenity Valley, during what turned out to be one of the bloodiest battles of the war. We held out against overwhelming numbers for seven weeks—two of those after our sorry-assed commanders had surrendered. Took sixty-eight percent casualties. Me and Zoe—her as is part of my crew—were the only two as came out of the 57th breathin'. I won't say alive.

"It was there I found that all a man should put his faith in is his ship, that which keeps him flyin'. Thus, the name, *Serenity*.

"As for knowin' some things about me. I'm a man of my word. If I take a job, I do the job. When I do a job, I get paid. If that don't happen, there's like to be trouble.

"I keep to the border planets, mostly. Stay away from the Alliance. I've been bound by law five times and the experience was not pleasuresome. Charges never stuck, though.

"I'm still flyin'."

—Conversation with Malcolm Reynolds

ZOE
FIRST MATE OF SERENITY

ATTRIBUTES

Agility d8

Strength d10

Vitality d8

Alertness d8

Intelligence d6

Willpower d6

Life Points 14

Initiative . . . . d8 + d8

Skills

Athletics	d6
Covert	d6
- Stealth	d10
Discipline	d6
Guns	d6
- Rifle	d10
- Shotgun	d10
Heavy Weapons	d6
Mechanical Engineering	d4
Medical Expertise	d2
Melee Weapons	d4
Perception	d6
Pilot	d4
Planetary Vehicles	d6
Ranged Weapons	d4
Survival	d4
Unarmed Combat	d6
- Brawling	d8

LIFE POINTS

W

S

WEAPONS & EQUIPMENT

Hogleg - Zoe's weapon of choice is handy both for shooting ornery folks and using the butt as a club. It holds up to 10 shells at once, and can fire up to 2 times per combat turn. Damage d10W. Range Increment 10 feet.

Armor - Whenever Zoe know she's walking into danger, she wears a ballistic mesh vest for protection. It converts up to 8 Wounds per attack to her torso from any gunfire attack to Stun, but slows her down slightly, reducing her Agility by –1 step for Athletics-based actions.

Zoe usually carries a utility knife (Damage d2W), a small compass, and a small personal comm-set that is tuned to *Serenity*'s standard frequency.

TRAITS

Fightin' Type (Major Asset) - As a career soldier, Zoe is ready for action.

Military Rank (Minor Assset) - She is a former corporal in the Independent army.

Steady Calm (Major Asset) - Zoe always keeps a cool head in dangerous situations.

Loyal (Minor Complication) - She would do most anything for her captain and her husband

Memorable (Minor Complication) - Zoe's exotic beauty makes her stand out in the memories of most folk.

Prejudice (Minor Complication) - As a former Browncoat, Zoe carries smoldering anger toward Alliance government officials, law enforcement, and military.

ROLE PLAYING NOTES

"First known to me as Corporal Alleyne. She was and is my right hand. She is as true a friend as a man can ever have. I've trusted her with my life more times than there are stars in the black.

"As to her raisin' and upbringing, I guess she'll tell you about that if she thinks it needful. What she generally says is that she was born in the black, raised to life aboard a ship. Like me, she volunteered to fight the Alliance and, like me, she was in Serenity Valley. Like me, she came out breathin'.

"Our views on life being much the same, she agreed to throw in her lot with me and come on board *Serenity* as First Mate. I must say that Zoe didn't seem to think much of the ship when first she set eyes on her. Nor did she think much of the man I hired as our pilot, a fellow called Wash.

"I've got to admit that he did take some getting used to, what with his palm tree shirts and fairly constant wisecracking, but, as I told her, he is good at his job. And I'm the captain.

"Well, Zoe and Wash flung Chinese cuss-words at one another on a regular basis and I thought that probably bullets was like to follow until I took to noticin' that all their rows seemed to end up in the bunk of one or t'other.

"Before I know it, Zoe—who can creep up on a man and slit his throat so fast and so silent that he's in the Bad Place before he knows what hit him—starts getting all melty and tearsome whenever Wash's name comes up. And he turns into a moon-brained calf at the sight of her. I don't recommend shipboard romances, as they tend to complicate things, but glad to tell they set about marrying each other, a sure-fire way to cure romance if I ever saw one.

"Now that they're hitched, we're mostly back to normal, what with the Chinese-flingin' and the bunk-sharing. There's a store of love between them, but since it doesn't get in the way of the flyin', I'm fine with it.

"Zoe is still my right hand.

"She and me stand back-to-back, always."

—Conversation with Malcolm Reynolds

WASH
EXPERT PILOT

HOBAN WASHBURNE

ATTRIBUTES

Agility d10

Strength d6

Vitality d6

Alertness d8

Intelligence d8

Willpower d6

Life Points 12

Initiative . . d10 + d8

Skills

Skill	Value
Athletics	d4
Discipline	d6
- Concentration	d8
Guns	d4
Influence	d6
Knowledge	d6
Mechanical Engineering	d4
Perception	d6
- Sight	d8
Performance	d4
Planetary Vehicles	d6
Pilot	d6
- Astrogation	d8
- Mid-bulk Transports	d12 + d2
- Short-Range Shuttles	d8
Technical Engineering	d4

LIFE POINTS

W

S

WEAPONS & EQUIPMENT

Wash doesn't normally carry a gun. He's typically dressed in a Hawaiian shirt, blue jeans, and sneakers. His billfold contains an Alliance 5 credit note and his shirt pocket holds a pack of cinnamon-flavored chewing gum.

TRAITS

Born Behind the Wheel (Major Asset) - Wash's reaction times are amazing when piloting a spaceship.

Lightweight (Minor Complication) - Wash gets drunk easily, and succumbs to other assaults on his constitution more quickly than most.

Sharp Sense (Minor Asset) - Keen eyesight is a great advantage when flying.

Talented: Pilot (Minor Assset) - Wash took to flying like a duck to water (not that he ever got to see a duck on his home planet, but hey).

ROLE PLAYING NOTES

"Wash often tells those that care (and those that don't) how he was raised on a planet that was so polluted he never saw the stars. Only black he saw came belching out of a smokestack. He says he turned space pilot for one reason and that was to breathe clean air. Given that space is a vacuum... Well, Wash thinks it's funny.

"He came to me with the reputation for being one of the best damn pilots in the 'Verse and I will say for him that he has more than lived up to that high claim. Which is the main reason I overlook such things as his taste in wearin' apparel, that tends to run to the garish and bright-colored, and his toys—namely dinosaurs—that have frequent rows on top of the control panel.

"Wash can fly anything that's space worthy and more than a few things that ain't. He can land this ship on a pocket handkerchief, should you care to set one down here on the bar. He can make *Serenity* give him more than she'll give anyone else, 'cept maybe me.

"Wash is a man I can count on to stay with the ship when Jayne and Zoe and me are out on a job. I know staying behind ain't easy for him. I know he worries about his wife considerable.

"I also know that Wash'll be where I need him to be when I need him to be there. And that's not nothin'."

—Conversation with Malcolm Reynolds

JAYNE
THE MERCENARY

ATTRIBUTES

Agility d6

Strength d10

Vitality d10

Alertness d6

Intelligence d4

Willpower d6

Life Points 18

Initiative . . . . d6 + d6

Skills	
Athletics	d6
- Dodge	d8
Covert	d6
Discipline	d4
Guns	d6
- Assault Rifle	d10
- Pistol	d8
- Rifle	d10
Melee Weapons	d4
Perception	d4
Ranged Weapons	d6
Pilot	d4
Survival	d4
Unarmed Combat	d6
- Brawling	d8

LIFE POINTS

W

S

WEAPONS & EQUIPMENT

Pistol - Jayne has an impressive gun collection and this piece is reliable and can be easily concealed. It holds 8 rounds per clip, and can fire up to 3 rounds per turn. Damage d6W. Range Increment 100 ft.

Vera - Six men came to kill Jayne one day, and the best of them carried a customized Callahan full-bore autolock. It's now his very favorite gun, and he named it "Vera." Vera can fire as single-shot or burst up to three times per turn, or full autofire as a full-turn action. Damage d8W. Range Increment 150 ft.

Jayne wears a t-shirt, trousers, and boots with a combat knife (Damage d4W) tucked away just in case.

TRAITS

Crude (Minor Complication) - Jayne is given to rude behavior and foul language. Good thing the Cap'n don't pay him to talk pretty.

Fightin' Type (Major Asset) - A professional mercenary, Jayne can handle himself in everything from a barroom brawl to full-scale gunfight.

Greedy (Minor Complication) - Jayne loves money more than most anything else. If the money's good enough, he'll get stupid.

Intimidatin' Manner (Minor Asset) - Jayne's physical presence and mean scowl can intimidate folk who don't know him.

Mean Left Hook (Minor Asset) - Years of hitting things have left Jayne's fists as hard as rocks.

Tough as Nails (Minor Asset) - Jayne can take more punishment than one might expect.

ROLE PLAYING NOTES

"Don't know much about Jayne Cobb, 'cept that his mother is still livin' and must think right highly of her son, 'cause she knits him these cunning little hats and sends them to him via the post. He must think right highly of his mother, 'cause he wears them.

"Jayne's not got over much fryin' in his brain pan, if you take my meaning. He does know one thing inside out and upside down and that's guns.

"Fact is, when Zoe and I first met Jayne, we were both of us staring down the wrong end of his gun after he and some fellows he was runnin' with got the drop on us. Now I could see right off that Jayne was the type of man what would always sell himself to the highest bidder. Just had to keep him listening long enough to promise of ten percent of the take and his own bunk. Jayne concluded a shift of allegiance was in order, along with a shift in his gun barrel from me to his late partners.

"He's been flyin' with me ever since.

"Jayne can handle any sort of firearm ever made. There's none better at shootin', 'cept maybe me. He's right handy with his fists, too. And he plays the guitar. Not sure why.

"Downside to Jayne—he has a crude mouth, a quick temper, and he's not altogether what you might call trustworthy. He's had a couple of chances to sell me out, but so far, the money hasn't been good enough. One day the money will be good enough.

"When it comes, that day will be an interesting day for us both."

—Conversation with Malcolm Reynolds

JAYNE COBB

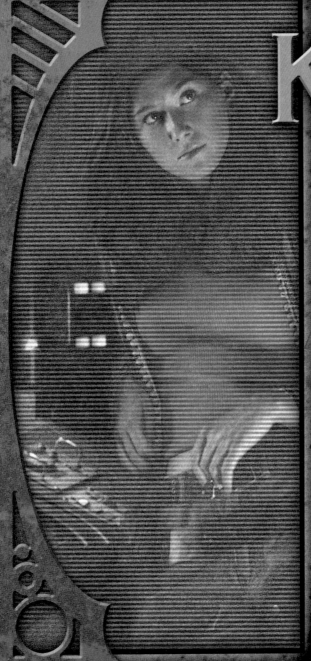

宁静角色扮演

KAYLEE
SERENITY'S MECHANIC

KAYWINNIT LEE FRYE

ATTRIBUTES

Agility d6
Strength d6
Vitality d8
Alertness d8
Intelligence ... d10
Willpower d6

Life Points 14
Initiative .... d6 + d8

W ○○○○○○○○○○○○○ **S**
LIFE POINTS

Skills			
Animal Handling	d4	Perception	d6
Artistry	d6	Pilot	d4
Athletics	d4	Technical Engineering	d6
Guns	d2		
Influence	d6		
- Persuasion	d8		
Mechanical Engineering	d6		
- Maintenance	d10		
- Repair	d12+d2		

WEAPONS & EQUIPMENT

Kaylee doesn't carry weapons unless the situation is dire. She wears a pair of loose-fitting trousers, work boots, and a brightly patterned blouse. (She loves things with flowers!) She usually carries a tiny screwdriver in one pocket.

TRAITS

Combat Paralysis (Minor Complication) - Kaylee tends to freeze up when bullets or fists start flyin'.

Mechanical Empathy (Minor Asset) - Kaylee's intuition regarding machines borders on the supernatural.

Straight Shooter (Minor Complication) - Lyin' may be easy for most folk, but Kaylee is normally honest and straightforward.

Sweet & Cheerful (Minor Asset) - No power in the 'Verse can stop Kaylee from being cheerful, and most find her a ray of sunshine in the cold and lonely black.

Talented: Mechanical Engineering/Repair (Major Asset) - Kaylee's way with machines is nothing short of astonishing.

ROLE PLAYING NOTES

"I had a 'genius' mechanic before Kaylee, fellow named Bester. Seemed promising enough at first, but kept dickin' around and offering up excuses instead of keeping us in the air. One day, I had reached the end of my considerable patience and went to the engine room to have words. I was not pleased to find him enjoying the naked company of a young local when he was supposed to be on the clock and, being plain-spoken, I said as much.

"Bester offered up yet another excuse and then it was as this young girl, who looks like someone's baby sister, up and tells me that she knows what's ailin' *Serenity*. Not only that, but, soon as she sorts her clothes out, she fixes the problem on the spot.

"I fired Bester on the spot and hired Kaylee.

"She has a way with machines goes beyond book-learnin'. They 'talk' to her, so she's says. I know for certain that *Serenity* talks to her way more than my boat talks to anyone else—includin' me.

"If our Kaylee has a fault, it's that she hasn't really learned that I'm a bad man and that the 'Verse is a bad place filled with bad people who aim to do me and mine harm. Kaylee is under the mistaken impression that I have a soft heart or, rather, that I have any kind of heart at all.

"Still, I have to say that her cheerfulness is welcome around the ship, though it does scrap a might on the nerves sometimes. That and she's gone all squishy and lovesome over the young doc, Simon Tam, former passenger and now crew.

"I'm hopeful she'll outgrow it."

—Conversation with Malcolm Reynolds

INARA
REGISTERED COMPANION

INARA SERRA

W
LIFE POINTS
S

ATTRIBUTES

Agility d8
Strength d4
Vitality d6
Alertness . . . d10
Intelligence d8
Willpower . . . d10

Life Points 16

Initiative . . d8 + d10

Skills	
Artistry	d6
Athletics	d6
Discipline	d6
Influence	d6
- Persuasion	d10
- Seduction	d12
Medical Expertise	d4
Perception	d6
- Empathy	d10
- Intuition	d8
Performance	d6
- Dancing	d8
Ranged Weapons	d6
- Bow	d8
Pilot	d6
Unarmed Combat	d4

WEAPONS & EQUIPMENT

Hair Pin - While Inara doesn't carry a weapon as such, she sometimes wears an ornate hair pin that can be used as a dagger when necessary. Damage d2W.

Bolt Thrower - Inara owns and is proficient with a bolt-thrower, a newtech weapon that uses the same skill and discipline of a bow but fires with nearly the force of a bullet. She may fire it up to 2 times per turn. Damage d6B. It takes 4 turns to assemble the bow.

TRAITS

Allure (Minor Asset) - Inara is beautiful, and is trained to use her presence to its best advantage.

Credo (Minor Complication) - The privacy of her clients and the importance of keeping her commitments are two things Inara will not breach without great reason.

Friends in High Places (Minor Asset) - As a respected Companion, Inara has contacts among many rich and powerful people on many worlds and moons.

Highly Educated (Minor Asset) - Inara was well-schooled in a Companion Training House on Sihnon from a very early age.

Memorable (Minor Complication) - Inara is a singular woman, one who tends to stand out in a crowd and in memory.

Registered Companion (Minor Asset) - The Companion Client Registry is only a keystroke away, along with many other benefits of Guild membership. However, it comes with a few responsibilities, as well.

ROLE PLAYING NOTES

"I can see you expressing some astonishment that we had a registered Companion on board *Serenity*. She wasn't a member of the crew, as such. Inara rented one of the ship's shuttles, not that you'd've recognized it for a proper shuttle, what with the fancy rugs and the velvet pillows, gold-gilt trappings and silk sheets. The business arrangement worked out fine for both of us. Her rent money helped keep *Serenity* flyin', while being aboard meant she could travel from planet to planet, where she met and entertained high-class, high-payin' clientele.

"Did I mention she was a whore?

"Inara helped me in other ways, too, though not what you're thinkin'. She made it a rule to never service the crew. There are some planets that wouldn't let *Serenity* land without her credentials smoothing our way. For that reason, I called her the Ambassador (call her other names less polite when I want to rile her. And I do take considerable pleasure in riling her!).

"I have to say, though, that Inara is a puzzle to me. Why would a beautiful Companion, who was, as I've heard rumored, on her way to becoming a High Priestess in the Guild House on Sihnon, choose to fly the black with lowlife such as ourselves? Why would a woman of her beauty and brains and talents, who could be sitting in the lap of some rich client dining on strawberries and cream, choose instead to eat canned protein at our table? Not to mention her life being endangered on more than one occasion when one of our jobs got a bit out of hand.

"Why would she? Fact is, she wouldn't. Wouldn't choose to be with us, that is. The Ambassador left us for good and all, so she says. Gone to train more little high-class whores. The crew misses her. A few more than others. Kaylee almost forgets how to be cheerful. Almost."

—Conversation with Malcolm Reynolds

BOOK
THE SHEPHERD

ATTRIBUTES

Agility d8

Strength d6

Vitality d6

Alertness d6

Intelligence d8

Willpower . . . d10

Life Points 16

Initiative . . . . d6 + d8

Skills

Athletics	d6
Covert	d6
Craft	d4
Discipline	d6
Guns	d6
- Shotgun	d8
Influence	d4
Knowledge	d6
- Alliance government	d8
- Criminal underworld	d8
- Religion	d8
Mechanical Engineering	d4
Perception	d6
Pilot	d2
Planetary Vehicles	d6
Technical Engineering	d4
Unarmed Combat	d6
- Karate	d10

W

LIFE POINTS

S

WEAPONS & EQUIPMENT

Though Book has displayed proficiency with all manner of firearms, he does not carry a weapon of any kind. The only possession he has with him at all times is his Bible, though he is known to sometimes smoke a long-stem pipe and he keeps an unlabeled Alliance IdentCard in his pocket.

TRAITS

Cortex Specter (Major Asset) - No information on Book can be found on the Cortex or any other accessible databank. The only hint of his true identity lies on the IdentCard he carries in his pocket.

Credo (Major Complication) - Book not only believes in Christian ideals, he practices what he preaches—following the Ten Commandments. He will sometimes skirt the edge of his rules if the cause is worthy. The Bible may have specific rules against killing, as an example, but it is a mite fuzzier on the subject of shooting kneecaps.

Religiosity (Major Asset) - A Shepherd less than two years outside the cloistered life of the Bathgate Abbey, Book is easily recognized as a man of God by his manner of dress and long, bound hair. While some don't take kindly to preachifying, most will treat a man of the cloth with respect.

ROLE PLAYING NOTES

"It was Kaylee, as you might figure, that landed us with a preacher on board *Serenity*. Now, I've nothin' against God, so long as He doesn't mix himself up in my affairs. And so long as Shepherd Book kept his sermonizing to those as wants to hear it, I had no problem with him shipping out with us.

"The Shepherd came on board at the Eavesdown Docks on Persephone. Said he'd been doing his shepherding at the Southdown Abbey and he'd been out of the world for a spell and would like to walk it a while. Kaylee took to him right off and brought him on board as a passenger. He paid his way with too-little cash and a load of fresh garden stuffs, which, I must admit, tasted fine after months of eatin' protein boiled, protein baked, and protein barbequed.

"It come as somewhat of a shock to Shepherd Book when he discovered how me and mine earn our living. And he was fair knocked flat on his backside when I introduced him to the Ambassador. I don't expect he figured to find a whore among his travelin' companions.

"I must say, though, that the Shepherd evened up the surprise score when he proved to be far and away more skilled and knowledgeable about fighting and guns and tactics and lawmen than one ordinarily looks for in a man of God.

"Besides being of considerable worth in a fight, Shepherd Book was a better than ordinary cook and the rest of the crew came to like him. He and Jayne spotted each other lifting weights. The Shepherd and Inara held forth about the ways of the 'Verse. She being a Buddhist by trade, their conversations were probably interesting to those who could stay awake. So long as he kept his Bible-thumping to himself, I had no problem.

"If he didn't see fit to talk about where he's walked in this life, I could honor that.

"You're askin' where the Shepherd is now. He left *Serenity*. Not sure why. Perhaps he saw that he'd done all he could in the way of salvation for us and he might ought to turn his attention to those in want of saving. We set him down at a mining colony on a backwater moon.

"Hope he finds what he's lookin' for there."

—Conversation with Malcolm Reynolds

SIMON
FUGITIVE DOCTOR

ATTRIBUTES

Agility d6

Strength d6

Vitality d6

Alertness d8

Intelligence . . d12

Willpower d8

Life Points 14

Initiative . . . . d6 + d8

Skills

Skill		Die
Athletics		d4
Discipline		d6
- Concentration		d10
Guns		d2
Influence		d4
Knowledge		d6
- History		d8
Medical Expertise		d6
- Neurology		d10
- Surgery		d12
Perception		d6
- Deduction		d10
Performance		d4
Scientific Expertise		d6
- Biology		d10
- Chemistry		d10
Technical Engineering		d6

W
LIFE POINTS
S

WEAPONS & EQUIPMENT

Simon does not generally carry weapons of any kind, unless one counts the scalpel in his Doctor's Bag. He wears the clothes he took with him from his previous life, which are the style of the upper class on Osiris. (This, sad to say, makes him often stand out on the border and outer planets.) While he was once a wealthy doctor, he now has only 25 Alliance credit notes left of his previous fortune, and usually spends his earnings as the resident medic of *Serenity*.

TRAITS

Deadly Enemy (Minor Complication) - Simon is a wanted fugitive (as a result of rescuing his sister from an Alliance-controlled facility), with warrants flagged monthy on the Cortex.

Easy Mark (Minor Complication) - Perhaps it's a result of a sheltered upbringing, but Simon never expects deception—an easy target for betrayal and pratical jokes.

Highly Educated (Minor Asset) - Simon is very smart, having graduated the top 3% of his class at the Medical Academy on Osiris and finishing his internship in 18 months.

Loyal (Minor Complication) - Simon's first instinct is to protect his sister, an impulse that goes so far that he ignores or pushes aside anything (or anyone) that he might want for himself.

Steady Calm (Minor Asset) - Even with the dangerous and unusual situations that seem to crop up as a member of *Serenity*'s crew, Simon keeps a cool head—looking for his moment.

Talented: Medical Expertise/Surgery (Minor Asset) - He was steered toward a medical career by his father, and Simon seemed clearly gifted from an early age.

ROLE PLAYING NOTES

"I don't mind saying that I took against the young doctor from the very start. Maybe it was the way he dressed—all wealthified—or the way he talked—all educated. Or maybe it was the fact that he chose *Serenity* as his ticket off Persephone. Though the ship looks fine to me, others tend to see her as sort of beat-up and disreputable. Not exactly the type of luxury cruiser I would guess the young doctor is accustomed to flying.

"I was suspicious of him from the start and I took considerable less to Simon Tam when I discovered that he landed me and mine in a world of trouble by smuggling his certifiable loony-bin sister on board my ship.

"Here's the doc's story, as he told it to us. If it's a little vague, I don't press him for the fine details. When you're wadin' hip deep through cow *mi tian gohn*, you're not much interested in the color of the cow.

"Simon Tam was one of the lucky ones. He was born to money and brought up with his sister, River, on the wealthy core planet of Osiris. Highly intelligent, Simon waltzed through medical school and, at a young age, was on the road to being one of the most respected and admired (and well-paid) surgeons at one of the most prestigious hospitals in Capital City.

"Simon was smart, but his little sister, River, was a hundred times smarter. There wasn't anything she couldn't do, from dancing to theoretical physics. Lookin' for an education program to challenge her, she went off to some high-powered Academy run by the Alliance. All was fine at first, and then Simon started receivin' letters that made no sense. On closer inspection, however, he discovered they were written in code. River told him that people were hurting her and she had to escape.

"Simon had money and he had influence and he spent both liberally to help free River. She was cryogenically frozen and shipped to Persephone—a place you go when you don't want to face a lot of questions, such as 'what do you have in that large box, sir?'

"Turns out, sadly, that the Alliance wants his sister back. They want her back so bad that they're not only offering good money for her, they've papered the 'Verse with wanted posters on these two. Now I don't mind makin' trouble for myself, 'cause I generally get paid for it. I do mind others makin' trouble for me.

"I've been tempted more than once to let Simon and his sister take a stroll in space without benefit of suits, but, I'll say one thing for him, the young doc is good at his job. And since our means of earning a living leads to a certain amount of scrapes and bruises, not to mention gunshots to the belly and the occasional knifing, I have decided to keep him on board. It's fair to say that some of us might not be here to breathe the air if it weren't for the young doctor.

"So far, he's earned a place on my crew. Not sayin' that'll last. But so far..."

—Conversation with Malcolm Reynolds

RIVER
FUGITIVE PSYCHIC

ATTRIBUTES

Agility..........d12

Strength........ d6

Vitality.......... d8

Alertness........ d6

Intelligence d12+d2

Willpower d8

Life Points 16

Initiative .. d12 + d6

Skills	
Athletics	d6
- Dodge	d8
Guns	d6
– Pistol	d10
Knowledge	d6
Linguist	d4
Melee Weapons	d6
Perception	d6
Performance	d6
- Dance	d8
Pilot	d6
Scientific Expertise	d6
Technical Engineering	d4
Unarmed Combat	d6
- Martial Arts	d12

Note: This version of River is designed to be balanced with the rest of *Serenity*'s crew, and may not match her abilities as seen in the film.

RIVER TAM

W
LIFE POINTS
S

WEAPONS & EQUIPMENT

River is not allowed to carry weapons on-board *Serenity* (after a few unfortunate incidents involving knives and guns), and does not carry anything other than random objects that catch her curiosity. She's not even given to wearing shoes, either.

TRAITS

Deadly Enemy (Minor Complication) - River has been pursued by the Alliance government (including specialized agents and contracted bounty hunters) since her escape from the "Academy" with the help of her brother, Simon. The Alliance seems to be ready to do most anything to re-acquire her.

Leaky Brainpan (Major Complication) - Whatever happened to her at the Academy—which certainly included unusual brain surgery, drug therapy, and psychological conditioning—has left River with an "altered reality matrix." She perceives the world differently than most folk, and has trouble communicating with others.

Loyal (Minor Complication) - Simon gave up everything he had and risked his life to save River, and now she would do anything for him.

Memorable (Minor Complication) - River, with her unpredictable behavior, mood swings, and bare feet, tends to stick out in most folks' minds.

Reader (Major Asset) - River is able to sense the world and thoughts of those around her with supernatural sensitivity. She does not have the know-how to shut her abilities off, however, and doesn't always understand what she sees or hears.

Total Recall (Major Asset) - River makes her gifted brother sometimes look like an idiot child. She remembers everything she sees and hears, making some things come as naturally as breathing.

Traumatic Flashes (Major Complication) - The abuse River suffered at the hands of the Alliance government, along with terrible secrets buried deep in her psyche, has left her with terrifying flashbacks and nightmares. These strike when unknown triggers set them off, or for no reason at all.

ROLE PLAYING NOTES

"Whimsical in the brainpan. That's the polite way of describing her. The not-so-polite way is to say the teenage girl's flat-out crazy. She hears things that no one says, sees things different than they truly are. One time she shot three people clean through the head with a single bullet each and her with eyes closed."

"She's a reader, I've come to believe. She reads minds. The doc, her brother, Simon, did a scan of her brain and discovered that the Alliance went in and cut on her—for what reason, best to ask them.

"She's quick-thinking, if sometimes odd-thinking. She does have her quirks, such as taking it into her head to slash Jayne with a knife because she didn't like the color of his shirt.

"Truth is, we never know what River's going to do next, and while that does perk up our lives, it is a mite unsettling. We never know but that we could wake up some morning to find she's murdered us all in our bunks.

"Still, none of us is perfect and River does have a kind of way about her, when she's not stabbing folk, and so long as the doctor keeps her drugged up and does his job, she and he can remain part of *Serenity*.

"You see, it's occurred to me that there are times when a girl with the ability to read minds might come in handy in our line of work..."

—Conversation with Malcolm Reynolds

RIVER TAM

CHAPTER 1

FIND A CREW

THE CLIENT

Inara had a client. She refused to tell the crew his name or anything about him and, in addition, stated that he had requested his visit be kept extremely confidential and she would appreciate it if they would give her some privacy. So, naturally, almost everyone on board the ship turned out to see him.

"Anyone know who he is?" asked Mal.

The man came on board alone, leaving his two body guards outside the Firefly. Inara was there to greet to him and guided him through the ship to her private shuttle. She cast the crew a baleful glance as she glided by.

"Oooh, if looks could kill," said Wash, hanging over the rail above the loading dock, "we'd all be laid out in our coffins."

"I have no idea who he is. And I don't blame Inara," said Simon, the young doctor, walking past with his sister. He paused long enough to comment. "Ogling this man is rude and indelicate."

"So no one knows who he is?" Mal persisted. "I've got a gut feeling..."

River placed her hand on the rail and stared down intently at the man. "He has a daughter," she said suddenly. "He *is* his daughter."

"So you know him?" Mal asked her, interested.

"No," said River, regarding him wide-eyed. "Do you?"

"But you just said—"

"Come along, River." Simon took firm hold of his sister. "We have better things to do than to stand here gawking."

He led River away. All the while, she kept her gaze fixed on the man, even craning her head to see him as Simon gently urged her back to their quarters.

"She said he was his own daughter." Jayne muttered, leaning over the rail. He thought about this, then twisted around to look at the others. "Hey! Ain't that impossible?"

"That can't be his own hair," Mal muttered.

"I think he's real pretty," said Kaylee. "That wavy black hair with those touches of gray at the side. He's not so old, neither. He's . . . distinguished. He and Inara make a sweet couple."

"Wasn't for that moneyed suit and store-bought hair, no one would look twice at him," Mal returned. "I ask again, in case no one heard me the first time. Anybody know anything about him? Kaylee? Inara confides in you. What did she say about him?"

"If she did confide me, it would be a confidence," Kaylee returned. "That means I'd be honor-bound not to tell."

"You'd tell your Captain if your he ordered you," said Mal, half serious and half not.

"But my Captain wouldn't order me 'cause he knows that wouldn't be honorable and my Captain's an honorable man," said Kaylee.

"No, he ain't," said Mal.

Kaylee patted his arm. "Got to go, Captain. That compressor's still acting up." She hurried away.

"Whatever gave her the idea that I was honorable?" Mal asked, looking around.

"I know that man," said Shepherd Book suddenly.

"Yeah, so?" Mal prodded. "Who is he?"

Shepherd Book cocked an eye at Mal. "Are you going order me to tell you, Captain?"

"Can't rightly do that, I suppose. 'though I do consider you crew, Shepherd, and, as such, I'd take it as a personal favor if you would pass on any information you might have about someone who is aboard my ship."

"I know"—Shepherd Book paused—"that he is Inara's client and that if she had wanted us to know, she would have told us." Opening his Bible, he walked off, absorbed in his reading.

Mal gazed after him. "Is there something wrong with me? Seems like a captain should strike terror into the heart of his crew, make them want to tell him things."

"I shake like a leaf, sir, every time you open your mouth," said Zoe.

"Me, too," said Wash, putting his arm around his wife. "I'm completely and utterly intimidated by your forceful and dangerous presence."

"That's good," said Mal, hooking his thumbs in his suspenders. "So you two will tell me everything you know about this guy."

Zoe and Wash exchanged glances.

"No, sir," said Zoe.

"We'll be in our bunk should you feel like having us whipped, Captain," added Wash, and the two hurried off.

"You'd tell me if you knew who he was, wouldn't you, Jayne?" Mal asked the only person left.

"I would," said Jayne, then he added with a wink, "'cept Inara paid me not to." Grinning, he sauntered off.

"There's definitely somethin' wrong with me," Mal said to himself and he shook his head.

Plenty of folk who want to explore the 'Verse will be eager to role play the crew of *Serenity*. After all, they are familiar characters, and odds are most of us can relate to at least one of them. It's a great way to start playing the game. We've also given you a shiny new crew and their ship, *Aces & Eights*, in case you want some variety.

Could be you're interested in creating your own characters. Ideas spin through your head. Perhaps your character is a hired gun, lured into danger by the thought of quick money. You might fancy a pilot, someone who escaped a Reaver raiding party and is now haunted by the tortured screams of her dead shipmates. You might even want to play an Alliance officer, bound and determined to bring these damn rebels under control (regardless of the fact you're on the run for desertion!).

Role playing a familiar character such as Jayne or Kaylee can be fun, but one of the most rewarding elements of role playing is creating and playing a character that is your own. A bunch of "stats" written down on a sheet of paper can fast become a living, breathing person, someone you know inside and out. The story you imagine for this person expands over the course of the game. And it is yours!

It's as much fun as pulling a Crazy Ivan. Jump aboard and we'll get started.

CREW BASICS

While the unwritten laws of the 'Verse dictate certain fundamental basics about who you are and why you are, the truth of the matter is that you can create most any type of character you can think up. Remember, though, the player characters in this game are called "crew" for a reason. They work together as a team, for survival's sake if nothing else. *Zhu tamin ya min zhu yi*, as they say. (And watch your friend's backside, as well!)

Campaigns can vary almost as much as a ship's crew. Your group could all be members of the Alliance or your group could be the owners and staff of a dance hall. Ideas for these types of campaigns can be found in Chapter Five: *Keep Flyin'*. Since these types of campaigns are more complex and take more time to develop, we're going to start with the easiest and likely the most popular. You and your crew are sailing the black aboard a ship. Since your game group makes up the ship's crew, you'll want to fill important roles to keep her flying. Cover the basics first, and perhaps one day you'll be able to afford a decent cook.

Pilot: Most folk can ride a horse, but you want a professional jockey to ride the money-race. Likewise most space travelers can fly a ship, but when the Alliance is on your tail or you're skipping through a debris field or trying to hold it together after the primary buffer panel flies off the nose during re-entry, you want a capable pilot. It ain't enough to know which buttons to push and dials to turn, it's love that keeps a boat in the air.

Mechanic: High class folk like to call them "engineers." No matter what name he goes by, someone's gotta keep the engine turning. Whether he comes all educated or just has a knowing way with machines, a ship's mechanic should know the boat from stem to stern. Things never seem to go smooth out in the black, so the person doing the fixin' should be ready to improvise at a moment's notice. Ship might break down a long way from civilized parts, and *wu de tyen ah* help you if you can't make full burn when a Reaver ship shows up.

Medic: If you run a peaceful passenger boat, you might well think you can make do with a simple first aid kit. 'Course, even passenger liners can get hijacked by scrappers or hit by Reavers. And then there's the inevitable gun fight that breaks out in the casino over a hand of poker. Best to have someone who can extract bullets, put a weave on cuts, and knows which salve will best heal flash-burns. Experienced trauma surgeons are a rare find. Still, the war created plenty of trained combat medics who will sell their skills for the right price.

Security: Someone on the boat should be handy in a fight—be it with guns, bar stools, or fists. Hopefully things are peaceable enough aboard ship. It's the rest of the 'Verse you have to worry about. Contract negotiations always seem to go better when the other side is looking at you and your big friend with the even bigger gun. Plenty of folk out there are ready for action, all for a fair cut of the profits and a private bunk.

Socialite: Your boat will most likely not have a state official—or even a registered Companion—on board, but a smart crew will have a *swai*—a smooth-talker. Such a respectable-appearing individual has a way with words that can secure invites to the right events, diffuse heated situations with dangerous enemies, or talk port control into releasing a land-lock when it's past time you left the world.

Captain: Someone has to make decisions, give the orders, and lead the crew into and out of hellacious circumstances. The captain makes the final call on all such matters, because his ship ain't the rutting town hall and this ain't no democracy. Downside is that he gets the blame when plans don't go as promised, and his name is usually the one remembered by potential enemies. Generally a ship's owner is the captain, though captains can be hired for the job by someone with more money than qualifications.

All this being said, most ships have to make do with crew pulling double or even triple duties. The captain and the pilot may be one and the same. The smooth negotiator could also be a fast draw and a dead shot. The reverse can also be said, as crew members can usually back each other up. Jayne certainly isn't the only person on *Serenity* capable in a fight, while Wash and Kaylee often work together to fix the ship's problems.

HEROIC LEVEL

Most folk on the job would like you to think they crawled out of their mother's belly ready to chew nails. Doesn't make it the truth, though. We all have to start somewhere. "What does not kill you, makes you stronger" or some such old saying from Earth-That-Was. A right to the jaw from the 'Verse makes you tough enough to bear more of the same.

When the Game Master begins a new campaign, he sets one of three heroic levels for the crew. This level is a yardstick that measures the crew's competence and experience, and sets the tone of the campaign. Most crews start out as Greenhorns—those who are still learning their way around the

'Verse. The difficulties they face are challenging, but not likely to get them killed (at least right away). As these characters gain more experience, they'll be ready to handle some real action. Of course, the GM can decide to skip all this and fly his crew straight into epic adventures filled with danger. Some crews may include a mix of characters at different heroic levels, though such a mix should be agreed upon by everyone before a campaign begins.

GREENHORN

As implied, you're still a bit wet behind the ears. Whether or not you are burdened with an overabundance of schooling, you lack experience. Some might say you know just enough to be dangerous. This usually means you're a *nyen ching-duh*, which ain't all bad. You could also be a person who's lived a relatively sheltered, quiet life. What the Greenhorn designation really means is that you've got plenty to learn.

Greenhorn crews know the basics of survival and they can handle lower-risk jobs. (Don't mean such jobs have to be boring.) The advantage to starting at this point is that the characters have room to grow. They can develop their lives through play instead of starting in the middle, giving them a sense of immense satisfaction when they survive and "graduate" to higher status.

A Greenhorn character begins with 42 Attribute points (see *Attributes* further on).

VETERAN

Much like a certain transport ship, you have accumulated some mileage over the years. You have experience and you are good at what you do. Probably learned a few tricks and can take some punishment before going down. You've gambled on life and won the first few hands, so you can now raise the pot a few times without too much fuss.

A Veteran crew is known in the business. They have a rep, whether it's deserved or not. They've moved on to bigger capers and they've made their share of dangerous enemies. Still, they are probably living hand-to-mouth, needing each job to keep from going on the drift. If you have a seasoned crew ready for some thrilling heroics, this is the level to start your campaign.

A Veteran character begins with 48 Attribute points.

> "I just get excitable as to choice, like to have my options open."
> —Jayne Cobb

BIG DAMN HERO

Ten armed men come to kill you, and you feel a twinge of pity for them before you start taking them out. You may have knocked over more than one Alliance facility in your unseemly career. A statue of you stands in some little town, where the folk sing songs for you each night in the local saloon. This being the case, you've earned the benefits along with the scars that come with hero territory.

Big Damn Heroes are legends, known throughout the 'Verse for deeds either good or bad. Heroes have flown into a mess of trouble and come safely out the other side. They are great—not good—at what they do, and they have dangerous enemies in both high places and low. Such reputations tend to make Big Damn Heroes big damn targets.

A Big Damn Hero character begins with 54 Attribute points.

CONCEPT

Today we meet the real you.

Hold off on the panic. No one is going to dangle you over a volcano or administer electric shocks. At least not until the campaign gets into full swing. What we're looking for is a Character Concept.

CREW CREATION

For experienced players ready to set sail right away, here's a no-frills checklist:

1. CHOOSE A HEROIC LEVEL

Determine the Heroic Level for your crew (the job of your GM). This gives you the amount of starting Attribute Points you have to spend.

2. CHOOSE TRAITS

You must choose, at minimum, one trait each in Assets (good stuff) and Complications (makes life interestin'). Assets can be bought with Attribute Points: 2 for a Minor, 4 for a Major. You may have a maximum of five Assets and five Complications.

3. GENERATE ATTRIBUTES

You have six attributes: Agility, Strength, Vitality, Alertness, Intelligence, and Willpower. Each is rated in die types ranging from d4 to d12 (the maximum for a beginning character). The cost matches the type in Attribute Points (4 points for a d4, 12 points for a d12, etc.).

4. CALCULATE DERIVED ATTRIBUTES

Tally and record your Life Points (Vitality + Willpower die types added together) and Initiative (Agility + Alertness, rolled frequently during combat situations).

5. CHOOSE SKILLS

You begin the game with 20 Skill Points plus the points provided by your heroic level. Every Skill is rated by a die type. General skills may advance only to d6, and are then improved upon by purchasing specialties (that begin at d8). Otherwise, the costs are equivalent to those for Attributes.

6. FINISHING TOUCHES

You may equip your character with gear using the rules in Chapter Three and the GM's plans for the campaign. Decide on personal details such as gender, height, weight, home world and the like. Spruce up your background and history a tad further.

Now you're ready to hit the 'Verse. Oh, got a name yet?

Your Character Concept is the flesh and muscle and other such that hangs on the skeleton. Without it, the skeleton will just fall into a heap of bones. The same reasoning applies to your character: without a little something extra, your character is just numbers and, between the two of us, numbers are downright boring. Suppose you have an idea for a Browncoat who's trying to carry on after suffering the bitter loss of the Unification War. Such a character might take any odd job—legal or not—to keep flyin' without submitting to the rule of the Alliance. Mix in a Firefly class ship and a fierce loyalty to his crew, and you have Mal. Dilute the bitterness, amplify the military discipline, add a husband, and you have Zoe. Tweak the concept a mite further, and you've created a unique character all your own.

The concept doesn't have to be over-complicated. A few words might sell the idea. "Former star athlete, running from his gambling debts" might be one way to start, or "Idealistic student who followed her boyfriend out to the Rim" is another. Start with a simple idea and let it grow from there.

RACE

Despite what sideshow barkers tell you, there is no evidence of alien life in the 'Verse. Though mankind has blazed a trail through the stars, and terraformed and colonized most of a new star system, the children of Earth-That-Was have only one deadly enemy—themselves. More on that later.

The races, nationalities, and cultures of the ancient world are vaguely remembered, but don't count for much anywhere. Fact is, the original settlers of our current star system were packed into their ships so tight that the old-world notions, feuds, hatreds, and prejudices got squeezed out of 'em. Races and cultures have blended so that it can be hard to tell one from another just by looking. A young doctor and his sister might appear Caucasian, but their surname, Tam, gives you a hint of their ancestry.

Ethnicity and background are important ideas to consider as you flesh out a character concept, but remember that the dividing lines are a might fuzzy and no one gives a damn who your great-grandpappy was anyway.

TRAITS

Numbers won't tell you everything about a person. It's human nature to remember people by certain qualities—both good and bad. On *Serenity*, we remember Jayne's greed, Inara's charm, and Simon's devotion to his sister. In the *Serenity Role Playing Game*, such qualities are known as Traits. Traits help define your character's personality, talents, preoccupations, and hidden secrets. Traits make your character either a gentle pacifist or a *shiong-muh duh duang-ren*.

Assets are generally positive Traits—those that give you some kind of edge in tense situations. Complications are negative and usually put you at a disadvantage in such situations. Both help define your character and both can often be a lot of fun to play! Traits can either be Major or Minor, depending on how much they help (or hurt) the character during an adventure. Think of Minor Traits as just a tiny quirk or flaw, while Major Traits are usually defining qualities that can be spotted from the next moon.

Traits are fully listed and defined in Chapter Two: *Traits and Skills*, so skip ahead if you want to take a gander at them.

ASSETS

Kaylee is able to do more than stick a screwdriver into a machine's workings. Engines speak to her. Wash can fly the ship through an ice canyon. Mal never gives up, no matter how hard things get. These are examples of how Assets define their characters.

> **"I'm the brains of the operation."**
>
> —River Tam

On the other hand, just remember: nothing in the 'Verse is free.

Each Asset you purchase for your character comes out of your starting Attribute points. A Minor Asset costs 2 points, while a Major Asset costs 4. You must purchase at least one Asset for your character, and you can't have more than five (either Major or Minor). Don't worry if you see your points dropping fast before you purchase Attributes, as you can gain back points by adding Complications.

COMPLICATIONS

Things just never seem to go smooth for Mal. If the money is too good, Jayne will get stupid. River is *fong luh* and ought to be institutionalized. These are complications at work, making things more interesting for your crew.

Each Complication you take adds points back into your pool for purchasing Attributes. A Minor Complication gains you 2 points, and a Major one is worth 4. You have to take at least one Complication, but you can't take more than five (either Major or Minor). Complications may seem bad, but not only are they worth points for your Attributes, good role playing of the bad stuff can earn you Plot Points. (Plot Points are important; more on that later.)

Once you've filled out your selection of Traits, you can determine your character's starting Attributes.

ATTRIBUTES

Jayne is strong as an ox and just as dumb. Inara could never lift heavy storage creates, but she can lift the emotional baggage of others and make them at ease. Simon is all manner of smart, yet River is known to make him look like an idiot child. Kaylee may back down when intimidated. Mal steps up to a fight—never avoiding the chance to spit the devil in the eye.

Attributes are the qualities that describe a character's physical and mental makeup. The physical Attributes are: Agility, Strength, and Vitality. The mental Attributes are: Alertness, Intelligence, and Willpower. Each Attribute is rated by a type of die—the more sides the better. Average yokels have a d6 for everything. Someone with a Strength of d4, for example, might be a ninety-pound weakling, while a d10 could be a muscle-bound weight-lifter. A d12 Attribute is the normal starting maximum,

though truly experienced characters might be able to achieve even higher scores.

When selecting your character's Attributes, you start with the Heroic Level selected by your Game Master. The points indicated are what you use to "buy" Attribute dice. Simply put, it costs you Attribute points equal to the die type you want for each Attribute.

For instance, your GM has decided that the crew will start as Greenhorns. (Don't fret, you're still better off than the "all d6" yokels.) You have 42 points to spend, that number adjusted depending on the Traits you selected. If you're set on a d10 Agility, then take 10 points out of your pool. 'Course you can purchase only die types that actually exist, so don't risk the GM's ire by picking a d7 in Intelligence—there ain't no such thing. If you end up with a couple of points left over, consider purchasing an additional Trait. Otherwise, leftover points become Advancement Points to be used later.

Greenhorn characters cannot start with an Attribute higher than d12. Veterans can go as high as d12 + d2. Big Damn Heroes can start with Attributes as high as d12 + d4. No matter where you start, you'll be able to improve Attributes later in the campaign. No one (not even Jayne) can start with an Attribute lower than d4.

Here's a table, just in case it isn't obvious at first glance.

Table 1-1: Attribute Die Costs

Die Type	Point Cost
d4	4
d6	6
d8	8
d10	10
d12	12
d12 + d2	14
d12 + d4	16

PHYSICAL ATTRIBUTES

Recollecting your Character Concept (and you did come up with a Character Concept, right?), let's say your character is better with his body

than his mind. Strong of arm, quick on the draw, or downright tough as a bull. For these concepts, Physical Attributes are a must.

Agility represents quickness and physical coordination. A high Agility could mean your character can twirl two pistols and leap on the back of a moving horse without screwing up either action. A low score might well mean you have four left feet—two on the ends of your legs and two at the ends of your arms.

Strength tells you just how strong your character is. A high Strength means you can kick down doors, win arm wrestling contests, or break someone's jaw with a good right hook. Low scores mean you have trouble carrying your own luggage.

Vitality is a measure of toughness and general health. High Vitality characters avoid catching the flu, can drink their buddies under the table, and run from the law without getting winded. Crew with low Vitality should stay away from people with colds and never drink the local water.

MENTAL ATTRIBUTES

Some characters have more brains than brawn. Mental Attributes are useful in those situations where honey is like to catch you more flies than vinegar.

Alertness represents intuition and observation. A character with a high score might hear the stealthy footsteps of an Alliance Operative sneaking up on the group, notice an important clue caught in the bushes, or know the instant a fellow is lying.

Someone with a low Alertness doesn't notice that his fly is unzipped.

Intelligence is smarts—plain and simple. Crew with high Intelligence are bright and inventive, able to think their way through complex situations, or solve puzzles that would confound lesser persons. Those with low scores might have trouble understanding big words or experience difficulty remembering complicated plans.

Willpower is about determination and force of personality. A high score means a character can resist intimidation (and even torture), can convince a person to do his bidding, and can push on even when his body is about to give up. Those with low Willpower might be easily fooled, back down at a threat, or take the easy way out.

DERIVED ATTRIBUTES

In addition to the six main Attributes, Derived Attributes come straight from the choices you've already made. You'll use them to know how quickly your character reacts in dangerous situations and just how much punishment he can take before dropping like a sack of oats. We call them Initiative and Life Points. Check the *Serenity* or *Aces & Eights* crews for examples of Derived Attributes in action.

Initiative is a roll that tells you who goes first in a given situation. Do you draw first or does your enemy have the drop on you? You'll make Initiative rolls during combat and other hairy situations where time is a major factor. When the GM asks for an "Initiative Roll," you roll your Agility + Alertness dice and tell the GM the result. Higher is better. Especially when a Reaver is rushing at you with a machete.

Life Points measure how much damage you can take before passing out or dying. When your character is punched, stabbed, or shot, the damage comes out of your total Life Points. If your damage is equal or greater than your Life Points, you're out of the action. Calculate your total by adding the die types of your Vitality + Willpower Attributes. For example, a character with a d8 Vitality and a d6 Willpower has 14 Life Points.

'Course, it's helpful to know whether you'll be needing a bandage or a tombstone. Damage comes in two types: Stun and Wounds. (See Chapter Five: *Keep Flyin'*.) If Stun damage puts you over your total, you are only knocked senseless and will recover with rest, though you may have bruises, nicks, and very minor injuries. If you continue to take Stun after being knocked out, you'll accumulate Shock Points that will keep you unconscious even longer.

Wounds are a bit more worrisome, as they represent serious injury—everything from flesh wounds to a bullet through the liver. A badly wounded character is distracted by pain and blood loss, so when you've taken half or more of your Life Points total in Wounds, you suffer a –2 step penalty on all Attributes until you've been patched up. If you've taken your entire total in Wounds, you'll be pushing up the daisies unless you receive help.

It's easiest to track the two types of damage by representing your character's Life Points with check boxes in two columns. (See the Life Point charts for the *Serenity* crew for an example.) Track Stun damage from the top going down and Wounds from the bottom going up. When the two columns meet, you pass out. When all the Wounds are checked off, you better hope the doc's around or it's time to think up your next character concept.

The effects of damage are discussed with more detail in Chapter Five: *Keep Flyin'*.

SKILLS

At this point you've got a handle on your crew's raw abilities and know something about their personalities, but maybe you still haven't got a clue what's rattling about in their brain-pans. Things like whether their knowledge is self-taught, learned from books, or gained at the feet of a master depends on the characters' own histories. Their level of competence is spelled out in skills.

Kaylee may have a talent with machines, but if she doesn't know the port thrust from a catalyzer, then the whole ship is in trouble. Inara may be beautiful and charming, but so are hundreds of other women. Her Companion training gives her the ability to handle her illustrious clientele. So how does this translate in game terms?

Each Skill, like the Attributes, is rated by a die type. A d2 represents basic familiarity with something. If you're flying a shuttle, for example, a d2 might let you steer, but be careful trying to land! A d6 Skill level represents a level of competence at which you could start to get paid an average wage for non-difficult work. Once your Skill level rises above d6, you really begin to stand out as someone who is very good at what he does.

Skills are broken down into two related groups. General Skills represent broad areas of knowledge that cover a lot of territory. Athletics is an example—you use it to run, jump, dodge, climb, and swim. The catch is that General Skills can advance only to d6. Beyond that, you have to specialize. Specialties branch off from the General Skills and allow you to excel in a specific activity—as many as you like, sky's the limit. For example, while your Athletics Skill is capped at d6, your former track star can advance his Run Skill up to d10 and his Jump Skill to d8.

To purchase your Skills, you get 20 points plus the total you used to purchase your Traits and Attributes (a Greenhorn character starts with 62 Skill points, a Veteran gets 68, and a Big Damn Hero gets 74). Purchase Skills just like you did with Attributes, by paying the point cost equal to the die type—just remember that while you only have to pay for the General skill once, you must buy each of its specialties separately. For example, in the previous example it costs 6 points to gain a d6 in Athletics. You could then add 4 points to those 6 to gain a d10 in Jump, and even add 2 points to gain a d8 in Run (all in addition to your d6 in Athletics).

Table 1-2: Skill Costs

Die Type	General Cost	Specialty Cost
d2	2	-
d4	4	-
d6	6	-
d8	-	2
d10	-	4
d12	-	6
d12 + d2	-	8
d12 + d4	-	10

See Chapter Two: *Traits and Skills* to take a look-see at the full list of Skills and their descriptions.

"I am a leaf on the wind. Watch how I soar."

—Hoban "Wash" Washburne

SKILL ROLLS

Skills don't stand on their own. They mix with Attributes to create a combined die roll. However, no single Attribute is married to a Skill, so you might be using different combinations depending on whatever mess you've currently stepped in. For example, suppose you're a ship's mechanic, trying to start up the gorram engine before the Alliance patrol boat arrives. The GM might tell you to roll Alertness + Mechanical Engineering to find the source of the problem, then roll Intelligence + Mechanical Engineering to try to fix it.

UNSKILLED ACTIONS

Nobody's good at everything. At his best, Simon's the 'Verse's worst liar. Put him on the spot and just watch the train wreck. Mal barely knows which end of a sword to hold, and Jayne will never win a spelling bee. Sometimes the crew members have to do things they are just plain bad at. When this happens, you roll just the Attribute die and hope for the best.

'Course, trying something you've got no talent for might work for some actions, though not others. Say you are trying to negotiate with a potential client. You can give it a go even though you lack the Influence Skill, since it doesn't require any special training to talk (or lie). You might be able to take a bullet out of a man's arm without any medical training, but if you attempt to re-attach a girl's leg and you don't have M.D. after your name, you fail without even getting a roll.

GEAR

Up 'til now, we've been alluding to figurative tools. Now you can get the literal kind—the physical objects you will use in an adventure.

The 'Verse currency is credits. You exchange credits for gear, weapons, services (Companion and otherwise), and perhaps little indulgences—such as fresh strawberries. As a beginning character, you're assumed to have the clothes on your back and perhaps a few personal items approved by the GM. Beyond the basics, you get a set amount of money (modified by appropriate Traits) to purchase goods from the equipment lists. A Greenhorn doctor will have 750 credits to stock up on medical supplies. A Veteran bodyguard of 48 Skill points has 1,500 credits as a starting fund to build a private arsenal.

For a list of gear and full descriptions, see Chapter Three: *Money and Gear*.

Any leftover credits after the purchases becomes your own stash, saved for slow times (there could be plenty) or to fritter away however you please.

CHARACTER DEVELOPMENT

Imagine Mal without his quirks. Alliance Feds don't bother him none. He lets Unification Day slide right past without a second thought. He doesn't feel a twinge of conscience when he robs folk. Imagine Kaylee minus the sunshine, Wash without a sense of humor, or Jayne with manners.

Personality lets the rest of the 'Verse know just who the hell you are. Motivation gives you a reason to have a personality. We won't go into the whole chicken-or-egg business because the end is the same. If you understand both your personality and your motivation for doing things, you'll have a real handle on your character and an instant feel for how your character will react in certain situations.

You started the character creation process with a concept, so now let's ask a few questions and flesh that concept out. Suppose you are a former pro athlete who's running from gambling debts. What made you quit the sport? Were you caught betting on your own team? Did you throw a game for the money? Did you refuse to throw a game and now you're running from a crime boss ? Do you have a gambling addiction, or did you bury your problem with your career? Use the answers to such questions to build you character's back story.

SECRETS

Face it, we don't actually know a lot about the crew of *Serenity*. Mal doesn't like to talk about his past, so we don't know much beyond his ranch upbringing and the battle of Serenity Valley. Inara left the Companion Guild House for a mysterious reason, abandoning her previous goals for a life on the move. River can't clearly remember everything that happened to her at the "Academy." Shepherd Book is a complete mystery—a man of God who's proficient with guns, unarmed combat, and disabling security systems.

While you might play an "open book" character such as Wash or Kaylee, it's also fun to play a character with something to hide. Let the details about your character's past trickle out slowly during the course of a campaign instead of proclaiming them at the start. Part of the fun of the game is learning about the rest of the crew. Reveal your secrets only in tense moments where the story hangs in the balance. You'll find that such revelations will create drama the group will remember for years to come.

And here's a secret about secrets and your character's past. You don't have to decide every little detail in the beginning. Give yourself enough to start with and let things work from there. Ideas will suggest themselves from the course of play, and your GM might also use elements from your unknown past. Your character will tell you things that you might not know about him at the beginning. Come to know your past during the game as you work to build the future with your actions.

PLOT POINTS

The sun shines on a dog's backside occasionally, and even a blind squirrel stumbles upon an acorn every once in a while. In stories, as in life, sometimes luck is on your side. Fate takes a hand. Things happen when you really need them to. Our game has a mechanism for this called Plot Points. When a character is in desperate trouble or really must succeed at an action, or is not keen on dying right at this moment, Plot Points ride to the rescue. When you have Plot Points to spend, no power in the 'Verse can stop you.

Plot Points allow you to add an extra die to your action rolls. The more points spent, the higher the die type, allowing you a greater overall range of possible results. This doesn't guarantee success, mind you, but the extra die gives you an edge that you wouldn't have otherwise.

You can also use Plot Points *after* the dice are thrown if the situation is truly desperate—such as when your ship would otherwise crash into a canyon wall. Spending Plot Points after the fact is more expensive, but it can keep the undertaker away. If you spend Plot Points after the die roll, each point adds only 1 to the die roll.

Another use of Plot Points is to keep your *pee goo* alive when things aren't going your way. You can spend points to avoid damage—to reduce a mortal

wound to something more survivable, for example. After learning the amount of damage you would take from an injury, you may spend Plot Points to roll a die and subtract the result from the amount of damage, first negating Wounds, then the Stun. Sadly, you can't use Plot Points to reduce damage from an old injury— you're stuck with that.

With the GM's approval, you can also spend Plot Points to influence the adventure in small ways. Perhaps your character has a contact on the backwater moon you've set down on, or could be that the man you danced with at the ball has fallen in love with you. If you have an idea, the points to spend, and the okay of the GM, then you can help shape the direction of the story.

Table 1-3: Plot Points	
Points Spent	Bonus Die
1	d2
2	d4
3	d6
4	d8
5	d10
6	d12
7	d12 + d2
8	d12 + d4
9	d12 + d6
10	d12 + d8
11	d12 + d10
12	d12 + d12

PLOT POINT POOL

You receive 6 free Plot Points at the beginning of the campaign, and you may keep up to a dozen (12) in your "pool" during the course of the game. (If you have 12 points, you can't earn any more until you spend some or a new game session begins.) They can (and should!) be spent, and can be earned back during play. You may keep up to 6 points in your pool between game sessions, while the remainder are immediately converted into Advancement Points, which you can use to improve your character. More details about Plot Points and all their uses can be found in Chapter Five: *Keep Flyin'*.

ADVANCEMENT POINTS

Your crew will grow and learn over time. Change is the only constant in the 'Verse, and while fate can be a *tah mah de* with one hand, it can be kind with the other. Advancement Points represent the accumulation of experience and are the building blocks for improvement.

Some of your Advancement Points will come from your Plot Point pool (see above), but you will also receive points from the GM during and at the end of an adventure. Advancement Points are your reward for a job well done—or at least survived. Depending on the length and difficulty of the adventure, you'll generally get 3 to 6 Advancement Points for your troubles, in addition to those you save from the Plot Point pool. You can then spend Advancement Points to increase an Attribute or a Skill, buy new Skills, or save them for a big upgrade spree during a big period of down-time.

Table 1-4: Advancement

Die Type	Skill Point Cost	Attribute Point Cost
d2	2	–
d4	4	–
d6	6	24
d8	8	32
d10	10	40
d12	12	48
d12 + d2	14	56
d12 + d4	16	64

CHARACTER IMPROVEMENT

Every Big Damn Hero began as a Greenhorn. Jayne wasn't always a crack shot, and there was a time when Wash didn't even know the startup sequence on a Firefly. Through the course of a campaign you will improve old skills and learn new ones. Advancement Points are the key to character improvement.

Generally, you may spend Advancement Points only to improve a character in-between game sessions, and only to improve a single Skill or Attribute by one die type or purchase a new skill at the d2 level. Advancement is a slow process. The exception might be that a long period of "down time" allows your character to train or otherwise gain experience outside the normal course of play—and is all done with the GM's approval.

Improving an existing Skill costs you the next die type up in Advancement Points. Raising from a d4 to d6 is 6 points, d6 to d8 is 8 points, d8 to d10 is 10 points, etc. Attributes cost four times the point cost as Skill improvement.

REMOVING COMPLICATIONS

First thing to understand is that you don't get jack for problems acquired during the campaign. If your leg gets cut off and thrown into a bog, that's a problem you have to square away on your own—no free points to ease the pain. You can, however, get rid of certain Complications by paying them off.

There are two elements in removing Complications. The first is to have the points you need to buy them off. Removing a Minor Complication costs 10 Advancement Points, while 20 points will rid your character of a Major Complication. A generous Game Master may also permit you to bargain down a Major Complication to Minor status for 10 points.

The second element is to work out a reasonable explanation with the GM as to why your problem isn't so burdensome anymore, which may cost you some in-game assets as well. If it makes sense and the GM gives it the okay, then you have one less problem to deal with. The crew member being hunted for gambling debts may sell off a priceless piece of stolen property and use the proceeds to get the *ching-wah tsao duh liou mahng* off his back. The process of buying off complications may involve adventure or role playing opportunities; if that's the case, so much the better. You'll gain more Plot and Advancement Points to do more of the same.

Note that some Complications aren't gonna go away by spending a few points and telling a pretty story. Mortal enemies aren't in the habit of suddenly forgiving and forgetting. Insane crew bound for the bug-house don't wake up with all of their loose screws tightened. Make up your mind to the fact that for some things, you're just gonna be stuck.

GET STARTED

Now that we know who you are, grab some gear, find the rest of your crew, and get your boat up into the sky. There's adventure to be had out in the black!

CHAPTER 2

TRAITS AND SKILLS

THE WARNING

The majordomo slid the fur coat from Hwa Ling's shoulders and deferentially removed Jack Leland's black, silk cape. The majordomo then handed them to a waiting servant.

"Mr. Leland," the majordomo murmured in subdued and well-bred tones, "Miss Ling, you are most welcome. His Grace, the Grand Duke Brunnhoff, and his guests are eagerly awaiting your arrival. You will find His Grace in the card room."

Leland removed his top hat and his white gloves and handed those to the majordomo. Hwa Ling, standing at Jack's side, cast a seemingly bored glance about the sumptuous entryway. In truth, her gaze missed nothing of importance, sizing up the servants, seeking out hidden cameras, taking note of the alarms, locating the exits. Although she was playing the role of Jack's paramour this night, she was, in truth, his bodyguard. His safety was her responsibility—a job she took quite seriously.

Hwa Ling turned to Jack with a smile and placed her hand lightly on his arm. The smile and the gesture told him all was well. If something had been wrong, she would have started a quarrel with him. Jack smiled in acknowledgement.

The two followed the majordomo, who walked with subdued and well-bred pace across polished marble floors. Portraits of olive-skinned nobles in lace and ribbons and supercilious smiles graced the walls.

"The Grand Duke's ancestors?" Hwa Ling asked in a low voice.

"As you well know from your research, the 'Grand Duke' started out as a boot-black boy on Persephone," Jack replied softly, a glint of amusement in his eyes. "He made his money in hog futures. The portraits are fake. The palm trees are holographic. The 'majordomo' is a two-bit actor hired on for the night."

"I trust his money is real," said Hwa Ling with an arched eyebrow.

"His money is excellent," said Jack complacently.

"Is 'His Grace' any good at poker?"

"I won't play with anyone who isn't," Jack returned. "It is not the winning so much as the game. You know that about me, my dear."

Hwa Ling did know it, though she could never understand it. For her, the game was inconsequential. The winning was everything.

As they continued down the long expanse of hallway, Hwa Ling took note of each person they encountered. She did this automatically, without even giving it conscious thought, registering their faces in her mind. A young servant walking down the hallway caught her eye. There was nothing remarkable about him. He was like a hundred others who had fled the Core worlds to find their fortunes on the Rim. His slanted, almond eyes did not even flick her direction as he passed. But he carried in his hands a vase filled with red lilies.

"You never once mentioned my new perfume," Hwa Ling said, suddenly petulant. She dropped her hand from Jack's arm and stamped her foot. "I spent all day shopping for it."

Leland's amiable expression never changed, though the glint of amusement left his eyes, replaced by concentrated alertness. He smoothed his hand over the left side of his dress jacket where he kept his derringer concealed.

"I meant to say something in the car, my dear. Tuberose, I believe. With a hint of jasmine? It suits you."

"A lot you know! It reeks! I can't stand it." Hwa Ling turned on her heel. "I'm going to the ladies room to wash it off. I'll meet you in the card room."

The majordomo indicated the way to the powder room. Upon entering, Hwa Ling found a female servant in attendance. Of Oriental extraction, the young woman kept her eyes properly lowered as Hwa Ling scrubbed off her favorite and extremely expensive perfume. When she was finished, the servant handed Hwa Ling a paper towel.

Hwa Ling opened the towel. She was preparing to dry off her throat and hands, when she saw Chinese characters, scrawled in lipstick, running up and down the length of the towel. Hwa Ling read, comprehended, and crumpled up the towel in her hands. She tossed the towel into the toilet. The servant stepped forward, pressed the handle, and the towel and its message swirled away.

Hwa Ling handed the servant a coin and walked out of the powder room, her stiletto heels clicking on the marble. Entering the card room, she cast a swift glance around. She spotted the five "hidden" security cameras with laughable ease and noted—with concern—that there was only one way in and one way out. She flicked her gaze over the assembled poker players: the Grand Duke in his phony finery and his five friends. She'd screened them all in advance, of course, and discovered nothing in their backgrounds to make her suspicious.

She'd screwed up.

She had screened these men to find enemies from Jack's past. She'd never thought to look for enemies from her own.

Jack sat at the table, shuffling a new deck of cards. The assembled men watched in admiration as the cards flicked through his long, agile fingers in a snapping blur.

"A kiss for luck, Hwa Ling, my dear?" he said to her, smiling.

She walked over to him. The admiration of the men shifted from the card-play to her. Placing her hands on Jack's shoulders, Hwa Ling bent down.

"Someone from the tong is here," she said softly, brushing his cheek with her lips. "He's going to try to kill me."

Any other man she'd known would have pitched a fit, insisted that she leave at once. Jack would never insult her like that. He merely twitched his eyebrows at the news and kept shuffling the cards. Hwa Ling strolled about the room in a bored manner before finally taking a seat behind Jack.

One of these men was in the pay of the Hip-Sing, the Tong that had murdered her father. She had taken her revenge on them, and now they'd sworn revenge against her. The servants who had warned her were members of her own tong, the red lilies her tong's warning sign of danger.

"Gentleman," said Jack in his deep, rich voice, "tonight's game is—"

Murder, thought Hwa Ling.

Every person in the 'Verse is unique. Even identical twins have different personalities. And just because folk are in the same line of work doesn't mean that they're cut from the same cloth. Take two doctors, both in the top three percent of the same prestigious school on the Core. One doctor might be soft-spoken, fussy about his clothes, and fiercely loyal to a crazy sister. The other could be barrel-chested, brash, and hides a drinking problem. While their medical capabilities are much the same, they are two very different folk.

Traits are the elements of a character's personality that help set each member of the crew apart from everyone else in the 'Verse. Defining a character's Traits is a good starting point when you're trying to get to know your character and create a unique persona. Traits also provide certain advantages and disadvantages that will help you better figure out your character's role in the action.

THE GOOD, THE BAD, AND THE BIG DAMN UGLY

Traits can come into play most any time, whether it's convenient or not. Beneficial Traits are called Assets. These enhance your ability to get things done either by improving the odds or providing opportunities that might not normally be there. On the flip side there's Complications, named such because that's exactly what they do—make your life complicated. Every character must have at least one Asset and one Complication. You can have more, but only up to five of each.

As explained back in Chapter One: *Find a Crew*, you acquire Traits before purchasing Attribute Points. Assets subtract points from your starting pool, while Complications add them. Many players like to balance the two types of Traits so they gain the normal starting Attribute points, but that isn't required.

Though you mostly have freedom to create your character as you like, the Game Master has final approval on your selection of Traits. He might also put a tighter cap on the number of Traits allowed. It's his job to give you all of that information 'fore you get started. After that, the decisions are all yours.

Picking Traits conforming to your history and background isn't exactly rocket science. Very often you'll realize what to take just by giving your concept the once-over. Could be you're a spoiled dandy from Persephone, who never spent much time outside the family estate. You ain't likely "Tough as Nails"—anymore than a border-planet dirt farmer would be "Highly Educated." Your pedigree and wealth might buy you "Friends in High Places" and "Moneyed Individual," but you might also be a "Lightweight."

After the obvious Traits are out of the way, spare a moment to ponder your character's personality, and what Traits you could take to reflect it. Perhaps you're one of those folk who never seem to get rattled, so "Steady Calm" sounds like a good choice. You're also a bona fide skirt-chaser, so "Amorous" is another Trait that fits like your custom-made dress coat.

Watch out for contradictory Traits. Some just don't go together. We'll leave it to common sense and the ruling of the GM (whose call on Traits is final) to determine if the ones you've chosen are suitable. You can't have "Heavy Tolerance" and also be a "Lightweight," anymore than you can be both "Portly" and "Scrawny."

Traits are tools used to solidify the profile and image of who you are. Treat them like a random grab bag and you end up with a patchwork rag doll best hawked at some cheap Rim tourist shop. There's a reason why Traits cost less during a character's initial creation than if they're purchased later—to encourage well-thought concepts and lay a good foundation for your role in the adventures to come.

Table 2-1: Traits

Trait	Point Cost
Asset, Minor	–2
Asset, Major	–4
Complication, Minor	+2
Complication, Major	+4

ASSETS

Assets are first acquired when your character is created (see Chapter One: *Find a Crew*). After that, you can purchase new Assets for your character during the course of a campaign using Advancement Points and through effective role playing. For example, if you undertake a series of clandestine missions for a member of Parliament, you could probably convince the GM you now have the Asset known as "Friends in High Places."

Many Assets grant you a straightforward advantage in a game situation, such as a step bonus to either a Skill or a Attribute die. For example,

you're playing a cute mechanic who has the Asset "Sweet and Cheerful." Normally, your Influence Skill die is only a d6. When dealing with folk who can't help but like you because you are "Sweet and Cheerful," your +2 step bonus kicks in and you roll a d10 instead.

On occasion, more than one such bonus might apply. As an example, you are a Registered Companion who has both "Allure" for a +2 and a "Good Name" for another +2. In a situation where you're having a romantic interlude with an interested party who has heard of your fame, you gain a whopping +4-step bonus to a Skill roll—which would change a d4 to a d12!

Some Assets grant you new ways to to use your Plot Points. (See Chapter Five: *Keep Flyin'* for a detailed explanation of how to use Plot Points.) Take your mechanic, who is not only sweet but has a way with machines. "Mechanical Empathy" allows you to spend Plot Points to determine exactly what's going on with that port compression coil. Other assets make the Plot Points you spend more effective. A preacher-man with "Religiosity" who spends Plot Points when interacting with the right folks gets more bang for his Plot Point buck (meaning his bonus die would be higher).

There are also Assets that affect your character in other ways. "Tough as Nails" gives you extra Life Points, while "Mean Left Hook" changes the type of damage you inflict with unarmed attacks. Read the description of each Asset and write the appropriate notes for it on your character sheet.

While Assets are part of a character's basic makeup, they can be rendered useless during the course of the game. A "Moneyed Individual" who has committed a crime and is now a fugitive could suddenly find her accounts frozen by the Alliance. A fellow with a "Sharp Sense" of hearing won't be able to eavesdrop in a bar if a grenade blast has blown out his eardrums. Such events are usually temporary, and the GM should give players an opportunity to make their Assets effective again.

Note that unless the description states otherwise, a character with the Major version of an Asset gains the benefit of the Minor version as well.

ALLURE [MINOR/MAJOR]

You are physically attractive, either a handsome fellow or a lovely woman. When you desire companionship you generally don't need to look far. Not only are you good-looking, but you know how to make your looks work for you in most situations.

> "She's a reader. Sees into the truth of things; might see trouble before it's coming. Which is of use to me."
>
> —Malcolm Reynolds

Only rarely does your *shwie* appearance attract the wrong sort of attention.

Benefit: With minor Allure, you gain a +2 step Skill die bonus on all actions keyed to appearance, such as: seduction, negotiation, persuasion, or winning beauty pageants. If you are gorgeous enough to have major Allure, any Plot Points spent on such actions are improved as if you had spent 2 additional points. (For example, if you are spending 2 Plot Points to improve a seduction attempt, your additional die is a d8 rather than a d4. If you spend 2 points after the roll is made, your final result is improved by 4 instead of 2.)

ATHLETE
[MINOR/MAJOR]

You know how to push your body past its normal limits for certain kinds of physical activity. You might pay the price in aching muscles later, but you're able to run farther, jump higher, lift heavier than most folk.

Benefit: Pick one Athletics Specialty. You may choose to exert yourself in the use of that Skill. If you voluntarily suffer Stun damage, you gain an extra die roll as if you had spent an equal number of Plot Points. You may spend up to the number of points that would render you unconscious, but no more. As a Major Trait, any Plot Points (not Stun) spent on physical activities are improved as if you had spent 2 additional points.

BORN BEHIND THE WHEEL [MINOR/MAJOR]

You learned to fly or drive before you learned to walk. You're never more at home than when you are seated at the controls of your favored type of vehicle. It's as if you and the machine unite to form a single entity.

Benefit: Choose either land or air/space vehicles. You gain a +2 step bonus to your Agility Attribute whenever you are at the controls of your chosen vehicle type. As a Major Trait, any Plot Points spent on actions involving your chosen vehicle type improve as if you had spent 2 additional points.

CORTEX SPECTER
[MINOR/ MAJOR]

There's almost no record of you in the Cortex. You're a ghost gliding through the system unseen. Simple clerical error could be the cause, or someone (perhaps yourself) went to the trouble to wipe the information clean.

Benefit: A Cortex search won't show much about your history besides your birth. Anyone attempting to dig up information on your past has a +8 added to the difficulty of their search. Casual searches will reveal almost nothing about you.

As a Major Trait, no official docket of you exists anywhere. Any Alliance, Fed, Interpol agent, or bounty hunter trying to look you up finds nothing. In most situations (applying for a liquor permit, making a purchase on credit) the officials will pass it off as a computer error, since everyone is on file somewhere. There could be disadvantages to this: credit could be denied or worse, you might have trouble checking into the emergency ward of an Alliance-run hospital. And if the Alliance finally arrests you on serious charges, it could mean a whole heap of trouble, for officially you don't exist.

FIGHTIN' TYPE
[MAJOR]

You know how to handle yourself in almost any combat-type situation—whether it's a rough-and-tumble brawl or a deadly shootin' match.

Benefit: You may take one non-attack action each combat turn without penalty. For example, if you move and shoot in the same turn, your shot will not suffer the normal –1 step Skill penalty.

FRIENDS IN HIGH PLACES [MINOR]

You know important people. You know important people who know important people. You dine with ambassadors, play golf with members of Parliament, and exchange holiday greeting cards with an Admiral in the Alliance fleet. When you need a favor, you know those who might be willing to help.

Benefit: Once per session, you can spend 1 or more Plot Points to call in a favor or secure a quick loan, either someone known from previous play or someone who occurs to you on the spot. The GM must agree on the nature and position of your "friend," as well on the possibility of that friend granting your favor, which favor must be appropriate for people in positions of influence or authority. (The member of Parliament can give you access to the gala opening of the National Gallery of Art, but she won't be any help in calling off the goons who are out to break your kneecaps over that little matter of the stolen stogies.) Remember that your contacts might call in favors from you. The cost in Plot Points depends on the the favor.

Table 2-2: Friends in High Places

Plot Points	Type of Favor
1-2	Small loan (up to 500 credits); loan of minor equipment
3-4	Medium loan (up to 5,000 credits); lifting a land-lock; invitation to important event
5-6	Large loan (up to 10,000 credits); security clearance; use of a ship

FRIENDS IN LOW PLACES (MINOR)

Similar to "Friends in High Places," except that your connections are of the shady, criminal, and underworld variety. You have contacts that could include: money launderers, fencers, thieves, cartel bosses, counterfeiters, and the like. They can set you up with jobs, tip you off to the latest word on the street, and offer you first-buy on recently smuggled items. Sometimes there's honor among thieves, but it's best not to assume anything.

Benefit: Once per session, you can spend one or more Plot Points to call in a favor from a local criminal contact, either someone known to you from previous play or someone you suddenly recall having met previously. The GM must agree on the nature and position of your "friend," as well on the possibility of your favor—which must be appropriate for such folk. (This friend will not be able to provide tickets to the opera, but could get you a sweet deal on a laser-sighted grenade launcher.) Note that your contacts might call in favors from you in the future. The cost in Plot Points depends on the favor.

Table 2-3: Friends in Low Places

Plot Points	Type of Favor
1-2	Small loan with interest (up to 500 credits); information; purchase imprinted goods
3-4	Medium loan with interest (up to 5,000 credits); a cut on a smuggling job
5-6	Large loan with interest (up to 10,000 credits); protection from rival crime lord

GOOD NAME [MINOR/MAJOR]

You've made a name for yourself through some heroic or charitable deed or have underworld credibility. One way or another, you've got a reputation that usually works in your favor.

Benefit: You are held in high regard within your social circle. You gain a +2 step Skill bonus to any social interaction in which your good name comes into play. As a Major Trait, just about everyone in the 'Verse has heard of you and your bonus applies almost all the time. 'Course, you don't get to apply this bonus to your enemies or people who see you *bie woo lohng*.

HEALTHY AS A HORSE [MINOR/MAJOR]

You just don't get sick. Even when the rest of the crew is down with coughs and sniffles, you feel wonderful. Serious ailments bounce off your iron constitution. On the off-chance you do get sick, you can count on a fast recovery. You might even heal faster than most when the damage wasn't caused by a germ, but something a might more potent (such as a bullet).

Benefit: You gain a +2 step Vitality Attribute bonus whenever you roll to resist or shake off illness or infections. As a Major Trait, any Plot Points spent on such rolls gain a bonus as if you had spent 2 additional points; you also heal damage (both Stun and Wounds) at twice the usual rate.

HEAVY TOLERANCE [MINOR]

Drugs and alcohol just don't affect you like they do most folk. You can drink a slew of husky fellows right under the table. Only downside is you have to pay for twice as many drinks to get a decent buzz, and you have to take more than the usual dose on most medications to get the desired effect. (You have to take double the dose of pain medication, for example, when the doc is stitching you up.)

Benefit: You gain a +2 step Vitality Attribute bonus whenever you resist the effects of alcohol, drugs, knock-out or lethal gasses, and poison.

HIGHLY EDUCATED [MINOR]

You were good in school, actually paid attention to the teachers, and retained what you learned. Comes in handy during social events and game-show appearances, though your extensive book-learning can sometimes make you stand out on a Border planet.

Benefit: You gain a +2 step Attribute bonus to Intelligence for any Knowledge-based Skill roll when you try to recall some information (though

it won't help you when you're taking actions).
For example, if you are a doctor trying to match
someone's symptoms to a particular disease, you
receive the bonus; it does not apply to rolls affecting
your treatment of the patient.

INTIMIDATIN' MANNER [MINOR]

You've got a steely-eyed stare. You have true
grit. Something about you makes folk think twice
before crossing you. Security guards call you "sir"
(even if you're a gal). Punks melt under your glare
and confess everything they know and most of what
they don't.

Benefit: You gain a +2 step Attribute bonus to
Willpower on any action that involves intimidating,
interrogating, bullying, frightening, and all manner
of awing other folks. You can also use this on your
rolls to resist similar attempts made against you.

LEADERSHIP [MINOR/MAJOR]

You are an inspiration to others. People look to
you in a crisis. You're able to motivate those around
you and encourage them to do what needs to be
done.

Benefit: Once per session, you can designate
a goal for receiving your leadership bonus.
Everyone working to achieve the goal gains +2
step Skill bonus on any one action directly related
to completing the task. (An example might be
focusing the entire crew on finding a stowaway.) As
a Major Trait, you may also spend any number of
your available Plot Points to improve the actions of
one or more characters other than yourself, so long
as those actions are related to your chosen goal.
These Plot Points must be used immediately by
each character who receives them in this way. The
characters may also supplement these Plot Points
with their own.

LIGHTNIN' REFLEXES [MAJOR]

You react to danger quickly. Folk rarely get the
drop on you. In a quick-draw contest, your gun is
out before the other fellow can find his holster.

Benefit: You gain a +2 step Attribute bonus to
your Agility on all Initiative rolls.

MATH WHIZ [MINOR]

Whereas others quickly run out of fingers and
toes, you have the answer all figured out. You can
solve *pi* out to more decimals than most folk care to
hear about. You can give the square root or the cube
root of any number tossed at you without benefit of
a calculator.

Benefit: You perform complex mathematical
calculations effortlessly, and solve most
mathematical problems without fail (and no need to
roll the dice). You gain a +2 step Attribute bonus
to Intelligence for all actions related to accounting,
engineering, and navigation—and in any situation
that requires immediate mathematic interpretation.

MEAN LEFT HOOK (MINOR)

Your fists are hard as rocks. You're capable of killing a man with your bare hands.

Benefit: Your unarmed attacks inflict Basic damage (split between Stun and Wound) instead of Stun. See Chapter Five: *Keep Flyin'* for more information on unarmed combat.

MECHANICAL EMPATHY (MINOR)

Machines talk to you. You have a way of fixing what ails them that goes way beyond the instruction manual. You are happiest when covered in engine grease.

Benefit: For the cost of a given number of Plot Points (as determined by the GM; see the table for guidance), you gain intuitive knowledge as to what's wrong with a particular mechanical device under your care, as well as a +2 step Skill bonus to Mechanical Engineering for any action attempting to fix said device. Certain unusual circumstances might block your ability (the machine turns out to be a hologram). When such is the case, you do not spend your Plot Points.

Table 2-4: Mechanical Empathy

Plot Points	Nature of Problem
1–2	Minor problem (dead battery, slipped belt)
3–4	Moderate problem (corroded wiring, blown gasket)
5–6	Major problem (faulty catalyzer, crack in the external fuel tank)

MILITARY RANK (MINOR)

You are a member of the armed services or you are a veteran and proud of it. You most likely fought in the war on one side or the other. Depending on whether you were Browncoat or Alliance, you'll earn respect in one locale and take your lumps in another. You have the know-how and the means to carry you through most tough situations.

Benefit: You are or were either an enlisted man or an officer. An enlisted military member or veteran gains a +2 step Attribute bonus to Willpower on all Discipline-based actions. Officers gain an equivalent bonus on all Influence-based actions.

MONEYED INDIVIDUAL (MAJOR)

You're loaded. Not only do you have a nice chunk of change on hand, you've got cash tucked away and rolling in on a regular basis. You sport a wealthy life style that can sometimes make you a target for those who want what you've got.

Benefit: Increase your starting credits by one-half (multiply your normal starting total by 1.5). Once per game session, you can make an Intelligence + Influence (or any appropriate Specialty) roll when making a purchase to see if you can afford it by dipping into your trust fund (instead of your money on hand). The Difficulty starts at Easy (3) for a purchase of up to 2,000 credits, and increases by 4 for every additional 2,000 credits of the purchase (see table). You may spend Plot Points on the roll.

Table 2-5: Moneyed Individual

Difficulty	Cost of Item
3	Up to 2,000 credits
7	Up to 4,000 credits
11	Up to 6,000 credits
15	Up to 8,000 credits
19	Up to 10,000 credits

NATURAL LINGUIST (MINOR)

You've got an ear for languages and can learn a new one with remarkable ease. You can pick up specific dialects and recreate accents with little effort. This talent helps you blend in with the locals no matter where you wind up. By listening to people talk, you get a pretty good idea where they're from (which might come in handy when they're not being perfectly honest about such!).

Benefit: You learn Linguist Specialties at half their normal cost. You can also imitate and detect specific accents and dialects, giving you a +2 step Skill bonus to Influence or Performance (and appropriate Specialties) whenever you are trying to pass for a native.

NATURE LOVER (MINOR)

You're in harmony with nature. Even though you are forced to spend most of your time in a crowded city or on board a cramped spaceship, you feel most in tune with your surroundings when you are sleeping on the ground under starlit skies or walking amidst the trees of a forest or riding your horse across the prairies.

Benefit: You gain a +2 step Attribute bonus to all Alertness-based rolls while in an outdoor setting, along with an equivalent bonus to a Survival-based skill die when applied to a natural environment.

NOSE FOR TROUBLE
[MINOR/MAJOR]

You've got a mental alarm that sounds when something's about to go wrong with the plan. You can tell when a no-good *guay toh guay nown* is lying his ass off. You have a creepy feeling that someone is standing behind that door.

Benefit: You can make an Intelligence- or Alertness-based roll to sense trouble even when circumstances might not normally permit it (you're dancing at a hoe-down), and you gain a +2 step bonus to either Attribute when the circumstances warrant (you're sneaking into the hide-out of the local crime boss). As a Major Trait, you may also spend 1 Plot Point to negate all effects of surprise, as you sense trouble just in the nick of time to avoid getting caught with your trousers down.

READER [MINOR/ MAJOR]

Your mind is open to the thoughts and emotions of folk nearby. Whether you realized your psychic potential by yourself or as part of a corporate or government program, being a reader can be both a blessing and a curse. *This trait is only available with GM approval, as it may not match all campaigns.*

Benefit: As a Minor Trait, your abilities are empathic in nature, letting you learn the general feelings and moods of those around you. You gain a +2 step Attribute bonus to Alertness whenever observing someone, trying to discern the truth from a lie, and in other situations where your talents might help you understand a person. As a Major Trait, the bonus increases to +4, and once per game session you may spend Plot Points to gain clues or other information.

Note: "Reading" someone is not as straightforward as reading a book, but rather comes across as visual or auditory information that you don't always understand. Use of Plot Points should always grant you some idea of what the person is thinking, but the image you receive may be symbolic. The GM may also require a character with this trait to take a Complication (such as Traumatic Flashes) to go with your character's unusual background.

Table 2-6: Reader

Plot Points	Information Gleaned
1-2	Minor information (trivial details, casual thoughts)
3-4	Moderate information (private details, significant thoughts)
5-6	Major information (vital details, closely guarded secrets)

REGISTERED COMPANION [MINOR]

You possess an active license in the Companion Registry, which legally permits you to do business throughout the system. *This trait is only available with GM approval, as it may not match all campaigns.*

Benefit: Most worlds open the doors for a Registered Companion. The Trait grants you a +2 step Skill bonus to Influence-based actions in dealing with those who respect your station.

Note: This Trait reflects only your status in the Registry. To maintain it, you must meet the obligations of Guild membership . Your other training and Skills are obtained normally through character creation.

RELIGIOSITY
[MINOR/MAJOR]

You follow the tenants of a particular faith and are either a faithful practitioner or a *bona fide* man or woman of your particular God. Faith gets you through the hard times and might help in dealings with others.

Benefit: Select a religious faith. (Most folk in the 'Verse are either Buddhist or Christian, though many other faiths exist in smaller numbers.) As a Minor Trait, you are a faithful worshipper. Your beliefs gain you a +2 step Attribute bonus to any one Willpower-based action per game session. As a Major Trait, you are priest, pastor, monk, rabbi, or other ordained figure and can easily be recognized as such by your garb (robes, collar, hat, etc.). In addition to the minor benefits, all Plot Points spent on Influence (and Specialty) actions when dealing with those who respect your station are resolved as if you had spent 2 additional points. For example, if you spend 2 Plot Points to gain an extra d4 rolled on a given action, you would actually roll a d8—taking into account the extra Plot Points. Had you spent the 2 points after the roll, you would add 4 points to the result instead of 2.

SHARP SENSE
[MINOR]

You have the nose of the bloodhound, the eyes of an eagle, or the taste buds of a wine connoisseur. One of your senses is especially keen, and you can use it to your advantage.

Benefit: Pick one of the five senses: Smell, Touch, Sight, Taste, or Hearing. You gain a +2 step bonus to your Alertness Attribute for any action utilizing that sense. You may take this Trait more than once during character creation, choosing a different sense each time.

STEADY CALM
[MINOR/MAJOR]

Some situations shake up normal folk and have them pissin' themselves, but not you. You keep a clear head while all around you are losing theirs.

Benefit: You gain a +2 step Attribute bonus to Willpower to avoid being shaken, frightened, or startled. As a Major Trait, you are never rattled unless extreme or unusual circumstances apply (such as the influence of drugs, terrifying nightmares, etc.).

SWEET AND CHEERFUL [MINOR]

No power in the 'Verse can stop you from being cheerful. You are so doggoned nice that most folks just can't help but like you.

Benefit: You gain a +2 step Skill bonus on any action in which your sweet and likeable nature works in your favor.

TALENTED
[MINOR/MAJOR]

Whatever it is, you're good at it. You demonstrate a knack for a particular Skill and are able to perform better than others who have equivalent training. (You are a talented pilot, a talented dancer, etc.)

Benefit: Pick one Skill Specialty. You gain a +2 step Skill bonus on every use of that Skill. As a Major Trait, each progression to a higher die costs you 2 points less than normal. (The latter benefit applies only to advancement during play, not character creation.)

THINGS GO SMOOTH
[MINOR/MAJOR]

Lady Luck has taken a liking to you. Things just always seem to go your way. You can wade through a swamp of *go se* and still come out smelling like a rose.

Benefit: Once per session, you may re-roll any one action except Botches (see Chapter Five: *Keep Flyin'*). As a Major Trait, you gain an additional re-roll (twice per session), including Botch results. Note that any roll, including those using Plot Points, can be re-done with this Trait.

TOTAL RECALL
[MAJOR]

Your brain stores all information you've garnered over a lifetime within easy reach. You remember just about everything you've ever seen or heard.

Benefit: You gain a +2 step Skill bonus to any action in which your Trait may come in handy. You may also spend a Plot Point to remember verbatim every detail of a past event or encounter with absolute photographic clarity. Note that some

repressed memories or traumatic events might be the exception to this rule.

TOUGH AS NAILS
[MINOR/MAJOR]

You're tougher than you look. You can take a beating and still spit in the guy's eye. If you get knocked down, you bounce up again, ready for some gorram revenge.

Benefit: You gain 2 extra Life Points over your normal total. As a Major Trait, you gain 4 points instead.

TRUSTWORTHY GUT [MINOR/MAJOR]

You've learned to trust your hunches. Instinct helps you out of bad situations and leads you into good ones.

Benefit: You gain a +2 step Attribute bonus to any mental Attribute roll when you are relying on intuition. As a Major Trait, you can spend 1 Plot Point to ask the GM a specific "yes" or "no" question related to your hunch. ("Do I get the feeling this guy is on the level?") Any follow-up questions cost 1 point each more than the last. (For example, if you ask the GM three questions, the first will cost 1 Plot Point, the second 2, and the third 3 for a total of 6 points spent.) The GM can shut down the line of questioning at any time, as even hunches have their limits.

TWO-FISTED [MAJOR]

You're a *jing chai* switch-hitter, able to write, pitch, and use a weapon with either hand equally well. Comes in handy during softball games and shoot-outs.

Benefit: You are ambidextrous. You can use weapons, write, hit, and perform other actions with either hand and incur no off-hand penalty.

WALKING TIMEPIECE [MINOR]

You never need to look at a watch to know what time it is. You are uncannily accurate. Your friends use you to set their clocks. A stopwatch ain't got nuthin' on you.

Benefit: Under normal circumstances you know what time of day or night it is without looking at a clock. You also have a good idea of how much time has passed between one action and another. (If you're supposed to wait ten minutes before entering the bank, you know when ten minutes is up.) If you're knocked unconscious or otherwise incapacitated, it takes a full-turn Intelligence + Alertness action at Average difficulty to get your internal clock ticking again.

WEARS A BADGE
[MINOR/MAJOR]

You represent the Law—at least somewhere. Though the badge lends you authority, it can also be a burden when those you are sworn to serve and protect actually expect some service and protection. And, sadly, that shiny badge makes a dandy target.

Benefit: You have the resources and power of your agency on your side, at least within your jurisdiction. Your authority gains you a +2 step Skill bonus to all Influence-based actions when dealing with those who respect your position. As a Minor Trait, you represent local law enforcement on one planet or region (a deputy sheriff, for instance). As a Major Trait, your authority covers most of the system (such as a Federal Marshal or Interpol agent).

COMPLICATIONS

Complications are the excess baggage the crew carries with them during the campaign. Sometimes the problem is physical—such as missing a perfectly good eyeball. Other times the problem is with your past. ("Did I mention, Captain, that my sister and I are wanted fugitives?") Such complications can make life real interestin' for both you and those around you.

Complications help define your character and offset your Assets. Complications can have negative effects on your character, but there are some compelling reasons to pick a few.

Complications provide great role-playing hooks, and a few faults make your character more believable. Because of this, playing out a Complication is a prime chance to earn Plot Points that could help get you out of the latest scrape. A Complication may suggest a certain course of action to you. (Jayne's "Greed" might lead him to betray Simon and River.) Even though it's not pretty, this action may enhance the game play. (The rest of the crew has to rescue Simon, River, *and* Jayne.) In this case, the GM should reward the player handling the character of Jayne with Plot Points for successfully playing his role.

Remember it's your job to portray specific faults in play. Playing out a minor fault could be worth a Plot Point all on its own. (You have an "Allergy" to perfume. The Registered Companion aboard your ship wears perfume. You start sneezing whenever she comes near you.) You might win more Plot Points if you use your complication to actually create trouble when things are otherwise going well. (You are holding your gun on the bank teller who is wearing enough perfume to choke a horse. You start to sneeze uncontrollably…)

Sometimes the GM will add a Complication to your character based on the events of the campaign. For instance, you accept a job from a major crime lord and then decide you're not going to go through with it. (Don't matter if you gave the money back, he's pissed!) You've gone and acquired yourself a Deadly Enemy. Complications received after character creation do not earn you any bonus points or new Assets, so don't ask.

You can use Advancement Points to "buy off" a Complication, with the GM's approval. In addition to the points, there are usually in-game requirements that must be met. See Chapter One: *Find a Crew* for more details.

Make the most of your Complications. Don't be tempted to ignore them. You'll find that they add immeasurably to the gaming experience.

ALLERGY
[MINOR/MAJOR]

Certain things mess with your body something fierce. A minor allergy might cause only a rash or a sneezing fit. A major allergy means that a bee sting, shrimp dinner, or a peanut butter sandwich might leave you pushin' up daisies.

Penalty: Pick an allergy. As a Minor Trait, your reaction is minor (hay fever, rash, sneezes) and you will suffer a −2 step penalty to your Physical Attributes (Agility, Strength, Vitality) for all actions in its presence, at least until you take medication. As a Major Trait, you suffer a life-threatening reaction to the substance, and you take d2 points of Stun each turn. When you have no remaining Stun, all additional damage is suffered as both Wounds and Shock Points. You likely carry an emergency injection to use in these situations, which will stop the damage in d4 turns.

AMOROUS [MINOR]

Sex might not be the only thing on your mind, but it definitely ranks up there at the top. You're always chasing skirts (or tight pants) and looking to find intimate companionship whenever possible.

Penalty: You'll make a pass at almost any person of your sexual preference and you don't put up any barriers when someone is coming on to you. This can cause a −2 step Skill penalty to Influence-based actions when the other party is offended by your advances. You also suffer a −2-step Willpower Attribute penalty when attempting to resist the wiles of someone who is your "type."

AMPUTEE [MINOR]

You lost an arm or a leg, either in the war or in an accident. Doctors weren't able to sew it back on, and you can't afford a fancy bionic replacement. You might have a prosthetic device, but it's utilitarian, meant to get the job done and nothing more.

Penalty: You are missing either an arm or leg. If you lack an arm, you can't perform any action that requires the use of two hands (such as shooting with two pistols). Actions that usually take two hands (opening the lid of a jar of pickles) suffer a –2-step penalty. If you don't have a leg, you make use of crutches, a cane or a crude prosthetic to walk. Your base movement is reduced to 5 feet per turn, and you suffer a –4-step penalty on movement actions.

BLEEDER [MAJOR]

You suffer a medical condition known as hemophilia or you take blood thinners for another medical condition. Your blood doesn't clot like most folk's blood, so try not to get cut, shot, or stabbed.

Penalty: If you suffer Wound damage, you'll begin to bleed (see Chapter Five: *Keep Flyin'*), and suffer 1 additional Wound each turn until the bleeding is stopped (Hard Intelligence + Medical Expertise action).

BLIND [MAJOR]

Could be you've been blind since birth or since a terrible accident. Either way, you have to rely on your remaining senses to get around. You might have a trained animal to assist you, though its training has limits and you are responsible for its care.

Penalty: Your character has difficulties moving in unfamiliar surroundings and suffers a –4 step Skill penalty on any action that normally depends on vision. (The GM can mitigate this for certain actions, as blind individuals can become surprisingly competent at many tasks.) The penalty is doubled to –8 step for any attempt at ranged combat. Because you've learned to rely on other senses, you gain the Sharp Senses asset for both Touch and Hearing at no cost.

BRANDED
[MINOR/MAJOR]

You are a bad, bad person and everyone knows it.

Penalty: You've got a bad reputation—fairly earned or not—in your home region. You suffer a –2 step Skill penalty to any social interaction when the story of your terrible misdeeds comes into play. As a Major Trait, virtually everyone in the 'Verse has heard bad things about you and the penalty applies almost all the time. You suffer no penalty when dealing with folks who know you personally, or those who feel you got a raw deal.

CHIP ON THE SHOULDER
[MINOR/MAJOR]

Your therapist told you that you have anger management issues—right before you punched out his lights. Your fuse is a mite short, and violence tends to ensue wherever you go.

Penalty: You're ready for a fight at the slightest provocation. You can't walk away from insults or taunts. You suffer a –2 step Skill penalty to all peaceable social actions with even a hint of tension. As a Major Trait, any time you suffer Wound damage you go completely berserk, concentrating only on taking down the *wang bao dahn* who hurt you—until someone else tags you, then you switch to that *chin-wah tsao duh liou mahng*.

CREDO [MINOR/MAJOR]

You live by a set of principles and you will not deviate from them without a damn good reason. And sometimes not even then! Not only are your principles likely to get you in trouble, people who know you can use your predictable behavior against you. (It might be worth noting that even though "Credo" might land you in hot *swei*, it could go hand-in-hand with the Asset "Good Name" or some such.)

Penalty: As a Minor Trait, pick a credo that will get you into minor trouble. Examples: You will always defend a lady's honor, you never run from a fight. As a Major Trait, your credo is a sure fire way to put yourself in danger. Examples: you never leave a man behind; the Captain goes down with the ship; you always protect the weak.

COMBAT PARALYSIS [MINOR/MAJOR]

You tend to freeze up when bullets start flying or fists start swinging. Your paralysis may come over you because you're afraid or because you have no idea what to do. Either way, it takes you a moment to collect yourself when violence breaks out.

Penalty: When combat begins, you are unable to take any actions for d2 turns. You may spend Plot Points equal to the number of turns rolled to shake it off. At the GM's discretion, someone with "Leadership" as an Asset might inspire you enough to jolt you to action. As a Major Trait, you are helpless for d4 turns. You can't even use Plot Points to act sooner.

COWARD [MINOR]

You are a firm believer in living to fight another day. You have no desire to be a Big Damn Hero. When a fight breaks out, so do you—in a cold sweat.

Penalty: When danger strikes, you look for the nearest exit. You suffer a –2 step Skill penalty on all combat actions in which you are in danger and an equal Willpower Attribute penalty on any action to resist fear, intimidation, torture, or other threats. You will fight when backed into a corner—unless there's some way you can crawl through the wall.

CRUDE [MINOR]

You're a gorram bull running amok in Society's rose garden. No matter what your social station, you prefer to tell it like is—using lots of colorful words in English, Chinese, or some mixture thereof. You don't care much about normal pleasantries. If you're sharpening your favorite knife at the dinner table, you'll hock a loogie on the blade right then and there.

Penalty: You cuss, put your elbows on the table, spit on the sidewalk, and engage in other crude behavior. You suffer a –2 step Skill penalty on Influence-based actions whenever refined social behavior is called for.

DEAD BROKE [MINOR]

You live in a state of perpetual poverty. Your pockets have holes the size of Alliance cruisers. If you have money, you will immediately spend it.

Penalty: You will never have any measurable amount of wealth. When taking this Complication, cut your normal starting credits in half. You must spend all that you have left immediately, buying whatever you think you must have, whether you need it or not. Because of your debts, you must give up one-half of all your income the first day in a town, spaceport, or sign of civilization. The circumstances of your money's disappearance vary based on your character background and the plans of the GM.

DEADLY ENEMY [MINOR]

You have made yourself a dangerous enemy— someone who'll go to great lengths to either capture or kill you.

Penalty: Someone is out to get you. You don't have to specify the nature of your nemesis, though your personal background may provide you or the GM with ideas. Your enemy might be extremely powerful and dangerous, posing a direct threat every 3 to 5 adventures, at the GM's discretion. You'll never be completely free of the danger until you buy off this Complication—so even if you think you've gotten rid of your enemy, the threat remains in one form or another at the discretion of the GM. For example, if you kill a major enemy, his brother or best friend will swear vengeance and take up the hunt.

DEAF [MAJOR]

You've lost the ability to hear. You can sign and read lips. Your ability to speak may or may not be impaired.

Penalty: You cannot hear anything and automatically fail any Alertness-based action involving sound. As an advantage, you are immune to sonic attacks that are designed to injure or disable hearing individuals, and you might be able to tell what people at a distance are saying by reading their lips. You can understand sign language and receive a +2 step bonus to any use of the Perception/Read Lips Skill.

DULL SENSE [MINOR]

One of your five senses is fried. Could be a chronic stuffy nose, bad eyesight, poor hearing, or desensitized skin. Whichever it is, best not rely on that sense in a tight spot.

Penalty: Pick one of the five senses: Smell, Touch, Sight, Taste, or Hearing. You suffer a –2 step penalty to your Alertness Attribute for any action utilizing that sense. You may take this Trait more than once during character creation, choosing a different sense each time.

EASY MARK [MAJOR]

Someone back on Earth-That-Was said that a sucker is born every minute, and here you are. You believe what people tell you, whether it's a get-rich-quick scheme, sob story, or other *fay-fay d'pian*.

Penalty: You generally believe what you're told. (At least the character does, and as the player you'll be rewarded with Plot Points for going along with this Trait.) In situations where you are attempting to distinguish the truth from lies, you suffer a –4 step Mental Attribute penalty.

EGO SIGNATURE [MINOR]

You think you're so damn clever that you invariably leave a token, clue, or some other mark as a calling card at the scene of a crime. You want everyone to be able identify and admire your handiwork.

Penalty: You consistently leave some sort of identifying clue at the scenes of your crimes. The clue doesn't necessarily have to lead straight back to you and it might not always be obvious, but it could help someone track you down, or allow someone to frame you by committing crimes, then leaving your calling card.

FILCHER [MINOR]

You've got a motto: "Anything not nailed down is mine. And anything I can pry loose ain't nailed down."

Penalty: If some piece of pretty catches your fancy, you'll try to take it—even if committing the theft is a really dumb move. You don't steal out of greed, but out of compulsion.

FORKED TONGUE [MINOR]

You lie like an Oriental rug. It's your nature to weave tall tales and tell wild stories to friends and foes. You will lie even when the truth might favor you—you just can't help yourself.

Penalty: You are a compulsive liar. Good luck getting those who know you to believe a word you say. You suffer a –4 step Skill penalty to all Influence-based actions in such situations.

GREEDY [MINOR]

Money is the root of all happiness, as far as you're concerned. You might get stupid if the money is good enough.

Penalty: You will take almost any opportunity to acquire money. Doesn't matter if you're dirt poor or filthy rich—what you have will never be enough. Your personal ethics become a mite flexible if the payoff is big enough. You will sell out your friends, your crew, even your dear old mother who knits such cunning hats.

HERO WORSHIP [MINOR]

You look up to one person, living or dead. That person can do no wrong in your eyes. You work hard to emulate him or her.

Penalty: You attempt to emulate your hero in dress and speech and will go to great lengths to feel physical connections to this person. (You might work hard to see him in person, for example, or visit the town of her birth.) This Trait doesn't always endear you to people, sometimes causing a –2 step Skill penalty to Influence-based actions when in the company of those who aren't as enthralled with your hero as you are.

HOOKED [MINOR/ MAJOR]

You're addicted to a substance—be it alcohol, tobacco, or some type of drug. You must get your fix on a regular basis or suffer serious problems.

Penalty: As a Minor Trait, you're either addicted to something not immediately dangerous (cigarettes, painkillers) or you have your problem somewhat under control (a "functioning" alcoholic). You must get a daily fix of your habit or suffer a –2 step penalty to all Attributes for one week or until you get your fix. As a Major Trait, your problem is more serious. You are abusing a dangerous substance or have a severe drinking problem. Your addiction interferes with everyday life, your relationships with people, and might possibly get you killed. If you go into withdrawal, the penalty is –4 to all Attributes for two weeks or until you get your fix. Note that you cannot "quit" your habit until you buy off this

CHAPTER 2

Complication, and when you do have the points necessary to do so, you'll have to go through a long withdrawal period (determined by the GM).

LEAKY BRAINPAN [MINOR/MAJOR]

You have more than a few screws loose. Your mind is not all there. It often wanders from one incoherent thought to the next without stopping to rest.

Penalty: As a Minor Trait, you are prone to occasional delusions and random, nonsensical outbursts—a bit startling to those who are not used to such, but not too serious. You suffer a –2 step Skill penalty to Influence-based social interactions. As a Major Trait, you're completely weird and creepifying. You're as likely to rub soup in your hair as slash a butcher knife across a crew mate's chest because you think he looks better in red. The GM might provide you with a completely different description of your surroundings than what the "normal" people are seeing in order to reflect your altered state of mind. Even in normal situations, your character perceives the world a completely different way. You suffer a –4 step Skill penalty to Influence-based social interactions.

LIGHTWEIGHT [MINOR]

You have a delicate constitution. You don't generally deal well with threats to your health.

Penalty: You suffer a –2 step Vitality penalty to any attempt to resist the effects of alcohol, diseases, environmental hazards, and poison.

LITTLE PERSON [MINOR]

You've been called vertically challenged, dwarf, midget, small-fry—you've heard them all. You stand about waist-high compared to most folks. On the bright side, you're a smaller target in the cross hairs. With the proper disguise, you might be able to buy the Kid's Meal at the local restaurant.

Penalty: You are only 3 to 4 feet tall. Opponents attacking you with a ranged weapon from more than 10 feet away receive a +4 to the Difficulty. Your base speed is reduced to 8 feet per turn, and you suffer a –2 step Skill penalty on movement actions. Being smaller than most folk presents challenges, but also opportunities, as determined by the GM.

LOYAL [MINOR]

Certain folks known to you can count on you no matter what—be they crew, war buddies, childhood friends, family, or fraternity brothers. You will do anything for their well-being, even it means going the extra mile—across Reaver space.

Penalty: Pick a group that can count on your loyalty. You will do anything short of sacrificing your own life to help and protect them (and you might even do that). With the GM's permission, you can be loyal to an individual—provided this person is another Player Character or an NPC who is a constant presence in the campaign.

MEMORABLE [MINOR]

There's something distinct about you that makes most folk remember you. You are easy to recognize or pick out of a crowd. This could be an unusually large nose, a bushy beard, a thick accent, peculiar mannerisms, striking beauty, recognizable scars, tattoos, etc.

Penalty: You're easily identified. Others gain a +2 step Alertness Attribute bonus when attempting to spot you or recognize your likeness.

MUTE [MAJOR]

You can't speak. You can communicate to others only through sign language and writing.

Penalty: You don't suffer any penalties to actions, though you must make use of non-verbal communication to get your point across. Whenever this causes you significant challenges, the GM should reward you with one or more Plot Points.

NON-FIGHTIN' TYPE [MINOR]

You don't believe in solving disputes through violence—either because of religious conviction or the way your mama raised you. You are only willing to engage in violence only under the most dire of circumstances.

Penalty: You will fight only for your own survival or in situations where there is no other choice. When you are forced to fight, you're not very good at it, and you suffer a –2 step Skill penalty to any combat actions.

OVERCONFIDENT [MINOR]

You've got a bold streak as wide as the Rim. You don't think you're smarter, stronger, and tougher than everyone else in the 'Verse—you know you are! Some term you "cocky," but you know that a person as wonderful as you are *should* be this confident and capable.

Penalty: You know that you're up for any challenge. You'll run, not walk, into deadly altercations. You'll pick a fight even when you're outnumbered. You'll bet all the credits you have on a single throw of the dice. You'll risk attempting a dangerous action even if you're not the least bit skilled at it.

PARALYZED (MAJOR)

A spinal cord injury nearly ended your life. You do not have the use of your legs, and spend most of your life sitting in a wheelchair.

Penalty: Without mechanical (or friendly) assistance, you can crawl at a speed of only 2 feet per turn. In a manual wheelchair, your base movement is 5 feet and you suffer a –4 step penalty to movement actions. An electric wheelchair can allow you to travel up to normal movement speeds. You might have difficulty in certain situations, such as going up or down staircases or crossing uneven terrain. You can use ranged weapons without penalty, but suffer a –4 step penalty when fighting hand-to-hand.

PHOBIA (MINOR)

Something scares the *mi tian gohn* out of you. Just the mention of this object sends a shiver up your spine, causes your knees to buckle, and your gut to clench. You fall to pieces when having to deal with it.

Penalty: Specify your phobia. The object of your fear is either uncommon and you have an extreme reaction to it (going to pieces at the sight of a corpse), or your phobia is more common (fear of needles, guns, heights, spiders, etc.). You become shaken in its presence, suffering a –2 step Attribute penalty on all actions.

PORTLY (MINOR/MAJOR)

You never met a pot roast you didn't like.

Penalty: As a Minor Trait, you are somewhat overweight. You suffer a –2 step Attribute penalty to all Athletics-based actions (except swimming) and Influence-based actions dealing with fitness and physical appearance. As a Major Trait, you are morbidly obese. The penalty increases to –4 steps and base movement is reduced to 5 feet per turn. You also suffer a –2 step Skill penalty to all Covert-based actions involving disguise and hiding.

PREJUDICE (MINOR)

You flat-out can't stand a certain group of people. Your dislike could be ideological, socio-economic, regional, racial, religious, or what have you. You have a hard time hiding your aversion to such folk.

Penalty: Pick a group of people based on race, religious views, region of space, which side they fought on during the war, etc. For whatever reason, you choose to dislike these people as a group. (They must be people with whom you could have social or business dealings, so you can't choose Reavers!) You will avoid interacting with them whenever possible, and if it's not possible, you won't be able to hide your disdain for them. You might even go out of your way to insult them. All Influence-based social interactions with the object of your prejudice suffer a –2 step Skill penalty.

SADISTIC (MAJOR)

Perhaps you believe firmly in the writings of Shan-Yu, or maybe you're just a sick bastard. Either way, you love hurting people. The sound of screams is music to your ears.

Penalty: Your cruelty knows no bounds, and you don't pass up any chance to express your sadistic side, including maiming and torturing those under your power. (**Note:** This is a Trait usually reserved for the bad guys. No aspiring Big Damn Hero should ever take it.)

SCRAWNY (MINOR)

You've either missed a few meals or else you've got a freakish metabolism, because you're the proverbial skin-and-bones. You run around in the shower to get wet.

Penalty: You're skinny. You suffer a –2 step Strength Attribute penalty to all Athletics-based actions and a –2 step Skill penalty on Influence-based actions dealing with fitness and physical appearance.

SLOW LEARNER (MINOR)

There's just some things that you're not good at and you're never gonna be. Best accept that and move on.

Penalty: Choose one general Skill. You pay 2 additional points for any improvement to the Skill or any of its Specialties. (This applies to advancement only, not character creation.) You also suffer a –2-step Skill penalty any time you try to use it.

SOFT (MINOR)

You are a sensitive flower. You have an extremely low tolerance for pain and if you stub your toe, you will carry on like you've been stabbed through the gut.

Penalty: You take 1 additional point of Stun every time you take any damage at all. You also must succeed an Average Willpower + Discipline action to keep from weeping and wailing whenever you suffer any Wound damage whatsoever.

STINGY (MINOR)

If you had two coins to rub together, you'd stick 'em in your mouth and pray for lockjaw. Some call you miserly or a tightwad, but you consider yourself practical and thrifty.

Penalty: No matter how rich you are, you never part with money you don't have to. You buy off-brand merchandise, haggle down shopkeepers, stash

cash in your boot. Charitable causes don't interest you, and only reliable friends will ever be considered for a loan—with interest, of course.

STRAIGHT SHOOTER [MINOR]

Normally considered a virtue, honesty is not always the best policy—especially in diplomacy, business, or barrooms.

Penalty: You speak the truth without regard for other people's feelings, or the circumstances involved. You might consider telling a falsehood only in dire emergencies, and even then you suffer a −2 step Skill penalty to Influence-based actions, as your lie is written all over your face.

SUPERSTITIOUS [MINOR]

You avoid black cats, dodge around ladders, and refuse to pick up a mirror for fear you'll drop it. You believe in omens and harbingers of luck—good and bad. You don't take any chances. If you spill the salt, you cast a pinch over your shoulder while counting backwards from five.

Penalty: You have a wide set of superstitious beliefs that affect your everyday behavior. Such beliefs can be self-fulfilling prophecies, however. Whenever you receive an omen of bad luck, you receive a −2 penalty to all of your Attributes for a set of actions (determined by the GM). Fortunately the reverse is true as well; when you receive an omen of good luck, the GM will determine a group of actions to receive a +2 Attribute bonus.

THINGS DON'T GO SMOOTH [MINOR/MAJOR]

Lady Luck hates your guts. For as long as you can remember, things never have gone smooth for you.

Penalty: Bad luck follows you around. Coincidences never work in your favor. Once per session, the GM can force you to re-roll an action and take the lowest of the two results. As a Major Trait, the GM can make you re-roll two actions per session.

TRAUMATIC FLASHES [MINOR/MAJOR]

Life would be a fair sight more convenient without the horrible dreams and visions that overtake you on occasion. These flashes might be residual memories of a traumatic incident from your past, messages from a disturbed conscience, or horrible recurring nightmares. You don't even always know what will trigger them, but they leave you shaken and unsettled.

Penalty: Once per game session, some trigger (determined by the GM) will cause you to suffer a traumatic flash. These episodes leave you incoherent, shaking, and screaming—rendering you incapable of action for d2 turns and causing you to suffer a –2 step Attribute penalty on all actions for ten minutes following the flash. As a Major Trait, these flashes happen twice per session.

TWITCHY [MINOR]

You're not paranoid. You know for a fact that everyone is out to get you! You spend most of your time watching your back. You trust no one except your oldest and dearest friends (and you trust them only to a point).

Penalty: You don't trust anyone, especially folk you don't know. If people are whispering, they're whispering about you. You don't believe it when people try to assure you that they're on your side. You are convinced that someone is watching you all the time. You suffer a –2 step Skill penalty to all Influence-based actions in social situations.

UGLY AS SIN
[MINOR/MAJOR]

Either you were born ugly or you've managed to make yourself look mighty hideous through scars, burns, or whatnot.

Penalty: You're unattractive, and suffer a –2 step Skill penalty to all actions keyed to appearance, such as seduction, negotiation, and persuasion. As a Major Trait, you're ugly to the bone and all Plot Points spent on such actions cost twice the usual amount.

WEAK STOMACH
[MINOR/MAJOR]

Blood oozing from a cut finger makes your knees go wobbly. You faint at the sight of a corpse. Therefore, you tend to avoid those situations where such is likely to occur.

Penalty: You cannot stand to be in the presence of blood, entrails, and dead bodies. You suffer a –2 step penalty to all Attributes until either the source of your discomfort is removed or until you leave on your own. As a Major Trait, you also have to make an Average Vitality + Willpower test for each five minute interval you are exposed to gory scenes or fall unconscious for 2d4 minutes.

SKILLS PAY THE BILLS

Just as Attributes represent your Crew's raw talents, Skills represent the training that helps best make use of that talent. The Skills you pick for your character reflect his or her origins, interests, and education. A quick glance at the Skills you choose can often tell a lot about the character, revealing either an upstanding, educated citizen of the Core planets or a hell-raisin' gunslinger from the Rim—or some such in between.

You purchase Skills during character creation and improve them later with Advancement Points (see Chapter One: *Find a Crew*). Skills are divided into two related types: General Skills and Specialties. An example of a General Skill is Athletics—a Skill needed for any type of physical activity from dodging to swimming. A General Skill can be improved upon, but may advance only up to d6. After that, you need to choose at least one Specialty Skill.

Speciality Skills start where the General Skill leaves off, allowing the character to improve in a specific area of expertise. For example, your former track star character has the Athletic Skill at d6, with the Running Specialty at d10. When you already have a d6 in a general Skill, your purchased Specialties start at d8, as you build on the expertise you have at the general level. There are no limits to the number of Specialties you may purchase.

If a character doesn't have a Specialty, he simply rolls using the general Skill (assuming he has it), or the Attribute only if he has no Skill in the action whatsoever. A Skill starting at d2 can be improved upon from there. Starting characters of any level rarely begin the game with more than a d12 rating in any one Skill Specialty.

BENCHMARKS OF PROFICIENCY

Since Skill levels are represented by dice, you might not have an immediate sense of just how good your character is at any one task. Use Table 2.7 (Skill Levels) to quickly see how your character measures up.

SKILL DESCRIPTIONS

Here you'll find a list of Skills for use in the *Serenity Role Playing Game*. Each entry includes the Skill name (followed by "Skilled Only" if it cannot be used untrained), sample specialties, and examples for each level of difficulty used in the game. Note that some examples are for simple actions, others are for complex (see Chapter Five: *Keep Flyin'*). Also note that some Skills may land under more than area of expertise. For example, dancing will come under Athletics if you are dancing in the Core Olympic games. If you are dancing in the Core ballet company, dancing comes under Perform. You and the GM should determine where your Skills lie and make the choice of either Athletics or Perform. You cannot do both.

NEW SPECIALTIES

You want to play a character who has a certain Skill and you don't see the Skill specialty you want on the list. Don't panic! Instead of filling this book with every possible Skill we could think of, we chose to list those that are most commonly used in game play. Feel free to create new specialties! If you want to be a master of origami or an expert of celebrity trivia—go right ahead! As long as you tie the specialty to a general Skill and the GM agrees, you can add whatever you like. Shiny!

ANIMAL HANDLING

You can make friends with any animal using this Skill. Caring for, feeding, riding, teaching the animal tricks, "whispering" to the animal—all things you learned growing up on a farm or ranch. Well, city kids can learn it, too, if they've got the heart for it.

Specialties: animal training, riding, veterinary, zoology.

Easy: Teach small domestic animals (cat, dog) simple tricks (come, beg, roll over); herd livestock (cattle, sheep); ride a pony at a trot; identify basic breed of a common animal (collie, greyhound, husky, Manx, Siamese).

Average: Teach domestic animals moderate commands (attack, guard, hunt, fetch); ride a horse at full gallop; drive teams of creatures, train tamed beasts or those born in captivity; diagnose common animal ailments and administer proper treatments; recall important creature facts and habits.

Hard: Teach domestic animals specific, complex commands (swim to the opposite side, leap and grab the sardine on the pole); ride through dense forest on horseback; ride an unconventional creature (camel, warthog) at top speed, approach a wild beast (wolf, mountain lion) without being afraid;

determine and treat serious bestial ailments and injuries.

Formidable: Teach tamed beasts complex commands; calm a pack of wolves; train domestic animals to do extreme tricks (count to ten, acrobatics); charge over dangerous terrain (quicksand, swamp) on horseback; perform intricate veterinary surgery with proper aftercare; identify behavior pattern of rare species.

Heroic: Perform experimental (or radical) veterinary surgery or treatments; tame a rare species of animal; jump a 50-foot chasm on horseback.

Incredible: Calm a cattle stampede on command.

Ridiculous: Successfully perform emergency surgery on a genetically altered or mutated animal.

Impossible: Take the lead in the Prime Minister's Derby riding a sick, blind mule with three legs.

ARTISTRY

You make artsy pretties that folks admire. Since aesthetic tastes vary quite a bit in the 'Verse, assume that the work is created to suit a target group or audience. (Your painting of the blue-faced woman with three heads and six arms is not likely to sell in the souvenir shop on Jiangyin, even though the art critics on Sihnon rave about it).

Specialties: appraisal, cooking, forgery, game designing, painting, photography, poetry, sculpting, writing.

Easy: Basic sketches and course projects for community college art classes; imitate a familiar yet simple signature; estimate worth of common art pieces; write a story for local writer's group.

Average: Produce marketable artwork (illustrations, comic books); elaborate on history and style of major art movements (surrealism, cubism); detect amateur forgeries of masterpieces; write a typical grant proposal, self-publish a novel.

Hard: Create gallery/exhibition-worthy artwork; authenticate obscure art; forge popular masterpieces (Mona Lisa, statue of David); falsify common documents (drivers licenses, diploma); estimate

Table 2-7: Skill Levels

Die Type	Proficiency	Comment
d2	Incompetent	"That ain't the 'on' button, is it?"
d4	Novice	"Don't pull the trigger, squeeze it."
d6	Competent	"Believe I know this dance. Shall we?"
d8	Expert	"I can reprogram this trash bin to go wherever we want."
d10	Professional	"The dermal mender will keep that ear on fine. Just don't fiddle with it!"
d12	Master	"A Crazy Ivan? Right now? Okay."
d12+	Supreme	"You're holding eights, low queen, jack, and ace. Your eyes gave it away."

worth of a good private collection; photograph objects and scenes with excellent artistic detail; write an enticing grant proposal or business plan; sell work to major publisher.

Formidable: Create critically acclaimed, universally recognizable original artwork; forge masterpieces of any style; photograph objects and scenes with perfect artistic detail; estimate worth of a historical collection; write novel that hits the best-seller lists; counterfeit official documents and files (state seal; identcard).

Heroic: Produce an instant classic; estimate exact worth of a national collection; photograph minute detail of a secured compound with an ordinary camera.

Incredible: Create a priceless masterpiece; create four-course gourmet meal using only basic ingredients and spices.

Ridiculous: Construct a long-form poem with perfect rhythm and meter on the first attempt; create a meal fit for royalty with only a few ingredients and only one available cooking method.

Impossible: Sculpt a perfect replica of an individual from only rough description; write a novel that tops the best-seller's lists for ten years running.

ATHLETICS

Whenever you are moving, most likely you're using athletics. This Skill allows you to run, jump, throw, climb, swim, and play sports.

Specialties: climbing, contortion, dodge, juggling, jumping, gymnastics, parachuting, parasailing, pole vaulting, riding, running, swimming, weight lifting. (**Note:** An individual sport can be its own Specialty, such as baseball or soccer.)

Easy: Complete a 50-yard dash; jump a knee-high hurdle; dive out of the way of a slow moving vehicle.

Average: Put ball through a 10'-high basket from close distance; complete a 100-yard dash; hurdle a chest-high fence; perform common acrobatics (somersault, handstand); balance on a narrow beam or ledge; swing across a hall on the chandelier; juggle 3 to 5 small, uniform objects; dive clear of a moving vehicle (21-60 mph speed).

Hard: Lift twice your body weight; juggle up to 5 palm-sized objects or 3 larger ones; perform complex acrobatics; land safely after a 15' fall; walk a tightrope; jump from one galloping horse to another; avoid a fast moving vehicle (61-120 mph speed).

Formidable: Jump off a 10-story building and survive the fall; dodge busy intersection traffic; bound over a 10'-tall wall; walk a tightrope in windy conditions; juggle multiple large and dangerous objects (knives, chain saws); complete a marathon or triathlon.

Heroic: Parasail upside down while holding the rope in your teeth; land safely after a 50' fall; walk a tightrope strung between two slow moving vehicles; juggle multiple large and dangerous objects blindfolded.

Incredible: score a hole-in-one; swim upstream against a raging current; rush head-on through a cattle stampede without a scratch.

Ridiculous: Jury-rig a malfunctioning parachute while in free-fall; pole vault from a rooftop across the street into a small open window two stories up; lift ten times your body weight in a military press.

Impossible: Free-climb a treacherous mountain while in handcuffs; bowl a perfect game without looking at the pins.

COVERT

Sneaky maneuvers, usually illegal. You can use this Skill to move silently, hide, blow a safe, or pick someone's pocket.

Specialties: camouflage, disable devices, forgery, infiltration, open locks, sabotage, sleight of hand, stealth, streetwise, surveillance.

Easy: Hot wire civic ground transports; move silently without waking up a sleeping person; pick a drunk's pocket; hide in full cover (behind boulder, large furniture, huge machinery).

Average: Pick common locks; deactivate normal home security systems; hide with partial cover (shadow, shrub, big crate); pick normal folks' pockets; disable a mid-size transport ship.

Hard: Open professional locks; defeat sophisticated, museum-level security systems; hide with limited cover (laundry bin, under table).

Formidable: Disable state-of-the-art security systems; decipher multipad combinations; sneak into a maximum security prison unnoticed; disable an Alliance cruiser.

Heroic: Crack the code to open Alliance treasury vault.

Incredible: Steal a priceless masterpiece from a Core-world art gallery.

Ridiculous: Single-handedly take over an Alliance destroyer.

Impossible: Break into a bank vault using only a butter knife.

CRAFT

Involves creating or altering items, often for commercial purposes—anything from the cheap china in a Jiangyn tourist trap to the million-credit remodeling of a mansion on Bellerophon. You must roll a Skill check to see how close you come to making a craft to the desired specifications. Note that most projects require complex Skill checks (see Chapter Two: *Traits and Skills*).

Specialties: architecture, blacksmithing, carpentry, cooking, leatherworking, metalworking, pottery, sewing.

Easy: Create a souvenir rain-stick or quilt; renovate a room in a modest house; tan leather; create a makeshift hammer.

Average: Make fresh bao; renovate a standard building; temper and forge steel; customize the exterior design of a sourcebox or datapad.

Hard: Forge a quality tool or weapon; cook a delicious four-course meal; rebuild a large structure; streamline a rifle or car; hand stitch a circus tent; create a hovering chandelier.

Formidable: Construct full medieval plate mail; rebuild a complex structure; improve the design of a starship or military installation; make or fix advanced tools or armor; build hazardous environment vehicles.

Heroic: Create/repair exotic tools, armor, and weapons; replicate a Ming-dynasty vase using only standard clay, a potter's wheel, and a few basic paints.

Incredible: Create innovative tools, armor, and weapons; bake a great-tasting chocolate cake using only protein packs; build a functional flying ambulance using only spare parts found in a junk yard.

Ridiculous: Create a meal that impresses a food critic using only canned vegetables and protein packs; forge a perfectly balanced katana using only a wobbly hammer and engine heat.

Impossible: Repair a faulty terraforming station without a schematic; draw reliable blueprints for the 'Verse's tallest skyscraper in half an hour.

DISCIPLINE

Usually obtained through some sort of training, such as that gained in the military or when learning martial arts—though the Discipline can be self-taught or learned through other circumstances. This Skill set allows you to resist interrogation, focus on the job at hand in the face of distraction, or scare the hell out of someone else.

Specialties: concentration, interrogation, intimidation, leadership, mental resistance, morale.

Easy: Study an interesting book in a quiet, well-lit room; scare off an annoying child; question a cooperative witness.

Average: Keep fresh recruits in line after they only went through one day of training; memorize medical jargon with a full day to practice; resist spilling the beans under the threat of violence.

Hard: Interrogate a hardened mercenary; memorize a stream of numbers while in the middle of a noisy party; lead a group of green recruits into battle the first time.

Formidable: Crack jokes while being tortured; stare down a ruthless bounty hunter; keep up troops' spirits in the face of overwhelming defeat.

Heroic: Stop a weaker friend from breaking under torture; lead troops in a charge against overwhelming enemy fire; memorize enemy positions with only a second to look.

Incredible: Intimidate a gang of thugs who have weapons trained on you; resist torture even when you have already died and been revived; perform complicated problem-solving while playing Russian roulette.

Ridiculous: Maintain morale on a corpse-laden battlefield after your side has surrendered to the enemy; memorize a full page of binary code with bombs exploding all around you; successfully frighten a hardened mercenary who fears neither death nor pain.

Impossible: Convince a group of unarmed farmers to charge marauding Reavers; refuse to go along with an enemy's plan after he has just kicked your friend through a jet intake; pick a set of handcuff locks while falling from a 30-story building.

GUNS

Anyone might be able to squeeze a trigger, but that's not the same thing as actually knowing how to shoot. The 'Verse is a dangerous place, and it's best not to strap on iron unless you have the know-how needed to use it.

Specialties: assault rifles, energy weapons, grenade launchers, gunsmithing, machine guns, pistols, rifles, shotguns.

Easy: Recognize ammo for different kinds of guns; hit an unaware, stationary target (broad side of a barn, man with his back to you) at close range; find the safety on an unfamiliar weapon.

Average: Identify special ammo (armor piercing, "smart" bullets, etc.); hit a smallish, stationary target (garden gnome) at close range; clear a jammed weapon.

Hard: Adjust the sight or make small modifications to a weapon; hit a small, stationary target (such as a Blue Sun Cola can) at close range; reload an unfamiliar weapon quickly under stressful conditions.

Formidable: Shoot a tiny, stationary target (the button of a coat) at close range; make significant modifications to a weapon (collapsible components, adding laser targeting).

Heroic: Shoot a miniscule, stationary target (a sideways poker card) at close range; make major changes to a weapon (adapting it to fire specialized ammunition), shoot at the guy who is holding your friend hostage and hit him dead square in the center of the forehead.

Incredible: Hit a person behind a closed door while aiming through the keyhole.

Ridiculous: Set the gun to autofire and stitch a fellow's outline without one bullet hitting him.

Impossible: Hit a buzzing bee several blocks away in the left eye.

HEAVY WEAPONS

This Skill makes it possible for you to bring the biggest gun to a fight—and use it! Some weapons require a crew of two or more to operate (see Chapter Five: *Keep Flyin'* for rules on Cooperative Skill use).

Specialties: artillery, catapults, demolitions, forward observer, mounted guns, repair heavy weapons, rocket launchers, ship's cannons, siege weapons.

Easy: Hit the broad side of an Alliance cruiser 50 yards away; set and time simple explosives (a few sticks of dynamite).

Average: Hit a slow moving vehicle; gauge and set charges for routine demolitions (single building/vehicle); make small modifications to heavy weapons or a ship's guns.

Hard: Hit a vehicle moving at fast speed; rig or disarm uncommon explosives; make considerable modifications to mounted weapons.

Formidable: Hit a vehicle moving at very fast speed; create or disable intricate explosive devices; make major alternations to mounted weapons.

Heroic: Hit a space ship retreating at hard-burn speed; neutralize a "tamper-proof" explosive device.

Incredible: Drill another ship right in the cockpit/engine room/specific vital part.

Ridiculous: Split a tiny gap between space cruisers to hit a nimble gunship.

Impossible: Launch shells to hit several distant, fast moving targets simultaneously.

INFLUENCE

Sometimes words are more powerful than a gun. This Skill can help you win friends and influence people, or if the situation demands, sweet-talk them into giving you what you need. (**Note:** Most uses of Influence can be opposed by the target's Attributes or Skills, so the examples below may not always apply.)

Specialties: administration, barter, bureaucracy, conversation, counseling, interrogation, intimidation, leadership, marketing, persuasion, politics, seduction, streetwise.

Easy: Bluff landlubber yokels into thinking you'll blow a crater in their backwater moon when your transport ship has no guns; grease the right palms of local underworld or government; intimidate a child; seduce someone who's already smothering you in kisses.

Average: Administrate daily business for a small business or town; promote products from a major manufacturer; negotiate shuttle rentals; bribe crime boss or state official you once crossed; fool townsfolk into doing something they're not opposed to doing; book passengers on your ship; dig up the latest scuttlebutt on a high-ranking government official; intimidate a non-violent person.

Hard: Run daily business for a large corporation, province, or large colony; negotiate a large purchase (property, vehicle); convince someone to do you a big favor; intimidate a stubborn individual; seduce an honorable person who is in a committed relationship.

Formidable: Handle an administrative crisis for a government or corporation; keep two bloodthirsty rivals from killing each other; work deceptive, but iron-clad fine print into a contract; try to seduce a trained Companion.

Heroic: Hornswoggle wealthy passengers into paying outrageous fares for standard passage on your *fei oo* vessel; convince two bloodthirsty rivals to kiss and make up; intimidate a hardened war veteran or mercenary; seduce a religious figure who has taken a vow of celibacy.

Incredible: Convince a peaceable person to risk his life for someone else's cause; win over a hostile crowd with a short, impromptu speech; find a tiny loophole that gets you out of an otherwise rock-solid contract.

Ridiculous: Convince a terrified, unarmed person to stand and fight oncoming Reavers; change the popular opinion of an entire planet with a short statement.

Impossible: Intimidate a Reaver; convince a village full of zealous hill-folk not to burn your crazy sister as a witch.

KNOWLEDGE

Some folk can tell you how many dimples are on a golf ball. Others know how to wash protein stains off a red flannel shirt. This Skill gives you a broad general knowledge of everything and detailed knowledge for each Specialty you take. Note that there is a difference between applied knowledge and "book learning." You can't have both. For instance, you can't have "Gunsmithing" because that's a Specialization of Gun Combat and counts as applied knowledge. (You might have once read a book on guns, but that doesn't mean you know how to manufacture a gun.)

Specialties: appraisal, cultures, history, law, literature, philosophy, religion, sports.

Easy: Recognize names of important Alliance Parliament senators; know common information about major worlds like Londinum and locate them on a system map; remember facts that are in primary school textbooks.

Average: Recognize names of local celebrities/legendary figures, and recount their deeds; know the origins and history of major artifacts or antiques; recall rules and etiquettes of culture in detail; quote popular scripture passages out of a major religious text ("The Lord is my shepherd…"); recall facts found in high-school textbooks.

Hard: Know the origins and recent past of minor artifacts/antiques; estimate the worth of a silk tapestry made in Sihnon; find Bathgate Abbey; recount the starting lineup for a champion sports team; remember information found in a college textbook (such as Mudder's Milk being similar to ancient Egypt's "liquid bread").

Formidable: Understand what the badges and sashes indicate for the nobility of Persephone; recall specific passages from scholarly papers written by distinguished professors.

Heroic: Recognize the betrothal/marriage ritual of a backwater settlement; remember the names of individual soldiers in a large army regiment.

Incredible: Recall facts of an absurd Earth-That-Was fad (such as pet rocks or disco music); recite verbatim entire books of religious scripture.

Ridiculous: Remember obscure figures from history with no context to work from; recite a long string of unrelated numbers in proper sequence.

Impossible: Recite all the dialogue of a childhood vidshow seen only once; recall exact survey statistics from a fifteen-year-long terraforming project.

LINGUIST [SKILLED ONLY]

Talking won't do any good if no one understands what you're saying. Just about everybody in the 'Verse speaks English and Chinese (to one degree or another). The Linguist general Skill covers basic familiarity with various languages, though its use won't grant you fluency—meaning you won't be able to follow a fast moving conversation in another language. Specialties represent familiarity or training with a specific non-native tongue. Note that you are automatically fluent in any language that is a part of your background.

Specialties: Arabic, Armenian, French, German, Hindu, Japanese, Latin, Portuguese, Russian, Tagalog, Swahili, Swedish, etc.

Easy: Essential words and phrases for a seasoned traveler ("Food?" "Where restroom?" "How much?" "No!"); basic grammar; simple everyday greetings.

Average: Basic conversation ("How is the weather?" "What is your wife's name?"); interpret basic ideas of a literature or film; identity one language from another in a similar group (Danish from Norwegian, Turkish from Hungarian).

Hard: Fluent conversation ("You must give me that Neptune Colony recipe for the Crescent Sea Oyster Graparon!"); translate foreign literature or verbal communication in detail; identify one dialect from another in the same language (Cantonese from Taiwanese; Titan Colony from Newbury Port).

Formidable: Native conversation, including expressions and colloquialisms; translate old, historical version of a modern language (Medieval English); interpret basic meaning of text recorded in an ancient language (Latin, Hieroglyphics).

Heroic: Comprehend full meaning of philosophical, religious, or scientific treatises written in an ancient language.

Ridiculous: Summarize complete work of Shakespeare in Greek, Chinese, and Apache simultaneously.

Incredible: Translate incomplete text written in a forgotten ancient dialect.

Impossible: Swear up a storm in Babylonian.

MECHANICAL ENGINEERING (SKILLED ONLY)

You know what they say: "there are always places to see, things to break." And with this Skill, you'll be there to fix 'em, so long as the things have nuts and bolts and don't run on fancy computers. You can handle very simple tasks such as changing a light bulb or tightening a screw without this Skill, but you'll need it to deal with more complicated workings.

Specialties: create mechanical devices, machinery maintenance, mechanical repairs, fix mechanical security systems, plumbing.

Easy: Set up pulleys, conveyors, axles, and other simple machines effectively; identify problems and make simple repairs to standard mechanical devices.

Average: Build an irrigation system; operate more complex mechanical devices such as a drill-press or laser-welder; disable standard machines and gadgets; fix moderate mechanical system damage; make standard modifications (install a vacuum pump system in an old engine).

Hard: Construct a Core ambulance from scrap-heap parts; operate/disable complex mechanical devices such as a catalytic cracking unit in an oil refinery; repair severe mechanical system damage; create a non-standard use of existing machines (such as setting up a Crazy Ivan maneuver).

Formidable: Reverse-engineer a mechanical innovation; boost the performance of a mechanical device (such as giving a short speed-boost to a Firefly Class transport ship).

Heroic: Go beyond double the performance limit of a mechanical system for a brief period of time; implement permanent, significant mechanical upgrades to a ship when you have limited resources.

Incredible: Repair catastrophic mechanical damage with scavenged parts; improvise a sophisticated mechanical device from spare parts; identify non-working components on a ship while you are recovering from a gun-shot wound that nearly killed you.

Ridiculous: Keep a mechanical system running despite a serious problem or damaged part (such as a burnt-out catalyzer); improvise a sophisticated mechanical device using non-standard components (such as chewing gum, tin foil, and a magnifying glass).

Impossible: Re-start a fusion engine cold before a plummeting ship hits the ground.

MEDICAL EXPERTISE
(SKILLED ONLY)

You know what they say: "there are always places to see, people to break". And when folk do break, you'll be there to put 'em back together with your bag of modern medical wonders. You can slap an aid-strip on a scratch and tell them to take two aspirins in the morning without this Skill, but anything more serious requires medical school, internships, residency, and knowing when to holler "clear!"

Specialties: dentistry, forensics, general practice, genetics, internal medicine, neurology, pharmaceuticals, physiology, psychiatry, rehabilitation, surgery, toxicology, veterinary medicine.

Easy: Give physical exam; use basic medical instruments (defibrillator, x-ray); administer treatment for common ailments and injuries (fever, broken ankle); perform CPR and handle minor emergencies (concussion, minor burns).

Average: Diagnose unusual ailments and injuries; recognize uncommon medicines and medical practices; use complex clinical instruments (CT scanner, respirator); handle most emergency injuries (bullet wounds, compound fractures, deep lacerations); graft a man's ear back on with a dermal mender; create a time-delayed drug dose.

Hard: Diagnose complex injuries and diseases; identify rare medicines; use specialized instruments (Neural Imager, Blood Gas Imager); treat lethal emergencies (bleeding out, toxic shock); reattach a limb.

Formidable: Treat unexpected, life-threatening complications; recall obscure medical theories and therapies; prescribe experimental treatment to alleviate "incurable" diseases; perform organ transplant and other intricate surgeries.

Heroic: Perform a radical procedure to stave off fatal injury or disease; perform open-heart surgery without adequate equipment or benefit of a proper medical facility.

Incredible: Perform intricate micro-surgery with improvised equipment.

Ridiculous: Restore a patient who has been clinically dead for almost half an hour.

Impossible: Cure a terminal disease with a radical, experimental remedy (curing lung cancer with a peanut-butter based treatment).

MELEE WEAPON COMBAT

Perhaps you swing a blade faster than the other guy can draw his gun. This Skill allows you to use weapons other than guns effectively in a fight. Note that actions taken against other characters are usually opposed rolls, so some of the examples might vary in actual use.

Specialties: clubs, knives, melee weaponsmithing, nunchaku, pole arms, swords, whips.

Easy: Know how to grip a rapier; use a butterfly knife; flail a pair of nunchaku slowly and without cracking your own skull; crack a whip impressively.

Average: Spank a novice fencer in the butt cheek with the flat of the blade; twirl open a butterfly knife; bat away an under-hand pitch; hit a slow moving target with a whip; gauge an opponent's Skill level with a given weapon.

Hard: Disarm a proficient fencer; deflect a quick, aimed strike; perform stunts and tricks (slice off the suspenders holding up an opponent's pants); feint; snuff out candle flame with a whip; identify exotic weapons; analyze opponent's fighting style with a given weapon.

Formidable: Disarm an excellent fencer; cut fruits tossed into the air into even pieces; hit a fly with a whip.

Heroic: Deflect arrows or crossbow bolts using your sword; strike a target with amazing precision; detect the weakness in a master fencer's style; disarm/trip multiple opponents with a whip.

Incredible: Block attacks coming from behind or from an unseen opponent.

Ridiculous: Deflect a bullet with a hand-held weapon.

Impossible: Cut off a section of a spaceship hull using a bowie knife.

PERCEPTION

This Skill helps you pick up on subtleties in your surroundings. You notice little things such as the tiny crack on the marble floor that less attentive folk could easily miss. Can't slip a gnat past you, if you get really good at it. Naturally, you can't take certain Specialties that rely on a particular sense if you are partially or fully disabled in that sense—awfully hard to justify takin' "sight" when you're blind, for instance–although a blind person might take this Skill in hearing. Note that Skill use against other characters is opposed, so some of the following examples could vary in actual play.

Specialties: deduction, empathy, gambling, hearing, intuition, investigation, read lips, search, sight, smell, tactics, taste, tracking.

Easy: Solve low-grade vidshow mysteries; spot a roadside billboard; eavesdrop on a conversation at the next table; know when a little kid is lying to you; follow footprints in light snow; detect a gas leak by smell.

Average: Collect fingerprints and gather other evidence; read the numbers on a license plate of a fast car; see someone hiding behind a bush; follow a muddy track.

Hard: Spot inconspicuous clues; surmise a culprit's physical and mental stats (height, weight, gender, hair color, level of education, etc.) from available evidence; sense a hidden emotion; solve a well-written mystery novel before final chapter; determine the best places for an ambush; trace faint or fading chemical scent.

Formidable: See through the deceits of a trained Companion; discern well-concealed emotions; decipher whispers in the next room through a closed door.

Heroic: Detect the lies of a master Companion; spot the tip of a handkerchief sticking out of a man's pocket in a large crowd; react instinctively to a battlefield maneuver.

Incredible: Determine someone's background and occupation from a cursory analysis of visible evidence (stains on a shirt, callus on a thumb, etc.); smell a burning circuit from the other side of the ship.

Ridiculous: Run through a hedge maze without taking a single wrong turn.

Impossible: See the tell-tale flash from a sniper's scope just before the shot is fired.

PERFORMANCE

You can hum a few notes, dance a few steps, or otherwise impress an audience with this Skill. Maybe you're even good enough to make a living. As with Artistry, your performance should fit a target audience. (Your rendition of the quartet from Rigoletto will not garner much applause in the local Whitefall saloon. In fact, it might get you lynched!) **Note:** con artists, fugitives, and other folk who want or need to pass themselves off as someone else will need to take this Skill.

Specialties: acting, dancing, costuming, keyboard instruments, impersonation, mimicry, oratory, percussion instruments, singing, stringed instruments, wind instruments.

Easy: Star in primary school stage plays; sing backup at the Abbey choir; strum basic guitar chords.

Average: Perform amateur productions and minstrel shows; sing lead vocal for a local band; win high school talent contests; write original songs; mask surface emotions.

Hard: Understudy in a professional production; write a film score or long orchestral piece; dance to

an unfamiliar number; emulate popular characters and recognizable voices on cue; disguise yourself as someone far older or younger than yourself.

Formidable: Headline a grand musical in a prestigious Core-world theater; receive critical acclaim for your performance in a major stage production; create a dead-on impression of any character; depict any emotion regardless of true feelings; disguise yourself as someone of a different racial background.

Heroic: Perfectly imitate the performance of an award-winning singer or actor; effectively disguise yourself as a member of the opposite sex; pretend to be a native of a remote location (such as the Triumph Settlement), though you've never been there.

Incredible: Portray perfectly two or more completely opposite personas in an instant; compose a classic symphony of true depth and beauty.

Ridiculous: Disguise yourself well enough to fool a member of your target's own family.

Impossible: Shatter spaceship porthole glass by blowing the perfect note on your flute.

PILOT

If it flies—either in atmo or out in the black—you're able to make the craft perform. In addition to simply flying, the Skill also covers charting a course, maintenance, and basic troubleshooting—though any serious problem is covered by Mechanical Engineering. You need a Skill roll to control the craft under adverse conditions, evade pursuit, or perform difficult maneuvers. A Botch roll does not mean you've instantly crashed your craft—but it certainly means you've made the ride a helluva lot more interesting!

Specialties: aerial navigation, astrogation, astronomy, astrophysics, space survival. (Note that specific types of craft are also Specialties. Examples include: gunships, hang gliders, helicopters, large cruisers, mid-bulk transports, patrol vessels, rocket shuttles, ultra-light aircraft, and short-range shuttles.)

Easy: Takeoff/land a good craft under normal conditions (fair to shiny weather, state-of-the-art port) with excellent instructions; set a short, simple course; switch autopilot on or off.

Average: Fly a functional craft through moderate conditions (fog, sensor static, turbulence), takeoff/land under typical condition (regular airfield, competent tower staff); plot a long, unusual course (one that avoids Alliance patrols, as an example); recognize specialized air and space vessels (Alliance gunship, medical ship).

Hard: Fly through harsh environment (deluge, dense asteroid cluster, high turbulence); takeoff/land under crappy conditions (low visibility,

under-serviced strip, incompetent tower staff); attempt an unusual maneuver (evasion, loop, maintaining altitude in howling wind); control craft under adverse conditions (ship damage, stellar electromagnetic phenomenon).

Formidable: Fly through very hazardous environment (electrical/ice storm, blizzard, restricted airspace) with a damaged craft; takeoff/land under extreme conditions (no visibility, short field, low fuel); attempting risky maneuver (rabbit through asteroid cluster at high speed, hard banks through canyon, multiple loops); perform a highly unconventional maneuver ("Crazy Ivan").

Heroic: Fly through a dangerous environment (ion cloud, tornado, relentless enemy air pursuit, flak); takeoff/land with critical malfunction (blown engine, stuck landing gear, out of fuel); attempting suicidal maneuver (hard banks while flying upside down, last-second vertical pull-up); maintain control of vessel while going to hard-burn in atmo.

Incredible: Navigate in atmo using only stellar constellations and magnetic compass to reach a precise destination halfway around the world; glide a powered-down ship from 6,000 miles away to successfully dock with a skyplex.

Ridiculous: Fly in atmo to a distant uncharted island without the aid of any navigational instrument; perform a "slingshot" maneuver using a planet's gravity with no computer calculations.

Impossible: Intercept a space yacht leaving atmo at escape velocity with a hang glider; outrun an Alliance cruiser in a short-range shuttle.

PLANETARY VEHICLES

Your ability to drive, operate, and maintain vehicles used planetside—on the ground, on or under water. Most folks are capable of driving a car, steering a boat, or riding a horse, but when things get a mite tricky, you'll need to roll the dice to see how well you perform. Note that basic maintenance for vehicles is covered under this Skill. Serious repairs must be performed by those with Mechanical Engineering.

Specialties: aquatic navigation, cars, canoes, equestrian, ground vehicle repair, horse-drawn conveyances, hovercraft, industrial vehicles, land navigation, large ground transports, military combat vehicles, powerboats, sailing, scooters, scuba diving, skiffs, submarines, yachts.

Easy: Take the vehicle for a spin around town up to speed limit; parallel parking; fix a flat tire or broken rudder; use global positioning systems to find the shortest route.

Average: Control the transport at high speed (hard turn at 50% max speed) under difficult conditions (slick ground, hard rain, fog) or through rough terrain (trees, gravel, choppy water); attempt tricks (sideswipe another vehicle); repair minor mechanical problems (replace timing belt, reconnect brakes, change lube).

Hard: Perform high-speed stunts (fast 90-degree turn, reverse); control the vehicle under adverse conditions (hail, snow); compensate for significant mechanical problems (failing breaks, reduced turning capability).

Formidable: Execute cinematic stunts (bootleg, ramp jump, drive in reverse through highway traffic; drive on two wheels); control the vehicle under hazardous conditions (pitch darkness, ice-coated roads, oil slick); compensate for major mechanical problems (flat tires, near-frozen steering).

Heroic: Perform daredevil stunts (drive off an overpass into traffic); drive vehicle into open hangar on a transport ship; compensate for disabling mechanical problems (missing wheels, acceleration jammed to full); steer a boat through a typhoon.

Incredible: Drive a car through a massive earthquake or meteor storm; coax a vehicle into exceeding its normal abilities; drive in reverse at top speed over unusual terrain while using only the rear-view mirror; scuba dive to record depth.

Ridiculous: Drive a car through traffic blindfolded while relying only on audio cues from a passenger; roll a vehicle at high speed to place it in perfect position so that you can then drive off in it; jump a cumbersome vehicle (such as a bus) over ramp or bridge.

Impossible: Stop on a dime while careening down a steep slope covered in ice without benefit of the brakes; keep leaky raft from capsizing during a hurricane.

RANGED WEAPONS

Any weapon that can be thrown or shot and is not a gun falls under this Skill. You make a Skill roll when trying to hit a target from a distance with a ranged weapon. There are places in the 'Verse where they still fire arrows from a bow or toss javelins at wild animals. Both are a whole lot quieter than a rifle and just as deadly between the eyes.

Specialties: blowguns, bows, crossbows, darts, grenade, javelin, ranged weaponsmithing, slings, throwing axes, throwing knives.

Easy: Match ideal ammunition to the right kind of weapon; hit a large, stationary target (such as the broad side of a barn) at close range; keep a bow pulled and aimed for a short length of time.

Average: Hit a medium, stationary target (such as a person standing still) at close range; make small modifications (tauter bow string, sharper arrow tips); identify origins and models of common ranged weapons.

Hard: Arm explosive or poisoned tips properly; hit a small, stationary target (such as a Blue Sun Cola can) at close range; recognize exotic ranged weapons (atatl, boomerang) and historical ones (Chief Shiny Oak's throwing knife); create new ranged weapons (razor-edged playing cards).

Formidable: Create mastercraft bows and arrows; hit a tiny, stationary target (the button of a coat) at close range); make significant improvement to a ranged weapon (infrared targeting, homing arrows).

Heroic: Shoot two arrows at different targets in the same shot; hit a miniscule target (a sideways poker card) at close range.

Incredible: Cut the ropes from around a man's neck on the gallows with one knife throw.

Ridiculous: Sling a rock into a moving airship's jet intake from 100 yards away.

Impossible: Split an arrow with another arrow fired from 300 yards away.

SCIENTIFIC EXPERTISE
(SKILLED ONLY)

You either got plenty of schooling or you were very well taught by your own self. This Skill measures your knowledge in the scientific fields, with each Specialty indicating a deeper understanding of that subject. Anyone who made it through the basic school years can recognize fundamental facts and theories without this Skill, but has no chance understanding concepts that are more complicated. Note the Specialties below represent major areas of study (earth sciences include chemistry, geology, as an example).

Specialties: earth sciences, historical sciences, life sciences, mathematical sciences.

Easy: Know who runs what renowned research institutions; relate the Theory of Evolution; re-enact famous experiments and discoveries; repeat common scientific formulae.

Average: Remember names of the foremost authorities on certain subjects and know where to find them; translate complex scientific jargon into common words; identify and operate advanced laboratory equipment.

Hard: Recall obscure discoveries and the parties responsible; explain the Theory of Relativity in detail and get it right; identify and operate specialized laboratory equipment; create complex chemical compounds in an inadequate facility; calculate advanced equations; teach advanced university classes.

Formidable: Recollect suppressed discoveries and who made them; produce complex chemical compounds in a makeshift facility; find and correct flaws in a popularly accepted equation.

Heroic: Go through a religious text and annotate scientific explanations for every inconsistency or miracle; synthesize a specific chemical compound using only household cleaners as base components.

Incredible: Re-create an unusual natural phenomenon (such as ball lightning) using only basic materials found in the galley.

Ridiculous: Use mathematical probability to predict the winning numbers for a planetary lottery.

Impossible: Calculate the precise location of Earth-That-Was using only a grammar-school history book and a crude telescope.

SURVIVAL

You never know when you're going to find yourself stranded buck-naked in the desert or drifting all by your lonesome in space. Whenever you find yourself in such a situation, you roll a Skill check to see how well you handle it.

Specialties: aerial survival, aquatic survival, general navigation, land survival, nature, space survival, specific environment (e.g., zero-G) or condition survival (e.g., heat, cold, toxic), tracking, trapping.

Easy: Build a campfire; recognize prominent star constellations; forage for food and water supplies on camp ground.

Average: Start fire with tindersticks; hunt deer or other common wild game; identify signs of creatures living nearby; perform minor first aid; find water supply in most environments; identify poisonous plants; set snares for squirrels and similar small animals.

Hard: Hunt boar and other ferocious wild game; survive quicksand or flash flood; find food and water supplies in bad weather; bandage a serious wound; apply a tourniquet correctly; treat frostbite and other harsh environmental hazards; adapt to temperature changes in a desert; set traps for panthers or other large beasts.

Formidable: Hunt polar bears on a glacier; evade killer sharks in an ocean; treat hypothermia and other lethal environmental hazards; neutralize deadly venoms; adapt to an unpredicted, drastic climate/temperature shift.

Heroic: Find food, water, and shelter in barren environment; locate trails on backwater planets you've only heard stories about.

Incredible: Survive for an extended period on the open ocean with no food or drinkable water.

Ridiculous: Track a jackrabbit through thick forest in a hurricane.

Impossible: Drift though deep space with low air reserves and no heat source—and live.

TECHNICAL ENGINEERING
(SKILLED ONLY)

With this Skill you can use machines that run on complicated electronics and computerized components, as well as engage in computer hacking and programming. You can wave-order deliveries and open programs without this Skill, though anything more complicated, and you'll be staring at a screenful of error logs.

Specialties: communications systems, computer programming, hacking, create/alter technical devices, demolitions, electronics, technical repair, technical security systems.

Easy: Repair a simple short-range wave comm; identify and fix standard electric and electronic devices; hook up a large computer network.

Average: Build a decent short-range wave comm; identify and operate advanced electric and electronic devices; override standard computer encryptions; reprogram a service drone or machine; repair moderate automated system damage; break into an unprotected computer system; pipe out comm static on all frequencies.

Hard: Build a functional long-range wave comm or a listening bug; identify and operate specialized electric and electronic devices; override security gate or airlock codes; repair heavy automated system damage; reconfigure a large computer network; identify hidden code embedded in a wave broadcast; implement advanced technical modifications such as photoelectric cells; hack into a small company's computer system.

Formidable: Build advanced technical devices; identify and operate innovative electric and electronic systems; override encryptions and codes of important government or corporate facilities; repair severe automated system damage; reconfigure a world-wide computer network; implement original technical modification; hack into a well-protected corporate security system.

Heroic: Build a sophisticated technical device from improvised components; override the encryptions of a Blue Sun secret file; repair a totally fried system with scavenged parts during battle; deactivate an assassin droid in combat using a remote.

Incredible: Hack into a government or military computer system; re-program a robot to fulfill a function it was not designed for.

Ridiculous: Send an overriding vid broadcast to every receiver in the system; track an encrypted wave message back to its origin terminal.

Impossible: Hack into an Alliance cruiser's controls and control it remotely.

UNARMED COMBAT

They say never hit a man with a closed fist, but it is—on occasion—necessary. And sometimes nothing brings more satisfaction to one's soul than delivering a good old-fashioned punch to the jaw. For those who relish those occasions, this is the skill to use, whether it's a knee to the groin, kick to the shin, hook to the chin, chop to the throat or gouge to the eye. Note that while Unarmed Combat doesn't involve the use of weapons, this and the Brawling specialty can allow you to use weapons of opportunity (beer bottles, etc.).

Specialties: boxing, brawling, judo, karate, kung fu, savate, wrestling.

Easy: Land a sucker punch; hit a head butt ("no one ever expects a head butt!"); kick to the groin; twist an arm; gouge eyes; elbow to the gut.

Average: Identify major martial art styles and techniques; hold average ranking (up to but not including black belt) in martial arts; fight for prize

money in local contests, hold your own in a bar fight.

Hard: Analyze opponent's fighting style, judging whether or not he's a better fighter; recognize exotic martial arts; black belt in martial arts; fight for prize money in Core world casinos, know specialized kicks and punches that can quickly disable an opponent.

Formidable: Break five thick boards with one strike; know specialized techniques that can quickly and silently kill an opponent; win a major boxing championship; hold a third-degree black belt or higher; disarm, disable, or kill an attacking, armed opponent.

Heroic: Break five cinder blocks with one strike; pick up Jayne and toss him out a window.

Incredible: Take on twenty Reavers unarmed and by yourself.

Ridiculous: Knock out a horse with a punch to the jaw.

Impossible: Kick a hole in the metal door of an Alliance cruiser using your bare foot.

Table 2-8: Traits & Skills

Assets	Complications	General Skills
Allure [Minor/Major]	Allergy [Minor/Major]	Animal Handling
Athlete [Minor/Major]	Amorous [Minor]	Artistry
Born Behind the Wheel [Minor/Major]	Amputee [Minor]	Athletics
Cortex Specter [Minor/Major]	Bleeder [Major]	Covert
Fightin' Type [Major]	Blind [Major]	Craft
Friends in High Places [Minor]	Branded [Minor/Major]	Discipline
Friends in Low Places [Minor]	Chip on the Shoulder [Minor/Major]	Guns
Good Name [Minor/Major]	Credo [Minor/Major]	Heavy Weapons
Healthy as a Horse [Minor/Major]	Combat Paralysis [Minor/Major]	Influence
Heavy Tolerance [Minor]	Coward [Minor]	Knowledge
Highly Educated [Minor]	Crude [Minor]	Linguist *
Intimidatin' Manner [Minor]	Dead Broke [Minor]	Mechanical Engineering *
Leadership [Minor/Major]	Deadly Enemy [Minor]	Medical Expertise *
Lightnin' Reflexes [Major]	Deaf [Major]	Melee Weapon Combat
Math Whiz [Minor]	Dull Sense [Minor]	Perception
Mean Left Hook [Minor]	Easy Mark [Major]	Performance
Mechanical Empathy [Minor]	Ego Signature [Minor]	Pilot *
Military Rank [Minor]	Filcher [Minor]	Planetary Vehicles
Moneyed Individual [Major]	Forked Tongue [Minor]	Ranged Weapons
Natural Linguist [Minor]	Greedy [Minor]	Scientific Expertise *
Nature Lover [Minor]	Hero Worship [Minor]	Survival
Nose for Trouble [Minor/Major]	Hooked [Minor/Major]	Technical Engineering *
Reader [Minor/Major] †	Leaky Brainpan [Minor/Major]	Unarmed Combat
Registered Companion [Minor] †	Lightweight [Minor]	
Religiosity [Minor/Major]	Little Person [Minor]	* Skilled Only
Sharp Sense [Minor]	Loyal [Minor]	
Steady Calm [Minor/Major]	Memorable [Minor]	
Sweet and Cheerful [Minor]	Mute [Major]	
Talented [Minor/Major]	Non-Fightin' Type [Minor]	
Things Go Smooth [Minor/Major]	Overconfident [Minor]	
Total Recall [Major]	Paralyzed [Major]	
Tough as Nails [Minor/Major]	Phobia [Minor]	
Trustworthy Gut [Minor/Major]	Portly [Minor/Major]	
Two-Fisted [Major]	Prejudice [Minor/Major]	
Walking Timepiece [Minor]	Sadistic [Major] †	
Wears a Badge [Minor/Major]	Scrawny [Minor]	
	Slow Learner [Minor]	
† GM Approval Required	Soft [Minor]	
	Stingy [Minor]	
	Straight Shooter [Minor]	
	Superstitious Things Don't Go Smooth [Minor/Major]	
	Traumatic Flashes [Minor/Major]	
	Twitchy [Minor]	
	Ugly as Sin [Minor/Major]	
	Weak Stomach [Minor/Major]	

MAL: "Zoe, is Wash gonna straighten this boat out before we get flattened?"
ZOE: "Like a downy feather, sir. Nobody flies like my mister."

CHAPTER 3

MONEY AND GEAR

THE IDEA

The door opened. Inara walked out. The door closed behind her with a bang. She flowed down the stairs with her customary grace, her elegant gown fluttering in the wind, her jeweled bracelets making soft tinkling sounds. But she was clearly annoyed. Her dark eyes flashed, her lips were pursed.

"That was fast, Ambassador," Mal quipped, though he looked uneasy. "Don't tell me there's some man in this 'Verse you couldn't seduce? Did he have a heart of steel?"

"A head of steel is more like it," stated Inara in disgust as she reached the bottom of the stairs where the rest of the crew waited. She cast a frustrated glance back over her shoulder at the entrance to the dance hall. "The guard is a robot. An armed-to-the-teeth robot."

Mal whistled. "Here, now. That's not good. What's the rest of the security set-up like?"

"What you might expect." Inara sighed. "Metal detectors, precious metal detectors, quasi-metal detectors, security cameras—you name it." She rearranged her bracelets. "We have to get into that club, Mal! Garibaldi is blackmailing my client's daughter and I promised we'd stop him. I don't break my promises."

"Not to mention the fact Stanchi is payin' us right well for this job," Zoe stated.

"Anyone got an idea?" Mal asked, looking around at the assembled group.

Jayne spoke up. "I do, Cap'n."

"Anyone else got an idea?" Mal asked.

"I dash in there," Jayne persisted, as if the others were paying attention, which mostly they weren't. "Guns blazin'. I shoot up security, shoot up the damn robot, and dash back out. I take off running down the street, and the rest of you mosey on inside like nothin's happened."

The group stared in stunned silence.

"Jayne," said Wash, awed. "That's downright brilliant!"

"It might just work, sir," said Zoe

"It might at that," Mal conceded. "Good thinkin', Jayne."

Jayne scowled. "Don't know why you're all looking so blamed surprised that I come up with a good idea," he stated defensively. "I graduated high school."

"You did?" Zoe raised her eyebrows.

"Almost," Jayne muttered.

"Okay," said Mal. "Here's what we do. Jayne runs in—"

"Sixth grade counts, don't it, Kaylee?" Jayne asked in an undertone.

"Sure, it does, Jayne," Kaylee said soothingly, as she gave his arm a pat.

Money may not be able to buy happiness, but it comes in useful when you need food, fuel, and the occasional pretty. A sum laid by for emergencies is always a good idea, and it'd be nice to have enough coin on hand for an impulse purchase every now and then. That's why some folk decide to take jobs as they come—they want just enough cash to keep flyin'. On the other hand, there are some folk like Jack Leland who figure that money buys freedom and the more of both they have on hand the better.

Hard to say who's right.

ECONOMICS OF THE 'VERSE

The central planets—them as formed the Alliance—have a complex and sophisticated economic system. Financial institutions such as banks hold the money for their customers in interest-bearing accounts, investing it at the exchanges on Sihnon and Londinum. Most money transfer in the Core is done by computer, with data bytes and pixels replacing cold, hard cash. Currency exists in the Core, to be sure, in standard paper notes issued by the Alliance. The notes are printed on special paper by fancy printing systems to discourage counterfeiters. Tracers on each bill allow the money to be tracked as it moves about. Paper bills and credit transfer are the only legal tender on Core planets, and those with gold or platinum coins must go to a licensed money changer. Purchasing goods with "hard coin" is illegal and untraceable, which is why it's preferred by black market merchants everywhere.

The Border planets, lacking the fancy trappings of "civilized" life, rely on precious metal coinage. While different planets have different standards and mint coins in different ways, some basic standards have developed. The coins most often used are made from set weights of silver, gold, and platinum. 'Course, coins aren't the only things used for business dealings. Barter is common practice, especially in transactions in which both sides have something besides cash to offer. While simpler, this economic system can also make prices and wages somewhat more fluid out on the Rim, as there aren't Cortex-accessible exchange rates to fall back on, thus making haggling an important skill to master. Debt is tracked with a signed I.O.U., and often collected at the end of a gun barrel.

CURRENCY

Simplest way to figure the worth of your credits or coins is to relate it to money you're most like to understand. It's useful not only to get a "feel" for how much your latest haul is worth, but also in determining the value of gear that's not found in this chapter. (More on that later.) First, understand that one standard credit authorized and used by the Alliance relates to roughly $25 U.S. dollars on Earth-That-Was.

Then take a gander at how credits and platinum coins equal out.

For those who like their cash to make a pleasant jingling sound, look over Table 3-2 for the rates of hard cash as they relate to credits and the ancient dollar—though I wouldn't bet your ship on these rates being near a sure thing.

Table 3-1: Currency

Credit	Dollar	Platinum	Gold	Silver
₡ 1	$25	2.5	5	250
₡ 0.4	$10	1	2	100

COSTS OF GOODS & SERVICES

If you're looking for this chapter to be a price guide to everything available in the 'Verse, you've come to the wrong place. The staggering variety of goods and services available make such a prospect nigh impossible. The good news is that many things in the 'Verse have equivalents for those of us still living on Earth-That-Was. A pair of tight pants is still pretty much a pair of tight pants, so if you really need to figure out the costs, just use the conversion rates listed above and do a little math! With this you

Table 3-2: Cash Equivalents

Coinage	Credit	Dollar	Platinum	Gold	Silver
Silver	₡ 0.004	$0.10	0.01	0.02	–
Gold	₡ 0.2	$5.00	0.5	–	50
Platinum	₡ 0.4	$10.00	–	2	100

can figure out the average costs for everything from a posthole digger (it digs holes for posts) to a pair of fancy sunglasses. For those of you who don't deal with dollars on a daily basis, a quick look at the exchange rates will give you the information you need.

The GM is the final word on whether a given item is available, what it costs, and what game effects it might have. As GM, if you know you're going to be faced with having to deal with prices, go ahead and make a quick comparison to items listed in this chapter and just wing it. Don't let details such as the cost of a plastic dinosaur figure slow down the game. If the players want to go on a shopping spree, they should provide you a list between sessions.

GEARING UP

So you've got a shiny new character, but he's as naked as the day he came cryin' into the world. Time to outfit him for his first trip into the black. Here are the starting credits for new characters based on the heroic level of the campaign. If you have the Moneyed Individual or Dead Broke traits, they affect your starting cash, so remember to take the right amount 'fore you spend cash you ain't got!

You can purchase just about anything you want with your money, though the GM can and may veto certain choices. Especially if you can't justify some purchases based on your character's background (or lack of one)! Once you have your stuff, it's time to get out there and find some jobs. Platinum don't grow on trees!

Table 3-3: Starting Cash

Heroic Level	Normal	Moneyed Individual	Dead Broke
Greenhorn	₡ 750	₡ 1,125	₡ 375
Veteran	₡ 1,500	₡ 2,250	₡ 750
Big Damn Hero	₡ 3,000	₡ 4,500	₡ 1,500

OWNING A SHIP

Every campaign is different. We've assumed that for this game your characters will crew a ship. (Not that you have to do this, but if you don't, your GM will have a mite more work to do!) Don't think

CHAPTER 3

you're going to be stuck in some rut—you'll still have plenty of chances for variation to keep things interesting. Take *Serenity* into consideration. The ship is owned and captained by Malcolm Reynolds—no questions asked (except by Jayne, and he don't count). *Aces & Eights* is owned by rich gambler Jack Leland, who hires Maxx Williams to captain the boat. Already, there's variety.

If you are using the *Serenity* model for the campaign, the crew and the GM will have to agree on what kind of ship you'll be flying and just who owns it before the game starts. A ship could be owned by the entire crew, with everyone holding "shares" (and working for their "fair" share of the profit). The crew might even work for someone else, someone who is not on the crew who owns the ship and pays you a wage to do what you do.

You might think that owning (or even just captaining) a ship is a huge advantage and should be an Asset, but ownership is a major decision that is a basic part of the campaign. The responsibility that comes with ownership or leadership usually offsets the perks (and if you're the GM, it's up to you to make sure that the perks are offset appropriately, if not fairly). Malcolm Reynolds, for instance, loves *Serenity* so much that if she goes down, he's going to go down with her. Maxx Williams is responsible for every member of the *Aces & Eights* crew, and he also has a commitment to his employer. These prevent him from having the same amount of freedom enjoyed by the rest of the crew.

GEAR

You've got the character, you've got the credits, and now you need the stuff (if you don't want to push up daisies just yet, that is). This section will get you most anything you need to outfit a crew, though of course we're waitin' for you to fork over the cash… and convince the GM, of course.

You won't find everything in the 'Verse there is to buy is on the lists and tables here. But you've got that handy-dandy conversion table to help you figure the cost of most things you'll want. What you will find in this section is the equipment that you're most likely to come across at some point in your unseemly career. If you don't see something you need, ask the GM if you can find it, 'cause, like as not, if people wanted it on Earth-that-Was, they still want it in the here and now.

Another important thing to remember is this: when humanity spread throughout the system, they brought with them corporations, businesses, and hot brand names. Keeping that in mind, the listings in this chapter are the average goods you might find on the outer worlds. The GM can decide such things as whether or not a gun does more or less damage than the average model or if the toaster oven is easier or harder to break. For assistance in the design of extremely advanced equipment and guidelines for prices, look up the section on Newtech at the end of this chapter.

CREDITS AND COINAGE

It may be apparent to you that some things don't quite match up on the tables below. If you were to do the math and work out all the prices, you'd find that sometimes the number of platinum pieces for an item doesn't quite match the credits. Why is that, you wonder?

There may be a fairly stable ('fairly' being the operative word) exchange rate between the two currencies, but hard cash and credits don't get spent the same way in the same places. In the Core, only credits and paper currency are legal tender, which means the gorram Alliance bankers could be tracking your every purchase. (And if they can, they probably are, right?) Because precious metal is not traceable, it is illegal tender for transactions in the Core—you try to flash some coin, and you may find yourself bound by law, pending sentence. Out on the Rim, most folk don't want to bother with their credit accounts (and money-watching Feds), so coin is what you'll generally need, unless you have goods or services to barter. The Alliance tolerates this 'cause none of them lily-skinned bankers feel like setting up branches that far from "civilization." But if you want to spend your hard-earned platinum on Ariel or Osiris, you'd better hit a money-changer first thing.

As a result of all this craziness, platinum values can get a mite fuzzy. Bartering with goods can make the prices of some things shift a bit. Since most people deal in platinum and not gold or silver for their big transactions, you won't find those smaller coins used in the tables here. That's not to say you can't use them on the Rim, but while you might buy yourself a soda or a fresh apple with those coins, no one's going to want to accept small change for anything much beyond that. Folk deal in platinum for real jobs.

BIG DAMN PRICES

Some things may seem much too expensive compared to others: food prices, Core medical expenses, and the costs of traveling (and shipping objects) between worlds are all high. That's just the way it is. Those big numbers you see are about right (though, perhaps, negotiable). Hopping around the system is pretty pricey. Owning and operating a ship can't be done on pocket change. Finding fresh food can be difficult on moons that have been suffering from a ten-year drought. MedAcad trained doctors

ECONOMICS OF A TRAMP FREIGHTER

Some game groups like to keep things simple in terms of the money. After all, drawing up a budget or working to balance costs and expenses are hassles we deal with enough in the real world. For most players, simply having an idea about how each character is doing, along with the group as a whole, is enough to get flyin' and have a good time.

Others like to enhance the reality of their play by knowing to the credit how much they have in the bank. After all, Malcolm Reynolds certainly has to worry about money. His crew works for shares of the profit, but often there's barely enough to refuel the ship and buy the food they need to stock the kitchen. For those who are interested in tracking money in a more detailed way, here are some general guidelines that can be molded to fit the situation for a specific ship and crew. The examples use a Firefly Class ship like *Serenity* as the baseline. Individual ships and crew will, of course, have unique jobs and bills to pay, but this will serve as a starting point.

POTENTIAL REGULAR EXPENSES

• The ship requires fuel (a primary cost). Fuel cells to power a Firefly for 30 days run ₡ 600.

• The crew requires provisions. A crew of five requires about ₡ 120 worth, if they eat mostly packaged protein and canned goods.

• Monthly payments (on a ship that is not wholly owned). A standard finance payment on a Firefly in good condition could run about ₡ 750.

• Supplies (ammunition, medical supplies, etc.). An average cost would be ₡ 200.

• Ship parts, upgrades to improve. These vary according to need and desire (see Chapter Four: *Boats and Mules*).

• Business expenses. This can fluctuate wildly, depending on the job.

• Salaries of crew (anyone who is not in for a "cut" of the profits). Monthly salary for skilled crew members can run about ₡ 200 each.

GETTING PAID

You do the job, you want to get paid. Below is a breakdown of standard rates for hauling cargo. These rates assume that a ship with the stowage capacity of a Firefly is filled to normal maximum or that they're carrying a full load of passengers (4-6 on a Firefly, depending on whether or not some of them share bunks). And remember, this is for Firefly quality transport. See the section on *Services* for more detailed info and a breakdown of the costs.

Even if you don't use these figures in the daily business of story and adventure in the 'Verse, they're probably worth a moment's consideration. Money is an important motivating factor for many crews.

Table 3-4: Cargo & Passenger Rates

Cargo / Passage	Legal Cargo	Illegal Cargo	Legal Passenger	Illegal Passenger
3 Day, Standard	₡ 175 - 250	₡ 200 - 275	₡ 50 - 85	₡ 75 - 115
3 Day, Complicated	₡ 225 - 3300	₡ 300 - 425	₡ 60 - 100	₡ 90 - 140
10 Day, Standard	₡ 575 - 850	₡ 675 - 975	₡ 170 - 255	₡ 195 - 285
10 Day, Complicated	₡ 750 - 1,000	₡ 1,000 - 1,250	₡ 215 - 300	₡ 245 - 350

CHAPTER 3

can charge pretty much what they please 'cause there are so few of 'em. Part of the expense of certain goods and services can be explained by the law of supply and demand: those who supply can demand what they like.

The other major reason for the high cost of some goods on the Rim is simple: the Alliance has the power and they aim to keep it. After a long and bloody Unification War, and a government mostly steered by major corporations (such as Blue Sun), the Alliance doesn't want no *wong ba duhn* from the Rim getting ideas as to his station in life and causing trouble. Consequentially, some prices are artificially inflated to make it more expensive to move things around on an interplanetary level. The corporations need some folk to run their goods, so it will never be impossible, but it can certainly seem that way.

AVAILABILITY

You can't find everything everywhere. Your average General Store on Whitefall stocks only the basic necessities of life. For pieces of pretty, you have to go to the fancy jewelry store on Persephone. You might find a gun dealer both places, but likely not sellin' the same quality weapon. Plain common sense should speak to most things like that. You can't just stop at one bitty little mart (or even a major triplex) and find everything you want.

Unfortunately, things get even less smooth when you have a whole 'Verse of planets and moons to shop on. The Core worlds manufacture pretty much everything you could want, but shopping on the Core has its own associated problems (see *Credits and Coinage*). Most of what you find out on the Rim is secondhand, a little worn, or flat-out *feh wu*. Wherever the crew goes, the GM will need to know what can and can't be found for credit, cash, or barter. To help the GM make those decisions, all of the equipment listed here has an "Availability" rating of Everywhere (E), Core Worlds (C), Rim Worlds (R) or Illegal (I). Whether or not a given item is actually available where these ratings suggest it is (or where it shouldn't be) is still up to the GM. So no hasslin' him when he tells you the gun shop is fresh out of Iskellian sniper rifles.

THE BLACK MARKET

Availability ratings of Everywhere, Core Worlds, and Rim Worlds are fairly self-explanatory, and it shouldn't take no genius to find most of these things—GM willing, that is. Illegal items, now, can be a mite trickier. Sometimes dealers sell these items under the counter, but just as often not, it may be near impossible to find some of them (unless a body has contacts of a less than reputable nature). Of

OPTIONAL RULE: ARBITRARY GEAR

The normal rules for starting cash and outfitting a new character usually work just fine, but sometimes the rules just don't support the campaign's story. One easy solution is to forget starting cash and make a list of character-appropriate gear—with the GM's approval, of course. For example, River was naked when she was smuggled onto *Serenity* in a cryogenic box, so she would not have any gear, just those possessions her brother brought on board. Here are a few more examples of how campaign concepts could change what new characters acquire for equipment:

• The crew are all in the military, so their standard gear is provided for them. They may have a few personal effects, but everything else is standard military-issue.

• The crew starts the campaign incarcerated on a prison ship on route to a penal moon. In a fight, they have to scrounge for whatever weapons they can find.

• The crew is vacationing in the rugged wilderness when they are kidnapped by slave-traders to be sold to an unscrupulous terraforming station. They must fight their kidnappers and take over the ship using only materials that are on hand.

course, when it comes to guns and the like, some types of weapons may well be illegal just because the Alliance wants to keep them out of the hands of the general populace. That kind of illegal may be overlooked if the perp is sufficiently generous (the "10-60%-over-the-normal-price" kind of generous), *dohn ma*?

Frequently, you can find things on the black market that you can't find elsewhere. 'Course, such things can get you dead by a variety of unpleasant means. Contacts can be made for some of the cheaper wants, but the more expensive your tastes run, the more likely a major boss—maybe from one of the tongs or the Syndicate—will have his hand in the acquisition. So . . . buyer beware . . .

GENERAL STORE

Here's where you'll find most basic goods: clothes, food, and such. On the Core, you visit a major triplex or market district to buy these things. Out on the Rim, find the local General Store and hope they've got what you need. Just remember

Table 3-5: Tools				
Item	Cost (Credits/Platinum)	Weight	Availibility	Notes
Fire Jelly	₡ 0.2 / 1p	2	E	Heating element for cooking
Garden Bunk	₡ 18 / 45p	45	C	Shipboard mini-garden
Gun Vac Case	₡ 2.6 / 7p	4	C	Allows a firearm to function in a vacuum
Gun Cleaning Kit	₡ 2.4 / 6 p	4	E	Gun and knife cleaning care and gear
Multiband	₡ 4.8 / 12p	–	C	Multi-function watch
Patch Tape	₡ 1.2 / 3p	3	E	10-yard roll of airtight cloth patching
Purification Cystals	₡ 0.4 / 1p	–	E	Prepares 20 gallons of water to drink
Trash Incinerator	₡ 7.4 / 19p	20	E	Disposes of organic trash

that there's a lot of gear not listed in this section. If you want a compass or pencils or tea bags, this is probably a good place to shop. Just ask the GM if you can find what you're looking for and either do a quick price conversion, or ask him to name a figure (such ordinary objects will most likely come cheap).

TOOLS

Fire Jelly: Sold in 8" tall tin cans, fire jelly was originally designed as an alternative to camp fires for soldiers during the Unification War. When lit, the jelly burns at 550 degrees at a rate of ½" per hour; the can is largely heat-proof, and putting the lid back on quickly snuffs the low-burning, smokeless flame.

Garden Bunk: When you can't afford to buy fresh vegetables, you can grow 'em–even on your boat where the 'garden bunk' has become moderately popular. Consisting of a plastic soil trough (sized to fit on a small bed), it comes with growing lamps and a small sprinkler system. Garden bunks don't afford a huge harvest, but when morale is down, a few fresh tomatoes can do wonders. The listed weight includes the soil and plants the unit will hold.

Gun Case: Since most weapons need atmo to fire, it stands to reason someone would think of a way to fire one in space, too. A gun case is designed for a specific type of gun. It closes around the front end, making it look like it's got a barrel about five times wider than it should be. The case pumps air into the chambers and barrel when you pull the trigger, allowing the weapon to discharge normally. Unfortunately, a lot of the internal atmo is wasted with each pull, so the air generally lasts for only 10 shots before the case needs to be refilled back on the ship.

Gun-Cleaning Kit: Every good soldier (and settler) knows that you need to take care of your weapons if you want them to take care of you. Guns need to be cleaned and sometimes repaired. This small kit includes all the tools necessary for such. Bought on the Rim, the kit most likely comes in a leather pouch about the size of a shoulder bag. Purchased on the Core, it will come in a professional-looking metal case.

Multiband: The evolution of the digital watch has led, at long last, to the Multiband. It's an all-in-one watch, digital compass, calculator, alarm, radio receiver, generic remote control, and voice memo. Unfortunately, multibands break easily and are mostly popular among students as a fashion accessory. The varieties range from cheap versions in plastic cases to gold-plated ones sold out of suitcases by shady men on street corners.

Patch Tape: A holdover from the war, patch tape looks like a roll of shiny rubber material. The thin tape is airtight, and the adhesive coating on one side provides a hold strong enough to seal a vacuum suit at full pressure. Hull breaches and the like usually can't be fixed in this manner, but if some *sah gwa* wants to try it, it's his funeral. Keeping a roll in a vac-suit pocket can often be a life-saver.

Purification Crystals: Frontier settlers and soldiers usually stock packets of these powdery, pale blue crystals. One packet (a box has 20) can cleanse up to a gallon of water for human consumption, killing pretty much all bacteria and parasites, just as if you'd boiled it.

Trash Incinerator: Most ships come equipped with some way to dispose of garbage, but there is always a market for ways to quickly and quietly get rid of refuse. The incinerator is a small metal crate fitted with electrical heating coils; it can destroy, in a matter of moments, almost any organic material that can fit into the 2'x2'x2' space. The resulting residue and ash is collected in a small filter that occasionally needs to be cleaned.

FOOD AND SUPPLIES

Crop Supplements: While terraforming has succeeded in making many planets habitable, the individual quirks of the various planets and moons make it difficult to predict whether or not a given crop will grow on each. Highly concentrated fertilizers and pesticides, packed into easily applied chemical pellets, are one of the more common

"Fruity Oaty Bars, Pow! Hey! Fruity Oaty Bars, make a man out of a mouse, make you bust out of your blouse, eat them now, bang! Ping! Zow! —Try Fruity, Oaty Bars."

—Advertisement

solutions to this problem. Settlers usually bring a fair supply of crop supplements with them in order to ensure bountiful harvests for the first few years. The pellets come in drums, bags, or boxes; one container is enough for five acres when mixed with the seeds before planting or tilled into the earth beforehand. The benefits usually last for two or three growing seasons, depending on the crops being farmed.

Drink, Fine Wine: A case of twelve bottles of extremely good wine; what more needs be said? Good wine is hard to come by, so it can get very expensive, but many folk consider it worthwhile.

Drink, Good Whisky: Wood alcohol is cheap. High-quality strong drink is a bit more costly.

Foodstuffs, Canned: While not as good as fresh food, canned or otherwise pre-prepared food is still a fair bit better than processed protein. Since such food keeps indefinitely (or at least a whole lot longer than the fresh stuff), food packs and canned fruit are popular among settlers and ship crews. The given price buys two or three boxes of different kinds of food, allowing one person to eat decently for about a week. Rationed, the food will go farther.

Foodstuffs, Fresh: This is what it's all about: fresh vegetables, fruit, and meat. Unfortunately, real food is fairly expensive; folk can't usually afford it unless things are going real smooth for them. Most often, fresh food is bought in small amounts or is carefully rationed over a period of time, at least by those who live in the black.

Foodstuffs, Luxury: This is the kind of fancy-pants yummies you can't even find most places on the Rim. A pound of fresh strawberries, a chocolate ice cream cake, caviar—such count as luxury goods to folk who live on the Rim. The units in which the goods are sold depends upon exactly what the food is. The price can vary as well, but whatever it is, it will almost always be quite expensive.

Foodstuffs, Nutrient Bars: Nutrient bars—a Newtech Alliance ration—are perhaps the most compact form of food ever developed. Each bar is about the size and shape of a gold ingot and each is wrapped in foil. The actual bar is a brownish compound, nearly tasteless, but at least it's better than protein paste. If sliced thinly, a single bar can provide 30 days' worth of nutrition for one person. The person will still need water and additional calories, but the vitamins, minerals, immune supplements, and so on will allow them to subsist on an otherwise minimal diet.

Foodstuffs, Protein Paste: Tubes of colored and (supposedly) flavorsome protein paste are the standard diet for spacefarers in the 'Verse. The paste is sometimes molded into different forms and cooked different ways. Sadly, it tastes about the same no matter what you do to it. Healthy, if boring, the paste stores a good long while.

Spices, Common: Whether it's protein paste, canned vegetables, or fresh meat, a sprig of rosemary can make your day a little brighter.

Spices, Rare: Popular in the Core for those who can afford high class dining, rare spices such as saffron can be extremely expensive. A good cargo to carry, and even better to have if you can afford it.

Table 3-6: Food & Supplies

Item	Cost (Credits/Platinum)	Availibility	Notes
Crop Supplements	₡ 300 / 750p	C	Fertilizer and growth-stimulating chemicals for most crop plants
Drink, Fine Wine	₡ 6.4 / 16p	C	One case
Drink, Good Whiskey	₡ 5.6 / 14p	C	One decanter
Foodstuffs, Canned	₡ 5 / 12p	E	Average cost for one person/week
Foodstuffs, Fresh	₡ 8 / 20p	E	Average cost for one person/week
Foodstuffs, Luxury	₡ 2 / 5p	C	Average cost for one 'unit'
Foodstuffs, Nutrient Bars	₡ 570 / 1425p	C	Case of 100 bars
Foodstuffs, Protein Packs	₡ 2.5 / 6p	E	Average cost for one person/week
Spices, Common	₡ 2 / 5p	C	½ lb package
Spices, Rare	₡ 5 / 13p	C	Five ounce package

Table 3-7: Protective/Emergency Gear

Item	Armor Rating	Agility/Alertnes Step Penalty	Cost (Credits/Platinum)	Weight	Availibility
Ballistic Mesh	1W *	–	₡ 46 / 115p	4	C
Chameleon Suit	1W	–	₡ 40 / 100p	17	I
Helmet, Infantry	4W	–1 Ale	₡ 16 / 40p	2	E
Helmet, Squad	4W	–2 Ale	₡ 35 / 88p	3	C
Mask, NBC	2W	–3 Ale	₡ 8 / 10p	3	C
NBC Body Suit	2W	–2 Agi / –2 Ale	₡ 32 / 80p	14	C
Plate Vest	4W *	–1 Agi	₡ 30 / 75p	10	E
Riot Gear	3W *	–1 Agi / –1 Ale	₡ 92 / 230p	24	C
HeartLine Health Suit	–	–	₡ 28 / 70p	3	C
Tactical Suit	5W	–2 Agi	₡ 110 / 275p	18	I
Vacuum Suit	2W	–2 Agi / –2 Ale	₡ 67 / 168p	35	E

* see description

TAILOR

Whether you're dressing for an evening shindig or just throwing on some overalls for grease-diving, you're gonna need something to wear.

Since you can figure the cost of most clothes by looking up the dollar price and doing a quick conversion, this section has a list of less-than-standard protective gear. If you want a fluffy pink ball gown or some tight pants to show off your backside, do a quick conversion to find the price.

PROTECTIVE/ EMERGENCY GEAR

Ballistic Mesh: Used much like the bulletproof vests of Earth-That-Was, ballistic mesh is a finely-woven cloth of metal and plastic over polymer sheeting. In basic dummy-talk, the mesh stops bullets, and it isn't as heavy or bulky as other armors. The mesh was often used by the Independents during the war, since it was hard for them to find heavier body-armor.

Ballistic mesh is meant to stop bullets and that's about it. The mesh absorbs 1 Wound point from *any* attack on an area covered by the suit (torso, arms and legs, usually), but it doesn't do much more than that to protect against knives, bombs, and so on. Against normal bullets, however, the mesh converts up to 8 Wounds to Stun damage (and Shock Points, if the victim takes too much Stun) per attack that strikes the protected area. This effect doesn't apply to arrows, bolts, or explosive ammunition.

Chameleon Suit: Snipers favor these to remain hidden while on the job. Mostly consisting of a baggy set of overalls with clumps of fiber optic wires sprouting here and there, the suit also sports a small computer and dozens of light sensors

placed around it. When activated, the suit attempts to match its color to the surrounding area. It does a fairly good job if the wearer is holding still. This effect adds +2 Skill steps to any Covert rolls to remain hidden while unmoving; it also protects as normal armor, though damage may cause its stealthiness to stop working (as determined by the GM).

Bryce

Helmet, Infantry: A basic metal or composite helmet with a cloth or mesh covering (to which the wearer can attach grass and foliage). Hits to a helmeted head do *not* add extra damage except on Extraordinary Success (though the character must still make the Survival test to avoid being dazed).

Helmet, Squad: This helmet originated with the Alliance during the war. It functions in the same way as an Infantry Helmet, but also includes a small communicator to allow members of a squad to stay in constant communication. Unfortunately, the design impedes hearing and peripheral vision.

Mask, NBC: A fancy gas-mask, this gadget lets you breathe safely in an area contaminated by nuclear, biological, or chemical hazards. Unfortunately, the mask doesn't let you see all that well, and it doesn't protect the rest of your body.

NBC Body Suit: A full-body, airtight, hazardous environment suit provides complete protection from nuclear, biological, and chemical hazards. The mask allows for slightly better vision than the NBC Mask. The bulky material makes it difficult to handle small objects or perform feats that require coordination.

Plate Vest: Ceramic inserts sewn into a ballistic mesh offer torso protection on both the back and the front. Any hits on an area covered by the vest do only Stun damage (and Shock, if necessary), as with ballistic mesh. Unlike the ballistic mesh, the plate vest will protect against sharp instruments (knives, axes), as well as bullets. Since the torso is the easiest target on a human, assume that most attacks would hit the vest, unless specifically targeted elsewhere on the body. The upside—the plate vest looks like a normal garment. The downside—the weight and bulk restrict movement slightly.

Riot Gear: Full law-enforcement riot gear consists of composite and ceramic plating sewn in various special pockets all over a specially made ballistic mesh suit. The effects of the mesh apply only to bullets, but the Armor Rating reduces damage from all attacks (the suit includes a helmet with face plate). Unfortunately, the helmet impairs hearing and vision, and the suit is bulky enough to be a mite cumbersome—but then, there's some as like to see the law slowed down a bit anyway.

HeartLine Health Suit: The HeartLine is an undershirt wired with sensors and other gadgets to monitor body temperature, heart rate, blood pressure, and so on. It generally transmits this data to a doctor or to a computer where it can be read by a doctor, who can monitor the patient's health.

Tactical Suit: This is the armor Alliance Federals wear, usually with a Squad Helmet. The suit covers the entire body and is armored with ceramic and composite plates, along with heavy padding. It will stop a heap of damage, but tends to rattle when you walk.

Vacuum Suit: Heavy, bulky, and generally restricting, vacuum suits are an absolute essential out in the black. They can be tricky to get on and

off, though, so allow yourself some time to get into it. You need to take good care of these to keep 'em working. A bullet hole or similar can be closed up with patch tape, but it is generally worthwhile to invest in a new suit when you have the credits.

ARMORY

Prayer for the Rim: "God grant me the serenity to accept the things I cannot change, the courage to change the things I can, and the firepower to make the difference." This is where you'll find the gumption to make the difference. Gun shops everywhere carry pistols, rifles, and shotguns; military surplus stores often carry more unconventional arms and melee weapons.

You should keep in mind that the Alliance strictly controls the sale of weapons on the Core. Permits are required for carrying weapons (especially concealed weapons) and many firearms and Newtech weapons are electronically tagged to make them traceable. Black markets exist on the central planets where you can buy illegal, untraceable firearms, but getting caught with such a weapon will land you on a penal moon.

On the Rim, folk aren't so picky. Gun shops are supposedly regulated, but, in truth, the government has better things to do than go around hasslin' gun

dealers and manufacturers. There is also a black market for guns on the Rim and these dealers tend to carry weapons with a bit more bang for a bit more buck. 'Course, there's always a good chance their previous owners are looking for 'em, so you might want to keep what you buy under wraps until you're back on the ship.

There are so many kinds of weapons in the 'Verse, we couldn't possibly list them all here. Then again, unless you're straying off into the realm of Newtech, most weapons tend to have the same in-game effects and stats as others in the same class (even if they look different). Spend some time figuring out what kinds of weapons your crew carries. A bullet fired from any type of gun can kill you, but folk tend to give more respect to those carryin' big, shiny guns, as opposed to those totin' derringers.

AMMUNITION & RELOADING

The amount of ammo you carry gets kind of important. Some GMs may want each crew member to keep track of how many bullets he has left, while others may just want to keep things simple by making the crew spend some cash every now and then and say, "I'm stocking up on ammo." Either way, if you're empty, your slug thrower won't mean *mi tian gohn* when the Reavers start gnawin' on your insides.

Most ammo can be bought at the same place you buy weapons. On the Core planets, bullets are sold only in gun shops and you have to produce the proper paperwork (though ammo can be found on the black market). On the Rim, most General Stores and similar will carry ammo. Because bullets are made of lead, there isn't exactly a shortage for most folk; though there are some who like to buy fancy, special-made bullets, such as explosive-armor piercing-hollow point-shaped charge shells of gruesomeness. That'll be quite a bit more expensive and most likely illegal, even assuming you can find it.

Disregarding that kind of extravagance, here's a pretty simple way to do ammo shopping on the outer worlds. Different guns use different caliber bullets, but the prices are basically the same. Players should know whether they're buying shotgun shells or pistol rounds, and how much they need. Figure the cost at about 0.2 Credits/ 1 Gold to buy 10 shots. If the guns are Newtech, the ammo will cost more—maybe a lot

more—but otherwise price shouldn't vary too much from there. Double the cost for ammo purchased on the Core from a licensed gun dealer and quadruple the cost for black market ammo on the Core.

When you buy the bullets, you probably buy them in a box and load your gun yourself. The number of bullets in the box depends on the weapon and how much you feel like spending. Common numbers are 20, 50, and 100 bullets.

HAND-TO-HAND WEAPONS

Baton, Security: The collapsible metal rod that extends up to two feet when unfolded is used for beatin' on folk who trespass where they ain't wanted. Usually has a rubber grip on one end.

Baton, Stun: Kinda like a standard security baton, but with more zap and less thwap. Instead of smackin' someone with this, you use it like a cattle-prod and poke 'em. A battery in the handle

Table 3-8: Hand-to-Hand Weapons

Item	Damage	Cost (Credits/Platinum)	Weight	Availibility
Baton, Security	d2 S	₵ 1.2 / 3p	2	E
Baton, Stun	d2 S *	₵ 12 / 30p	2	C
Brass Knuckles	*	₵ 0.8 / 2p	1	E
Club	d6 B	₵ 0.2 / 1p	3	E
Hatchet	d6 W	₵ 16 / 40p	4	E
Knife, Combat	d4 W	₵ 1.6 / 4p	1	E
Knife, Utility	d2 W	₵ 0.8 / 2p	–	E
Machete	d4 W	₵ 3.2 / 4p	3	E
Sword, Combat	d6 W	₵ 24 / 60p	6	E
Sword, Gentleman's	d4 W	₵ 26 / 65p	1	C

* see description   B = Basic Damge; S = Stun Damage; W = Wound Damage

CHAPTER 3

Table 3-9: Ranged Weapons

Weapon	Damage	Range Increment (feet)	Max ROF (Magazine)	Cost (Credits/Platinum)	Weight	Availibility
Bow	d4 W	70	1 (-)	₵ 6 / 15p	6	E
Crossbow	d4 W	150	1 / 2 turns	₵ 8 / 20p	13	E
Crossbow, Powered	d4 W	175	2 (6)	₵ 24 / 60p	15	C
Derringer	d4 W	30	1 (2)	₵ 14 / 35p	1	E
Grenade Launcher	*	40	1 (8)	₵ 106 / 265p	12	I
Pistol	d6 W	100	3 (8)	₵ 18 / 45p	2	E
Pistol, Laser	d10 W *	100	3 (10)	₵ 330 / 825p	1.5	I
Rifle	d8 W	225	3 (30)	₵ 30 / 75p	9	E
Rifle, Assault	d8 W	150	3 (40) †	₵ 40 / 100p	11	I
Rifle, Sniper	d8 W	1,000 *	3 (20)	₵ 160 / 400p	15	C
Rifle, Sonic	d8 S	15	2 (50)	₵ 140 / 350p	6	I *
Shotgun	d10 W	10	2 (10)	₵ 50 / 125p	10	E
Submachine Gun	d6 W	60	3 (35) †	₵ 36 / 90p	4	I

* see description   † Can fire single shot, burst, or autofire   B = Basic Damge; S = Stun Damage; W = Wound Damage

discharges a fairly large jolt, enough to shock without doing' much real damage to the poor guy on the other end. All the damage done by it is converted to Stun (and Shock Points if it knocks 'em out). The batteries cost 1 Gold, and last for up to 10 shocks.

Brass Knuckles: This little piece of hand hardware converts unarmed damage into Basic damage instead of Stun damage (see Chapter Five: *Keep Flyin'* for information on unarmed combat). A nasty little surprise in a bar fight.

Club: A good, old-fashioned heavy stick. A bit more brutal than a baton, since doin' some serious damage is now an option. You can buy a metal one, but if you're okay with something a little less deadly, you can fashion a club out of wood that works the same, but does only d4 damage (Basic).

Hatchet: One of the most versatile hurtin' tools ever invented, you can also use it to cut down trees and chop firewood. You can even upend it and use it like a club. (Just don't grab it by the sharp part!)

Knife, Combat: A 6"-to-10" long blade is standard. Combat knives make deadly weapons. Can be used to stab or cut, and can also be thrown with some accuracy if you practice at it.

Knife, Utility: A paring knife or pocket knife *can* be used as a weapon, but not so well as others.

Machete: A broad, heavy knife used as both an implement and a weapon. Settlers on the Rim use machetes for chopping through brush.

Sword, Combat: Weapon made of metal with a long blade and a hand guard. The art of swordsmanship is considered a gentlemanly sport in the Core and for the wealthy on the outer worlds, where some indulge in the tradition of dueling to the death. Might be troublesome if you don't even know which end to hold.

Sword, Gentleman's: Swords like this are all fancied up with extra frills and decorations, and are more prone to breaking. Many gentlemen wear these to fancy-dress shindigs, to show what bad taste they have in weapons.

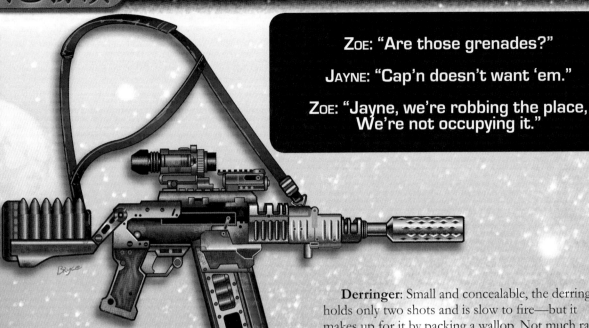

> ZOE: "Are those grenades?"
>
> JAYNE: "Cap'n doesn't want 'em."
>
> ZOE: "Jayne, we're robbing the place, We're not occupying it."

RANGED WEAPONS

Bow: Like the sword, the longbow has become a fashionable weapon of sport in the Core. Most quivers hold 20 arrows, costing about 5 Silver per arrow. The Alliance does not regulate the sale of bows and arrows. (Leastwise as of now.) Learning to skillfully use the bow and arrow can be part of the training of a Registered Companion.

Crossbow: A little more practical than the longbow, the crossbow is used as a hunting weapon. A case usually holds 20 bolts that cost about the same as arrows.

Crossbow, Powered: High-powered, fancy crossbows are used almost like sniper rifles by some, though they were meant for hunting game, not people. The bolts for these cost as much as bullets.

Derringer: Small and concealable, the derringer holds only two shots and is slow to fire—but it makes up for it by packing a wallop. Not much range to be had with one of these, though.

Grenade Launcher: These nasty devices can be loaded with any normal grenade, allowing them to be fired from a considerable distance. The damage done by the grenade is the same as the grenade used, but because the launcher is more inaccurate than most guns, range penalties are doubled.

Pistol: The staple of gunfighters everywhere, pistols come in all shapes and sizes. Most folk on the Rim are allowed to carry them in even polite society, since having a gun shows you've got good sense.

Pistol, Laser: A highly coveted piece of Alliance Newtech, laser weapons are illegal for all except those on the central planets who can obtain special permits for them (and that ain't easy!) and the Alliance military, who don't often use them anyway, because of the high cost involved. Laser pistols inflict more damage than a normal weapon, and the Wounds they inflict are considered burn wounds and thus are much harder to heal. Laser weapons require extremely high-density batteries, which cost

Table 3-10: Explosives

Weapon	Damage	Range Increment (feet)	Cost (Credits/Platinum)	Weight	Availibility
ChemPlast (CP-HE) Charge	3d12 W	5	₡ 6 / 15p	1	I
Grenade, Concussion	4d6 B	10	₡ 1.4 / 3p	1	I
Grenade, Flashbang	2d6 B *	5	₡ 0.8 / 2p	1	I
Grenade, Fragmentation	5d6 W	15	₡ 1.8 / 5p	1	I
Grenade, Smoke	d4 S	20	₡ 0.6 / 2p	1	C
Grenade, Gas	3d6 S	5	₡ 1.2 / 3p	1	I
Mining Charge	5d10 B	2	₡ 20 / 50p	5	E
Seeker Missile	2d8 W	5 *	₡ 95 / 238p	4	I
Squadkiller	4d12 W	15	₡ 48 / 120p	8	I

* see description

B = Basic Damge; S = Stun Damage; W = Wound Damage

2 Credits each and are very difficult to find. Laser pistols don't sit on the black market for long.

Rifle: Whether used for hunting or combat, the rifle is a very deadly weapon. Unfortunately, carrying one of these around is a might conspicuous.

Rifle, Assault: Full-auto weapons are definitely frowned upon by most authorities ('cept when they're the ones using them), but the attraction of being' able to saw a man in half is right strong in some. Most Feds carry a Newtech assault rifle as their main weapon.

Rifle, Sniper: Used by those who prefer one shot, one kill. Remember, though, that the range increment listed is for someone bracing the rifle and using the scope. If you try to use this like a normal rifle, it uses the range increment of a normal rifle (225 feet).

Rifle, Sonic: The standard issue weapon of choice for law enforcement on the central planets, the sonic rifle looks like a fancy shotgun with a couple of nested radio dishes about five inches across where the barrel ends. The sonic rifle fires a sonic burst that stuns the target, potentially knocking him down (or out). Armor works at only half effectiveness, rounded down, and there is no risk of damaging any but the most fragile of goods. The gun has a very short range and is inoperable in a vacuum. Like a laser weapon, it runs on hard-to-find batteries (1 credit each), and like most government equipment it is usually equipped with a transponder chip that allows it to be tracked.

Shotgun: Two barrels of death. 'Nuff said.

Submachine Gun: SMGs are popular in the criminal underworld. Machine guns eat ammo, but at least you can sleep better at night knowing your enemies are carrying around two pounds of lead.

EXPLOSIVES

ChemPlast (CP-HE) Charge: A high-yield plastic explosive, these charges let loose their energy in a relatively small area. Shrapnel isn't an issue (unless whoever set the charge packed it full of nuts and bolts and the such), but the blast wave is apparently a lot like being struck by a cruiser.

Grenade, Concussion: Used offensively because their smaller blast radius is less dangerous in the open, these grenades can still clear an area very effectively.

Grenade, Flashbang: Designed to stun enemies, flashbangs do relatively little damage, but everyone within 20 feet of the grenade is automatically stunned for one turn, and then they have to make a Survival roll against a Difficulty of 15. If they fail, they are stunned for 2d6 more turns. If they succeed, they are stunned for only 2 more turns. The only way to deal with this effect is complete ear and eye protection, which gives

a +2 Vitality Step bonus to the roll. Flashbangs don't always have to be grenades. Certain creative individuals have disguised these explosives in such innocent lookin' objects as a stick of incense.

Grenade, Fragmentation: Sharp fragments of metal rip through everything and everyone in the area. The only effective protection usually involves diving behind something—or someone—big and thick and heavy.

Grenade, Smoke: Inhaling the smoke does some damage, seeing as you get less air that way, but mostly the smoke obscures vision inside and through the cloud (counting as Thick Smoke, giving +8 to the Difficulty to hit any target through more than 10 feet of smoke). The smoke fills the blast area and dissipates slowly (usually in about two minutes). NBC masks prevent the damage.

Grenade, Gas: The grenades release a special nerve-gas designed to knock out those who breathe it. The effects are like several hours of hard drinking on an empty stomach. An NBC mask will prevent the damage. The gas dissipates in a few rounds.

OPTIONAL RULE: SIMPLIFIED WEAPON DAMAGE

To some, having to make a damage roll may seem more complicated than it's worth. The general assumption is that having a damage roll adds more excitement to the game, but there are those who don't like the extra rolling and prefer the option of giving weapons a flat damage rating. Rather than rolling the weapon's Damage and adding it to the Stun or Wounds (or both) when a hit is scored, just add half the max roll on the Weapon's damage die, rounded down.

Table 3-11: Optional Damage

Die Type	Damage
d2	1
d4	2
d6	3
d8	4
d10	5
d12	6

Mining Charge: Used to blast mine shafts, these charges are perfect for demolition of all kinds, and often come with a remote detonator or a timed electric fuse.

Seeker Missile: A Newtech weapon from the war, Seekers are automated, flyin' grenades. They use a small hover-drive to move around, and look a lot like a two-foot-long tadpole that wants to splatter you across the scenery. They tend to move toward motion and heat, and explode when they think they're near a target—any mobile heat source not transmitting the proper transponder signal. Tossing a flare tends to fool Seekers, but the blast can still be deadly at a range.

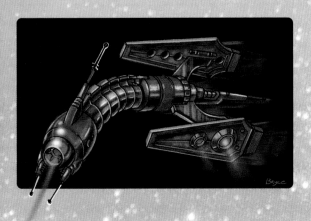

Squadkiller: A horrific little surprise left by retreating Alliance forces during the war, squadkillers are about the size of a large book, and are usually buried or hidden at a major intersection or common areas where people are likely to congregate. Built-in sensors wait until there are at least 12 warm bodies within 15 feet of this bomb, and then boom! Folk are all dead, just like that.

HEAVY WEAPONS

Heavy artillery—auto-cannons and the like—aren't included on the weapon list. That don't mean you won't ever run into them, but they're not as common as pistols or grenades. Of course, it is possible to beg, borrow, buy, or steal big guns. Or your crew might be military, in which case they will have access to them.

Generally speaking, a man who takes a direct hit from a shell fired by an autocannon won't be gettin' up afterwards. The damage is just too massive for a body to withstand. However, if he gets caught in the blast wave of a shell, or in a near miss, or he's hit while inside an armored vehicle, he might have a chance to survive. Below is a sample weapon—an artillery piece meant for destroying enemy aircraft.

"Mjolnir" Mk II Cannon / Damage: 1d4 (ship) / Range Increment: 250 / Max ROF (Magazine): 1 (10)

The workers on the mining moon of Haven have posted guards around their community and mounted an anti-aircraft cannon at the edge of town. The Mjolnir sits on a rotating platform that is usually mounted on a defensive emplacement or a hover-vehicle (which must be grounded while firing). The large shells take two turns each to load, but can be fired once per turn. The cannon can be aimed and fired by one person, though you might want to consider adding another person to continually reload. Note that the damage listed is for ship scale. The damage is multiplied by 10 for use against vehicles, and multiplied by 100 against individuals. Any person taking a direct hit will be an instant splotch! (See Chapter Five: *Keep Flyin'* for details on damage.)

TECHSHOP

When humanity's home in the 'Verse was established, the tech-heads began working on an interplanetary communications network. If the central planets are the beating heart of the system, then the Cortex is its nervous system. Nodes have been placed around every planet—even newly terraformed outer worlds—with communications lines along most every trade route and shipping lane. Only those who deliberately go out of their way to avoid bein' noticed (flyin' under the Alliance radar, for instance) will find themselves cut off from their fellow folk.

The Cortex can be accessed by anyone with the right equipment, which means to say anyone with the cash to afford an access terminal, or—for something even more shiny—a handheld access device. Once on the Cortex, a 'Verse full of talk, news, information, and entertainment is waiting to be had.

Most Cortex-based communication comes in the forms of "waves," which can be as simple as text messages, but are more often viewed on flat-screen video. And for those with the right equipment, three-dimensional holographic imaging is possible. Most waves are delayed messages, though if two parties are close enough, the communication can be live and direct. While a source-trace can locate the origination node for each end of the signal, the trace cannot specifically track where a particular wave came from in the first place.

The Alliance government works to control content on the Cortex, and they are adept at doing so for the most important and sensitive material. But the sheer volume of information means that if some file or document is broadwaved from a

> "You can't stop the signal, Mal. Everything goes somewhere, and I go everywhere."
>
> —Mr. Universe

location with the right equipment, it will reach every data node strung throughout the system and can be accessed by anyone ready to receive.

One important thing to remember about Cortex access points is that every screen serves also as camera and microphone. Watch your favorite episode of Razor Frog and someone on the other end could be watchin' you pick your teeth. Privately owned devices are harder to pull feeds from, though someone with the right know-how can do it. Public terminals are supposedly private, but it's widely known that someone could be watching you at just about any time. However, since there are so damn many screens in the 'Verse, no one could watch every one all the time. The truth is out there. You can't stop the signal.

Laws against electronic crimes are heavily enforced and law breakers punished, but the potential rich rewards of the bits and bytes still encourage hackers and the like to keep on tryin' their luck. Black market tech helps the nefarious stay one step ahead of the Feds.

COMPUTERS, HARDWARE AND PROGS

Cortex Terminal, Black Box: An illegal terminal, designed to disguise the user from Alliance snoops. Unfortunately, since so many features of

the Cortex are closely monitored, pretty much everything interesting is locked up tighter than the First Allied Bank. About all you can do with this clunky unit is send anonymous waves (basically voice and video mail) and read the news.

Cortex Terminal, Personal Access: What most Core citizens use. Essentially a 2'x 2' touchscreen monitor, 5" thick, with a moderately sized base to allow for the rest of the equipment, Cortex terminals are a phone, a computer, and a TV all rolled into one—to put it in the terms of folk back on Earth-that-Was. You can surf the Cortex, access almost any information (assuming you can pay for a pass code), send waves, use progs, store almost limitless amounts of data… assuming, of course, that the gorram thing wants to cooperate. Since a terminal is just that—a terminal—sometimes you can lose Cortex access if a satellite or transmission station goes down, and then you lose whatever you were working on, and have to hope your connection gets going mighty quick, because you have no storage capacity.

Cortex Terminal, Public Access: These terminal panels can be found in all sorts of places. Generally they serve a specific purpose, and can access only a limited number of functions. Police, Telofonix (a local-area communication service), and emergency calls (direct to a hospital or ambulance) are three standard options. Docking berths on the

Table 3-12: Computers, Hardware, & Progs

Item	Cost (Credits/Platinum)	Weight	Availibility	Notes
Cortex Terminal, Black Box	₡ 747.2 / 1,868p	20	I	Illegal, nonstandard Cortex access terminal
Cortex Terminal, Personal Access	₡ 100 / 250p	15	C	Allows access to profiles on Cortex for data storage
Cortex Terminal, Public Access	₡ 52 / 130p	15	E	Allows access to profiles on Cortex for data storage
Data-library, Standard	₡ 22.8 / 57 p	–	E	Annual renewal costs ¼ original price
Data-library, Professional	₡ 92 / 230p	–	C	Annual renewal costs ¼ original price; may require Alliance certification
DataBook	₡ 30 / 75p	2	E	Low-storage display unit; reads data discs and can interface with Cortex terminals
Data Disc	₡ 0.2 / 1p	–	E	Stores electronic data or recordings
Dedicated Sourcebox	₡ 154 / 385p	30	C	Allows access to Cortex, but also acts as a local Cortex hub and database
Encyclopedia	₡ 60 / 150p	2	C	Official Encyclopedic Data-library (OED)
Holo-Image Development Suite	₡ 64 / 160p	5	C	A software bundle with additional computer hardware
SubKelvin	₡ 80 / 200p	–	I	A security-destroying software link
XerO Security	₡ 7.2 / 18p	–	C	Computer security software; 5 credit annual fee

Table 3-13: Communications & Security Equipment

Item	Cost (Credits/Platinum)	Weight	Availibility	Notes
Barrier Field	₡ 1,062 / 2,655p	450	C	Up to 50 feet of force-barrier fencing
Commpack, Long Range	₡ 37.8 / 95p	10	C	Allows communication up to 300 miles
Commpack, Short Range	₡ 22.4 / 56p	7	E	Allows communication up to 20 miles
Distress Beacon	₡ 31 / 78p	14	C	Automated distress signal, range of 750 miles, self-powered for 10 hours
Emergency Signal Ring	₡ 300 / 750p	-	C	A Newtech, miniaturized distress beacon, worn as a ring
Fedband Scanner	₡ 19.8 / 50p	3	I	Reads most official frequencies
Gunscanner	₡ 132.8 / 332p	220	C	Security device
Micro Transmitter	₡ 8 / 20p	-	C	Wearable comm. unit
Motion Sensor Array	₡ 22 / 55p	12	C	Redeployable security system
Ship-linked Handset	₡ 3.2 / 8p	1	E	Handset linked to ship's comm. system, 10 mile range
Surveyor's Box	₡ 230 / 575p	65	C	Scanning and detection equipment for laying out mineshafts
Transmission Station	₡ 2,200 / 5,500p	3,000	C	License is ₡ 1,000/year; can process Telofonix and other Cortex signals
"Jabberwocky" Signal Blocker	₡ 13.3 / 34p	10	I	Powerful communication jamming unit

surface usually have public terminals for ship specs and for logging travel plans, which can be useful if you want to advertise for cargo or passengers.

Data-library, Standard: Knowledge is power, and power costs money. If you want access to a vast library of literature, history texts, recipes, and so forth, then paying for a data-library subscription is the way to go. These can provide a lot of information; how general or specific is up to the GM.

Data-library, Professional: The latest in medical science, gravitic engineering, ship construction, and pretty much anything else can be had by those who feel the urge to pay for it. Sometimes a fellow needs to be licensed to get access to such, but at least you can be guaranteed to get pretty much all the information the Alliance doesn't feel it's too dangerous for you to know.

DataBook: The exact appearance can vary, but these data readers range in size from a paperback novel to a hardback textbook. They can store up to 5 terabytes of data (enough for a few useful progs or 3-D schematics or such), read data discs, and link to the Cortex through a terminal or sourcebox. They can even be linked to other electronic devices to be used for programming or control purposes, though that's less of a sure thing. Not many on the Rim bother with such a posh bit of gear, but it has its uses.

Data Disc: These crystalline hexagonal discs can be clicked into a data reader for access at most

any terminal or computer station. The standard disc holds enough information to store even short holographic recordings and can be reused.

Dedicated Sourcebox: Expensive sourceboxes that not only act as terminals, but can also store up to 200 terabytes of data and maintain a terminal link for up to a mile around.

Encyclopedia: Another expensive little toy, these devices are slick Core databooks with their own extensive data-libraries. While the common features are Languages, Human History, and Universal Encyclopedia, different models come with up to three other libraries. For example, a doctor might get one with Medical Science, Anatomical Engineering ,and a Bio-Physical Atlas in addition to the standard three. Otherwise, it functions as a normal DataBook.

Holo-Image Development Suite: Holographic tech is expensive, but not uncommon in the 'Verse. This device allows you to produce holographs. A bunch of progs and a 3-D manipulator (little box you stick your hand in, so you can move it about and shape the images) lets you make durn near anything you put your mind to (if you have the right skills).

SubKelvin: Where there's a will, there's someone workin' against it. SubK is a well-known (and thus almost useless) security-removal utility. It works well against Core softies who don't know their operating matrix buffer from their main feedback path, but that's about it. There's better stuff out there, if you know where to look.

XerO Security: One of the most popular Cortex Profile Protection Utilities, XerO self-updates, auto-runs, and jumps through hoops on command.

COMMUNICATIONS AND SECURITY EQUIPMENT

Barrier Field: Force barrier technology may once have been just *bie jih mone*, but now it's just extremely costly. Some of the wealthier families on the Core and the outer worlds can afford to surround their homes with the 10" tall, square projector pillars that make up the generator system, but not many. A pillar has to be situated at each corner and end point—as the fields only project along straight lines—and the tech is expensive. However, once operational, the barrier field is extremely durable: it takes at least 50 Damage inflicted in one turn to overload it. Attacks on the barrier generally alert a security system to the problem. Even if the security is disabled, the fireworks may attract unwanted attention. Normally invisible, the barrier field is highlighted by timed energy surges to show that it's active; when you start pounding' on it, the energy flow can get a lot brighter.

Commpack, Long Range: A backpack-sized transmitter capable of sending and reading on a range of frequencies. The batteries for the Commpack will last for up to two months of normal use, and are relatively cheap (between 40 and 50 Silver each), so this unit was often used by the Independent Faction during the war, despite the unfortunate fact that the signal isn't exactly secure.

Commpack, Short Range: Essentially the same as the long range version, the difference in the short range Commpack is that the signal is heavily encoded. The drawback is that this reduces the range available at the unit's power level.

Distress Beacon: A pre-set common distress signal transmitted at extremely high power will generally attract the attention of the Feds or police if you're on the Core. Out on the Rim, Alliance patrols may hear the call and, if so, they'll respond. Since patrols are pretty few and far between, though, the chances are they may not hear it or they may have other priorities. The beacon is only about the size of a duffle-bag, so moving it around isn't too much of a problem for most folk.

Emergency Signal Ring: A Newtech distress beacon miniaturized down to where it can be worn as a ring, and activated without any overt movement. Wealthy folks find them useful to protect them against kidnappings and the like, since they can be tracked easily and a personal code built into the ring lets the authorities identify them. When the police

get an emergency code call, they tend to respond in force.

Fedband Scanner: A ship's communication system can be tuned in to most frequencies, but civilian ships do not typically pick up the official government and police channels. There are ways around this, if you feel like tinkering, but for most folks, a wave-scanner such as this does the trick.

Gunscanner: A fairly standard security device in the Core, most banks and government buildings have a gunscanner installed at security checkpoints. Of course, folk with the proper permits can carry weapons, but all others will have their weapons confiscated. The scanners can be calibrated to detect a lot of things, though most look for a concentration of metals, traces of common propellant chemicals, and the ID chips installed in most legally acquired firearms. Newtech gunscans are even more efficient, and could include barrier field tech to keep out anyone with a weapon.

Micro Transmitter: Usually a hard-to-spot earpiece, micro-transmitters are used by the majority of security forces in the 'Verse. The transmitter's range is generally limited to a few hundred yards, but it makes up for that by allowing easy and discreet contact.

Motion Sensor Array: A main hub unit about the size of a small databook monitors the transmissions from the eight motion sensors. The sensors are 1" cubes with glass panels over the sensors and can be stuck to walls, stashed in tree branches, or wherever. They just need to be placed within 100 feet of the hub.

Ship-linked Handset: A clunky little walkie-talkie handset, this is the standard device used for keeping crew members in touch with their ship. Most ships come with several handsets, but generally additional or replacement units are needed—there's always some lummox who sits on his handset and smashes it.

Surveyor's Box: A local area geoscanner combined with a mapping utility prog make this device, that is about the size of a foot locker, useful for surveyors laying out mine shafts and tunnels. Some are sold to nonprofessionals, but what uses they find for 'em isn't always apparent.

Transmission Station: Offering franchises for carrying the Cortex signal has become an extremely popular way for the Alliance to spread and maintain the Cortex farther out on the Rim. Of course, once you own a Transmission Station and the license, you still need an approved place to put it—usually that means on an orbital station somewhere, and that usually means high rent and living costs, since you'll be paying spaceport prices for food and services. Not a choice for those looking for an exciting, high-paying life, though if you can afford to finance one of these (and a few operators), they can be a good way to make money.

"Jabberwocky" Signal Blocker: The Jabberwocky box is only one of any number of illegal devices used by some folk to prevent other folk from hearing what they figure they have a right to say. Once activated, the box can scramble all to hell any signal within five miles. If you use it for more than a minute or two, it quickly becomes obvious to the authorities that something isn't quite right. The Jabberwocky is difficult to locate, but it will be eventually be found.

THE OUTFITTERS

Some folk who are professionals in their particular field require gear that is specially designed for their needs. Such gear can generally be effectively used only by those who have been professionally trained in the operation of the equipment. Specialty equipment can either be very expensive and difficult to come by (such as a Cryo Chamber), or it may be fairly commonly found (such as lock picks). Those who are professionals in their chosen fields will know where to obtain the equipment they need and how to obtain it. (Doctors will know where and how to acquire medical supplies; engineers will know where to obtain cutting torches, etc.)

MEDICAL EQUIPMENT

Blastomere Organs: Cloning and growing organs for those needing transplants has become a viable practice in the Core, but Blastomeres—a recent Newtech creation—could make this practice

obsolete. Designed to be acceptable by any human body, the synthetic organs could eliminate the time needed to grow a cloned organ. Blastomeres are longer-lasting and are more durable than normal human organs, potentially improving the body and increasing the lifespan of the recipient. Needless to say, they are extraordinarily expensive and, since they are still undergoing testing, they are not yet available to the public.

Cryo Chamber: Designed originally to put patients in stasis until they can be properly treated (or a cloned organ can be grown), cryogenic freezing chambers have a number of other uses. Slavers sometimes transport their victim in cryo, though this is expensive and can pose a problem if the people handling the cryo unit don't know how to use it properly. Putting a body in cryo requires giving the person a carefully measured set of injections, depending on how long the stasis is supposed to last. Removing the person from cryo requires a careful "warm-up" procedure. Not following these procedures doesn't necessarily mean that the subject will die, but this can happen if the user bungles it badly.

Dermal Mender: Another fancy medical innovation, this is for those who don't like stitches and can pay to avoid scarring. Through a combination of regenerative stimulation and the application of artificial skin, the dermal mender can close almost any wound in a matter of minutes. Unfortunately, while the mender works well for tissue bond (don't fiddle with it and it should be good as new in a few days), the dermal mender can't fix bone, cartilage, or organs. It'll patch up your skin (and maybe even help put an ear or a nose back

Table 3-14: Medical Equipment

Item	Cost (Credits/Platinum)	Weight	Availibility	Notes
Blastomere Organs	₡ 18,000 / 45,000p	5	I	Newtech replacement organs; can extend lifespan
Cryo Chamber	₡ 1,300 / 3,250p	275	I	Suspended animation unit
Dermal Mender	₡ 800 / 2,000p	15	C	Newtech wound-sealing equipment
Doctor's Bag	₡ 27.4 / 69p	7	R	Simple case with tools and supplies
Doctor's Bag (MedAcad)	₡ 210 / 525p	8	C	A full set of portable Core MedAcad tools and supplies
First-Aid Kit	₡ 0.6 / 2p	3	E	A basic first-aid kit
Immunization Packet	₡ 3 /7 p	–	C	Powerful but short-lived inoculation against most common diseases
MedComp	₡ 312 / 780p	23	C	Vital-status diagnostic computer
Medical Supplies, Emergency	₡ 110 / 275p	20	C	Most commonly needed emergency supplies for one month
Medical Supplies, Standard	₡ 46 / 115p	15	C	Standard medical supplies to keep an infirmary stocked for one month
Operating Theatre, Modular	₡ 346 / 865p	1,250	C	Base camp or shipboard infirmary; installation costs ₡ 25

on, at least partially), but that's it. After surgery, the dermal mender can close the incision (maybe healing some of the Wound damage) and prevent infection. The GM is the final arbiter as to what Wounds inflicted on a character can be healed with a dermal mender.

Doctor's Bag: A collection of basic medicines, antibiotics, scalpels, extractors, etc. Everything a doctor needs to perform minimally in house-call environments, though far from enough to treat everything he might encounter. Out on the Rim, this may be the best there is. The GM will assign a –2 to –4 Skill step penalty for trying to perform any surgery or complex procedure equipped with only the supplies found in this bag.

Doctor's Bag (MedAcad): A doctor who graduates from one of the major Medical Academies (on Osiris, Londinum, or Sihnon) will almost certainly have one of these. Technically, they are available to any licensed practitioner in the Core (as are most medical supplies, if the buyer can pay), but that means that the person much have attended one of the major MedAcads or has his training certified by one, which is no mean feat. These more advanced doctor's kits include the best in portable instrumentation, the latest in commonly needed medicines (though in small amounts), and so forth. The penalty for any surgery with this is reduced to between –1 and –3 Skill steps from a normal doctor's bag, though some things (such as major open-heart surgery) still require more than is available here.

First-Aid Kit: A standard first-aid kit containing several pain killers, weaves, smelling salts and other minor but useful items. At the GM's option, someone using a first-aid kit can staunch bleeding, apply painkillers to reduce Wound penalties, and so forth. It counts as "standard equipment" for first-aid rolls.

Immunization Packet: These little foil packets contain several hypos of medicine and a couple of chewable tablets. Using a packet will help prevent the user from being infected by almost any known disease. The effects last for only about 48 hours.

MedComp: While a bit big to carry by hand (being a little bigger than a Cortex terminal), the medcomp combines most necessary medical scanners with a set of diagnostic progs. Most of the sensors operate via a plastic-cased finger sleeve attached to the medcomp by a wire; someone hooked up can have his heart rate, body temperature, blood chem levels, and so forth monitored by the computer. Use of a medcomp gives a doctor +2 Skill Steps to diagnose a problem or disease, and the monitors may allow a doctor extra time to react to and treat emergency situations (if a patient's heart stops, for example).

Medical Supplies, Emergency: The doctor who pays the monthly cost for keeping these on hand should be equipped to deal with most major medical situations he could reasonably expect to encounter (serious gunshot wounds, major infections, massive blood loss, etc.). Being well-stocked with emergency medical supplies gives +2 Skill steps to rolls to treat both major and minor medical problems—as long as the GM rules the situation is not so unusual that the doctor is unprepared for it—and the bonus stacks with that when the doctor has Medical Supplies, Standard, when applicable. Constant use may require that the supply be restocked more often than once a month.

Medical Supplies, Standard: Paying the monthly cost to keep an infirmary stocked with the basics allows the doc to make rolls without penalty to treat most common or mild problems, such as a cold or a bullet in the leg. For treating a minor wound (usually 1-4 Wound points), using such supplies can even give a +1 Skill step bonus.

Operating Theatre, Modular: Developed during the war so that base camp hospitals could be set up quickly almost anywhere, a Modular Operating Theatre equipped with a MedComp and standard and emergency medical supplies counts as Superior Supplies/Ambulance Conditions for first-aid and surgery purposes. Since many ships were equipped with them during the war, most ships use a similar model for their infirmary.

COVERT OPS GEAR

Debugger: A palm-sized signal scrambler, these generally won't interfere with high power transmissions, such as the Cortex, but they play merry hell with most electronic bugs in a 15' radius.

Disguise Kit: A suitcase filled with makeup, hair dye, wigs, fake beards, plasticskin, noses, ears, etc. Basically everything a professional spy might need, including several bottles of pills designed to alter the user's skin tone and a few sets of 'John Doe' artificial fingerprints that adhere seamlessly and remain good for 24 hours.

Eavesdrops: If you want to know what people are saying behind your back, this is the way to find out. The microphones (no larger than the size of a pinhead) can be hidden anywhere within 30 feet of the transmission hub. The hub collects the audio data and stores it (up to 48 hours from each eavesdrop) or transmits it all in one burst. It can also transmit constantly at a range of up to half a mile.

Fake IdentCard: Alliance IdentCards are extremely hard to actually fake, since they are embedded with hardwired microchips containing important data about the holder. As a result, it's easier to steal someone else's card and apply your face to the picture, even though this means the card will likely get you caught if anyone puts it through a card-reader. A truly usable fake IdentCard can be obtained only at obscenely high cost, and even then it won't match Cortex records, meaning careful examination will reveal the fraud.

Laserlight Mist: A small can of mildly reflective aerosol mist will reveal security alarms and barrier fields, laser trip wires, and so on without setting off alarms. The mist dissipates within two turns.

Lock picks: An assortment of small picks and wrenches for opening locks rolled up in a piece of cloth. Not worth much, since old-fashioned mechanical locks are rarely used where there's anything worth stealing.

Lock picks, Electronic: Especially in the Core, most locks are electronic in nature and require either overriding a keypad or transmitting a code before they'll open. This little pack of gadgets can help accomplish both.

Mag Charge: A short-range, electromagnetic pulse charge, about the size of a large battery.

Unless the electrical equipment is hardened against EMP waves (which is extremely difficult, if not impossible to do fully), all electrical equipment in the 10' affected radius will short out and stop working until repaired. Most ships possess enough redundancies so that one of these will not cause fatal problems, but using them aboard a space vessel or atmospheric craft is not advised.

Optical Bomb: A bundle of LEDs and fiber-optic cabling around a capacitor, optical bombs are designed to temporarily blind an opponent (and possibly nearby security cameras), making it easier to disable said opponent. To be truly effective, the bomb must go off within 15 feet of people and 10 feet of cameras and must be within line of sight. An NBC mask will protect a person's eyes, while more expensive security devices have an auto reactive coating to protect cameras from such attacks. It otherwise functions like a Flashbang grenade, except that only eye protection is required.

Poison, Kortine (Debilitating): If a dose (usually about two milliliters) of this poison enters a victim's bloodstream, it will do 1d8 Stun damage each turn for six turns, with extra Stun counting as Shock Points. Unless a further dose is applied, the poison will not raise a victim's Shock Points high enough to put him into a coma (so maximum Shock Points from Kortine is equal to a victim's Life Points −1). If ingested, the effects are the same, but the Damage is only 1d4/turns.

Poison, Cyanol (Lethal): Equally lethal by ingestion or injection, a milliliter of this poison will do 2d12 Wound damage and the victim must make a Hard Endurance roll (see Chapter Five: *Keep Flyin'*). Failure indicates death by heart attack.

Table 3-15: Covert Ops Gear

Item	Cost (Credits/Platinum)	Weight	Availibility	Notes
Debugger	₡ 20 / 50p	1	C	Single scrambling hub; 15' radius
Disguise Kit	₡ 65.6 / 164p	5	C	Refill for ₡ 5 per 10 uses
Eavesdrops	₡ 47.2 / 118p	3	I	Includes 4 bugs and transmission hub
Fake IdentCard	₡ 4,000 / 10,000p	–	I	Illegal and hard to obtain
Laserlight Mist	₡ 1.8 / 4p	1	C	One can, good for about 25 cubic feet
Lock Picks	₡ 14 / 35p	–	I	Required for mechanical locks
Lock Picks, Electronic	₡ 35.4 / 88p	1	I	Required for electronic locks
Mag Charge	₡ 27 / 68p	1	I	Shorts out electronic devices
Optical Bomb	₡ 16 / 40p	1	I	Wide-spectrum; may disable cameras
Poison, Kortine (Debilitating)	₡ 11 / 27p	–	I	Price per dose
Poison, Cyanol (Lethal)	₡ 12.6 / 32p	–	I	Price per dose

Table 3-16: Engineer's Supplies

Item	Cost (Credits/Platinum)	Weight	Availibility	Notes
CAD Board	₡ 27.2 / 68p	5	C	Design and schematic display tablet
Cutting Torch	₡ 4 / 10p	8	E	Will cut through most metal
Gravcart	₡ 485 / 1,212p	150	C	Can carry up to one ton
Scrapware	₡ 5 / 12p	50	E	Junked parts, for repair materials
"Sticky" Scrapper's Gel	₡ 2 / 5p	2	C	Used to cut sheet metal, bulkheads, etc; price per 10 yards of gel
Tool Kit, Basic	₡ 14.4 / 36p	15	E	A full set of basic hand-tools
Tool Set, Electronic	₡ 138 / 345p	45	C	Used for computer and electronic device or circuit work
Tool Set, Mechanic's	₡ 284 / 710p	130	E	A moderately well-furnished workshop

ENGINEERING SUPPLIES

CAD Board: About the size of a dinner tray, this device operates much like a databook. The large screen is meant to aid engineers and architects in the creation of plans and schematics, and allows in-depth examination of building plans, ship layouts, and the like.

Cutting Torch: Whether you're working on your ship or cutting your way into someone's vault, this is the tool of choice for most folk. The small energy pack can be worn at your hip, and the device includes a face mask to keep you from burning off your eyebrows. Requires atmo to work.

Gravcart: A six-inch thick platform, two yards long and one yard wide, the gravcart uses a small grav-drive to float and carry up to one ton. It does not supply its own lateral motion, requiring it to be pulled or towed.

Scrapware: Salvagers sell crates of good condition materials such as wire, metal sheeting, springs, etc., at junkyards and spaceports. Scrapware won't help you all that much if a catalyzer or some other complex part busts, but it can allow a good mechanic to perform basic repairs on the fly, so you can make it back to port.

"Sticky" Scrapper's Gel: When cutting your way into derelict ships, sometimes you have to do it with no atmo around—and then your trusty cutting torch won't work. The solution is Scrapper's Gel. The device lays down a line of the goo that has a conductor embedded inside. When a small surge of energy is applied, the goo turns into a powerful acid that can eat its way through most metal. Since it doesn't work in atmo, someone bent on cutting a hole in the hull with gel will have to go outside to do it.

Tool Kit, Basic: Hammers, saws, wrenches, screwdrivers, and the like (and their powered equivalents) can be used by most folks and are good to have around. A carpenter, mason, metalworker, or similar will find that these are the right tools for the job. If you want a big workshop with table-saws, sandblasters, and powered arc-welders, then you need one of the bigger tool sets.

Tool Set, Electronic: A full set of equipment for working with modern electronics in the 'Verse. If you're a computer designer, a holo-set repairman, or something along those lines, this is what you need. Most of the tools will probably fit in a utility belt, but there are one or two bigger pieces that are a bit more difficult to carry around.

Tool Set, Mechanic: A full set of mechanic's tools used by ship's mechanics, engineers, and those working in garages. You need this setup to do any real repair work on a vehicle of any sort from a mule to a full boat.

ROBOTS

Robots are an interesting type of gear. They could be just about any shape and size. They can do a helluva lot that real folks can't. But before we get to talking about robots, let's get one thing straight: there aren't any thinking robots in the 'Verse! Sure, lots of progs and robots can sound like a person, maybe even act like a person in some way, but they're not people. Scientists and programmers are working long and hard making robots ever smarter, but there's a big difference between convincing programming and being sentient.

Robots in the 'Verse are much like they were on Earth-That-Was. Generally, a robot is designed with a specific job in mind, and it can do only that job. Some have completely pre-set commands, and some are smart enough to make simple decisions (such as "stop," when they'd run into something). Some of the more common models are described here, but there are other types in use, especially in heavy industries. Prominent manufacturers push

> "I have a commitment to my LoveBot. It was a very beautiful ceremony.
> Lenore wrote her own vows. I cried like a baby. A hungry, angry baby."
>
> —Mr. Universe

Table 3-17: Robots

Item	Cost (Credits/Platinum)	Weight	Availibility	Notes
AgriCultivator	₡ 2,240 / 5,600p	1,300	C	Automated farming robot
Automated Secretary	₡ 1,600 / 4,150p	100	C	Receptionist; can take and transfer Telofonix calls, greet visitors, etc.
LoveBot	₡ 1,960 / 4,900p	120	*	Personal companion robot
Excavator	₡ 2,350 / 5,875p	950	R	Designed for mining and digging
Household Assistant	₡ 1,344 / 3,360p	55	C	Cleans floors thoroughly
Scout Drone	₡ 640 / 1,600p	12	I	Military reconnaissance robot

their prototypes in mass advertising, so they pop up on the Cortex as commercials. The Foreigner Corporation (Cybernetics & Robotics Division) has more then a few models they'd like to see get some sales.

ROBOTS

AgriCultivator: A brilliant design, the AgriCultivator has all the necessary tools to till, plant, tend, and harvest a field. It runs off rails suspended above the field on which it is working. This robot has become colloquially known by the shortened name, AgriVator, because of its propensity for breaking down.

Automated Secretary: To all appearances a pleasant-looking young person (man or woman, at the buyer's option) sits behind a desk, answering the

Telofonix calls and greeting visitors. If you were to steal a peep around the desk, though, you would find the person has no legs—just the wheeled chair it's built in to. The unit can answer simple questions related to its function, such as giving directions, typing memos, and filing documents. When faced with something it doesn't understand, it will ask politely if it can refer the person to a more capable party, usually a help-desk or other human in the area. To operate, the automated secretary must be plugged into the local power grid.

LoveBot: No self-respecting robotics manufacturer makes such a self-indulgent toy, but there's enough demand to keep a small but steady underground market supplied with these extremely expensive 'bots. Usually built to custom specs (desired sex, build, skin tone, hair color, etc.), the

LoveBots are designed for companionship. They are capable of a slow walk, simple conversation, and the physical acts for which they are primarily designed. They generally lounge quietly on sofas or beds, and remain plugged into the power grid by a cord (which can be detached; a LoveBot can run on battery power for 12 hours). As a concession to practicality, LoveBots have an internal emergency signal beacon, and are capable of summoning the police or an ambulance if they detect the need. They can also be used to record and play back simple messages. Anyone known to own such a device automatically earns a black mark in the Companion Registry.

Excavator: One of the few robots manufactured and operated almost solely on the outer worlds, Excavators are used in most mining concerns. Capable of identifying, cutting, and loading minerals and ores into an attached cart, the unit runs on tracks that guide it and supply it with power. Humans still have to do the truly dangerous work of mining, since they still have to blast through rock, shore up tunnels, bring in and construct the tracks, and identify areas in which to concentrate operations. After that, the excavators are brought in to do the rest. The arms that fold in to the rectangular body contain laser-saws, mining-charge layers, measurement and cutting tools, sensors and claw-like manipulators.

Household Assistant: Not much bigger than a trash can, this angular little robot has a vacuum, a static dust-cleaner, bays for polishes and waxes, and so on. It can clean a room fairly well in a matter of minutes, assuming it doesn't bungle its sensors and start running into things. Popular as a show of wealth in the Core, the Assistants are owned by many of the wealthiest families (even though they still employ housekeepers). Consequently, the

wealthy Core-wanna-be's living on the Rim consider them status symbols and will pay well for them.

Scout Drone: A newly modified expansion on the Seeker missile, the scout drone is slightly larger than its explosive predecessor. Capable of both automated seeking and manual guidance, the drone can travel up to two miles from its launch-point and return safely on a full battery charge. It carries several cameras, an infrared sensor, and a variety of other sensory instruments, all of which constantly transmit data back to base. These drones have yet to undergo a real field test, since they went into mass production after the war ended.

NEWTECH

Not all gear is created equal. Sometimes your rusty old six-shooter looks mighty shabby compared to the fancy new piece the Alliance has just issued to the Feds. Both guns do about the same thing—put a hole in a man—and yours has sentimental value. But while you're having a sentimental gun jam, the Feds have slapped you in cuffs and hauled you off.

Because it would be too cumbersome to list all the brands, makes, and models of each and every bit of equipment in the 'Verse, the tables here give the average stats for most things. If a character (or NPC) needs a pistol with a little more kick to it, a computer with a bit more power, or a med kit with the latest in bandages, the GM can let them find (or buy) a Newtech version of what they'd normally use.

While it's all well and good to design custom equipment, it can get pretty complicated. Technological developments require experimentation, and things usually don't go smooth when you're trying to invent a newfangled gun. So, to keep things simple, the basic Newtech system breaks technological development time into three levels based on how much the object costs, which will be two times, four times or ten times the normal price.

Of course, these levels can fluctuate. Unique or truly dangerous items may cost considerably more. Basically, the crew decides what they're looking for, and the GM will let them know if it exists and, if so, how much it costs. The guidelines below should serve to work out the price, though there's sure to be add-ons and gadgetry that aren't listed, so don't feel limited by the following.

NEWTECH DESIGN

When you are trying to put together Newtech equipment, first try to find something—either in this chapter or from Earth-That-Was—on which to base your invention. If you can't think of just the perfect thing, try to come up with some basis for it and work out the particulars with your GM.

That done, decide how much more advanced you want this new item to be. If you see something in the descriptions below that matches, that's great. If not, tell the GM what you want the object to do and let him set the cost multiplier. It might even pay the GM to make up his own Newtech chart for his game, since everyone's take on the 'Verse may be a bit different.

Then work out exactly what makes that item special: does it shoot farther, last longer, or weigh less than its real life counterpart? There are a lot of possibilities at each level, but don't go hounding your GM to cram every single bonus onto one piece of gear. In other words, don't get greedy. And remember, the GM can modify these lists however he sees fit, and that includes disallowing anything he finds might cause an issue in his game.

COST X2

Items at this level of Newtech are not all that hard to find. They're just a little too expensive to be the standard of the day. Most Alliance military gear is at this level (and is also tagged and tracked).

Suggestions: +1 Step to damage, magazine size increased by 50%, range increment increased by 50%, durability doubled, usable lifetime increased by 50%. Modifications to equipment might include: silencers, computerized scopes, automatic firing action, fancy ammo, computers, mechanics miniaturized down to half the normal weight, experimental medicines, holographic technology.

The "Gilgamesh" shot-rifle: Essentially a shotgun with incredible range, the Gilgamesh is an experimental weapon originally commissioned by a private party, but now available to others through special orders. An on-board computer uses a laser sight to determine the range to the target and sets a charge on the slug to explode about 1 ½ feet prior to impact. When the charge detonates, the slug releases a cloud of shot similar to a shotgun blast. To create this gun, take a normal rifle from the ranged weapons table and add +1 damage Step (makes it d10, same as a shotgun), increase the range increment by 1/2 (to 150), add a computerized scope, and top it off with fancy ammo. It costs 60 credits, but hopefully will keep its owner alive.

COST X4

This level of Newtech is the high end of what retailers in the Core might be able to find. The exceptionally wealthy can get their hands on it to show off or give themselves an edge on their opponents. The crew are not going to find this kind of equipment just lying around.

Suggestions: +2 Steps to damage, magazine size doubled, range increment doubled, almost impossible to break, usable lifetime doubled.

Modifications to equipment might include: auto-target "smart" tracking, miniaturization down to 1/10 normal weight, biotechnology (cloned or genetically improved replacement organs, body-enhancing gene therapy, etc.), cybernetics (robotic prosthetics and the like). The item may also integrate the features of more than one normal item or possess capabilities generally beyond its scope (subject to GM approval, of course).

Note: Cybernetics and biotechnology are both developing sciences in the 'Verse. While they can make a person's body better than it might be, they aren't perfect. They're also hard to find, especially outside the Core. Even on Londinum and Sihnon, cybernetic limbs, better hearts, and muscle-boosting gene therapy are usually reserved for the military and the very wealthy.

Eyetap Computer. Looks like a standard set of nondescript reading glasses that come in a bulky case. The eyetap allows the wearer to view what might almost be considered a new level of reality. Any flat surface can be turned into a "screen" in the wearer's vision (or a "screen" could be conjured up in the middle of empty space). Anything the wearer sees can be downloaded and recorded. The information can then be called up at any time, so long as the glasses are being worn. Essentially this mimics a photographic memory, though some folks may wonder why the wearer is staring blankly before speaking!

Casual observers will not be able to detect the fact that the eyetap computer user is accessing data, for the "screen" and its contents are visible only to the person wearing the glasses. Commands can be entered through a keypad on the inside of the glasses' case or via a small touchpad device that can be palmed or kept in a pocket.

To make this nifty little device, take a databook and miniaturize it down to 1/10 the weight, add some holographic tech as part of the display, and incorporate the features of a video camera. It'll cost 300 Platinum, which is quite a hefty sum, but it might escape notice, and allow those folk who bought it to make good on their investment.

COST X10

Anything this advanced will be extremely rare. Perhaps the basic technology is widely used, but this Newtech level represents the cutting edge of achievement. Equipment at this level, especially weapons, might be worth a lot more than just ten times their old value. For example, the laser pistol in the weapons listing costs a whole lot more than a normal pistol.

Suggestions: +3 Steps to damage, magazine size tripled, range increment tripled, almost never wears out, never runs down. Extremely dangerous ammo (armor piercing, high-explosive rounds, etc), miniaturization down to 1/100 normal weight, force field technology, laser technology, gravitic technology (other than for shipboard artificial gravity).

Zero-G Thruster Cane. Not everything at this level is deadly dangerous. Conceived of by an eccentric ship's mechanic, the ZgTC appears to be a gentleman's fancy dress cane, metallic black with a white tip and a silver handle. Unlike most canes, however, the ZgTC has a small compressed air thruster built into one end (the tip of the cane acts as the jet) and a magnetic grapple in the other (the cane's handle can be sent shooting out to up to 50 feet, attached to a thin cable). The cane is used for dramatic entrances, quick getaways, and impressive party tricks.

To make it, you have to combine two items. Assume the GM rules that the actual cane costs basically nothing, with the thruster and the grapple costing as much as a vacuum suit, this would ordinarily be a x4 cost Newtech item. However, because of the miniaturized machinery involved, the GM decides it will be a x10 cost item. So add the miniaturization and combine two items, and you have spent ₡ 670 for a walking stick—but a very nifty one, all told.

SERVICES

Some folks have special talents that others are willing to pay good platinum for. Knowledge can turn straight into cash if someone else needs the knowing you've got in your head. This is the place to look for such services. If you can't find it here or you can't afford it, don't despair—poke around the odd spaceport, look through the Cortex listings, maybe post a sign. You'll find someone with the know-how you need at a price you can manage.

SERVICES

Allied Postal Service: The Allied Postal Service is a fairly reliable way to send small parcels on interplanetary freight. The maximum possible load is 500 pounds for a cost of ₡ 5 per 25 lbs, or fraction thereof, beyond the 10 lb limit. If the recipient does not have a permanent home address or lives on a ship (at least currently), the receiver will be sent a wave and then have 2 weeks to pick up his parcel from a nearby Postal Office, though service and quality depend on the individual franchisee.

Companion: Companions are trained in all the arts, at least rudimentarily (though they must demonstrate skill at several), as well as games, and pastimes of all manner, including fencing and archery. Schooled in music, dance, etiquette, languages, and, of course, the physical skills required, Companions provide comfort and care to their clients. Companions choose their own clients and may reject and even blacklist those who cross the line.

The Companion's Guild has transformed the sex trade into an established and respected industry. The Guild is very powerful and protects its own (and its reputation) through networks of contacts that they have established over the years.

Interplanetary Freight: Running cargo and passengers from one place to another is a necessary part of the industry of the Alliance, and most other organizations in the 'Verse. A reputation for speedy and reliable service, as well as the quality of the transport can be weighty factors in the negotiation of prices. The rates given on the chart represent the level of quality and comfort a Firefly or similar vessel can provide—which is to say, not all that much. A luxury liner like the *El Dorado* could charge up to ₡ 300 per day, providing fresh food, entertainment, private suites, and the like to its customers.

Table 3-18: Services

Item	Cost (Credits/Platinum)	Availibility	Notes
Allied Postal Service	₡ 1.2 / 3p	E	Up to 10 lbs
Companion	–	–	A Companion may be requested but Guild law states a Companion chooses the client
• Evening	₡ 350 / 875p	C	
• Full Day	₡ 450 / 1,125p	C	
Interplanetary Freight	–	–	
• Cargo Run	₡ 70 / 175p	E	Basic rates per day, not counting expenses
• Passengers	₡ 20 / 50p	E	
Medical Care			
• Antibiotic Course	₡ 10.4 / 26p	E	Medical treatment is not always available on the outer planets
• Full Physical	₡ 8 / 20p	E	
• Surgery, Major	₡ 600 / 1,500p	C	
• Surgery, Minor	₡ 150 / 375p	E	
Ship Repair	₡ 640 / 1,600p	E	Price per hour of labor; parts may cost extra

Sailing the black can be mightily expensive. The ship needs to be in good condition to be space worthy. Since help may be far away, you need to keep supplies on hand for all sorts of emergencies. Parts, supplies, and fuel are more expensive for spacecraft than for planet-side vessels. You can make a lot of money hauling cargo for the Alliance (and maybe a lot more hauling it without the Alliance finding out), but one big breakdown, a problem with a major crime boss, or a run-in with the law can cost you your ship—and maybe even your life. Things often don't go smooth, so the trick is to stay five minutes ahead of the posse and hope there's a Shepherd praying for you.

Cargo Run: People pay to have cargo shipped. The cargo may be legal, in which case they are likely also paying government tariffs (cutting into profits on all sides). The cargo may be illegal, meaning you might have to split the profits with a middleman, but you might well get more money due to the danger involved. If the goods are legal, then you'll have to settle for less so the owner can get a tax-break (otherwise she'd just use legal channels). Banned goods bring in a heftier profit, but can get you jailed for possession. Either way, you'll probably stand to make money.

Passengers: Aren't generally worth as much as cargo on lower-class ships, but they can pay for the cost of a fuel cell or two, and sometimes folk can't afford better or they want to move around without much publicity (in which case they might even be willing to pay a bit more!). However, since a passenger eats food, takes up space, and uses air (unless stowed away in a cryo chamber, in which case you definitely want to keeps the Feds' noses out of your business), the prices for travel still tend to be high.

Medical Care: Medical care on the Rim can be spotty or nonexistent at times. Not many MedAcad-trained doctors want to move out where there's nobody with the money to pay 'em. If you can even find a local doctor, chances are he's a crackpot or a drunk, a self-taught "talent" or maybe even a fugitive on the run. In any case, this doc probably won't charge as much as doctors on the Core. Then again, you get what you pay for.

Sometimes a local baron might hire his own personal physician and pay to transport him from the Core. If he allows the locals to use his M.D., the doctor will likely charge 10 times the going rate. The baron will get his cut, of course.

Antibiotic Course: A basic treatment course for an infection. Pop one pill once a day for about two weeks. Unfortunately, sometimes you can't find even common antibiotics out on the Rim.

Full physical: A basic exam. Generally, it's a good idea to get checked out regular.

Surgery, Major: Major surgery can mean anything from extensive cosmetic alterations to heart replacement surgery. The price varies widely between different operations, but the listed price can serve as a median for surgery of this nature, which probably requires at least three medical personnel and an extended stay in a hospital.

Surgery, Minor: Minor surgery refers to reattaching ears, laser surgery on eyes, appendix removal, or other operations that are potentially serious, but do not require extraordinarily advanced equipment, extended hospital stays, etc. However, the prices can still vary, so use the listed cost as a baseline.

Ship Repair: The listed price refers to the time spent on repairs. Much of the higher costs come from replacing expensive parts. Generally, replacing major parts (engine components, etc) should cost about 1% of the value of the ship. Systemic repairs (replacing the entire drive system) should cost 10-20% of the value of the ship. For routine maintenance costs of a specific model, see Chapter Four: *Boats and Mules*.

CHAPTER 4

BOATS AND MULES

THE TELL

"Money buys freedom."

Plato said that, way back on Earth-That-Was.

Money also bought trouble. Plato had not said that. Jack Leland said it, though he found very few who believed him.

Most folk figured that if a man was filthy rich, like Jack Leland (professional gambler by trade), that man had no problems, because he could buy his way out of them. That was true sometimes. Jack was able to buy the best ship, the best pilot, the best crew, the best body guard.

He needed them because he had long ago discovered that having money tended to create problems, the reason being the more money you had, the more some folk came to believe that you didn't deserve to have it—and they did. Which tended to complicate a man's life.

Leland considered his life's current complication as he carefully scrutinized the faces of those gathered around the poker table. He was looking for the "tell"—those little twitches, jerks, and fidgets a man gets when he's playing cards. Mostly a person doesn't even know he's doing it, but such habits can be a dead give away to whether a man's holding a full house or if that pair of queens on the table are all by their lonesome.

Jack recalled a fellow he'd met not long ago. Captain of a Firefly name of Reynolds. Malcolm Reynolds. He'd been a fair to middling poker player, but Jack had found Reynolds amusing and he'd let him win in payment for a pleasant evening. Besides, he could see that Reynolds needed the credits. Reynolds was the type who would go through his life always needing the credits.

Because Malcolm Reynolds was an unusual man. He was a thief who was too honest for his own good, a smuggler with honor when honor wasn't what was needed to pay the bills. A man of faith, who didn't believe in anything. If Malcolm Reynolds did a job for you, he fully intended to keep his end of the bargain and he fully intended that you should keep yours. If you crossed him, he shot you. Simple as that. Yes, there was a man with an uncomplicated life.

A life Jack Leland envied right about now. If he'd been Captain Reynolds, he would have pulled out his six-gun and shot every son-of-a-bitch at the table. Jack Leland couldn't do that, though. He was wealthy and famous, with powerful friends and more powerful enemies who were just waiting for him to make a mistake to take him down and worry his carcass like ravening wolves.

Leland's body guard, the drop-dead (and she knew numerous ways to make that happen) gorgeous woman, Hwa Ling, had just informed him that a member of a rival Tong was planning to have her assassinated tonight. And, of course, if they took out Hwa Ling, they'd have to take out Jack Leland.

He looked around at every man seated at the table. He looked at a man's eyes, looked at his fingers, looked at what a man did with those fingers, those eyes. He looked at a jaw, saw a nerve twitch. He looked to see a bead of sweat trickle down a man's neck.

Jack Leland looked for the tell.

Not to find out which man was going to beat him at poker.

To find out which man was nerving up for the kill.

As often as not, characters in the 'Verse are always on the move. They are on the job, looking for work, or trying to stay ahead of the competition—or possibly the Feds. Since hoofing it only gets you so far, a crew is gonna need a ship.

A boat in the *Serenity Role Playing Game* is a precious thing to a crew—or at least should be. A ship is more than a mode of transportation. The ship is home, the source of work, the way to stay mobile, and the key to freedom. The focus here is on the vehicles that sail the black, though most of the rules apply to other craft as well.

SHIPS

As far as folk in the 'Verse are concerned, traveling the black means traveling between the worlds and moons of a single star cluster. Maybe in the future someone will come up with ships that can make it to other stars in less than a lifetime. (But don't that sound like science fiction?) For now, it's hard enough sailing between a small group of planets and stars. To get us through the basics, read the following information, courtesy of Christopher Rush of the Celestine Engineering University, Osiris.

Spacecraft are made for interplanetary voyages. They travel a lot slower than the speed of light, taking anywhere from hours to weeks to reach their destination. If you search the history of Earth-That-Was for a parallel, you'll find it's somewhat like the days of steamship travel, when sailing from Marseilles to London was a relatively short, safe trip, while rounding the Cape of Good Hope to California could be long and risky—and China might as well have been on another planet. Sad to say, though, space is even less forgiving than a stormy ocean. Make one wrong move, and you could be sucking vacuum instead of just taking a swim.

No matter the risks (or mayhap because of them), there have always been brave souls who sail the black. To understand these folk, what they do, how they do it, and how they live, you need to give ship technology a moment's consideration.

GRAVITY CONTROL

In the nine hundred years since folk dreamed about traveling to other worlds, all kinds of fancy scientific inventions have played their part in making

that happen. If you had to pick just one that was most important, it would be the grand unification of the theories of gravity and electromagnetism. This breakthrough led to a relatively cheap means of controlling gravitic attraction and inertia that changed the old notions of space travel and propulsion. Previously only elite astronauts could fly into the black. Now ordinary folk take such trips every day. The math behind all this will surely hurt your head, so we present the short version—the three techniques that cover most all of the basics:

Screening reduces the pull of one object (usually a planet or moon) on another (a spaceship, hovercraft, or maybe a chandelier) and essentially the other way around as well. This allows heavier-than-air vehicles to float without the need for wings and rotors and such. Putting up a screening field takes time and energy, but once the field is going, it doesn't take much energy to keep it that way. Since aircraft no longer have to fight gravity every moment, and they can take advantage of the almost total lack of friction when flying, aircraft are now practical for all sorts of jobs—from freight handling to rubbernecking. Spacecraft can save their fuel for getting up to orbital velocity.

Note that screening by itself doesn't change the inertia—the resistance to motion—that heavy objects have, else ships would be blowing away in the least little breeze. Screening does put every object within the field in what amounts to zero gravity, which would be awfully inconvenient for ladies in them fancy hooped skirts, if it weren't for artificial gravity, which is next.

Artificial gravity works the other way, pretending to be a planet-sized mass and pulling on everything in its range. Artificial gravity provides nearly the same effect as normal gravity inside a screening field and also on ships in free fall. Although artificial gravity can't actually change the forces of ordinary acceleration, careful handling of the artificial g-field can cancel out most of the tossing caused by movement and—so long as the pilot doesn't get too crazy—make for a smoother ride. Artificial gravity has also been used on a grand scale in the terraforming of small worlds and moonlets, allowing them to keep a breathable atmosphere despite how dinky they are.

One last benefit of g-fields has to do with fusion, which we'll get into in a bit under the *Power* heading.

> "You can learn all the math in the 'Verse, but you take a boat in the air you don't love, she'll shake you off just as sure as the turning of worlds. Love keeps her in the air when she oughta fall down, tells you she's hurting 'fore she keens. Makes her a home."
>
> —Malcolm Reynolds

All this was a big improvement over brute-force rocketry and early space flight. Sailing to the nearest planets would have still taken months if it weren't for the third technique: inertia reduction. Artificial g-fields and g-screening wouldn't normally affect the inertia of a ship, but setting them against one another in a particular manner made it possible to drop the ship's resistance to motion in a specific direction to next to nothing. Spaceships designed to take advantage of this trick have gained greatly in speed and efficiency, though there are some limitations (which we'll discuss under *Propulsion*).

Even though screening, artificial gravity, and inertian reduction are three distinct effects, most folks just call the whole gorram thing a grav drive.

POWER

Fusion power is nothing new: life on Earth-That-Was, or any planet, has always looked to free energy from the sun and other stars—the biggest damn fusion reactors in the 'Verse. Harnessing all that energy into a power supply without blowing everyone up was the joker that taunted four generations of high-energy physicists back around the last millennium. What finally did the trick was artificial gravity, which let scientists recreate the intense pressures and temperatures in the center of a star, where fusion happens on its own.

Fusion power plants consist of an electro-magneto-gravitic "bottle" that contains plasma (protons from hydrogen) at super high temperature under tremendous pressure. The protons fuse together to produce helium, releasing energy in the process. The hot plasma is tapped off the bottle and run through a magneto-hydrodynamic generator to produce electricity. Other designs employ nanotech materials to convert heat energy directly into electricity (and cool the power plant in the process).

Because there are almost no moving parts, a fusion power plant can run for many decades without a major overhaul. All you have to do is occasionally replace the containment jacket (a sandwich of lithium alloys, boron, and plastics) that surrounds the core and absorbs the stray neutrons produced in the interior; else the jacket gets brittle and breaks down over time. Without core containment, these high-energy neutrons would shoot right through you, poisoning you and turning the ship into a glow-in-the-dark deathtrap through secondary radiation effects.

Contrary to what you read in books, fusion plants don't explode, even when severely beat up. Despite the extremes of temperature and pressure in the core, the density of plasma is surprisingly low. The amount of hydrogen used to produce power is likewise close to none. Not that a plasma leak won't still barbecue anyone unlucky enough to be caught in the same compartment, of course. Which is why it's important to have a backup power supply for when the main fusion plant is offline.

Hydrogen-oxygen fuel cells, which combine the two gases to produce electricity without "burning" them in the ordinary way, are popular aboard ship because they are cheap to run and the exhaust is clean, potable water. The vapor condensers have other uses as well, for the imaginative. Many ground vehicles also use hydrogen-fueled motors, due to their high power-to-weight ratio and the ease of manufacturing. Power cells—loops of high-temperature super conducting wire storing loads of electrical energy—make good backup aboard ship, as well as being the primary power source for small electric vehicles and hand lasers. They are too finicky to bet your life on entirely, however, as they sometimes run out of juice before they ought to.

Along with power goes thermal management: all that power-using equipment generates heat, and dumping it into the perfect insulating vacuum of space is a problem. Big ships, with a generally lower ratio of surface to volume, have an even harder time with heat, and are designed with a lower power budget per ton than smaller ones. Spaceships ordinarily have nanomaterial heat pump wiring running through their structure into radiator grids embedded in parts of their hull plating.

PROPULSION

There are basically two kinds of propulsion systems for air- and spacecraft in the 'Verse: reaction thrusters and pulse drives.

Reaction thrusters are the most commonly found. They include any sort of engine that produces thrust in one direction by throwing energy out the other—remember Newton's Third Law? Rockets, air-breathing jets, and airscrew propellers all fall into this category. The most common type of reaction thruster found on spacecraft is a "rocket-based combined cycle engine," or simply a pod.

Pods are often mounted on movable hydraulic swivels that allow them to shift direction quickly and easily. An engine pod runs in one of three modes. In atmosphere, it's open on both ends like a jet engine. Heated plasma from the fusion power plant is routed to the pod, heats up a mass of air, and blows it out the back to produce thrust. At low speeds, the heated air also spins a turbine that sucks in still more air from in front to get the cycle started. Once the ship goes supersonic, these turbine blades fold back out of the way and the pod continues in scramjet mode. Running the engine in air-breathing mode is very efficient, since most of the thrust comes from the air itself, and not from the plasma.

CHAPTER 4

WASH: "If she doesn't give us some extra flow from the engine room to offset the burn-through, this landing is gonna get pretty interesting."
MAL: "Define interesting."
WASH: "Oh god, oh god, we're all gonna die?"

When the ship breaks atmo, there isn't enough air for the engine to work on. The intake irises shut, and the pod switches to pure rocket mode. Extra hydrogen "fuel" is routed through the fusion plant to produce a steady stream of high-energy plasma, which the pod pumps out at extreme speeds to produce thrust. This uses a lot of hydrogen and is good for only limited "burns." In between those burns, a ship can either coast or use her pulse drive (keep readin').

Smaller boats and aircraft don't carry big fusion plants, and use other kinds of reaction thrusters that have the additional advantage of being simpler to build and operate. These thrusters range from hydrogen-oxygen rocket engines to hydrogen-burning jet engines to big electric turbofans run off power cells. Rockets like these can be very powerful and fast for their size, but are extremely inefficient with their fuel, thus limiting them to short range and shallow orbits. Attitude control jets on spacecraft, and chemical rocket engines on missiles are also widely used. The air-breathing types are, of course, restricted to atmo.

Pulse drives, now, are another animal entirely, separating deep space boats from short-range orbiters.

Take a ship equipped with regular grav and reaction drives. Tweak the grav and add some control hardware so it can work the inertia reduction trick. Strap on a high-impulse (but low-efficiency) rocket motor to give her a big initial "kick" and keep her moving, and *voila!*—pulse drive.

Pulse drives are very fast (around 60 times faster than reaction drives), but with that speed comes some severe limitations.

First, the ship is mostly lacking in inertia (thanks to screening), and so the extra speed she gets from the pulse drive isn't real. That is, the ship keeps moving only as long as the drive is running. Shut it off, and she goes right back to drifting. Since you don't want to be on the drift, pilots run the reaction thrusters as well as the pulse drive for some part of the journey to get the ship moving.

Second, because the inertia reduction works directly along the drive axis, the ship's course is more or less fixed when you turn on her pulse drive (though it's not strictly a straight line, due to gravity effects). The pilot can bend the heading, but only very slowly. To make a radical course change, you have to drop out of pulse drive, turn the nose, and

re-initiate. This can use up your fuel real quick. *Tian tsai* navigators will plot a course to use as little extra fuel as possible, carefully choosing start and end points, and taking advantage of any planet along the way to change direction without having to burn by using a gravity slingshot.

Third, though the pulse drive is fast, it's not very precise. Going from burn to off takes more than a couple of seconds—a ship can travel 10,000 miles in the interval. In deep space this doesn't matter so much, but close to a planet (flying from one moon to another,) it is easier and safer to just use the reaction drives.

LIFE SUPPORT

People who spend their whole lives on the surface of a Core planet have a hard time appreciating how lucky they are. There's air to breathe all around. Most places, fresh water falls from the sky. Meat animals and veggies are just there for the taking. Even if there's an accident—a forest fire or a toxic chemical spill—a planet's ecosystem is big enough to absorb the damage, spread it around, and recover.

For the folks living on the newer Rim colonies (where the finer points of terraforming are just starting to sort themselves out) life don't go that smooth. Sometimes the rains don't come.

But that's nothing like venturing into the Black with just a thin metal and ceramic wall between your precious hide and all manner of hurt: no air, no water, nothing living, too hot, too cold, too little gravity, too much radiation. A ship in space is a little world unto herself. Life support has to provide everything needed to sustain life for a ship's crew and her passengers.

HULL

A ship's hull is more than just a box to hold all her parts. It's a complex system that serves several critical functions. On the simplest level, the hull is a giant air tank that holds in atmosphere and keeps out the black. The hull wouldn't be of much use, though, if you couldn't get in or out of it, so this shell has access points—hatches, airlocks, ports, vents—through it. These have to be specially designed, so that you don't lose pressure on the inside. Together with decks, bulkheads, and internal bracing, the hull provides a framework for mounting other parts. It has to protect the ship's contents from damage (stellar radiation, micrometeorites, debris) and act as a conduit for the artificial g-field. Waste heat and comm signals have to go out through the hull and sensor data has to get in, so some sections of the hull are transparent to specific kinds of radiation. Selected panels may allow a g-field to pass through, too, but the strength drops off pretty rapidly. Finally, the hull must absorb noise and vibration, which would otherwise damage equipment and drive the crew nuts.

ATMOSPHERE

Maintaining breathable air aboard ship is a tricky proposition. Not only do you have to pull carbon dioxide and excess water vapor from the air, replace it with fresh oxygen, and circulate it evenly throughout the ship, you also have to balance temperature and humidity, filter out dust and pollen, scrub away more than one hundred trace contaminants, prevent the growth of bacteria and mold, and replace the inevitable losses from leaks and absorption. Fire detection and suppression is also part of the atmo system. To save weight, most long range vessels use a closed-loop air recycling system, with specialized algae tanks doing most of the work, helped along by mechanical and chemical processes. Purely physical recycling systems exist, but use a lot of power and are difficult to keep up. On short range boats, air is supplied from storage tanks and regulated by passive filters; this also serves as an auxiliary or back up system on deep space craft.

WATER

Some really big ships have closed-loop water systems. They recycle some waste water through the algae tanks, but distill most of it through heat exchangers attached to the power plant. Smaller ships make do with tanked water, supplemented by vapor condensed from the air and fuel cell exhaust. Water for drinking, cooking, and minimal cleaning runs to 6 pounds per person per day; washing and showering can add up to another 30 pounds, while laundering uses 30 pounds per person per day on its own. Clearly, the less used the better. Livestock carried as cargo have their own requirements.

FOOD

Growing fruits and vegetables in space has turned out to be too time consuming for all but the very largest ships, or those family-run vessels that have lots of extra hands. Most food production on shipboard is actually a by-product of the air recycling system. With just a little bit of artificial sunlight and some nutrients, tanks of blue-green algae take in carbon dioxide and give off oxygen

as they grow. The algae is an almost perfect food, providing most of the proteins, vitamins, and calories a person needs to stay healthy. Eating the algae is a last-ditch survival effort for most, however, because the algae tastes like the pond scum it is. No amount of flavoring or bulk additives can make it taste like steak. Most folk think even protein paste is better. Needless to say, crews purchase real food planet-side when they can afford it. This can include shelf stable food packs, fresh meat, fish, and produce. Serving fresh, high-quality foodstuffs is the definition of "First Class" in space.

WASTE MANAGEMENT

Waste water is collected in septic tanks and spun to remove the solids. The water goes to the distillation rig to be purified; the leftover sludge is pumped out at each refueling stop. Big ships sometimes bake the sludge to sterile ash in a furnace first, to save on storage and get all of the water back. Trash and solid waste are compacted into standardized garbage bins that are swapped out in port. Docking fees pay for waste disposal, although some organic-poor moons have been known to offer discounts, since they can use it for the fertilizer.

NAVIGATION, SENSORS, AND COMMUNICATIONS

Guidance, navigation, and control are the brain and nerves of a ship. Sensors and comms are her eyes, ears, and voice.

NAVIGATION

Virtually all spaceships and aircraft have some kind of computerized fly-by-wire system installed that lets novices handle the controls without killing themselves. You may call yourself a great pilot, but unless you switch off the nav comp and go to manual, the ship is flying herself. You're just telling her where you want her to go. Of course, she's going to be fairly conservative about it. The mark of a true pilot is the ability to fly manually and get that last 3% out of her performance.

Long before the war, the Alliance established a network of powerful navigational beacons throughout the Core, extending out to the Rim, though only in "high traffic" areas. Once you get out on the "edge", there are fewer beacons around. This network is deliberately separate from the Cortex for safety and redundancy. Comparing the time-stamped signals from four or more of these satellites will tell a ship where she is and where she's heading without having to shoot the stars with an astrolabe or something similar. In an emergency, coded advisories can be sent out over the beacon signals. All nav systems are required to be able to read the signals and inform the crew.

Worlds have their own, short-ranged systems linked into their communications networks, and ships use these when available to recalibrate their backup inertial guidance systems once they come off pulse drive. Even the poorest moon will have an electronic benchmark left by the initial exploration team somewhere near the docks that gives enough data for a rough update, so the ship doesn't have to fly by guesswork.

SENSORS

It's hard to be sneaky in space. The black is very, very cold, and a ship with any kind of power running stands out like a bonfire on the desert in a pitch dark night. The only place to hide is near something bigger than you are or (if your pilot is that good) in the blind spot caused by a ship's hot drive wake.

Sensors come in two modes: simple detectors, designed to tell you that something is out there;

and scanners designed to provide enough detail to tell you what that something is. Both types use a mix of active (transmitting) and passive (receiving) techniques spread pretty much across the electromagnetic spectrum. The actual hardware—antenna blisters and frequency generators and such—matters less than the signal processing that turns the entire ship into one big phased array antenna that allows you to hear and understand the softest whisper.

COMMUNICATIONS

The Cortex is a vast signal network that ties all the worlds in the 'Verse together. It uses any and all available channels—laser, maser, broadcast radio—to ensure that a message is routed to the right destination. Due to the speed of light lag caused by the distances involved (up to eight hours to send out to the Rim and get a reply), messages, called "waves" because of the way they spread throughout the system, tend to be pre-recorded. Real-time conversations are limited to less than about 100,000 miles.

WEAPONS

Most ships in the 'Verse are unarmed. Since the war is over, there's little enough need for one ship to shoot down another, and the Alliance has always been touchy over the notion of private citizens totin' cannons in space.

Alliance ship are armed, of course. You never know. Might be some bad people about. Military weapons fall mainly into four categories.

SPACE MINES

Space mines are small robotic spaceships launched from a larger vessel. They are instructed in what ships to attack and when. Their range is kept short on purpose, to prevent them from becoming a hazard to ships other than their intended targets, and thus they rely on proper placement to catch their prey. Due to their programming and the intentional lack of outside contact they are very hard to spoof or shut down remotely.

MISSILES

Missiles (high-thrust chemical rockets with autonav, sensors, and a lethal payload) are the main offensive military weapons. Missiles come in many sizes, from 50-pound "come-hithers" carried by gunships on enforcement patrol, to multi-ton battleship-killers. Missiles carry every kind of warhead, and can be mounted in simple tube or box launchers (disposable, often packaged with the missile) or on external rails. Target information is provided from the firing vessel, however, missiles can be ordered to operate in either command-guided (to ensure positive control) or fire-and-forget mode. Because of the guidance linkages, missiles are more vulnerable to counter-measures than other weapons systems.

BOMBS

A bomb is a warhead with minimal sensors and nav systems for terminal guidance. Bombs depend on a combination of gravity (falling) and aerodynamics (gliding) to reach their targets. Since they are dropped from a flying ship—which is why they are often called "drops"—bombs are only useful on or near the surface of a world. Bombs are mostly dropped on structures and other stationary targets, since they are cheaper for this role than missiles, and easier to carry. Bombs come with every variety of warhead (although kinetic bombs require high-speed attack runs), and are generally only slightly larger than the warhead itself.

CANNONS

A cannon is any device mounted on a ship or vehicle that provides the energy to launch a warhead (and sometimes guidance system) externally. Cannon can be chemically powered (like a gun) or electromagnetic (a coilgun or railgun). The limited maneuverability of cannon-launched warheads restricts their range to short or point-blank, and their military use to self-defense. They are often rapid-fire weapons, making up in volume what they lack in accuracy. Since cannons are considered primarily defensive weapons, a civilian ship can sometimes get away with carrying one, whereas carrying a missile launcher would result in automatic impounding and confiscation. Cannon are rated for the size of warhead they fire, ranging from 1 to 200 pounds, though only 20-pounders and above are really spaceship grade weapons.

WARHEADS

The deadly cargo that weapons systems deliver, warheads comes is a variety of types and uses.

Kinetic: A kinetic warhead is just a bullet: a solid bar of metal that does damage by slamming into the target at high speeds. At 2 miles per second (common for missiles and cannon), a kinetic warhead does as much damage as an equivalent amount of high explosive, and it's harder to disrupt.

Explosive: Explosive warheads are dual-purpose. They have a shaped charge for maximum damage on a direct hit and enough power to shake up the target even with a near miss (although this works much better in atmosphere).

Canister: A defensive warhead consisting of a large number of dense ball bearings (up to an inch across) surrounding a bursting charge. Once the warhead is directed at the target and reaches optimal range, the charge scatters the balls in an expanding cloud along its path like a giant shotgun shell. This is usually enough to trash the guidance systems of missiles and bombs, and can damage light vehicles (and people), as well.

Magnetic: More properly an "electromagnetic pulse" warhead, these use an explosive charge to generate an extremely powerful, short duration electric current in a coil of wire. The current sends out a wave of magnetic energy that will fry anything electronic—computers, nav systems, sensors, comms—within range. Mag warheads can be used offensively or defensively against incoming missiles.

Jammer: A warhead that puts out signals or highly reflective materials (chaff, "sand," or smoke) designed to confuse sensors or shut down comms on a wide variety of wave lengths. Jammers may try to overwhelm the target with noise, imitate and distort signals they receive to give false returns, or send out low-level signals to cover up the target without being noticed.

Decoy: This warhead attempts to mimic the sensor signature of a particular ship, usually to draw fire away from her. At engagement ranges, this involves flares, spoofing sensor signals, and sometimes smoke or chaff to provide a false target. Larger decoys can produce a larger and more varied signature. Beyond easy visual range, size does not matter so much. An effective decoy may depend more on psychology than engineering to dupe its target.

Nuclear: Unlike conventional explosives, nukes are effective proximity weapons even in space, although the damage mechanism is somewhat different. "Dirty" bombs that scatter radiation over a large area inside of atmo aren't effective in space because normal shielding protects those inside.

LIFE ABOARD SHIP

Working on a spaceship is pretty much like any other job except that you live where you work. You're cooped up with the same folk for weeks at a time, and there's often few places you can go to get away from them. A crew is like family: you may not like each other, but you're stuck with each other, and you have to find some way to get along. (Some spaceships are owned and crewed by real families, with kids and pets and all. These ships tend to be comfortable and well-maintained, but are not known for taking on passengers.)

As to how many people you need for a crew, you hire as many people as you need to do the job. This can be as few as two on a short-range orbiter. Deep space vessels generally have at least four crew members to stand watches and perform routine maintenance. Freighters will get by with as few crew as possible to save money: a 100,000-ton bulk carrier might have three or four officers and only a dozen hands, contracting most repairs at a shipyard. Passenger ships will have large crews, but most all of these (up to one crew for every two passengers on a luxury liner) are dedicated to taking care of the passengers. Military vessels will fall somewhere in the middle: they rely on automated systems to reduce their numbers, but carry extra crew for damage control and replacements in battle.

Crew positions and titles vary with requirements, available skills, and taste. Officers normally have some professional qualifications, and can be expected to know the theory behind the work as well as the practical aspects. Spacehands tend to learn on the job, and may have experience ranging from complete novice to decades of hands-on knowledge. Large crews may be divided into "deck" (fly the ship), "engineering" (fix the ship), and "cargo" (load/unload the ship). Smaller ships can't be bothered.

One position will always be filled, however: the captain or ship's master. He or she has authority over and is responsible for everything the ship and her crew does or fails to do. In flight, the captain's word is Law. A passenger or crew member who poses a danger to the ship can be tossed out the nearest airlock, and the only thing the Alliance Board of Inquiry will care about is that the incident was properly noted in the log and arrears of pay were sent to the next of kin. On the other hand, any violations of Alliance law found on shipboard are presumed to have been committed with the captain's knowledge until proven otherwise.

DAILY ROUTINE

Planet-side, there's always a lot to do: unload, refuel, pick up new passengers and freight, scrounge spare parts, negotiate with local authorities, and hit the town. On the ship, space travel can alternate between long stretches of sheer boredom and short moments of sheer terror with nothing much in between. The terror part tends to take care of itself—either you survive or you don't. But having a lot of time on your hands can also be trouble.

Even though the ship can fly herself, it's a good idea to have a designated person, awake and alert and sober, standing watch at all times, ready to respond to unforeseen problems. This is particularly important near the beginning and the end of a voyage where space tends to get a bit crowded. Those on watch don't have to stay on the bridge, as long as they carry a pager so that emergency messages can be routed wherever they may be. Some ships split the entire crew into equal shifts. Others maintain a "day" shift and go to minimum manning at "night."

Routine housekeeping and maintenance takes up a fair amount of crew time. There's always some compartment that needs cleaning or a filter that needs replacing. You won't see too much painting on shipboard; fumes are hard on the air scrubbers. Unless the crew can afford a steward, they probably take turns cooking and doing dishes afterward. Mealtimes are often a source of entertainment for passengers and crew alike.

A good captain will make certain that his crew has something to occupy hands and minds. Exercise is important to keeping the body in good condition, and most ships will have exercise equipment. Most crew have some kind of hobby they pursue in their spare time. This can be anything from weight lifting to meditation—as long as it doesn't pose a hazard or an annoyance to anyone. Many people take up musical instruments, practicing them daily, and even forming bands or chamber orchestras. Books, movies, and other information can be retrieved off the Cortex, though comm lags can prove a source of continual irritation depending on location and quality of the equipment. Ship-born kids get their education from the Cortex, and many spacers have picked up a good deal of knowledge on a wide variety of subjects for the lack of anything better to do. A ship sometimes becomes its own subculture, with its own slang, traditions, and sense of style—going even beyond the connection of a family.

OPERATING COSTS

Once you own a spaceship you now have to keep her running. Operating costs include: salaries, fuel, supplies, port fees, etc. (For figuring the costs of maintaining the ship, refer to the section, "The Ship As a Character".) As with much else in the 'Verse, the figures provided are a guide. Costs will vary depending on a variety of factors. Parts or services on the Core worlds will be close to what's listed. A backwater planet may charge next to nothing for the same services, or gouge every credit the market will bear. Many poor settlements don't have the equipment to liquefy and store hydrogen fuel, for example. In general, you can count on most everything being harder to come by on the Rim.

PORT FEES

Docking for up to one week, administrative costs, power hookup, septic flush, and fresh water fill costs 1 credit per 100 tons of ship. Each week thereafter is 0.5 credits per hundred tons.

FUEL

Liquid hydrogen delivered to the ship's tanks costs 5 credits per 1 ton of fuel. Fuel is available on Core planets and only on those frontier worlds with well-developed economies where hydrogen is used to run a wide variety of smaller vehicles. Liquid hydrogen is unavailable elsewhere on the Rim. Hydrogen is normally cracked from water or petrochemicals, then run through a series of refrigerations to liquefy it. Liquid hydrogen must be kept extremely cold (-423 degrees F) and under pressure, which makes storage a challenge. Leaks are a festive occasion for everyone—forcing immediate attention to the problem.

PROVISIONS

Costs for "real" food can be found by reading up on the subject in Chapter Three: *Money and Gear*. Ships taking on a large load of supplies or doing repeat business with the same supplier may be able to negotiate a discount.

SALARIES

How the crew takes their pay is between them and the captain (or owner, if he or she prefers). Spacehands on salary make 10 to 20 credits a month depending on experience and skills, plus free room and board. Officer's pay is roughly double this. Captains and owners normally take shares of the ship's profits, although a liner captain may receive a flat 100 credits a month. The crew may be offered shares instead of some or all of their pay, which gives people an incentive to work hard—and keeps overhead down.

OTHER COSTS

Insurance: Fancy liners and ships belonging to big companies are insured at around 10 credits per ton per year for small vessels and double that for large ones (more than 100,000 tons). This covers not only accidents and damages, but also mechanical breakdown of major parts. A captain running a Firefly like *Serenity* normally won't be able to get such insurance on a bet.

Dock Workers: Crews requiring help loading or unloading can usually hire manual labor at half-a-credit a day per person. There are always laborers hanging around the docks looking for work, though dealing through the local union or tong (which may be the same thing) rather than hiring directly is sound business practice.

Rental: Equipment needed, but not on hand can like as not be rented. Rentals cost 1% of purchase price per day, and require a substantial guarantee in the form of cash (a bond) or collateral (usually the ship) to insure that the equipment will be returned in its original, undamaged condition.

Dry Dock: Repairs and maintenance can be contracted from local shipyards (if available). This costs double what similar work would cost for parts and materials alone, and may involve substantial delay if there's a lot of work already scheduled. But it is much faster than do-it-yourself. The cost is one week per 100,000 credits, rounded up.

Fines: Various infractions of Alliance law and local regulations are punishable by fines, which run from 100 credits for something minor to fines that equal more than the value of the ship. Game Masters are encouraged to be especially creative when the question comes up.

PAYING THE BILLS

Running a ship costs money and there are only a few ways to make it. The most common is to sell either goods or services. Typical rates are given below. It's important to realize that time is money—more trips and less time in port mean more revenues—and that even a little money is better than none at all. It can be better to offer a big discount or take a bad deal than to have no deal at all and fly a ship with empty holds or cabins. (This is how really low-value cargo winds up getting shipped.) Transportation is figured from origin to announced destination. Arrival date is a good faith estimate rather than a promise, and some deviations from the schedule are to be expected.

FREIGHT

Ships carrying cargo are paid one of two ways:

If the cargo belongs to someone else, the crew is paid for bringing it from origin to destination. The usual rate is 1 credit per ton of general cargo, assuming the trip doesn't take more than a week. Longer trips or those involving danger or difficulty will charge more accordingly; as will those where the crew has to take a more active role in collecting payment or making delivery. Some shippers will offer bonuses for timeliness or charge penalties for delivery beyond a certain date.

The captain can buy the cargo and then try to sell it at the destination for enough to cover the costs and risks involved. This is far more common out on the Rim, where banks are scarce and demand for goods tends to be somewhat irregular. Payment may be in cash or barter or a combination of both. Quick turnover is the key to making a profit, so a smart captain will have a buyer in mind before purchasing the goods.

PASSENGERS

First class passengers pay 100 credits per person, and they expect spacious quarters, fresh food, and attentive service. Second class passengers pay 50 credits per person, and generally are found on transports. They expect the same quality of life as the crew. Steerage passengers pay 20 credits a head, take what they can get for comforts, and may have to provide their own food. As with freight, voyages over a week with guaranteed express service or into known dangers are worth an additional premium.

CHARTER

Sometimes a customer wants to hire an entire boat; this is called a charter. It is also possible to charter a shuttle craft aboard a larger vessel for private use. If the chartered ship comes with captain and crew, and the captain pays all normal expenses, the cost is based on the ship's potential revenue: 3 credits per ton of cargo hold plus 150 credits per passenger cabin, per month, with the usual surcharges for hazardous duty. If the charter covers only the vessel itself (a "bare-hull" charter), the cost is 1% of the ship's purchase price per month, payable in advance. The customer provides a crew, pays all operating expenses, and keeps the profits.

A bare-hull charter usually requires substantial guarantees against theft (collateral or a bond in escrow for a significant portion of the ship's value) and assurances that the customer will use the ship in a reasonable and prudent manner, keep her in good repair, etc.

GETTING AROUND

It's difficult to provide exact distances and travel times in the 'Verse, because the moons and planets are moving in their orbits, and their relationships change. The table below gives general ranges for travel times. The Game Master should determine where in the range the voyage falls. Divide by the ship's Speed Class (keep readin') to get actual travel time; minimum time is always one hour. Communication lag is the time it takes for a Cortex message to cover the distance one way. Receiving a reply takes at least twice as long.

TABLE 4.1 TRAVEL TIMES AND COMMUNICATIONS LAG

Journey	Travel time	Comm Lag
Between moons of the same planet*	1-600 hour	0.1-10 seconds
Between moons of the same planet	1-20 hours	0.1-10 seconds
Between planets in the same system	20-1,500 hours	2.5 minutes-2 hours
Between planets in adjacent systems	500-2,500 hours	1-4 hours
One side of the 'Verse to the other	3,000-6,000 hours	4-10 hours

* Using reaction drive only, rather than pulse drive.

Spaceships generally carry enough fuel for at least 600 hours of normal cruising, utilizing either reaction drive only, or pulse and reaction drives together. Each use of the pulse drive burns 100 hours' worth of fuel. Pushing a ship to her max speed (known as "hard burn") adds 2 to her effective speed class, but increases fuel use by 50% (both initial burn and cruise rate).

SHIP AS A CHARACTER

When you spend as much time with a piece of equipment as a crew does with their spaceship, you get to know her like you would a person—her good points, her moods, her flaws. After a while, it might come to seem to you that she *is* a person—another member of the crew. Before you start playing the game, take the time to get to know your ship. Spend some thought on the little quirks and curlicues that make her real.

One point: there's no "the" in front of a ship's name. It's not a title, just her name.

Some GMs may want to use the Ship Characters that are provided in this book. That's shiny! This section is for those GMs and/or players who want to create their own ship from scratch. What follows in this section is a method of creating ships as characters using mechanics that are similar to those used when creating people-type characters: Attributes, Traits, Skills. While not a comprehensive spaceship design system, this does allow the GM to come up with new ships or modify the samples given to fit his concept of the 'Verse, and then describe them in enough detail to play.

To illustrate this process, we will follow the creation of a ship using a basic design.

Note: while the crew's ship is properly treated as a character, she is always an NPC. It's important that the GM does not allow the ship's Attributes and Traits to overshadow the actions of the crew.

CONCEPT

Before you start crunching numbers and piecing together Attributes, you'll want to have an idea of just what kind of boat you're talking about. Is she a small, four-man craft built for speed rather than comfort? A slow-moving cargo hauler? Retired military craft sold at auction and rebuilt from scrap? Get a few ideas in your head first, and the rest of the process goes a lot smoother.

Our example ship is the Firefly Class transport, *Hotaru*. She looks a bit like *Serenity* on the surface, but has less specialized features.

SHIP ATTRIBUTES

Ships have the same 6 Attributes as characters, though their interpretation is different from the same Attributes for people. Some ship Attributes can have an undamaged rating of 0, as indicated in the descriptions. Ships do not have a set number of points based on Heroic Level as do characters. Instead, the more Attribute points used to describe the ship, the greater her Complexity and cost.

AGILITY

The Agility Attribute represents a ship's reaction speed and maneuverability. Agility—not Speed Class—determines movement in combat. An Agility of 0 is used for an orbiting base or space station that has only minimal attitude control thrusters. An average Agility for ships required to make more than the most basic maneuvers is d6—anything higher is certainly a plus in a difficult situation.

TABLE 4.2 Spaceship-scale Agility

Agility	Description	Example
d2	Slow, unresponsive maneuverability	Alliance Cruiser
d4	Ungainly, slow maneuvering	Cruise Liner
d6	Average maneuverability	Military Patrol Boat
d8	Good maneuverability	Firefly Class Transport
d10	Exceptional maneuverability	Alliance Gunship
d12	Near perfect maneuverability	Hummingbird Fighters

Example: Firefly Class ships have a good Agility at d8.

STRENGTH

The Strength Attribute represents the size of a ship and her resistance to damage. Strength usually equates to tonnage, but can vary.

TABLE 4.3 SPACESHIP-SCALE STRENGTH

Strength	Tonnage	Example
d2	10-100 tons	Escape Pod, One-Man Shuttle
d4	100-1,000 tons	Small Transport, Standard Short Range Shuttle
d6	1,000-10,000 tons	Mid-bulk Transport, Firefly Class ships
d8	10,000-100,000 tons	Large Transport, Blockade Runner
d10	100,000-1 million tons	Alliance Warship
d12	1 million-10 million tons	Alliance Cruiser

Example: *Hotaru* is average size at 4,000 tons with a Strength of d6.

VITALITY

The Vitality Attribute represents the a ship's repair and maintenance status. Vitality may be temporarily reduced to 0, but only as a result of neglecting routine maintenance.

TABLE 4.4 Spaceship-scale Vitality

Vitality	Description
d2	Barely holding together
d4	In need of regular service
d6	Performs well with standard maintenance
d8	Newer model or design requires low maintenance
d10	New model or design has redundant systems built in
d12	Fresh-off-the-line model or design has auto-repair systems built in

Example: *Hotaru* may not look like much, but she's a Firefly, and will run forever if her mechanic is half-awake. She has an above-average Vitality of d8.

ALERTNESS

The Alterness Attribute represents the range and resolution of a ship's sensors and communications equipment. Civilian vessels tend to skimp on electronics, installing only the bare minimum. Military ships tend to the opposite extreme.

TABLE 4.5 Spaceship-scale Alertness

Alertness	Description
d2	Rudimentary; only the barest nav-sat, Cortex access, and communications equipment
d4	Basic; typical needs for a privately-owned civilian vessel, including long range emergency beacons for distress situations
d6	Average; standard commercial vessel
d8	Good; standard military vessel
d10	Excellent; military listening post
d12	Amazing; expensive sensor or communications gear designed to send/receive broadwave messages, scan all spectrums, and analyze all frequencies

Example: *Hotaru's* basic comm/sensor suite is pretty cheap at d2.

INTELLIGENCE

Virtually all ships have some type of autopilot—smart enough to follow simple course instructions, and keep the ship from crashing during routine operations. The Intelligence Attribute represents the expert systems available in a ship's control, navigation, and guidance suite. Intelligence is also used to determine how easy it is to spoof her. No ship in the 'Verse is really "intelligent," though, in the sense of being self-aware. An Intelligence of 0 indicates manual controls with no autonomous capability at all.

TABLE 4.6 Spaceship-scale Intelligence

Intelligence	Description
d2	Bare-bones; can make only basic corrections, stop in emergencies, or sound an alarm
d4	Substandard; can handle mundane flight details, and issue automated responses to communication attempts
d6	Average; can auto-calculate a flight plan with correct input, account for unusual (but not unheard-of) anomalies during flight
d8	Good; fast response and crash avoidance, auto-landing routine on predictable terrain
d10	Excellent; auto-checks sensor information to verify its accuracy, extensive emergency response programming
d12	Amazing; sophisticated systems can handle most flight details without pilot assistance

Example: *Hotaru* has the average Firefly autonav systems which are fairly primitive at d2.

WILLPOWER

The Willpower Attribute represents the redundancy and safety margins built into a ship's design. This is the measurement of the ship's ability to operate despite damage, the ability to bypass malfunctioning systems and jury-rig temporary substitutes, and a measure of how far a ship can be pushed beyond her design limits.

TABLE 4.7 Spaceship-scale Willpower

Willpower	Description
d2	Rudimentary; auxiliary life-support and little else
d4	Basic; automatically seals bulkheads at critical sections, backups available for the most critical systems
d6	Average; often able to maintain optimal function after modest damage
d8	Good; most ship systems have an auxiliary backup
d10	Excellent; damage containment protocols and redundant backup systems may allow ship functions to continue after significant damage
d12	Amazing; modular, redundant system designs and integrated emergency procedures allow ship to often function even after extensive damage

Example: *Hotura* has the standard Firefly poor design of d2. She's tough, but has little in the way of backup systems.

SPECIFICATIONS

Specifications are the physical statistics of a ship's design. These include dimensions, tonnage, fuel and cargo capacity, and accommodations for passengers. While many of these details aren't strictly necessary for play, they can be useful in determining what a ship might look like, how much cargo or how many passengers it could carry, and other details.

(Here's a hint for busy GMs: look up the specifications on an historical ship from the period 1850 to 1950 of about the same type as the one you have in mind and use those specifications. The spaceship won't look like the steamship, but the end result will be similar.)

We use as much information as possible gleaned from the film in the sample description of Firefly Class ships. *Hotaru* is a basic transport model, however, and so she will lack many of *Serenity's* special features.

DIMENSIONS

These are the overall length, beam (width), and height of the ship given in feet. Ships that expect to enter and leave atmo cannot generally have a length more than 20 times longer than the beam (width) or height. Ships designed to function only in the black don't have to take gravity and aerodynamics into account, and don't worry about it.

Example: *Hotaru's* dimensions:
Length: 191 feet
Beam: 128 feet
Height: 53 feet

TONNAGE

The overall mass and volume of a ship is measured in tons. For those interested in specific numbers, you can determined "block volume" by multiplying the three dimensions in feet together (length x beam x height) and dividing the result by 100. Actual tonnage will be smaller, from one-half the number for a bulky ship up to one-sixth for a truly sleek design. Otherwise determine the tonnage based on the ship's Strength score, above.

Example: The volume of a Firefly Class ship is approximately 2,400 tons.

SPEED CLASS

Ships are rated for Speed Class, which is a measure of both how fast she travels on her pulse drive and how efficiently she burns on reaction drives. (This does *not* determine maneuverability in

combat. That's covered by Agility.) Speed Class is a number, normally between 1 and 10. Speed Class 1 is very slow, suitable for short range scows and bulk cargo transports. At Speed Class 10—suitable for fast couriers and racing yachts—a ship can reach anywhere in the central planets in a day, and most anywhere in the system in 25 days.

A boat has a "cruising" speed, which uses a normal amount of fuel and does not push the ship past its normal limits, and a top speed (often called "full burn"), that is 2 points higher, but uses 50% more fuel and can stress the ship if run for long periods of time.

Example: *Hotaru* has a Firefly's Speed Class of 4. Her maximum (full-burn) is Speed Class 6.

FUEL CAPACITY

A boat's fuel capacity is generally a measure of its size, and is a measure of hydrogen for the ship's fusion engine, represented in tons. Since hydrogen is light, the tanks required to store it are larger. Fuel capacity can be higher or lower depending on the design. Just remember that the required storage volume is always 5 times the capacity. A fuel tank provides 600 hours of cruise endurance, give or take. Volume dedicated to fuel storage above what is required increases the number of cruise endurance needed before refueling.

TABLE 4.8- Fuel Capacity

Strength	Tonnage	Average Fuel Capacity/ Storage Volume
d2	10-100 tons	1 ton / 5 ton tank
d4	100-1,000 tons	12 ton / 60 ton tank
d6	1,000-10,000 tons	125 ton / 625 ton tank
d8	10,000-100,000 tons	1,250 ton / 6,250 ton tank
d10	100,000-1 million tons	12,500 ton / 62,500 ton tank
d12	1 million-10 million tons	125,000 ton / 625,000 ton tank

Example: With a Strength of d6, but only weighing in at 2,400 tons, *Hotaru* is on the low end of the scale for this class. It is determined she has only half of the average fuel capacity for a Str d6 ship: 60 tons, which requires 300 tons of fuel tank space.

CREW QUARTERS

Crew members require living space. This ranges from dinky (8 tons per person) to plush (30 tons per person). This space is split between individual rooms and common areas. The captain will often be allocated a larger cabin, which doubles as the ship's office.

Example: *Hotaru* has three single crew cabins and two doubles, one of which is the captain's. This is the equivalent space for seven persons at a generous 210 tons. The rooms take up 90 tons, while the common area is 120 tons.

CARGO AND PASSENGER CAPACITY

Most ships are designed to haul cargo and/or passengers, though the amount of space dedicated to this purpose varies. Small, dedicated transports should hold roughly 25% of their total tonnage in cargo and/or passenger space (but can be higher according to design). Large, bulk transports can have up to 80% of the ship's tonnage dedicated to hauling. Note that dense cargos give more bang for the storage buck.

Passenger cabins take the place of cargo capacity at 8 tons per second class passenger and 16 tons (or more) per first class. Passengers on small ships share the crew's common areas. Luxury liners may allocate extra space for common areas and for entertainment (theaters, casinos, cabarets, dining rooms). Steerage passengers travel in the cargo hold as freight (at one person per 4 tons' capacity), although some large liners may have barracks-style quarters installed for steerage passengers.

Example: As a Firefly of 2,400 tons and lacking an infirmary or passenger cabins, *Hotaru* has a 600 ton cargo capacity (2,400 x 25%).

SHIP TRAITS

Spaceships have extremely complicated systems that interact on many different levels. Quality control varies from part to part, and fluctuates over the life of the ship. This tends to make for individual differences in performance that will not show up on official spec-sheets. Crews call this a ship's "personality," and treat her accordingly. In game terms, a ship has two personality types: Quirks and Assets/Complications:

Quirks: A ship as character may have one or more trivial quirks that have no direct game effect, but which could gain Plot Points for those players interacting with the ship character. For example, a spacecraft may groan or shudder throughout her length whenever she makes contact with atmosphere. Her hull may pick up a slight static charge whenever the drive is engaged. The Game Master is encouraged to invent bits of flavor like this from time to time, then leave it to the players to discover which of these unusual happenings are simply quirks and which are indications that

TABLE 4.9 - Ship Traits

Trait	Type	Description
Allure	Asset	A great-looking ship. The bonuses come into play when the ship's appearance is a factor.
Branded	Complication	Ship gained negative notoriety. If this factors into a social situation, the penalties apply.
Cortex Specter	Asset	Few records of the ship exist, though actions of the crew can quickly change that!
Dull Sense	Complication	Penalty applies to one type of sensor or piece of communications equipment.
Everybody Has One	Complication	Extremely common model of ship.
Fast Throttle	Asset	Ship flies faster at hard-burn
Fuel Efficient	Asset	Uses less fuel than typical.
Gas Guzzler	Complication	Uses more fuel than typical.
Good Name	Asset	Ship gained some positive notoriety. If this factors into a social situation (with an admirer), the bonuses apply.
Healthy as a Horse	Asset	[Minor Only] Vitality bonus applies to maintenance.
Hooked	Complication	[Minor only] Ship constantly requires something (hydraulic fluid, voltage regulators) or suffers the listed consequences.
Lightweight	Complication	Penalty applies to maintenance rolls.
Loved	Asset	Crew feels a deep connection with their boat.
Memorable	Complication	Unique feature easily identifies the boat.
Soft	Complication	Prone to easy damage
Tough as Nails	Asset	Resists damage
Ugly as Sin	Complication	Boat is plain ugly.

some system is starting to go bad. Of course, if playing the quirk results in a Complication (e.g., a static spark distracts the pilot's attention at a critical moment), the GM is justified in awarding Plot Points to the player (the pilot) for it. Plot Points should be awarded only when the crew is interacting with their ship. A crewmember being held prisoner on board an Alliance cruiser will not receive Plot Points if the cruiser shudders causing him to fall off the catwalk.

Asset/Complication: A boat may have Traits (either Asset or Complication), just like characters of the two-legged variety. These Traits are the more significant features that distinguish one Firefly Class transport from another. The GM should determine these modifiers ahead of time and reveal them to the players slowly as they gain experience with their vessel. (Even a crew that's been flying a ship for a long time can still be unpleasantly surprised!) Following are a list of Traits suited to a ship. Most of the "people" Traits work in a similar fashion to those found in Chapter Two: *Traits and Skills*. Those Traits listed in **bold** are ship-specific Traits, not meant for folk.

Example: Hotaru starts out with the "Everybody Has One" Trait and "Healthy as a Horse" at the minor level, same as all Firefly Class transports. Because of her age, she adds a major level of "Seen Better Days".

EVERYBODY HAS ONE (MINOR COMPLICATION)

This model of ship is extremely common—ubiquitous, in fact. Although there are some advantages (parts are easy to find), what this really means is that everyone knows how you operate and what to expect from your ship—specifications, performance, weak spots—just by looking at her. A minor Trait of "Everybody Has One" means production runs were in the hundreds. Models that number in the thousands or tens of thousands have "Everybody Has One" as a major Trait. Military vessels, other than the very smallest, do not qualify for this Trait, due to the way they are ordered and built.

Penalty: Anyone attempting to exploit the known features of the design receives a +2 step Skill bonus to his action—though he must have some knowledge of the model in question. (A GM may allow an Intelligence + Knowledge or Mechanical Engineering at Average difficulty to recall the right details.)

FAST THROTTLE (MINOR/MAJOR ASSET)

Though the ship performs normally at cruising speed, she flies faster than she should when pushing to hard-burn.

Bonus: As a minor Trait, the ship gets a +1 to its speed rating at hard-burn. As a major asset, the ship receives a +2 to the rating instead.

FUEL EFFICIENT (MINOR ASSET)

Through a miracle of good design or dumb luck, the boat doesn't burn fuel as fast as most its size.

Bonus: Standard space devoted to fuel yields 800 hours of cruise endurance.

GAS GUZZLER (MINOR COMPLICATION)

The boat just ain't economical when it comes to fuel, and either needs larger tanks or more regular trips to a refueling station.

Penalty: Standard space devoted to fuel yields only 400 hours of cruise endurance.

LOVED (MAJOR ASSET)

This ship knew it was loved from the day the crew first saw her, when everyone else thought she should be on the scrap heap. The "Loved" ship may throw the occasional tantrum, suffer from health issues, or even have a nervous breakdown. But if the crew believes in her and nurses her and keeps on lovin' her, she'll come through for them when it counts. Note that in order to retain this Asset, the crew must perform standard maintenance on a regular basis, keeping the ship in good repair as well as their means will allow. The Asset can be lost if a crew with means falls behind on maintenance. A dirt-poor crew who still cares for the ship as best they can (going without fresh food in order to purchase spare parts) will still retain the Asset, even if maintenance suffers somewhat.

Bonus: Members of the crew can spend Plot Points from their personal pool for rolls whenever the ship's Attributes or Skills are called into use, even if their characters aren't directly involved.

SEEN BETTER DAYS (MAJOR/MINOR COMPLICATION)

The ship is old and showing obvious signs of wear. At the minor level, a ship that has "Seen Better Days" is more than 20 years old. She's been around the 'Verse some, but is still basically sound. Purchase price is 25% of the original price. Maintenance costs are increased by +50%. As a major Trait, the ship has really "Seen Better Days"—more than 40 years' worth. To anyone with an ounce of judgment, she's clearly a piece of *luh-suh*. She probably wasn't working when you found her, and might be worth more as scrap. Purchase price is 5% of the original price, if that. What it takes to get her runnin' again is up to the GM. Double maintenance costs.

Penalty: The ship suffers a –1 step Attribute penalty for Vitality on monthly maintenance rolls. As a major Trait, the penalty increases to –2 steps. An equal bonus applies to Influence rolls for characters in social situations where their ship's age comes into a factor. (These penalties are cumulative with "Ugly as Sin.") Note also the cost differences listed above.

SHORT RANGE
[MINOR COMPLICATION]

The ship is equipped with only reaction thrusters (engine pods, chemical rockets, etc.), and not a deep space pulse drive. Range is limited to wide orbit, though travel among the moons of a single planet is possible. Travel to another planet or system will take months or maybe years. Short Range vessels are generally not equipped with regenerative life support systems, and thus have limited supplies of air and water.

Penalty: With no pulse drive, cruising speed is limited to 1 (and "full burn" to 3). Life support will run out without access to a mothership or space station.

SLOW THROTTLE
[MINOR/MAJOR COMPLICATION]

The ship functions normally at cruising speed, but her pulse drive doesn't really accelerate like she should.

Penalty: As a minor Trait, the ship gets a −1 to its speed rating at hard-burn. As a major Complication, the ship is not able to achieve hard-burn at all.

SHIP SKILLS

Skills for ships (and other vehicles) represent the programs and relational databases executed by the controlling computer and its expert systems. Ordinarily, these systems lack the creativity and flexibility to go beyond the general into specializations; their Skills are limited to d6 unless the GM grants an exception.

TABLE 4.10 - Ship Skills	
Skill	**Description**
Athletics	Collision avoidance systems
Covert	Stealth programming
Heavy Weapons	Automatic targeting
Knowledge	Internal encyclopedia/ database
Mechanical Engineering	Interactive maintenance manual
Perception	Sensor routine and internal security checks
Pilot	Autopilot/Autonav

Ships have a variety of available Skills, but the hardware and software necessary to make good use of them are expensive. Each ship receives Skill points equal to twice her Intelligence Attribute for free. After that, Skills are purchased with Attribute

CHAPTER 4

points like Assets, which may result in added costs due to Complexity.

Example: With a d2 Intelligence, *Hotaru* begins with 4 "free" points for programs. Her owners install 4 additional points for a total of 8. The ship has Aerial Transport Operations d2 (bare minimum autopilot), Space Navigation d2 (bare minimum autonav), and Perception d4 (internal security system). The 4 additional points used will be noted for use in calculating *Hotaru's* complexity.

COMPLEXITY

Complexity measures the overall capabilities, integration, and expense of a ship's systems. Total all the points used for Attributes, Skills, and Traits, (positive and negative), in the same manner as given in Chapter Two: *Traits and Skills*, and consult the table below.

TABLE 4.11 - Ship Complexity

Attributes	Complexity	Cost
12-24	Very Low	x0.4
26-30	Low	x0.6
32-36	Average	x1.0
38-42	High	x1.6
44-48	Very High	x2.4
50+	Extreme	x4.5

Ships designed for the military are normally two levels of Complexity greater than an equivalent civilian ship.

Example: With 28 points in Attributes, −4 points in Traits, and +4 points in Skills, for a total of 28 points, *Hotaru* rates a Low Complexity and a cost factor of 0.6.

DERIVED ATTRIBUTES

Initiative is calculated for ships the same way as for characters. Initiative is used only when the ship is taking some action on her own (executing a preprogrammed flight plan, for example). Most times, the Initiative of the captain or pilot is what matters.

Life Points for ships are based on Strength + Willpower, rather than Vitality, due to the role that sheer mass plays in absorbing damage. Stun points represent minor system overloads that will reset themselves in short order if not messed with further. Wound points represent substantial damage.

A ship that has lost all her Life Points is "dead"—drifting, unable to move or perform any action—but not destroyed. Total destruction requires Wound damage equal to double the ship's Life Points. Stun damage heals normally, but ships do not "heal" Wound damage without "surgery" from a qualified mechanic.

Example: *Hotaru's* Initiative is d8+d2. She has 8 Life Points.

GEAR

Unlike more integrated systems, weapons and armor for ships can be purchased and installed, usually at the expense of cargo capacity. Other gear, particularly auxiliary craft (shuttles, hovercraft, etc.) can also be installed on the same basis.

Example: *Hotaru* has neither armor nor weapons, and she lacks the shuttles that come standard on some Firefly models.

MAINTENANCE

The ship requires constant upkeep—changing filters, replacing worn out or damaged parts, cleaning and lubricating and adjusting every moving piece. Each ship has an average annual maintenance cost based on size, type, and age. See the individual ship descriptions for this amount or consult *Maintenance Costs*.

Monthly maintenance costs are detailed in the ship descriptions. Each month the mechanic (or the person taking care of the ship's systems) must make a Hard (11) Skill roll using the ship's Vitality + the mechanic's Mechanical Engineering/Maintenance. (If others help with upkeep, they can assist on the roll per the rules in Chapter Five: *Keep Flyin'*.) The cost per month to keep flyin' normally are determined by the roll.

TABLE 4.12 - Monthly Maintenance

Result	Cost
Botch	x 2
Failure	x 1.5
Success	Normal
Extraordinary Success	x 0.5

Example: The Firefly Class transport *Hotaru* has a monthly maintenance cost of 320 credits. Her mechanic, Bester, rolls *Hotaru's* d8 Vitality and adds his own d6 for Mechanic Engineering/Maintenance. The final result is a 4—coming up quite a bit short. It will cost 480 credits to keep *Hotaru* flying

CHAPTER 4

KAYLEE: "Everything's shiny, Cap'n. Not to fret."
MAL: "You told me entry couplings would hold for another week!"
KAYLEE: "That was six months ago, Cap'n"

normally, barring any further problems. Time to look for a better mechanic.

The GM should describe a particular system or part that needs attention. If the crew does not spend the cash (or find the parts some other way) to make the repair, the ship's Vitality is temporarily reduced by -1 step, cumulative each month of missed maintenance. Once the Vitality reaches 0, the ship breaks down completely and cannot move or perform any other action without fixing the problem. This assumes fairly regular use. If a ship is placed in mothballs or lies dormant for long periods, maintenance costs and the effects of such neglect are based on years, rather than months.

WEAPONS SYSTEMS

Warhead cost and damage are based on weight and type. Bombs have the same weight, cost, and damage as the equivalent warhead type.

TABLE 4.13 - Spacecraft-Scale Warheads

Weight	Cost*	Damage**
10 pounds	10	0
20 pounds	20	d2
50 pounds	50	d4
100 pounds	100	d6
200 pounds	200	d8
500 pounds	500	d10
1,000 pounds	1,000	d12

* Multiply cost by 5 for decoy, jammer.

** Damage is Wound for kinetic, explosive, and canister; Stun for magnetic, jammer. Decoy does no damage.

Missiles are classified by range, as Short, Medium, or Long. Weight is a multiple of warhead weight. Cost is 1 credit per 100 pounds of missile, plus warhead cost. Missile launchers have negligible weight and cost, but tonnage must be dedicated to them (at one ton per 2,000 pounds of missiles). In a pinch, missiles can be carried as cargo, kicked out an airlock, and fired by remote. This is very slow and requires enough crew in pressure suits to manhandle the missiles, but this may be the only option for an unarmed vessel.

TABLE 4.14 - Spacecraft Missiles

Type	Range	Weight
Short	6 miles	x5
Medium	10 miles	x10
Long	16 miles	x20

Example: Missile launchers are due to be mounted over *Hotaru's* over-wing bays. These are short range missiles with 100-pound warheads that weigh 500 pounds and could cost 600 credits each for kinetic, explosive, canister, or magnetic; 1,000 credits for decoy or jammer. Figure 20 x 2,000 / 500 = 80 in each bay at no additional cost or weight.

Cannons are either conventional or electromagnetic. Specify the number of ready rounds carried in the cannon's magazine (additional rounds may be carried as cargo). If conventional, the weight of one round is double the weight of the warhead; magazine tonnage is total weight of all rounds divided by 2,000. If electromagnetic, round weight is the same as warhead weight, but the weight of the magazine is twice the total weight of rounds to allow for power and cooling systems. Cannon firing warheads smaller than 10 pounds are vehicle weapons—see Table 4.18.

TABLE 4.15 SPACECRAFT-SCALE CANNON

Warhead	Weight	Cost
10 pounds	1,000 pounds	10,000 credits
20 pounds	1 ton	20,000 credits
50 pounds	2 tons	50,000 credits
100 pounds	5 tons	100,000 credits
200 pounds	10 tons	200,000 credits

ARMOR

One point of Wound armor (damage resistant hull plating) weighs 5% of ship tonnage, takes up 1% of ship's tonnage as volume, and costs 10 credits per ton of weight. One point of Stun armor (electronic hardening, radiation shielding, etc.) takes up 1% of ship's tonnage (both mass and volume) and costs 1,000 credits per ton.

Example: Adding one point of W armor to *Hotaru* would weigh 2,400 x 5% = 120 tons, take up 2,400 x 1% = 24 tons of cargo space, and cost 120 x 10 = 1,200 credits. One point of S armor would cost 2,400 x 1% = 24 tons and 24 x 1,000 = 24,000 credits.

PRICE

The original purchase price for a spaceship is 10 credits per ton, multiplied by Speed Class and the cost factor for Complexity, plus the cost of installed gear. This is *not* the price you would be quoted in a contract from the shipyard for a new build; rather, it represents the approximate market value of a nearly new ship currently in operation. This price may be reduced for age and wear, as in "Seen Better Days".

Example: *Hotaru's* original purchase price was around 20 x 2,400 x 4 x 0.4 = 38,400 credits. Since she's 40 years old and has "Seen Better Days", she went for just 5% x 48,000 = 1,920 credits at auction.

MAINTENANCE COSTS

Each year, routine maintenance (not due to battle damage) costs an average of 2 credits per ton of ship multiplied by the cost factor for Complexity (and modified by "Seen Better Days", if appropriate). Divide by 12 to determine the monthly maintenance cost.

Example: If she were new, *Hotaru* would have maintenance costs figured at 2 x 2,400 x 0.4 = 1,920

credits a year on average. Due to her age, that cost is doubled to 3,840 credits a year, average. That leaves a monthly maintenance cost of 320 credits.

INCREASING ATTRIBUTES

Making permanent improvements to a ship's Attributes, Traits, or Skills is not as simple as doing the same for a character. Upgrades require replacement parts, new hardware, shipyard time, and extensive reintegration. In game terms, calculate the difference between the ship's original (not purchase) price and what her new price would be, based on increasing Complexity. That is the cost for the upgrade, in addition to any Progression Points required. The ship will be in dry dock for one week for every 10,000 credits of the upgrade.

Example: Upgrading *Hotaru's* avionics suite and thereby increasing Alertness from d2 to d8 will bring her Attribute point total up to 30, raise her Complexity from Very Low to Low (cost factor 0.6), and increase her original purchase price to 72,000 credits. This is an additional 24,000 credits for the upgrade, which will require two and a half weeks at a shipyard to install (assuming things go smooth).

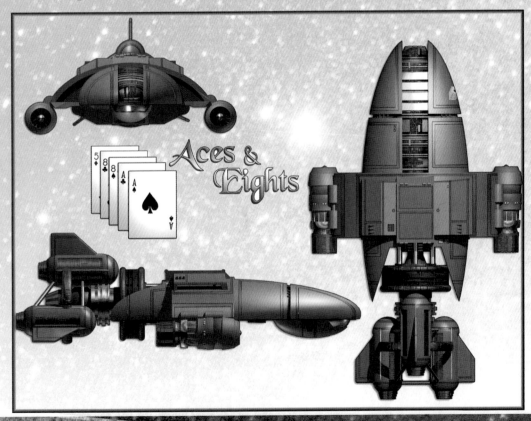

Aces & Eights

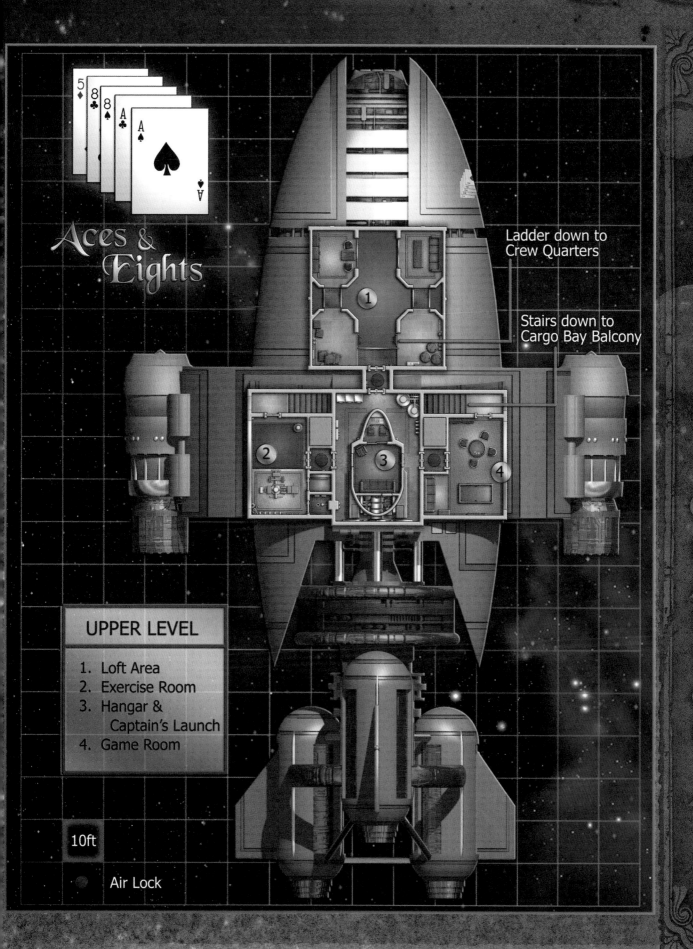

Aces &
Eights

Ladder down to
Crew Quarters

Stairs down to
Cargo Bay Balcony

UPPER LEVEL

1. Loft Area
2. Exercise Room
3. Hangar &
   Captain's Launch
4. Game Room

10ft

● Air Lock

CHAPTER 4

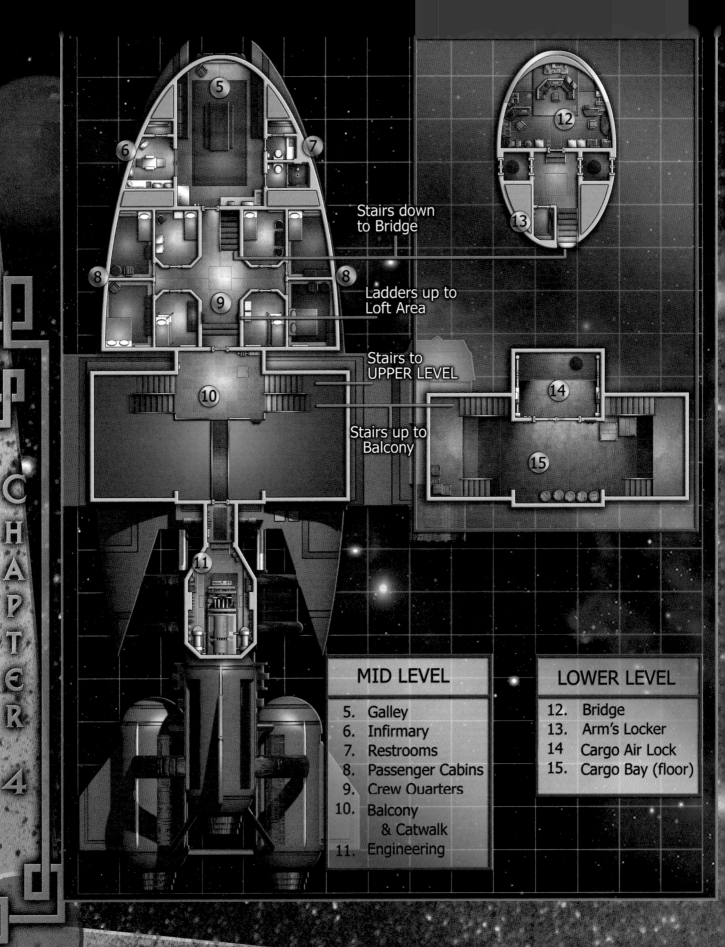

Stairs down
to Bridge

Ladders up to
Loft Area

Stairs to
UPPER LEVEL

Stairs up to
Balcony

MID LEVEL

5. Galley
6. Infirmary
7. Restrooms
8. Passenger Cabins
9. Crew Quarters
10. Balcony
    & Catwalk
11. Engineering

LOWER LEVEL

12. Bridge
13. Arm's Locker
14. Cargo Air Lock
15. Cargo Bay (floor)

CHAPTER 4

SAMPLE SHIPS

The following ships just scratch the surface of what a crew might encounter flying out in the 'Verse. They can be used as is or modified to create unique ships with features a crew won't be expecting. Just be especially careful to watch for those ships painted red and flying without reactor core containment!

HOTARU (FIREFLY CLASS TRANSPORT)

Dimensions (LxBxH): 191 x 128 x 53 feet.
Tonnage: 2,400 tons.
Speed Class: 4 cruise/6 hard-burn
Crew Quarters: Two double, three single cabins.
Fuel Capacity: 60 tons (600 hours).
Cargo Capacity/Maximum Deck Load: 400/460 tons in hold #1; 200/490 tons in hold #2. Two small-capacity storage lockers.
Passenger Capacity: None, crew quarters only.
Price: ₡ 2,400 at auction.

Agi d8, Str d6, Vit d8, Ale d2, Int d2, Wil d2; Init d8+d2, Life 8. Healthy as a Horse; Everybody Has One; Seen Better Days. Aerial Transport Operations/Firefly d2; Space Transport Operations/Firefly d2; Perception/Security d4. Complexity: very low. Maintenance costs ₡ 3,840 a year.

A basic transport model Firefly, without any fancy frills.

ACES & EIGHTS

Dimensions (LxBxH): 195 x 125 x 65 feet
Tonnage: 6,000 tons.
Speed Class: 5 cruise/7 hard-burn
Crew Quarters: 2 singles, 2 double bunks.
Fuel Capacity: 125 ton (800 hours)
Cargo Capacity: 4-ton bomb bay; 8 tons of external weapons.
Cargo Capacity: 300 tons.
Passenger Capacity: 2 singles, 2 queen beds.
Armament: Two 100-pound short-range explosive missiles secretly mounted in the undercarriage; missile mounts go "live" by entering the correct code sequence from the bridge or engine room; Formidable Alertness + Perception/Search action required on a search to find the missile bay during inspection.
Price: Unknown.

Agi d6, Str d6, Vit d10, Ale d8, Int d8, Wil d8; Init d6+8, Life 14. Allure (minor), Good Name (minor), Memorable (minor). Aerial Transport Operations/Gunship d4; Perception/Search d6; Space Transport Operations/Gunship d6. Complexity: extreme. Maintenance costs ₡ 54,000 per year.

A privately-owned vessel, *Aces and Eights* is known throughout the Border and outer worlds as the personal transport ship of an eccentric, rich, roving gambler by the name of Jack Leland. Though officially the ship is his preferred accommodations for taking high-stakes poker games outside of the Core, many folk are familiar with the fact that the crew is for hire for certain jobs—hand-picked by level of personal interest as much as money by the owner and Leland's hired-gun, Captain Maxx Williams.

Aces and Eights, though a mid-size transport, has many expensive amenities. A loft area with low ceilings and exposed pipes allows for incidental storage and an out-of-the-way spot for meetings. The rec room comes complete with exercise mats, punching bag, and full set of weights. The galley is a combination kitchen and dining room. A large Cortex access terminal dominates the bow end of the room. The ceiling has four enormous skylights, allowing for an excellent view of the black. The infirmary is rather small for a mid-bulk transport, and is suited to short-term care only.

The hangar holds the Captain's Launch—a small short-range shuttle that normally integrates into the ship during normal operations. (The roof of the ship opens up to allow the launch exit and entrance to the body of the ship.) Captain Williams and the owner, Jack Leland, are the only two who have access to the launch area. High-tech retinal imaging will lock out all but the most skilled and determined.

The room most often talked-about on the ship is the Game Room, where Leland holds high-stakes poker games when the worlds he visits do not have casinos or hotels suitable to his standard of living. The game room has a card table, billiards table, and liquor cabinet stocked with only the best booze in the 'Verse.

ESCAPE POD

Dimensions (LxBxH): 8 x 4 x 4 feet.
Tonnage: 1 ton.
Passenger Capacity: 1.
Life Support: 5 man-days.
Gear: Heat shield (armor, 1W).
Price: ₡ 100.

Agi d4, Str d2, Vit d6, Ale d2, Int d6, Wil d6; Init d6+2, Life Points 8. Sharp Sense (Radio). Expendable; Short Range. Aerial Transportation Operations/Missile d6; Space Transport Operations/Missile d6. Complexity: very low.

Escape pods using high-thrust chemical rockets carry survivors away from the site of a disaster in space. Once away, the pod's computer takes over. If there is a world within range, the computer heads for it, picks out a likely landing spot, and makes the best entry possible, using the ablative hull of the pod for a heat shield and aerobrake. If a world cannot be found, pods will swarm together to wait for rescue. The pod carries life support for five days, but living in a space the size of a coffin for that long is not particularly comfortable. It is possible that a skilled pilot could override the computer, take control of an escape pod, and guide it in for a landing. Only pilots familiar with the pod's system would know the proper codes, etc.

Well-equipped spaceships (Alliance vessels and high-end passenger liners) provide escape pods for 150% of the crew and passenger complement.

SHORT-RANGE SHUTTLE

Dimensions (LxBxH): 25 x 13 x 10 feet
Tonnage: 20 tons.
Speed Class: 1 cruise/3 hard-burn (reaction thrusters only).
Crew: Pilot, Copilot.
Life support: 20 man-days.
Fuel Capacity: 1 ton (1,000 hours).
Cargo and Passenger Capacity: 12 tons, or up to eight passengers on fold-down benches.
Price: ₡ 480.

Agi d8, Str d2, Vit d6, Ale d2, Int d2, Wil d4; Init d8+d2, Life 6. Healthy as a Horse; Short Range. Aerial Transport Operations/Shuttle d2; Space Transport Operations/Shuttle d2. Complexity: very low. Maintenance costs ₡ 16 per year.

A basic model space-and-atmosphere shuttle, this boat is capable of reaching any moon around a planet, or the planet itself, and returning. Can be based on a ship, planet, or moon.

ALLIANCE SHORT RANGE ENFORCEMENT VESSEL [ASREV]

Dimensions (LxBxH): 83 x 48 x 20 feet
Tonnage: 40 tons.
Speed Class: 5 cruise/7 hard-burn
Crew: Command Pilot, Weapons Officer, two Marshals.
Crew Quarters: 4-seat cockpit, with 2 cramped bunks located behind.
Fuel Capacity: 1 ton (500 hours).
Cargo Capacity: 4-ton bomb bay; 8 tons of external weapons.
Armament: One 1-pound autocannon with 200 rounds. Up to 8,000 pounds of bombs and 16,000 pounds of missiles.
Price: ₡ 3,400 plus ammunition.

Agi d10, Str d2, Vit d6, Ale d6, Int d4, Wil d4; Init d10+d6, Life 6. Everybody Has One (the only military ship to have this Complication). Aerial Transport Operations/Gunship d4; Perception/Search d4; Space Transport Operations/Gunship d4. Complexity: average. Maintenance costs ₡ 80 per year.

The most common vehicle for Alliance Federal Marshals, sometimes referred to as a "gunship," ASREVs have three principal roles: anti-boat and anti-missile patrols around Alliance bases and warships, airspace dominance over planetary settlements, law-and-order quick response missions. Although ASREVs are equipped with pulse drives and the range for deep space flight, limited cockpit space and slow speed make ASREVs a poor choice for long stern chases or courier duty.

The Independent faction fielded an essentially identical vehicle prior to and during the Unification War. Captured models have been assigned to Federal bases on remote moons. Some few are in private hands and see a variety of uses from personal shuttles to survey ships.

SMALL TRANSPORT [WREN CLASS]

Dimensions (LxBxH): 60 x 25 x 20 feet
Tonnage: 100 tons.
Speed Class: 3 cruise/5 hard-burn
Crew: One, who acts as captain, pilot, and mechanic, with room for one co-pilot/relief.
Crew Quarters: Bridge doubles as cabin and living space for two.
Fuel Capacity: 10 tons (3,000 hours).
Cargo Capacity: One standardized 40-foot container (25 tons) in external frame.
Armament: none.
Price: ₡ 1,600.

Agi d4, Str d4, Vit d6, Ale d4, Int d2, Wil d4; Init d4+d4, Life 8. Aerial Transport Operations/Transport d2; Space Transport Operations/Transport d2. Complexity: very low. Maintenance costs ₡ 80 per year.

As long as cargos are bound for the frontier, small transports will always be able to make a buck. A Wren Class ship is essentially an oversized cockpit with reaction engine pods and a pulse drive mounted to a universal structural frame. Cargo is loaded in a single, standard 40-foot container attached to the frame, which can be dropped at the destination. The Wren can then pick up another load for the return trip, haul back an empty container, or fly back clean.

Ships of the Wren Class are relatively small, can be operated by a single individual, and have an operations and maintenance costs lower than any other class of ship known to the frontier. Different containerized load-outs can be mounted into the frame depending on the task at hand. A prospector looking for a new claim might want extensive survey capabilities, while a scout going into dangerous territory will want some defensive capability. Of course, this makes load-out something of a gamble, as one never knows what one is going to find beyond the frontier. It takes a savvy spacer with a nose for what's coming next to make it in this kind of life. If the salvage is on the very fringe of the black, odds are these guys will bring it back first—if they get back at all.

HOMESTEAD TRANSPORT
(BUMBLEBEE CLASS)

Dimensions (LxBxH): 140 x 80 x 80 feet
Tonnage: 1,000 tons.
Speed Class: 1 cruise/3 hard-burn
Crew: Pilot, co-pilot, mechanic.
Crew and Passenger Quarters: Four double cabins.
Fuel Capacity: 20 tons (1,200 hours).
Cargo Capacity: 400 tons of external modules and loose cargo.
Armament: Armor 1W.
Price: ₡ 850.

Agi d4, Str d4, Vit d6, Ale d2, Int d4, Wil d6; Init d4+d2, Life 10. Aerial Transport Operations/ Transport d4; Space Transport Operations/ Transport d4. Complexity: very low. No maintenance costs.

Not all settlers of the frontier come via commercial transport. Historically, settlers and homesteaders came West in their own wagons. A classic example is the Conestoga wagon of the nineteenth century—the "prairie schooner" of the North American West on Earth-That-Was. The wagon was used for a one-way trip, then served as the basis for the new homestead. This was the theory behind the Bumblebee Class homesteading ship from Munroe Heavy Industries.

A minimalist vessel, a Bumblebee has a small pulse engine and weak reaction thrusters on a long spire, set at a right angle to the circular descent shield. The crew and passenger accommodations cluster behind the heat shield. In traveling configuration, the top and bottom decks contain two double cabins each. The mid-deck includes the drives, common areas, and access through a long boom to the flight deck, which is located in front of the shield.

"Cargo modules" are attached externally to the spire. These are not standardized; shipping crates, freight boxes, feed silos, water tanks, tractor-mules, and tools are held in place with straps and occasionally cable netting, making the whole overburdened and haphazard and the oversized heat shield a necessity.

A unique feature of these ships is their ability to "circle the wagons" when traveling in groups of six or more. Fore and aft universal structural clamps allow them to dock together to form stable geodesic "balls" so as to allow free movement among them during the trip, providing a measure of security and redundancy. The clusters then split apart for landing.

A Bumblebee is designed for one trip and one planet fall, using an ablative heat shield to unload most of her descent energy. She lands "head down" and then unfolds the basic homesteading structures and equipment from around her central access core.

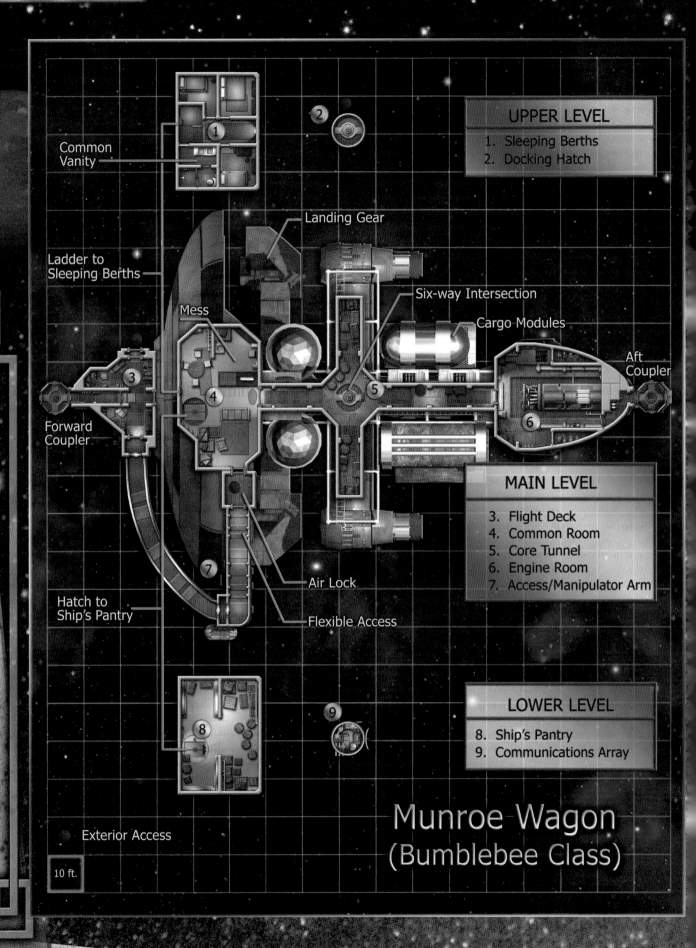

Common Vanity

Landing Gear

Ladder to Sleeping Berths

Mess

Six-way Intersection

Cargo Modules

Aft Coupler

3

Forward Coupler

4

5

6

7

Air Lock

Hatch to Ship's Pantry

Flexible Access

8

9

Exterior Access

10 ft.

UPPER LEVEL

1. Sleeping Berths
2. Docking Hatch

MAIN LEVEL

3. Flight Deck
4. Common Room
5. Core Tunnel
6. Engine Room
7. Access/Manipulator Arm

LOWER LEVEL

8. Ship's Pantry
9. Communications Array

Munroe Wagon
(Bumblebee Class)

CHAPTER 4

The Bumblebee essentially cannibalizes herself to establish the homesteader's farm. Structural panels and framework are also modular and designed to be disassembled into standardized components with hand tools and then reassembled as needed.

FIREFLY

Dimensions (LxBxH): 191 x 128 x 53 feet.
Tonnage: 2,400 tons.
Speed Class: 4 cruise/6 hard-burn
Crew Quarters: Two double, three single cabins.
Fuel Capacity: 60 tons (600 hours).
Cargo Capacity/Maximum Deck Load: 400/460 tons in hold #1; 100/220 tons in hold #2.
Passenger Capacity: Four double cabins aft of #2 hold.
Gear: Two 20-ton shuttles.
Price: ₡ 48,960.

Agi d8, Str d6, Vit d8, Ale d2, Int d2, Wil d2; Init d8+d2, Life 8. Healthy as a Horse; Everybody Has One. Aerial Transport Operations/Transport d2; Space Transport Operations/Transport d2. Complexity: very low. Maintenance costs ₡ 1,920 a year.

Caravel, outrigger, Douglas DC-3, Liberty Ship, UH-1 "Huey"—every great era of exploration and commerce has a signature vehicle, common as dirt and used for everything and anything. For the last great wave of colonization, the Firefly Class mid-bulk transport is that symbol.

The Firefly design was the brainchild of celestine architect, Jennifer Yamadera, of Beaumonde. She wanted to build a simple, cheap Everyman freighter for folk to use on the newly opened frontier worlds. By combining all the major power-using systems—gravitics, pulse drive, life support—into one big, elegant package, she cut down on production costs and developed the signature spinners-and-bulb engine layout that gives the class its name.

This design makes a Firefly Class one of the easiest ships of its size to maintain, and accounts for its popularity to this day. The only drawback is that all the main systems run together—if one goes, they all go (although there is auxiliary life support, and

the g-field may take some hours to relax completely). Yamadera licensed her design to at least half-a-dozen different shipyards over the 34 years the Firefly stayed in production, and there were several copycats, as well.

The original Firefly was designated 01-K64, for model 01 and the year she first flew (2464). The "K" in the type class is a pun: "kei" is a Japanese word for "firefly." More than 20,000 of the 01 model were constructed between 2464 and 2473. The design tended to shake badly in atmosphere, however, due to turbulent air from the forward fuselage being sucked into the engine pods.

A second model (02-K64) in 2468 tried to fix the problem by having the engine pods swing up instead of down, but that just caused her to be unstable on the ground, and the model was dropped after only a handful were launched. The solution—to extend the wings to move the engine pods about 2 feet outboard—was incorporated in the 03 model in 2469, and production continued until 2498. In all, more than 93,000 Firefly-class transports were constructed; maybe 40,000 are still in the air.

The ship's layout is complicated by the systems package design. The bridge sits high and well forward on a gooseneck. The bridge includes stations for pilot, copilot, and flight mechanic on the main level, and for sensor/comms operator on tandem step-down in the nose. Aft of the bridge, in the gooseneck connecting to the main body, the crew quarters are located beneath the corridor leading to the common room. The common area itself dominates the top third of the ship's midsection and includes a full galley, storage, and shower facilities. Further aft, behind the constriction caused by the external portion of the grav spinner, are the engine room and the internal portions of the combined drive—pulse, power, and life support.

The main (#1) cargo hold is located directly beneath the common room in the midsection. Catwalks lead to the port and starboard over-wing bays and down into the hold. In the most common version, the over-wing bays hold two 20-ton shuttles; in other designs these bays are plated over

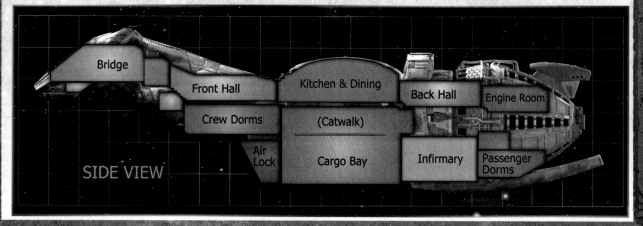

Bridge · Front Hall · Kitchen & Dining · Back Hall · Engine Room · Crew Dorms · (Catwalk) · Air Lock · Cargo Bay · Infirmary · Passenger Dorms · SIDE VIEW

SERENITY

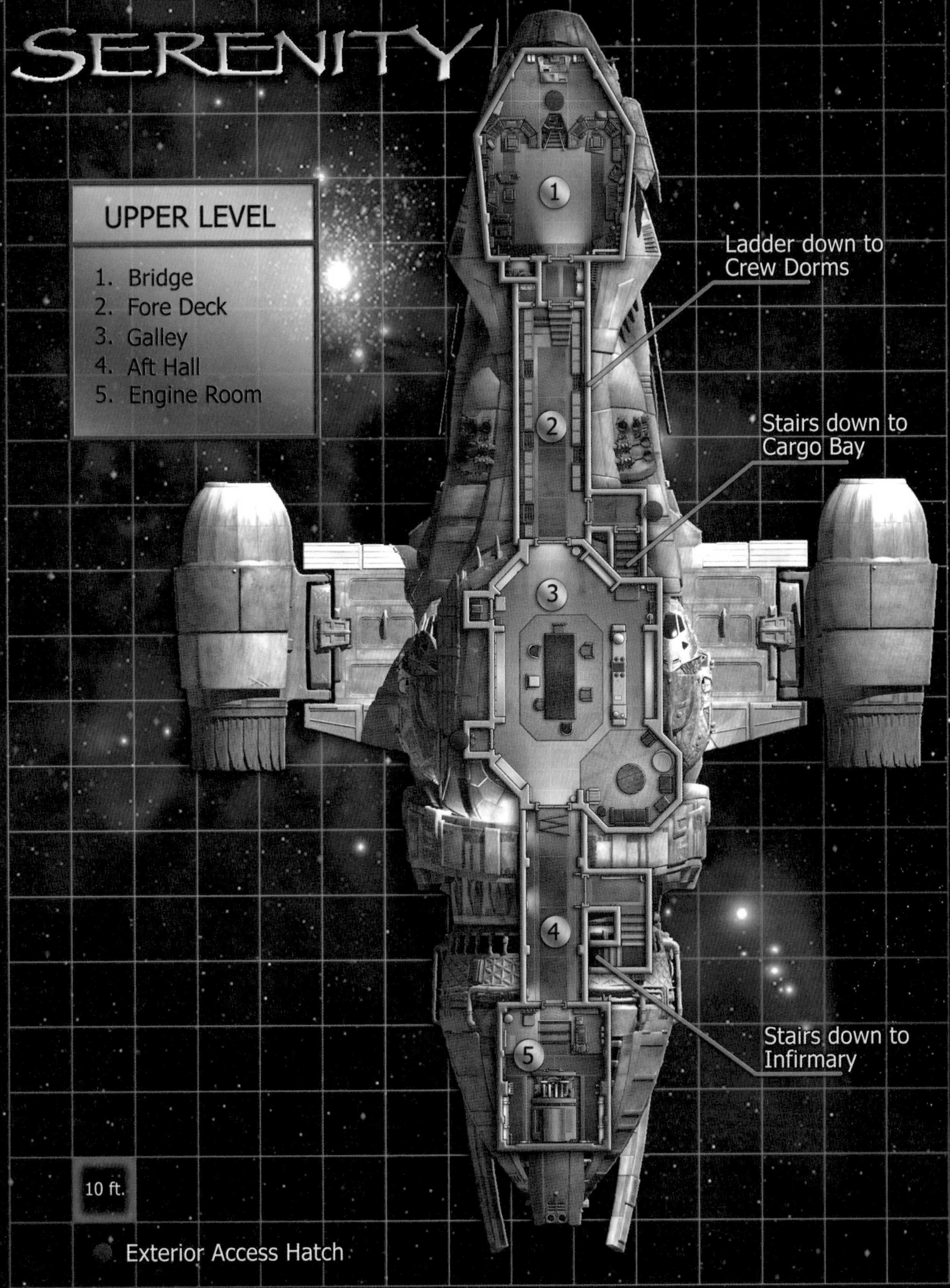

UPPER LEVEL

1. Bridge
2. Fore Deck
3. Galley
4. Aft Hall
5. Engine Room

①

Ladder down to
Crew Dorms

②

Stairs down to
Cargo Bay

③

④

Stairs down to
Infirmary

⑤

10 ft.

● Exterior Access Hatch

CHAPTER 4

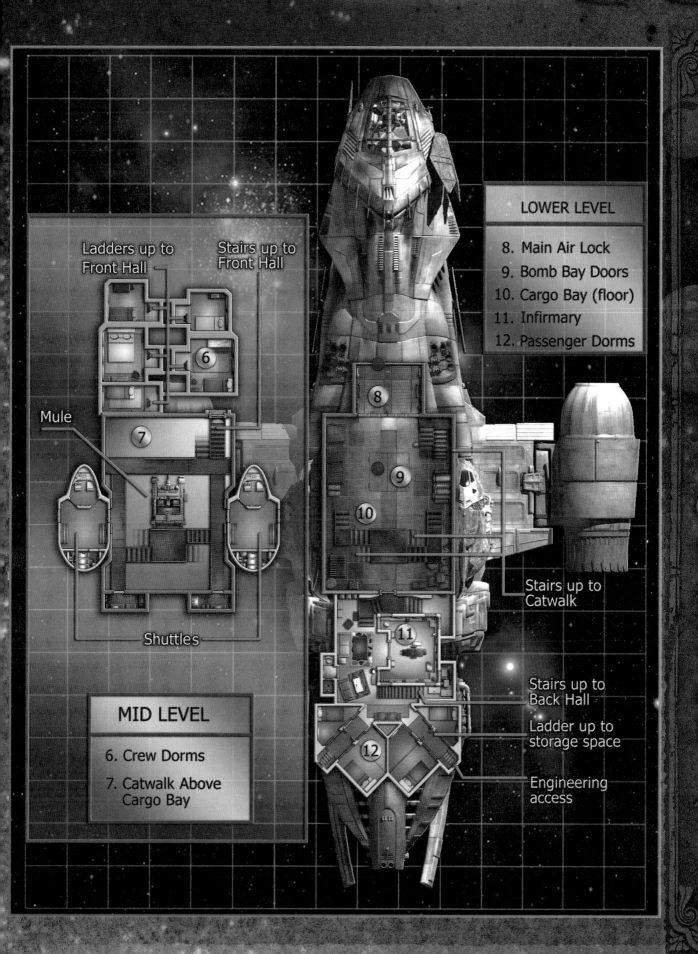

Ladders up to Front Hall

Stairs up to Front Hall

LOWER LEVEL

8. Main Air Lock
9. Bomb Bay Doors
10. Cargo Bay (floor)
11. Infirmary
12. Passenger Dorms

Mule

Shuttles

Stairs up to Catwalk

Stairs up to Back Hall

Ladder up to storage space

Engineering access

MID LEVEL

6. Crew Dorms
7. Catwalk Above Cargo Bay

CHAPTER 4

and converted to additional passenger or cargo space. The rest of the engine section surrounding the drive room was originally devoted to fuel tanks, but later modifications (made standard on the 03-K64) included a second cargo hold on the lowest level. This sometimes causes weight and balance problems with loading heavy cargo in the after hold.

The main hold opens through the forward airlock onto a cargo ramp, with a built-in postern hatch for personnel access while the ramp remains up. An additional hatch in the underbelly allows cargo to be slung into the hold at a hover. When the ship is on the ground, drive-protective skids and landing stabilizers make that hatch unusable.

VARIANTS

Because of its simplicity and low cost, the basic Firefly transport has been modified and adapted to a number of roles over the years. The specifications at the top of this entry are for the most common design: two cargo holds, some passenger space, and two shuttles for moving personnel or freight.

All-cargo: Carries 640 tons of freight, but has no shuttles or passenger space. Original price: ₡ 48,000.

Blockade Runner: Not seen since the war, this variant added 2 points of armor and 80,000 pounds of missiles (in the over-wing bays) at the expense of shuttles, passengers, and cargo space. Carried 360 tons of high-value cargo per trip through Alliance lines. Original price: ₡ 51,600, plus ammunition.

Bulk: Reconfigures the cargo holds to carry bulk products such as ore, grain, or liquids. The fore and aft access ladders are converted to feed chutes to receive the cargo, and the forward airlock and cargo ramp adapted to pump out the holds. Original price: ₡ 50,000.

Container: The 02-K64 model's up-swung engines allow this version to carry 16 standard 40-foot containers (total 400 tons) in place of the #1 hold. This design retains the original fuel tanks for 100 tons (1,000 hours) total, and uses the over-wing bays for 40 tons of supplies. Fewer than 30 of this variant remain. Original price: ₡ 48,000.

Medship: This variant places a modular infirmary in the #2 hold (making it useless for cargo), and uses the passenger dorm to house a forward support medical team (trauma surgeon, nurse, and two medtechs). The shuttles are fitted out for aeromedical evacuation, with the ship's crew doubling as ambulance drivers. Original price: ₡ 52,000.

Personnel Carrier: Used for passenger service or for transporting troops during the war, the personnel carrier variant holds 50 persons in relative comfort or up to double that many in cramped conditions ("hot-bunking," and so on). ₡ 54,000.

SERENITY

Dimensions (LxBxH): 191 x 128 x 53 feet.

Tonnage: 2,400 tons.

Speed Class: 4 cruise/6 hard-burn

Crew Quarters: Two double, three single cabins.

Fuel Capacity: 60 tons (600 hours).

Cargo Capacity/Maximum Deck Load: 400/460 tons in hold #1.

Passenger Capacity: Four double cabins aft of #2 hold.

Gear: Two 20-ton shuttles. Infirmary in #2 hold. Hover mule. At least six 50-pound, short range decoy missiles in cargo.

Price: Unknown, but probably no more than 2,500 credits.

Agi d8, Str d6, Vit d6, Ale d2, Int d2, Wil d4; Init d8+d2, Life 8. Loved (Major); Healthy as a Horse (Major); Everybody Has One; Seen Better Days. Aerial Transport Operations/Firefly d2; Space Transport Operations/Firefly d2. Complexity: very low.

Maintenance costs: ₡ 3,872 credits a year.

This 03-model Firefly may have started out life as a standard version, but she has been converted and reconfigured several times over her working life. At least one security-minded previous owner added a number of hidey-holes for high value cargo. Her final conversion was as a medship for the war, and she served in that capacity until Armistice. With the war ended, she was decommissioned and sold to a scrap yard on Boros, where she remained until purchased by her current owner, Malcolm Reynolds. *Serenity's* Vitality and Willpower have been raised by her ship's mechanic. A Quirk-level problem with the ship's heat management wiring led to the installation of aftermarket radiator panels at several points around the hull.

Survey: Retains the original fuel tanks (for 100 tons/1,000 hours) and adds an excellent sensor suite. Alertness d8, Complexity: low. Original price: ₡ 72,000.

Tanker: Retains the original fuel tanks and converts the mid-section to liquid hydrogen storage. Carries 180 tons of fuel (enough to fill 2 additional standard Firefly Class ships), plus 40 tons of cargo. Some models add an articulated fueling arm to avoid suiting up, allows for servicing a variety of ship configurations. Original price: ₡ 48,000.

ALLIANCE PATROL BOAT

Dimensions (LxBxH): 340 x 155 x 45 feet.
Tonnage: 3,955 tons.
Speed Class: 5 cruise/7 hard-burn
Crew Complement: 4 officers, 12 space hands.
Crew Quarters: 8 quad cabins, 2 double cabins, 2 single cabins.
Fuel Capacity: 200 tons (1,200 hours).
Cargo Capacity: 20 tons.
Gear: Eight 100-pound short range missiles (500 pounds each). Ten 10-pound short range missiles (50 pounds each), with decoy or jammer warheads. One 20-pound cannon with 160 rounds. Two 1-pound autocannon with 1,000 rounds each. Two shuttles. Two ASREV. 25 escape pods. Infirmary with four beds.
Price: ₡ 140,000, plus ammunition (11,000 credits per full load).
Agi d6, Str d6, Vit d6, Ale d2, Int d6, Wil d6; Init d6+1d2, Life 12. Perception d6; Pilot d6. Complexity: high. Maintenance costs ₡ 10,560 a year.

The work horse of the Alliance enforcement arm, patrol boats can be encountered anywhere in the 'Verse (though they are mainly found concentrated around the Core planets). Patrol boats perform customs duty, search and rescue, anti-smuggling patrols, and maintain general control of the space lanes.

Patrol boats saw service on both sides during the war, being one of the few classes the Independent worlds had on hand at its outbreak. Those that were captured intact have been returned to Alliance service (or at least that's what was supposed to happen!).

INDEPENDENT BLOCKADE RUNNER

Dimensions (LxBxH): 529 x 85 x 67 feet.
Tonnage: 10,000 tons.
Speed Class: 9 cruise/11 hard-burn
Crew Complement: 24 officers, 340 space hands.

Crew Quarters: 85 quad cabins, 42 double cabins.
Fuel Capacity: 1,250 tons (1,500 hours).
Cargo Capacity: 3,000 tons.
Gear: Sixteen 100-pound long range missiles (2,000 pounds each). Eight 100-pound medium range missiles (1,000 pounds each). Twelve 100-pound short range missiles (500 pounds each). Eighty 10-pound short range missiles (50 pounds each), with decoy or jammer warheads. Two 20-pound cannon with 160 rounds each. Four 1-pound autocannon with 1,000 rounds each. Armor (1S). Two shuttles. Infirmary with ten beds.
Price: ₡ 4.6 million, plus ammunition (66,000 credits per full load).
Agi 1d2, Str d8, Vit d6, Ale 1d2, Int d6, Wil d8; Init 1d2+1d2, Life 18. Tough as Nails. Aerial Transport Operations/Warship d6; Space Transport Operations/Warship d6. Complexity: extreme. Maintenance costs:
₡ 90,000 a year.

Before the war, the Independent worlds didn't have a navy—just a few patrol boats for customs duty or search and rescue, and some police gunships. After the war started, there was never much chance to catch up. The Independents tended to avoid directly confronting the vastly superior Alliance navy in space, relying on stubborn ground campaigns to wear down the Alliance's will.

That is not to say they gave up the fight in space entirely. The Independent's celestine strategy concentrated on raiding the Alliance shipping and supply lines using hit-and-run tactics, and on smuggling troops and material through the Alliance blockades. While unsuccessful, these have created stories remembered in the many years since the war. These operations required ships that relied more on speed and maneuverability rather than heavy weapons and armor. Virtually all Independent ships were converted merchants with beefed up drives, increased manning, and weapons.

The only class of blockade runners the Independents managed to launch were the 10,000-ton Nu Hai Dao Class. Besides Nu Hai Dao, there were nine others in the Lady Pirate Class, each named for famous female pirates or other notorious women from Earth-That-Was: Lai Choi San, Anne Bonney, Mary Read, Grainne Ni Mhaille, Ching Shih, Charlotte de Barry, Alvilda, Rachel Wall, and Jane de Belleville. Three of these vessels remained at large at the end of the Unification War and were never accounted for. Official records claimed they were destroyed, but, in truth, the Alliance has no idea where they are. Official accounts of the ships' last known locations vary widely, and have become the subject of barroom tales for years.

CHAPTER 4

ALLIANCE PATROL BOAT

Equipment Locker

Captain's Office

Air Locks

Restrooms & Showers

Gurney Lift

UPPER LEVEL

1. Bridge
2. Escape Pods
3. Crew's Quarters
4. Recovery Ward
5. Engineering (upper level)

10 ft.

Exterior Access

Ladder to lower level

MID LEVEL

6. Lounge
7. Rec. Room
8. Conference Room
9. Weapon Lockers
10. Galley
11. Medical
12. Launch Bay
13. Hangar
14. Engineering

LOWER LEVEL

15. Cargo Hold

Storage

Restrooms

Ramp down to
Cargo Hold

Air Lock

Missile Tubes

Storage

CARGO LINER

Dimensions (LxBxH): 396 x 262 x 101 feet.
Tonnage: 35,000 tons.
Speed Class: 1 cruise/3 hard-burn
Crew Complement: Four officers, ten space hands.
Crew Quarters: One double, fourteen single cabins.
Fuel Capacity: 700 tons (1,200 hours).
Cargo Capacity: 21,000 tons.
Gear: A mobile crane/container lifter, four forklifts, and a flatbed truck are standard pieces of equipment to move the heavy loads this spaceship normally carries. When first commissioned, this cargo vessel comes standard with two 20-ton shuttles, configured as lifeboats.
Price: ₵ 420,000.

Agi d6, Str d8, Vit d6, Ale d2, Int d2, Wil d6; Init d8+d2, Life 8. Aerial Transport Operations/Transport d2; Space Transport Operations/Transport d2. Complexity: low. Maintenance costs ₵ 42,000 a year.

This is a fairly typical medium-to-large transport of the sort used by big shipping companies to move cargo on scheduled runs among the Core planets. The Polaris Class was made famous by the Trans-Universal Shipping Company before they went out of business in the wake of a war-profiteering scandal.

ALLIANCE CRUISER

Dimensions (LxBxH): 1,200 x 1,000 x 2,500 feet.
Tonnage: 5.5 million tons.
Speed Class: 1 cruise/3 hard-burn
Crew/Passenger Complement: 40,000, and two squadrons of ASREV.
Minimum Crew: 40.
Fuel Capacity: 55,000 tons (600 hours).
Price: ₵ 0.5 billion.

Agi d2, Str 1d2, Vit d8, Ale 1d2, Int d6, Wil d8; Init d8+d2, Life 20. Healthy as a Horse. Aerial Transport Operations/Cruiser d6; Perception/Security d4; Space Transport Operations/Cruiser d6. Complexity: extreme. Maintenance costs: ₵ 50 million a year.

After winning the war, the Alliance moved quickly to consolidate its hold over the outer planets. The Tohoku Class was conceived as a mobile base for pacification operations, and a visible symbol of Alliance power and prestige. In essence, each Tohoku is a self-contained city in space, providing a platform for the Alliance to bring the benefits of civilization to the backward worlds of the Rim. The cruisers are manned more like a city than a spacecraft: information and development specialists, economists and financiers, public administrators, and the staff to support them all. A few high-ranking officials even bring their families aboard.

The Tohoku design consists of four towers (two large, two small) projecting out of a wide, flat base. The base provides primary support services, including engines, power, and life support. On the underside of the base and inverted with respect to the rest of the cruiser is the landing field; a control tower projects downward to provide oversight. The main towers—hundreds of feet across at the base and hundreds of levels tall—offer maximum surface area for heat management and contact with the outside.

Listing all the capabilities and gear for one of these fortresses would be pointless. Suffice to say that while virtually any sort of defensive weapon is available in quantity, Tohoku Class ships are unarmored and rely on their gunships for defensive actions.

EL DORADO

Dimensions (LxBxH): 397 x 160 x 52 feet.
Tonnage: 10,000 tons.
Speed Class: 5 cruise/7 hard-burn
Crew Complement: 8 officers, 16 space hands, 50 crew dedicated to passenger care, 10 entertainers.
Crew Quarters: 24 double cabins, two 40-ton suites (captain, chief mate/chief engineer).
Fuel Capacity: 600 tons (1,200 hours).
Cargo Capacity: 800 tons.
Passenger Capacity: 43 double cabins, three 40-ton VIP suites.
Gear: Six 20-ton passenger shuttles. Sixteen 20-ton shuttles configured as lifeboats. Auditorium/theater with 500 seats and full stage. Two salons (dining room and casino). Infirmary with three beds.
Price: ₵ 1 million.

Agi d4, Str d8, Vit d6, Ale d6, Int d6, Wil d6; Init d4+d6, Life 14. Allure; Good Name. Aerial Transport Operations/Transport d4; Perception/Security d4; Space Transport Operations/Transport d4. Complexity: high. Maintenance costs ₵ 32,000 a year.

Passenger liners and personnel carriers can be found throughout the 'Verse, connecting the Core planets to each other and to the outer worlds. Passage on one of these ships is like a stay in a moderately priced hotel: clean, efficient, safe. The ship has a dining room, a small bar, and maybe a sundries shop. Most passengers take their entertainment in their rooms. Such ships are simple, economic ways to reach a destination.

By contrast, the cruise liners of the Floating World Class have been designed for those who want to enjoy the journey. Cruise liners come from a few select classes, but all have common elements: luxurious, well-appointed state rooms; fabulous restaurants; theaters; spas; and casinos that offer high-stakes gambling for those with the credits, and low stakes good-time gambling for those who just want to try their luck. The captain and crew are experienced and attentive to the needs of their guests. Security is paramount.

El Dorado is representative of the Class, though individual models vary. Along with her sister ships *Nu Du Shen* (Queen of Gamblers), *Lotus Blossom*, *Galaxy Princess*, and *Truthful James*, *El Dorado* sails a route throughout the system, taking her time, stopping long enough to give the passengers a look at the "exotic" surroundings, take on food and water, exchange passengers, and change theatrical troupes.

Guests visiting *El Dorado* for the first time enter via the long gangway leading to the reception area on Deck 1 (if the ship is docked) or are brought aboard by the passenger shuttles to the promenade on Deck 4. One of two enormous staircases leads the visitor to the Grand Salon on Deck 3, in the heart of the ship. That deck has the theater (with 500 seats and a full-depth stage for live performances), the main dining salon (seating 60 guests at a time in 5-star luxury), and, of course, the gambling salon and casino. There are 17 passenger staterooms on this deck.

Deck 4 (above) is primarily passenger staterooms (26, plus the three VIP suites). The bridge and senior officers staterooms are on Deck 5, along with the ship's complement of lifeboats. Deck 2 is split between crew aft and cargo forward, with the lower drives arrayed outboard. It also features more "access tunnels" than strictly called for by accepted standards in celestine architecture, which lead to two special storage vaults (often called the "lady holes"). The lowest level, Deck 1, is given over to cargo, reception, a few crew cabins, and pulse drives. Four cargo lifts serve to bring baggage and provisions aboard.

VEHICLES

There will be times when the crew will make landfall (or perhaps the characters live on land). The crew will need transportation, and this section provides information on both ground and air transport. Since this will be similar to the players' every day experience, this section will concentrate on the differences that are found in the 'Verse, and on the minimum rules needed to play the game.

SURFACE TRAVEL

On the Core worlds, most citizens get around on foot, or by excellent and cheap public transportation—buses, subways, air taxis, maglev trains, etc. Private vehicles are discouraged, simply

because the sheer numbers would clog up the airways. Private vehicles are also highly taxed, making them incredibly expensive to own. The elite use personal aircraft as their daily means of transportation. Police and military forces also rely on aircraft as their primary means of transport.

On the Rim, people walk or ride horses. The common person doesn't have much call to be traveling. Roads are primitive or non-existent in most places—most often unplanned, growing up wherever there is a need through use. Horses, or old-fashioned carriages pulled by horses, mules, or the owners themselves provide transport from farm to town. More prosperous individuals may own a ground car powered by power cells, hydrogen fuel, or even steam. Wealthy landowners might own a modern hovercraft or skiff.

For long distance travel, rail (maglev trains) and water (hydrogen-powered flatboats and wherries) are available on worlds that can afford the infrastructure.

AIR TRAVEL

Between the black and ground there's a lot of blue (or green or brown, depending on how well the terraforming is progressing). Going up and down in that ocean of air is easy—all but the largest spacecraft can make a ground landing. Horizontal travel is a bit more difficult.

Some smaller vessels, like the Firefly Class transports, are maneuverable enough to fly horizontally, even to threading their way around surface obstacles. On remote worlds, such vessels may be pressed into duty as air transports, carrying cargo from one surface location to another. That isn't the most cost effective practice, however. Air travel is best performed by aircraft, be that jet-powered grav vehicle (by far the cheapest and most reliable) or propeller-driven plane. Helicopters, ultralights, and hot air balloons still exist, mainly as toys for the rich hobbyist or in special niche applications. Some developing worlds may find that dispersed settlements favor a network of grav vehicles, rather than investment in roads and rails, but this requires a large amount of money from the start.

VEHICLE STATISTICS

Land vehicles can be described in the same sort of game terms and statistics as spacecraft, adjusted for their generally smaller size. Specific changes are noted in this section. Game Masters are encouraged to adapt existing vehicles to the 'Verse as needed, using the examples provided as guidelines. Physical attributes are listed as "P" while Mental are noted with an "M" and are provided by die type.

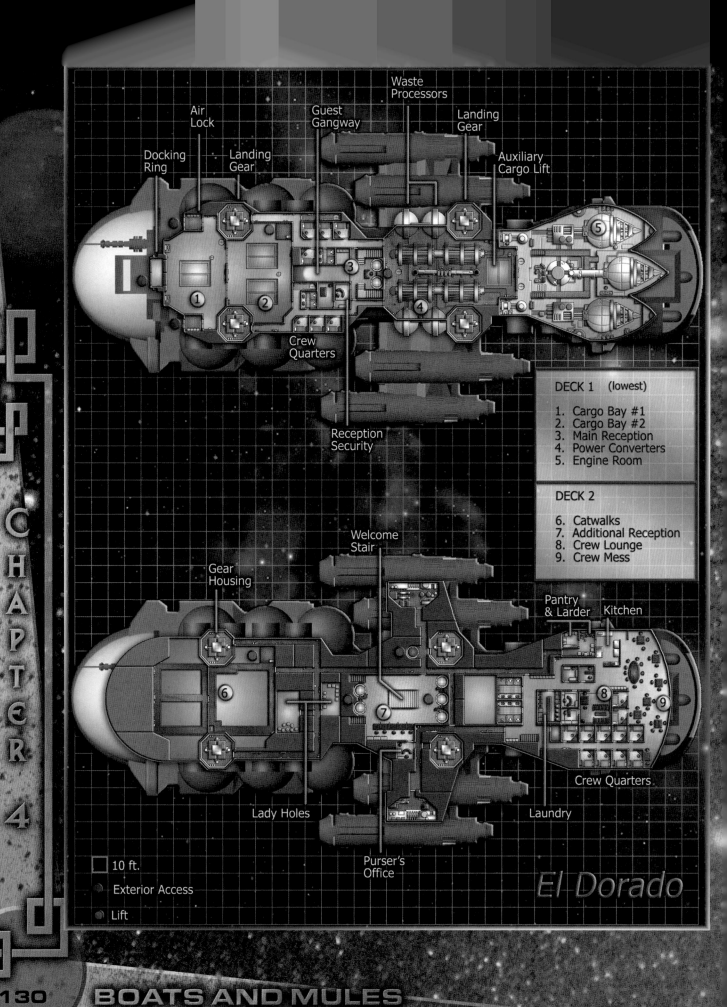

Waste
Processors

Air
Lock

Guest
Gangway

Landing
Gear

Docking
Ring

Landing
Gear

Auxiliary
Cargo Lift

1

2

3

4

5

Crew
Quarters

Reception
Security

DECK 1   (lowest)

1. Cargo Bay #1
2. Cargo Bay #2
3. Main Reception
4. Power Converters
5. Engine Room

DECK 2

6. Catwalks
7. Additional Reception
8. Crew Lounge
9. Crew Mess

Welcome
Stair

Gear
Housing

Pantry
& Larder

Kitchen

6

7

8

9

Crew Quarters

Lady Holes

Laundry

Purser's
Office

10 ft.

Exterior Access

Lift

El Dorado

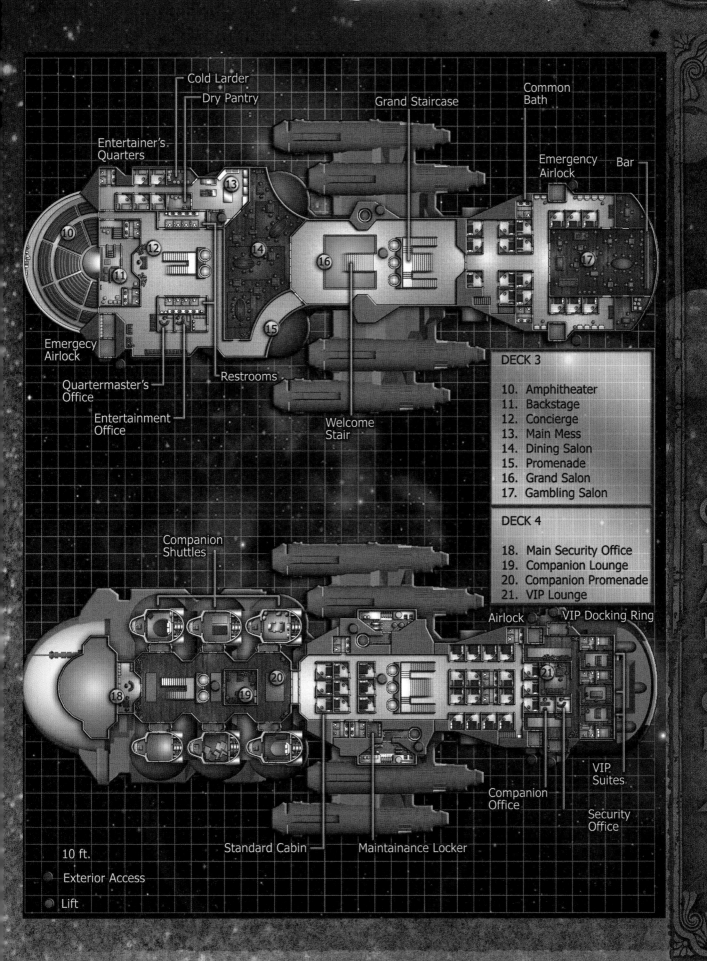

Cold Larder

Dry Pantry

Entertainer's Quarters

Grand Staircase

Common Bath

Emergency Airlock

Bar

13

10

12

11

14

16

15

17

Emergecy Airlock

Quartermaster's Office

Restrooms

Entertainment Office

Welcome Stair

DECK 3

10. Amphitheater
11. Backstage
12. Concierge
13. Main Mess
14. Dining Salon
15. Promenade
16. Grand Salon
17. Gambling Salon

DECK 4

18. Main Security Office
19. Companion Lounge
20. Companion Promenade
21. VIP Lounge

Companion Shuttles

Airlock

VIP Docking Ring

18

20

19

21

VIP Suites

Companion Office

Security Office

Standard Cabin

Maintainance Locker

10 ft.

Exterior Access

Lift

C H A P T E R 4

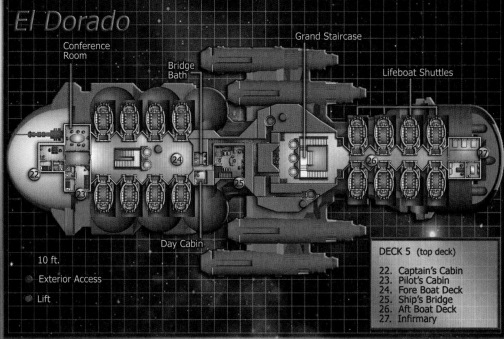

El Dorado

Conference Room

Bridge Bath

Grand Staircase

Lifeboat Shuttles

Day Cabin

10 ft.

⬭ Exterior Access

⬭ Lift

DECK 5 (top deck)
22. Captain's Cabin
23. Pilot's Cabin
24. Fore Boat Deck
25. Ship's Bridge
26. Aft Boat Deck
27. Infirmary

TABLE 4-16 VEHICLE-SCALE STRENGTH

Strength	Tonnage
d2	20-100 pounds
d4	100-500 pounds
d6	500 pounds-1 ton
d8	1-5 tons
d10	5-20 tons
d12	20-100 tons

TABLE 4-17 VEHICLE-SCALE WARHEADS

Weight	Cost*	Damage**
0.1 pound	0.1	0
0.2 pound	0.2	d2
0.5 pound	0.5	d4
1 pound	1	d6
2 pounds	2	d8
5 pounds	5	d10
10 pounds	10	d12

* Multiply cost by 5 for decoy, jammer.

** Damage is W for kinetic, explosive, and canister; S for magnetic, jammer. Decoy does no damage.

TABLE 4-18 VEHICLE-SCALE CANNON

Warhead	Weight	Cost
0.1 pounds	100 pounds	100
0.2 pounds	150 pounds	200
0.5 pounds	220 pounds	500
1 pound	300 pounds	1,000
2 pounds	500 pounds	2,000
5 pounds	700 pounds	5,000
10 pounds	1,000 pounds	10,000

Multiply weight by 2 for ground-mounted versions, and by 20 for towed versions.

Multiply cost by 1.5 for ground-mounted versions, and by 5 for towed versions.

For comparison, a 0.1 pound cannon is equivalent to a .50 caliber machine gun; a 1-pound cannon to a 1.5" or 37mm gun; and a 10-pound cannon to a 3.5" or 90mm gun.

SAMPLE VEHICLES

MULE

Horses are the All-Terrain Vehicles of the 'Verse: they can live on forage and a little bit of grain, and you don't need a factory to make more. Where keeping horses is impossible (on a hostile moon, or aboard ship), mechanical "mules" fill the gap. Mules come in a wide array of types and sizes, but most are pretty much a 1-man or 2-man vehicle with open seats, hydrogen motor, and three- or four-wheel drive.

Small Mule: P d4, M –. Seats: 1. Speed: 40 mph. Weight: 500 pounds. Cost: ₵ 35. Capacity: 500 pounds (on racks); 1,000 pounds (towed).

Large Mule: P d6, M –. Seats: 2. Speed: 40 mph. Weight: 1,000 pounds. Cost: ₵ 50. Capacity: 1,000 pounds (on flatbed in back); 1 ton (towed).

HOVER MULE

Wheeled vehicles are simple and cheap, but they are always limited by terrain. Hover mules use g-screens to stay aloft and ducted fans for propulsion. Power is usually supplied by power cells charged off the ship's electrical system between uses. Different makes of hover mule include: flatbeds, forklift tines, cranes, or buffers for carrying, lifting, or pushing cargo. Lift capacity is less than a ground vehicle of similar size, and towing a ground trailer is a pain.

Small Hover Mule: P d6, M –. Seats: 2. Speed: 60 mph. Weight: 1,000 pounds. Cost: ₵ 70. Capacity: 500 pounds.

Large Hover Mule: P d6, M –. Seats: 4. Speed: 60 mph. Weight: 1 ton. Cost: ₵ 100. Capacity: 1,000 pounds.

HOVERCRAFT

Hovercraft are passenger vehicles designed for speed over cargo capacity. Grav vehicles with significant free-flight capability, using hydrogen-powered turbofans for extra power, they are most frequently encountered on the central planets as private transportation, air taxis, or emergency vehicles. Cockpits may be open or enclosed in a canopy during bad weather, dust, or when traveling at high speeds. Hovercraft often fly only a few feet above ground for extra efficiency.

Small Hovercraft: P d6, M –. Seats: 2. Speed: 150 mph. Weight: 1 ton. Cost: ₵ 100. Capacity: 500 pounds.

Medium Hovercraft: P d8, M –. Seats: 4. Speed: 150 mph. Weight: 2 tons. Cost: ₵ 150. Capacity: 1,000 pounds.

Large Hovercraft: P d10, M –. Seats: 6. Speed: 150 mph. Weight: 10 tons. Cost: ₵ 350. Capacity: 2 tons.

SKIFF

A skiff is an armored hovercraft used in military operations. They come in a variety of configurations for different missions: command, reconnaissance, personnel carrier, ambulance, heavy weapons platform, recovery. Skiffs are powered by hydrogen fuel cells with power cell backup, and use armored turbofans for propulsion. The basic model comes unarmed.

Folk from the outer planets claim that Reavers have converted military skiffs for their own use. Carried by larger carriers, the skiffs are dropped on planets for raids.

Small Skiff: P d10, M d2. Armor 4W. Seats: 4. Speed: 60 mph. Weight: 5 tons. Cost: ₵ 400. Capacity: 1,000 pounds.

Medium Skiff: P d10, M d2. Armor 6W. Seats: 6. Speed: 60 mph. Weight: 10 tons. Cost: ₵ 600. Capacity: 1 ton.

Large Skiff: P d10, M d2. Armor 8W. Seats: 10. Speed: 60 mph. Weight: 20 tons. Cost: ₵ 800. Capacity: 2 tons.

Reaver Skiff: Pd12, M –. Armor 6W. Seats: 6. Speed 60 mph. Weight: 10 tons. Capacity: 1 ton. Weapon: Harpoon launcher (short range only, d2 W vehicle-scale.)

Harpoon Gun

Cockpit

Hanging Racks

Seating Ledge

Access Hatch
(below window)

High
Window

Drive Core

Equipment Locker

Engines

10 ft.

Side View

SPACESHIP AND VEHICLE COMBAT

Combat in the *Serenity Role Playing Game* is about character decisions and dramatic action. The same is true of battles involving transports. The difference is simply a matter of scale.

SCALE

Spacecraft are armored against the perils of space flight. By the same token, spacecraft in vacuum move much more quickly than vehicles in atmosphere, and spacecraft weapons are designed to do far more damage than a man-portable or vehicle-mounted weapon.

To represent these differences, combat in the game involves three different scales: Personal, Vehicle, and Spacecraft. Personal combat is covered in Chapter Five, *Keep Flyin'*, and includes any battle fought primarily with hand weapons against people and animals. Combat for armed vehicles and spacecraft uses the same basic rules, but adjusts the ranges and damage factors to reflect the larger, faster targets involved.

VEHICLE SCALE

Vehicles range in size from 20 pounds (a tiny robot) to 100 tons (a large aircraft or tank). This intentionally overlaps with "Personal Scale" and "Spacecraft Scale" at either end. It's up to the Game Master to determine which scale best fits the action.

In Vehicle Scale combat, ranges are increased. On an Earth-sized planet at ground level, any target beyond about 5 miles is below the horizon and out of sight. On smaller worlds and moons, the distance is correspondingly less.

TABLE 4-19 VEHICLE-SCALE RANGES

Range	Feet	Miles
Point Blank	1,000	0.2
Short	5,000	1
Medium	10,000	2
Long	20,000	4
Extreme	40,000	7.5

CHAPTER 4

SPACECRAFT SCALE

Spacecraft range in size from 1 ton and up; there is no theoretical limit, although vessels get progressively weaker for their size at the top end and so as a practical matter are limited to around 10 million tons.

Combat in space can take place at tremendous ranges, and is limited only by sensor and time-of-flight lags. Most space battles in the game will take place at the pace of Personal Combat (roughly 3 second combat turns), which sharply restricts the range:

TABLE 4-21 SPACECRAFT-SCALE RANGES

Range	Miles
Point Blank	3
Short	6
Medium	10
Long	16

COLLISION DAMAGE

When a spacecraft or vehicle collides with another object, the damage it causes is equal to its Strength. Game Masters should adjust up or down by steps, based on relative speed and angle—a head-on collision at full speed will do much more damage than sideswiping when traveling at nearly the same speed.

MIXING SCALES

For purposes of figuring damage and Life Points, Vehicle Scale is roughly 10 times greater than Personal Scale, and Spacecraft Scale is roughly 10 times greater than Vehicle Scale. When using a weapon from one Scale on the next higher Scale, treat the damage as 0 (that is, only the basic damage applies). When going from higher Scale to lower, multiply damage points by 10. If using Spacecraft Scale weapons on personnel, any hit is pretty much an automatic kill (unless Plot Points or the GM decide otherwise).

CHAPTER 5

KEEP FLYIN'

PAYDAY

"'Hands and knees and heads bowed down! Everybody! Now!'" Captain Malcolm Reynolds ordered the group of frightened bank customers.

This scene might have come from the movie, Serenity. In fact, it was coming from the living room of Margaret's house, where the group had gathered to play the Serenity Roleplaying Game. Sean, playing Captain Reynolds, was comfortably seated at the game table.

"What sort of folks are these?" Sean asked Jim, the Game Master.

"Looks to be about fifteen people in the little trading post, mostly farm folks and a few kids."

"Should be easy pickings," said Margaret in the character of Jayne.

Jim grinned. "Would be, except for the two farmers who leap to their feet. They are rushing straight at both of you—one going for Mal and a younger fellow going for Jayne. What are you both doing?"

"I wave my pistol at the guy and stare him down," Sean said, picking up his dice. "Maybe he'll think better of the notion."

Margaret had a different idea. "Hell with that! I grab the older guy and sit his ass down head-first!"

Jim scooped up his dice. "Roll for Initiative!"

Margaret and Sean rolled their dice and announced their numbers. Jim rolled the dice for the farmers.

After looking at the farmer's numbers, Jim said, "These hayseeds aren't fast enough to get the drop on you. Sean, you're up first."

"Like I said, I'm staring at him down the barrel of my pistol."

"Roll Willpower plus Discipline to see if you cause him to have second thoughts."

"I'm grabbing hold of this guy," Margaret said.

"Go ahead and give me a Strength plus Brawling roll." Jim turns to two other players. "Renae, what is Zoe up to?"

"I'm checking over the hostages to see if any of them have any bright ideas," Renae answered, playing Zoe.

Sean rolled a 10 for his intimidation attempt, while Margaret rolled a 17 for Jayne's unarmed combat. Jim rolled for the non-player characters and compared the numbers.

"Sean, your farmer backs up and swallows hard," Jim said.

"Figures." Sean grinned.

Jim turned to Margaret. "Extraordinary success! You clothesline the guy as he rushes forward, hitting him so hard he spins upside-down. You're able to grab his legs and pile-drive him right into the floor. You're pretty sure he's not getting back up anytime soon."

Jim turned again to Renae. "You've walked through about half the bank and taken a hard look at seven people. Roll Alertness plus Perception."

Renae rolled her dice and got a 6. She looked up at Jim, a bit worried.

Jim shrugged. "No one seems about to make any trouble."

Sean stood up from the table. "I raise my pistol and make a slow turn. 'You folks want to be looking very intently at your own belly buttons. If I see a head start to rise, violence is gonna ensue.'"

Margaret rubbed her hands together. "Looks like this is the place."

Sean took a drink from his soda can. "So, Jim, do the people listen?"

Jim nodded. "Yep. Everyone sits down and stares at the floor, including the guy who rushed you a moment ago. At this moment, River steps up to the door. She's bare-foot and wide-eyed."

"I motion for her to come in," Renae said. "I'll watch to see how she reacts to the people inside. Maybe she can read the insides of their heads, see if they're gonna try something."

"Jayne, what are doing?" Jim asked.

"I'm heading to the vault."

"Mal?"

"I'll step a bit closer to River, so I can watch her back in case someone tries any funny business. Time for another announcement." Sean raised his voice. "'You've probably guessed we mean to be thieving here, but what we are after is not yours. So let's not have any undo fussing.'"

Jim checked his notes and looked over at Margaret. "Vault's locked up."

"I tell the others."

Jim, who is playing River as Non-Player Character, makes another dice roll and announces, "River looks troubled for a moment, then points over to a young man. Looks like he's reaching for his gun."

"Handy having a reader around! I stick the barrel of my hogleg in his ear and say to him, 'You know what the definition of a hero is? It's someone who gets other people killed. You can look it up later.'"

"The young man tosses the gun across the room," said Jim.

Renae grinned. "Thought so."

Jim turned his attention back to Sean. "The trade agent stands up, his hands raised. 'This is just a crop moon. Don't think you'll find what you—'"

"I tell him to shut up and make us wealthy," Sean interrupted.

"The old man sighs, then he shuffles over to the wall and punches in a code. A tiny little wall safe pops open, revealing a few bundled bills, some scattered coins. Not very impressive, and definitely not what you came here to find."

Renae turned to Sean, her voice dripping sarcasm. "'At last. We can retire and give up this life of crime.'"

Sean laughed, then addressed Jim. "I look around for the secret catch that Mingo told me about in his wave."

"Roll Alertness plus Perception."

"I'm not taking any chances. I'm going to spend some Plot Points on this roll." Sean slid four poker chips over to Jim, and added an extra die to those in his hand. Everyone stared eagerly as the dice hit the table.

"14!" Sean said, pleased.

"The floor opens up just a few feet away, revealing a six-foot-wide entrance and stairs leading down to a corridor. Everything is gleaming metal and blue lights. You've found the vault."

Sean turned to Renae. "You were saying? . ."

A ship brings you work. Your crew helps you run the ship. Your gun helps you keep all of it. And in this game, sort of like in life, a roll of the dice will determine whether you succeed or fail.

Now we get to the rules of the game. If the *Serenity Role Playing Game* were a ship, this chapter would be the engine. Just remember that there's only one law in these parts: the rules serve the story. (If a Shepherd tells you different, pay him no mind.) The game rules are meant to support game play and game play is supposed to be fun. The rules are guidelines for the Game Master to use, modify, or discard in pursuit of that goal.

There's a flipside, of course. A bad GM may decide to ride roughshod over the rules, changing them at a whim and enjoying newfound megalomania. If that happens, the bad GM will have a hard time convincing the players to come back for more. The rules are here for a reason. They are meant to simulate life in the 'Verse, allowing the crew to get shot, stabbed, or blown out an airlock while those playing the crew sit comfortably at the gaming table. Rules allow players to understand how the crew interacts with the rest of the 'Verse.

If you're a player, feel free to casually browse this chapter and check up on the subjects important to your crew. Only one person needs to be intimately familiar with all the rules, and that's the Game Master.

PLAYING THE GAME

So you've broken out of a torture chamber run by a sadistic madman and you are trying to sneak past his guards to get the hell off this skyplex. Or perhaps you're flying a small transport ship through a narrow canyon with an Alliance short-range enforcement vessel hot on your tail. Could be that the catalyzer on your port compression coil has completely blown out, and you're trying to jury-rig a replacement. Might find yourself dueling with pistols, staring a man down and hoping you'll be the one to draw first. What do you do?

Answer's easy. Pick up the dice and roll. Our game is designed to provide the players with fast, dramatic adventure. While some actions in the game are automatic (eating a Fruity Oaty Bar, for instance), others have a chance of failure (keeping from heaving up your Fruity Oaty Bar when you stumble upon victims of Reaver attack). When you want to take action that may or may not succeed, you roll some dice and add the numbers together. Higher is better—trust me.

'Course, things don't always go your way and that's especially true when it comes to dice. But your crew won't be left helpless in the face of fickle Lady Luck. Crew and GM alike get shiny Plot Points. Plot Points let you bend the normal rules of the game in your favor. If you really need to hide from those guards, you can spend a Plot Point and roll an extra die toward your total. Maybe that shot coming at you is going to blow right through your brainpan, ending your unseemly career. A few Plot Points may turn that mortal wound into a minor graze. Don't go hogwild with Plot Points, though, because you start with just a few. Earning Plot Points can be a mite tough.

The basic play of the game is pretty darn simple. You state what you want to do. You'll probably have to roll some dice, maybe spend a few Plot Points, then tell the Game Master your total. After that, you find out what happens—good or bad.

USING THE DICE

There is an element of chance in almost every action. Talent, skill, planning, strategy—they all play an important role in a bank job, for example, but if you're trying to intimidate the teller and you're only rolling a d4 for Willpower, you've likely tripped on your own boot lace and fallen flat on your face in front of the teller's window.

'Course, if you're rolling a d12 for Willpower, you have a much better chance for a happier result. But that depends on your character. Jayne picking off his enemies with a sniper rifle is much more likely than Kaylee accomplishing the same. The numbers that pop up on those dice tell a story, if you've got the imagination for it.

Each Attribute and Skill in the *Serenity Role Playing Game* has a die type. If you're a lummox, you might have an Agility of d4, while a ballet dancer could have a d10. Skills work the same way. A d2 means you know just enough to be dangerous, while a d12 indicates true mastery. This is all explained back in Chapter Two: *Find a Crew* and Chapter Three: *Traits and Skills*, so flip back if you need a little review.

Most actions require that you roll the Attribute die and the Skill die. If you don't have that Skill (and decide to try anyway), then you roll the Attribute only. Add all the numbers together and find out if you've saved the day or just made things worse.

THE REAL BASICS

You'll find lots of examples, modifying circumstances, and optional rules in this chapter. Important thing to remember is the basic mechanic of the game:

Attribute + Skill = Result

When someone tries to do something, he rolls the appropriate dice and generates a total. High numbers generally mean success, low numbers indicate failure. The game situation and the number rolled give the Game Master a starting point to describe how a given action plays out—the more imaginative and descriptive the better.

That's it. *Dohn ma?*

WHEN TO ROLL

The roll of the dice is a fun element of the game, but only a *b'n dahn* would roll them for every single action attempted. Truth be told, most actions in the game don't require the use of dice at all. The rule of thumb: if an action might fail, you should roll for it. Most of the time, actions that aren't important to the overall story simply happen, nice and simple. Those that are crucial to the story require a toss of the bones.

Jayne doesn't need a Skill roll to reload Vera. Simon doesn't require a roll to give someone an injection. Folks don't need the dice in order to talk, walk, sleep, eat, or go about the other mundane business of an average day. But change the circumstances just slightly, and suddenly the same action might be call for a dice roll. If Jayne is riding on the back of the mule flying down a dusty trail at high speed, he might find it a little trickier to reload his prize rifle. If Simon's patient is flailing about in the operating theater, then he'll discover that administering the medication becomes a mite harder.

Most actions are judged a success or failure by comparing the numbers to the Difficulty Chart. If the total of your dice equals or exceeds the Difficulty, the action succeeds.

"Bit of a rockety ride. Nothing to worry about."
—Malcolm Reynolds

Table 5.1: Action Difficulty

Action	Difficulty
Easy	3
Average	7
Hard	11
Formidable	15
Heroic	19
Incredible	23
Ridiculous	27
Impossible	31

Examples of actions attempted at different Skill levels can be found in Chapter Three: *Traits and Skills*. Circumstances can make actions harder or easier, and the number required higher or lower. Other factors can change the type of dice rolled to get the job done.

EXTRAORDINARY SUCCESS

Some folk don't want to know that they did good, they want to know just *how* good. This optional rule is an easy way to determine when Extraordinary Success is achieved. The rule is pretty simple to understand, but the GM is the final word on just what Extraordinary Success means at any given moment. Note that on opposed actions, the opposing roll is the Difficulty Number.

Difficulty Number + 7 = Extraordinary Success

Example: Jayne is running for his life through an Alliance-held complex and he comes up on a door. He decides to kick it open. The GM determines the door is Hard, but Jayne's player rolls the dice and totals a 19! Extraordinary Success! Jayne not only kicks the door open, the door flies off its hinges and smacks a guard who was about to open it from the other side.

Table 5.2: Extraordinary Success

Action	Ordinary	Extraordinary
Easy	3	10
Average	7	14
Hard	11	18
Formidable	15	22
Heroic	19	26
Incredible	23	30
Ridiculous	27	34
Impossible	31	38

Complex Actions: Extraordinary Success does not apply during complex actions (see below).

EXTRAORDINARY SUCCESS & DAMAGE

When folks get hurt, healing them is often a bit more complicated than applying a bandage. Bones get broken and bullets hit major organs. Severe head trauma can put a fellow into a coma. Here's how Extraordinary Success works with damage. (See *Taking Damage* later in this chapter.)

If an attack gains an extraordinary success, the victim must make an Average Endurance action (Vitality + Willpower). If successful, the damage is taken normally. If the action fails, the damage is taken along with the following (based on the type of attack):

Basic: The character suffers a debilitating injury, either a broken limb (which is useless until treated), or he has been rendered blind or deaf. The exact nature of the injury is determined by the GM, depending on the situation.

Stun: If the damage is Stun-based, the character falls unconscious immediately, taking a number of Shock Points equal to the Stun damage inflicted during the attack.

Wounds: If the damage is Wound-based, the character has suffered a serious injury. Without successful treatment, the character will suffer an additional d2 Wounds every ten minutes.

ATTRIBUTE ROLLS

Some actions the crew might attempt don't require skill at all. These are tests of a character's raw Attributes. They are rolled with Attributes only, and depending upon the situation, may either be two Attributes rolled together or one Attribute rolled twice. A modifier to an attribute roll always affects the lower attribute only. Here are a few examples.

Burst of Strength: Strength + Strength. Made to see if you can perform a brief feat of physical strength, such as shoving a heavy object out of the way.

Endurance: Vitality + Willpower. Rolled when you're taken more Wounds than Life Points to see if you stay alive.

Get Out of Harm's Way: Agility + Alertness. Made when reacting to sudden danger, such quickly holding your breath when poison gas enters a room.

Initiative: Agility + Alertness. Determines how quickly you react each combat turn.

Long Haul: Strength + Vitality. Made when trying to perform an extended feat of strength that has to be maintained more than a few seconds, such as carrying a heavy load up a hill.

Memorize: Intelligence + Alertness. Used to commit important information to memory.

Recall: Intelligence + Willpower. A check to remember an important event or fact.

Resistance: Vitality + Vitality. Made to resist environmental hazards, diseases, alcohol, and toxins.

SKILLED ACTIONS

Most actions in the game are those related to Skills. (That doesn't mean, however, that you always have the Skill you need in a given situation!) When a player declares an action, the Game Master determines the appropriate Attribute and Skill required. Remember that when you don't have the specialty, you can always use the General Skill instead. The dice are rolled, added together, and the total is compared to the Difficulty chart to determine success.

Example: Kaylee is trying to repair *Serenity's* navigational controls in mid-flight. The GM secretly determines that this is a Hard action (Difficulty 11), and decides Intelligence + Mechanical Engineering/Repair are the Attribute and Skill required. The player rolls the dice and hopes for the best.

There is no universal pairing of Skills with any one Attribute. As circumstances change, so do the rolls required. The GM is the final word on which Attribute and Skill go together for a particular action.

Example: Kaylee continues to work on the navigation system and might have a chance to discover that it has been sabotaged. The GM asks Kaylee's player to roll Alertness + Mechanical Engineering/Repair to see if she spots the problem.

Another simple example involves running across a room, with varying details:

• The room is empty, requiring only speed to make it to the other side. Strength + Athletics/Running.

• The room has obstacles, requiring some maneuvering to avoid them. Agility + Athletics/Running.

• The room has caltrop-mines scattered all about, requiring extreme care not to set them off. Alertness + Athletics/Running.

UNSKILLED CREW AND SKILLED ACTIONS

Sometimes you just don't have the know-how needed for a situation. A ship's mechanic may have to pick up a gun to defend herself. A doctor may have to take the helm of a shuttle and attempt an emergency landing. A mercenary thug might be asked to give a speech in the town square. When this happens, you gotta roll anyway. When you have an Attribute but no Skill, you roll the Attribute alone. Best hope a Shepherd's praying for you! Note that you can always spend Plot Points on a roll when you're desperate for success.

OPPOSED ACTIONS

Most actions are easy or difficult based on the situation. (Baking a tasty chocolate cake using only leftover protein packs is Hard!) Others are even trickier because someone is working directly against you, and you have to be the better man—or woman—to succeed. Resolution on these actions is simple. Both players make the appropriate rolls, with success granted to whichever player rolls highest. Sometimes the Attributes and Skills are the same for both (individuals in direct competition) or they may be completely different (two characters attempting different yet opposing actions). Examples include:

• Mal and Jayne arm wrestling at the dining room table. Both roll Strength + Athletics/Arm Wrestling.

• Zoe slips past an Alliance Fed, hoping he doesn't hear her. She rolls Agility + Covert/Stealth, while the Fed rolls Alertness + Perception/Hearing.

• Mal haggles with Badger over the worth of his salvage, both trying to get the better of the deal. Both roll Willpower + Influence/Negotiation.

BOTCHING

Just as Lady Luck sometimes smiles upon you, she can also spit in your face. In game terms, you've rolled a "botch." A botch happens when all the dice you rolled come up as ones. This means Something Bad happens, giving the GM free reign to be both creative and fun-loving as to just what this failure means in the story. In combat, a botch usually means that you lose your next action. Perhaps your gun misfires, or you drop it, or you slip on the deck plating and it takes a moment to regain your footing. Here are a few examples:

• Jayne attempts to be on his best behavior at a social engagement, but he rolls all ones on his dice. He intends to pass the gravy boat, but passes gas instead.

• Zoe lifts the butt of her hogleg to smash a drunk's face, but she rolls all ones. The sawed-off shotgun slips out of her hands and goes flying across the room.

• All alone on *Serenity*, Mal tries to replace a crucial engine part, but he botches his roll. He drops the part through the grating and has to go down below to retrieve it.

Sometimes a botch means you've endangered yourself or someone else. The GM may ask you to make an attack roll to see if you accidentally hit an unintentional target. And may the Maker of the 'Verse protect you if you fumble while you're lobbing a grenade!

COMPLEX ACTIONS

A standard action is one that can be accomplished in a short period of time. Complex actions require more time, and are more difficult to perform: open-heart surgery, major engine overhaul, defusing a bomb, hacking into an Alliance security system.

Complex actions are handled slightly different than standard actions. Complex actions have a Difficulty Threshold—a number that is usually too high to succeed in one roll. Good news is this: you can roll multiple times, and you keep adding the results together. Each roll represents a block of time that varies, depending on the circumstances

"Kaylee, you got a day's work to do and two hours to do it."
—Malcolm Reynolds

(determined by the GM) and might be minutes, hours, or days. Difficulty Thresholds are five times the Difficulty of standard actions.

Table 5.3: Complex Actions	
Action	Difficulty Threshold
Easy	15
Average	35
Hard	55
Formidable	75
Heroic	95
Incredible	115
Ridiculous	135
Impossible	155

A botch rolled on a complex action (see below) does not mean automatic failure, but it does tend to have unfortunate side-effects: your roll for that time-block does not count at all, and you've increased the difficulty by one category. For example, an Average complex task becomes a Hard complex task after a botch. Rolling two botches in a complex action results in automatic failure.

Example: Kaylee is engaged in a lengthy repair, trying to get the grav boot working properly without shutting down the main engine. The GM assesses the difficulty as Hard (55), and requires Intelligence + Mechanical Engineering/Repair rolls, assigning each roll a 15 minute increment. The first three rolls (45 minutes!) go well, and get her close to the total. Unfortunately, the player rolls a botch, which raises the total to Formidable (75). It takes her three additional rolls to reach the new threshold. It takes Kaylee an hour and a half to complete the repair.

AIDING OTHERS

When your friend is in need, you can pitch in and help out. How much your help counts depends on the nature of the action. Not every action benefits from assistance, but many can. Aiding actions function exactly the same way for either simple or complex actions.

Direct Assistance: When your efforts directly contribute to the success of an action (for example, helping to lift a heavy load), you roll as usual and your total is combined with the total rolled by the person who is receiving your aid.

Indirect Assistance: When you can only offer aid to another character—such as assisting during

surgery, acting as a copilot, or helping someone bake a chocolate cake—rolls are not totaled together. Instead the totals are compared and the highest is used.

Table 5.4: Dice Steps
d2
d4
d6
d8
d10
d12
d12 + d2
d12 + d4
d12 + d6
d12 + d8
d12 + d10
d12 + d12

LIFE GETS EASIER OR THE JOB GETS HARDER

It would be shiny if we all lived in a 'Verse where things go smooth all the time, but that ain't like to happen. Instead, circumstances are always changing. In game terms, that means you have to make a few adjustments now and then. Glad to tell you it's pretty darn easy. Only thing you really need to know is whether the circumstances are outside your character's ability to control (a sudden dust storm) or whether your character has the ability to control the circumstances (starting up the mule's engines).

Change of Circumstance: If things change for better or for worse, and if the changes are outside the crew's control (or the control of the character about to roll the dice), then the Game Master simply adjusts the Difficulty of the action. A quick glance at the chart can give the GM an appropriate target number, or he may simply make an arbitrary increase or decrease. Generally, a Difficulty is adjusted in 4-point jumps. Larger numbers make reaction to the change more difficult. Smaller numbers mean that it's easier to handle.

Example: Jayne is engaging in a drinking contest against the local champ, with some hard-earned credits down on the table. Lucky for Jayne, the lady bartender is a bit sweet on him, so she starts weakening Jayne's drinks to give him the edge. The GM lowers the Difficulty of Jayne's Resistance rolls by 4.

Personal Edge: If the factors that change are within a character's control, then the Difficulty stays the same, but the dice that are rolled change. If that sounds nonsensical, think of it more like this: if you've got an advantage, you roll bigger dice. If you're hindered, you roll smaller dice. The changes to the roll are called "steps" (as in a ladder or staircase).

Thusly, if the original die is d10, then a 1-step bonus results in a d12; a 2-step bonus to the d10 becomes d12 + d2. A 1-step penalty results in a d8, while a 2-step penalty means a d6. Step bonuses can go as high as they need, with each increase over a d12 adding a new d2 and starting a new progression. If ever a die is penalized one or more steps below a d2, the die is eliminated from the roll entirely. If that means no dice at all, then the action automatically fails.

Traits and equipment often provide step bonuses or penalties to a given die roll. It's always important to note, however, whether you are modifying the Attribute or Skill. If something affects a Skill that you don't have, the modifier is ignored. Sorry.

Example: Wash is trying out a fancy new flight simulator while killing time at a refilling station. He decides to make life easy, and sets the simulator on Beginner level, giving him a 2-step bonus to his Aerial Craft Operations/Starship roll. Shiny! Wash's performance score is amazing. A bit later, Kaylee goads Simon into giving the flight simulator a try. Simon has no flight training whatsoever. Even at a Beginner level, with no Skill to modify, Simon's results are *jao gao*. He crashes his virtual ship into a virtual asteroid.

PLOT POINTS

The crew in our game are the heroes of a story (even if they don't always act the part). While they don't always succeed (or even survive) every situation, the game wouldn't be much fun if they always failed miserably at everything they tried to do. Plot Points are a way for major characters in the game to add a little drama to the story. Plot Points can be used to improve the odds for important

actions, prevent someone from getting killed or badly injured, or even used to alter the story. Just note, however, that the Game Master gets a few Plot Points for his important Non-Players Characters, too!

Plot Points should be represented by something physical in the game: colored beads, poker chips, or pieces of hard candy. (Watch out for the latter, though, as players might be tempted to eat their reward!) Giving and taking Plot Points is easier and less distracting if you use something that can be handed out. In fact, we recommend that once everyone understands just how Plot Points work, stop talking about them. While they have a big impact on the game, you don't want to hear or say the words "Plot Points" every few minutes. Players and the GM are encouraged to translate the use of Plot Points into imaginative game play.

Example: Wash is doing some tricky flying through significant cloud cover, hoping *Serenity* can evade a small Alliance gunship. His player decides to spend 3 Plot Points on his next action, so he hands 3 poker chips to the GM and then adds a d6 to his next action roll. The extra die saves him from a Botch, so the GM announces that the gunship is still hot on *Serenity's* tail. Wash then decides to pull a rapid deceleration—essentially "putting on the brakes" so the Alliance boat will fly past them. The GM is pleased with Wash's clever maneuver, and quietly hands the player two Plot Points as a reward.

GAINING PLOT POINTS

Every character starts a new campaign with 6 Plot Points, as explained in Chapter Two: *Find a Crew*. Plot Points can be spent or saved as the player sees fit, but only 6 points can be saved between game sessions. The rest become Progression Points and are used to improve Skills, Attributes, and either add or remove Traits. Plot Points are the primary reward in the game, and are handed out for good role playing, good ideas, and succeeding in goals.

COMPLICATIONS IN PLAY

Complications are meant to provide a continual source of "interesting times" for a given character, and as such, they become a regular source of additional Plot Points when they affect the story. Note that when a Complication becomes an issue,

MAL: "I am a lost lamb. What in the hell happened back there?"
WASH: "Start with the part where Jayne gets knocked out by a ninety pound girl. 'Cause I don't think that's ever getting old."

the reward should happen only once per given situation.

If Jayne succumbs to his Greedy nature and attempts to cheat at cards, he is rewarded once with a few Plot Points. He doesn't gain any further points for later slipping an ace up his sleeve. However, if he were to sneak into Simon's room in order to rifle through Simon's clothes for cash to make up for what he lost at cards, that would be worth a few more Plot Points. 'Course, Jayne had better watch his back if the rest of the crew finds out!

Character-Initiated: Many Complications are factors of a character's personality. As such, they kick in when the player role plays his character's less-than-perfect personality traits. When this happens, they should be rewarded accordingly (see the Jayne example above).

GM-Initiated: Traits that deal with a character's personal history often become a factor only when the GM so desires. Even if an entire story revolves around such a Complication (such as a Deadly Enemy plotting the crew's demise), the points are rewarded to the player only the first time the truth (or the bad guy) is revealed.

Example: Mal has a Deadly Enemy—a certain sadistic old man who runs a skyplex. Mal's player does not receive the Plot Points when the old man's anonymous goons first show up and haul him off— but gets several when the old man tortures him!

Situational: Some Complications come into play only when the circumstances are right and, as such, are generally out of the player's control. The players should be rewarded with Plot Points only if the situation places them in direct danger or causes some other difficulty.

Example: Kaylee is guarding the entrance to the airlock while the rest of the crew has gone into a skyplex. When several guards show up and start shooting, her Combat Paralysis kicks in, and she freezes up. Her player gets a few Plot Points, since the cute mechanic is now in *f'n zse*.

Constants: Each Complication is a bit different. Some are constant—such as a character's disability (blindness, missing limb, etc.). The players with a constant Complication should not be rewarded in ordinary situations, but only when the Complication becomes a significant hindrance.

Example: A character with a missing leg does not receive a reward for walking through the cargo bay, but does so when she is running away from a ticking bomb!

One more thing—if the GM has a story that makes life especially un-fun for a particular character (even if the player is enjoying the extra attention!), it might be worth a few Plot Points for that player even if there is no Complication involved. This should be done rarely, and the Plot Points given only in extreme circumstances.

REWARDS

Plot Points are awarded throughout the game, and their allocation is solely at the discretion of the GM. The general rule is that Plot Points should be given out as a reward for good role playing. Here are just a few possible rewards:

• **"That was cool!" (1)**: The player comes up with a great idea, engages in some superior role playing, or just does something so gorram cool it must be acknowledged. Toss him a Plot Point to encourage that sort of thing!

• **Complication in Play (1-3)**: A character's Complication makes life more difficult for her. Plot Points ease the pain.

• **Completed a Challenge (2-4)**: The character or group makes it through a threatening situation or overcomes a significant obstacle. This could be something physically dangerous—such as a fight, defusing a bomb, preventing the ship from crashing. It could also be a mental or social challenge, including completing a difficult negotiation, gaining access to a forbidden location, etc. The more challenging the situation, the more points awarded.

• **Personal Goal (3-5)**: A character achieves an important personal goal in the current story. This could be anything from gaining a piece of information to acting out vengeance on a hated foe. Note these are personal goals specific to a smaller story. If a character achieves a life-long personal goal, such as buying his own Firefly, the rewards should be substantially higher!

• **Crew Goal (4-6)**: This is a reward for each player for succeeding in an important mission. For example, the crew of *Serenity* obtains some illegal salvage and successfully outmaneuvers undercover Alliance marshals, Reavers, and Niska's thugs to get paid. When they do, everyone deserves the Plot Point reward (and hopefully a share in the cash).

Each player can decide how to make use of his hard-earned Plot Points. Some players will want to use most of them in the current session to improve their chances at succeeding in the short-term, while others will hoard them and use them for Progression Points to improve Skills, increase Attributes, buy off Complications, or even purchase new Assets. There's no right or wrong approach. Just remember that only 6 Plot Points can be saved in between game sessions—the rest become Progression Points.

SPENDING PLOT POINTS

The only thing more fun than gaining Plot Points is spending them. Use them to stay alive, pull off some heroic feat of daring-do, or affect the story in a tangible way. Here are the basic uses of Plot Points, though these can be expanded upon by the GM.

IMPROVING ACTIONS

When a character spends Plot Points on an action roll, the player gains an extra die that is added to his dice pool before he rolls. A few Plot Points spent might gain an extra couple of points, while a bunch of points spent could potentially lead to amazing success. There are no guarantees with this, however. Even if you spend 6 Plot Points for an extra d12, there is always a chance you could roll a 1!

Table 5.5: Plot Points and the Bonus Die

Plot Points	Die Type
1	d2
2	d4
3	d6
4	d8
5	d10
6	d12
7	d12 + d2
8	d12 + d4
9	d12 + d6
10	d12 + d8
11	d12 + d10
12	d12 + d12

Plot Points "After the Fact": You can also spend Plot Points to affect an action *after* the dice have been rolled. This is generally much more expensive, but can still make a difference on really important actions. Each Plot Point spent improves the die total by only 1. Note that you are allowed to spend Plot Points both before and after the roll.

Example: Mal is riding horseback through some light scrub with an angry lynch mob hot on his tail. (Why can't things ever just go smooth?) He sees a small ravine up ahead. Mal decides to make the horse jump the ravine. The GM decrees that this is a Hard action, and Mal's player needs an 11 to succeed. Mal's player decides to spend 5 Plot

Points and gain an extra d10 to the action. *Tzao-gao!* Even with the extra die, the total is only 7—failure! Instead of allowing Mal and the horse to plummet into the ravine, Mal's player decides to go ahead and fork over 4 additional Plot Points to achieve bare minimum success. Mal's horse makes it over, sending a cascade of rocks and dirt clods down into the ravine.

Complex Actions: When using Plot Points to gain an extra die on complex actions, the bonus die counts for only one roll during the series. To gain the die multiple times, you have to spend more Plot Points each time.

STAYING ALIVE

There will come times during a game when you'll want your character to *not* be dead. As we've said often enough—the 'Verse is a dangerous place. One bullet might put you over the top as far as Wounds go, and some *hwoon dahn* out there is using auto-fire against you! Whenever you take damage, you have the option of spending Plot Points to reduce it. Essentially, you're doing a quick re-write of the story—making sure you live to the next scene.

Plot Points spent to reduce damage grant you a die roll exactly the same as a bonus die for an action (see Table 5.5). Take the results and subtract it directly from the damage dealt—counting Wounds first, then Stun. And just in case you were wondering, you don't gain Life Points back if your roll ends up higher than the damage dealt on an attack.

You can use Plot Points to deal with damage, but you have to do so as soon as the GM announces it. You can't go back later and decide you would like to reduce damage dealt from a previous injury. Another thing to keep in mind is that you're stuck with the results of the roll. If it comes up as a 1, deal with it and call for a medic.

Example: Shepherd Book is caught in the crossfire when a negotiation between Mal and a potential buyer goes south. Book catches a bullet that does 7 Wounds and 4 Stun—some serious damage! Book's player opts to spend 5 Plot Points, and rolls a d10 to reduce the damage. He lucks out and rolls an 8, completely eliminating the Wounds and reducing the Stun damage to 3. Book is hit but the bullet lodges in his copy of the Bible, stunning him slightly from the impact.

Note that the GM does not announce that Book saved himself by spending 5 Plot Points! The GM provides an exciting account of Book diving head-first into a ditch as the bullets kick up dust all around him.

COVERING YOUR ASSETS

Some Assets require that you spend Plot Points in order to use them to their full effect. If you've got "Friends in High Places", you'll need to spend at least 5 Plot Points to obtain that large loan from one of your buddies. Someone with "Mechanical Empathy" can spend Plot Points to get right to the heart of a problem. Using Plot Points in this way is explained in Chapter One: *Find a Crew*. The GM may adjust the required number of points or even disallow the use of an Asset in a given situation if it doesn't suit the story. Don't fret, though—you don't have to spend Plot Points for actions when you don't gain the benefit of the Asset.

Example: The catalyzer on the port compression coil has completely burned out on *Serenity's* engine, leaving the ship on the drift and life support completely out. Kaylee's player is able to spend a few Plot Points to learn the nature of the problem. Realizing how crucial the situation is, Kaylee's player attempts to spend even more points to figure out a way to fix things. The GM has secretly determined that *Serenity's* mechanical woes are the heart of the adventure, so when Kaylee's player attempts to spend the Plot Points, the GM hands them back to her and says that the ship has nothing more to say.

While players are free to burn Plot Points on actions that might still fail, players do not have to lose them when using Assets that don't apply to the current story.

STORY MANIPULATION

It's no secret that you are playing characters in a story being mostly told by the Game Master. But Plot Points give you the power to change the story line in small ways. This is often done to your character's advantage and should always be done to make life more interesting for your character and the crew. That being said, Plot Points won't let you rewrite the story in the middle, change the nature of an important character, or any other stuff like that. Best let such notions go.

What you can do with Plot Points is stretch the story in a convincing and believable way, leastwise to the GM's satisfaction. It's not hard to believe that a Border world bumpkin might fall in love with a beautiful, registered Companion. A character who hails from Persephone might remember he has a cousin who works at the Eavesdown Docks. A former Independent soldier tracking down a bounty on a fellow Browncoat could easily find out that they were both in the same outfit.

When you want to use Plot Points in this way, make your suggestion and give the GM the number of Plot Points you are willing to spend, based on how far you are stretching the realm of believability. If he's not agreeable to the notion, you'll get your points back. If he likes the idea, but thinks that you didn't spend enough Plot Points to gain the impact you were hoping for, he could determine the Points spent and devise a slightly different version of events. (Perhaps the dockworker is not actually your cousin, but you did go to school with the fellow.)

Table 5.6: Plot Points and Story Impact

Cost	Impact
1-3	**Inconsequential**: "The bartender is a former Independent. I'm sure he won't mind a fellow Browncoat running up a large tab."
4-6	**Minor**: "I completely forgot I'd hid that hundred credit note in my boot!"
7-10	**Significant**: "Rosco! Ain't seen you since the reunion back on Shadow. So you're a Federal Marshall, now. How ya been, old buddy?"
11+	**Major**: "We've been drifting through the black without power for nigh onto two days. Amazing that your ship just happened by this outta the way spot!"

It's important to remember that at no time does the use of Plot Points let you take over the story. The GM gets to play with your idea, and things may not exactly turn out like you plan. The bartender may let you run up a large tab, but when you're unable to settle up, he may decide you're a disgrace to the Independent forces and call in his bouncers. Your cousin may let you hide at his place, but it turns out he owes a local rail baron a ton of platinum and the kneecap-breakers arrive that very night. The folks who pick you up on the drift may decide to shoot you and strip your ship! The GM isn't going to hump your character over (we promise!), but don't expect things to be all roses and sunshine just because you forked over a few Plot Points. That just ain't the way of the 'Verse.

Here are a few ideas about how you can use Plot Points, now that we have the costs out of the way.

- **Attack of Stupidity** – Everyone gets stupid sometimes, makes a really moronic decision. This is that moment.
- **Can't Hire Good Help** – Folk neglecting their duties. ("The guards are drinking and playing dice!")
- **Deception** – Someone has lied about his true identity or background. ("Turns out he's an Alliance undercover officer.")
- **Dissension in the Ranks** – A formerly solid group ain't lookin' so unified. ("I get seven percent and I have to share my bunk with that fellow.")
- **Green-Eyed Monster** – Jealousy is an ugly thing, and someone is lookin' mighty ugly.
- **Good Fortune** – A stroke of good luck, just when it was needed!
- **Hatred** – Or at least strong dislike. Someone is really itching to beat (or shoot!) the tar out of another fellow.
- **It Broke!** – A supposedly reliable object fails to perform. The pistol misfires, the rope snaps, the saddle slips.
- **Love is the Air** – Well, maybe it's just lust. But sparks are definitely flying!
- **Overly Cautious** – Instead of assuming the obvious, she's going to make sure everything's exactly right before she shoots you.
- **Remember Me?** – You knew him from the old days. And after a moment's consideration he may remember you, too. Might be a good thing. Might not.

- **Twinge of Conscience** – Maybe he's not so bad after all. It may take him all of a moment to decide whether to finish you off now or let you crawl away on your belly.
- **Unexpected Consequences** – Something you did before had unforeseen results. ("Those thugs you shot back on Whitefall once attacked my wife. I'll help you however I can.")
- **Unprepared** – An NPC is plum caught off guard. It will take a moment for him to get his act together!
- **What the—?** – Something unexpected happens. The trigger-man sneezes, a snake spooks the horse, or something else upsets the whole shebang.

COMBAT

It's an unfortunate truth that sometimes it takes a gun or a fist to get things done. Even peaceable folk may be forced to defend themselves when conducting business, traveling, or trying to have a quiet drink.

The combat rules—like the rest of the game— are meant to convey fast, cinematic action. It's up to the players and the GM to keep things lively and descriptive, and not make combat just a bunch of numbers and die rolls. While combat does slow down the flow of time (in game terms), fights should be dramatic and quick-paced, whether it's a one-on-one gun duel, or a barroom brawl with twenty combatants.

> **"Can I make a suggestion that doesn't involve violence, or is this the wrong crowd?"**
> —Hoban "Wash" Washburne

The vast majority of times these rules are used in a game is when fists, bullets, and knives are flying. But there are other, non-lethal situations where the combat rules also come in handy. These rules come into play any time the GM needs to "zoom in on" the action and deal with it in short segments, or needs to know who goes first and does best.

TIMING—COMBAT TURNS

When all hell breaks loose, life can get a mite complicated. To prevent combat from becoming a *lun bei jo jei*, the game breaks combat down into turns. Each turn lasts about three seconds of game time, long enough for folks to take one careful action—or multiple actions that are less-than-careful! Initiative is rolled to determine in what order everyone will act. Each character takes his actions in sequence. Pretty simple, huh?

INITIATIVE

When combat first breaks out, the GM determines who acts first—usually the one who initiates the ensuing violence. That person (or group in the case of an ambush situation) gets a "free" turn ahead of everyone else. Otherwise, everyone rolls Initiative for their characters. As explained back in Chapter One: *Find a Crew*, this is an Agility + Alertness roll, though it can be modified by Traits and other factors. This roll determines the turn order—highest goes first. Ties result in simultaneous actions, with opposed Agility rolls made when it's really important to know who's faster. If a character is waiting for something, he can hold his action until later in the turn, though if the turn gets to the end and he still has not acted, he loses the chance to act that turn entirely.

RESOLUTION

Actions are resolved in order. Things are happening fast, so there isn't time for a lot of questions and table talk! If a player asks too many questions or can't make a quick decision (determined by the GM's discretion), then the character spends the combat turn looking around and trying to assess the situation.

ACTIONS

Each turn allows for one action without penalty. This action can be most anything that could be accomplished in the short time frame. You can run across the room, throw a punch, shove another magazine into the pistol, or perform a similar action. But let's say you want to run across the room *and* punch a fellow in the face, or you want to fire off several rounds. You can't perform simultaneous actions at the same level of skill that you use for just performing one action, but you may not have the luxury of time to do this perfect, especially if the guy across the room is holding a gun on your partner!

MULTIPLE ACTIONS

Every action beyond the first taken in a turn brings a cumulative –1 step Skill penalty to all actions in the turn. Two actions bring a –1 step penalty, three actions –2, etc. If a reduction would reduce your Skill die below d2, you lose that action entirely—so don't try it! (Though many actions can be attempted unskilled, trying to do something you're not good at while simultaneously doing something else is ill-advised.) The GM may rule that you're trying too many actions for one turn, and put a limit on how many you can do. In addition, most weapons have a limit on how many rounds can be fired (see Chapter Three: *Money and Gear*).

You can include defense actions in your total if you want for the turn ("I dodge out of the way and shoot the thug in the face!"). You may decide to add defense actions even after your turn is over, but those will count against your total for the next combat turn.

FREE ACTIONS

Not everything you do counts as an action against you. You can take a quick look around the room, speak (or holler) a short phrase, or drop to the ground. All these are considered "free" actions. Note that **reaction rolls** (innate defense rolls or any other roll made in resistance to something that happens during the turn) do not count against your total actions for the turn.

OPTIONAL INITIATIVE

Maybe your group decides that rolling Initiative each and every turn takes too much time or the GM thinks it is slowing the pace of the game. Here are a few alternatives:

Merry-Go-Round: Initiative is determined normally, but everyone goes in the same order each turn until the battle is over. Characters who "sit out" an entire turn trying to get their bearings can re-roll the Initiative roll to establish a new place in the turn order. This has the advantage of speeding things up, but can seem repetitive.

Action as Initiative: Instead of a separate Initiative roll, everyone rolls the first action of the turn. (If the actions do not normally involve a die roll, the player rolls Agility + Alertness.) This roll serves as both Initiative and the result of the first action—with secondary actions resolved normally with separate rolls. This is another way to speed up combat. The main drawback is that the most successful actions always go first, which means that those most likely to fail always go last.

OPTIONAL SECONDARY ACTIONS

Generally, each player resolves all the actions for the turn at once. One alternative is to let all players take their first actions in the turn in order of Initiative, and then go back through the order again for secondary actions. This can sometimes create more "realism" in the order of actions, but has the potential to slow things down.

MOVING ABOUT

Most folk have a base movement speed of 15 feet per turn. This number represents a leisurely walk and doesn't count as an action during a turn. Anyone can pick up the pace and go twice his base speed (hustle), or he can break into a run. Use the following table for determining movement and the number of actions taken. Note that a run uses an Attribute + Skill roll to calculate speed for the turn. The GM determines which Attribute to roll based on the situation. A flat run without any obstacles in the way usually relies on the better of either an Agility or Strength roll, while any maneuvering requires the use of Agility.

There is one exception to the multiple action rule listed above: if a character's only action in a turn is movement, then there is no penalty to the Skill roll. If the character attempts other actions in addition to movement in a turn, the character receives the normal penalty to all actions. (A character who is running does not take a penalty to his Athletics/Running Skill die if movement is the only action for the turn. A character who is running and attacking in the same turn is penalized for taking three actions, incurring the usual –2 step penalty to all Skill dice.)

Table 5.7: Movement

Pace	Actions	Speed
Walk	0	Base (normally 15 ft.)
Hustle	1	Base x 2 (normally 30 ft.)
Run	2	(Base x 2) + (Attribute + Athletics/Running)

Example: Hwa Ling takes one look at the explosive and realizes she only has moments to run for her life. She breaks into a full run, so the GM asks for an Agility + Athletics/Running roll. Since Hwa Ling does not have the Running specialty, she must rely on the Athletics general Skill. A quick glance at the character sheet reminds the player that Hwa Ling's base speed multiplied by 2 is 30 ft. Her player rolls a d10 + d6 and gets a total of 11. Hwa Ling makes it only 41 feet before the explosive charge detonates. (Perhaps she should have spent a few Plot Points!)

DEFEND YOURSELF

No one enjoys being stabbed, shot, or kicked in the groin (especially the latter!). While standing there taking the beating may prove you're tough, most folk would just as soon dodge, block, or dive behind some cover. A wise man once said: "You can't get paid when you're dead." And if you can't avoid the fight, you can at least try to avoid the bullet.

You can incorporate defensive actions into your regular actions during the turn. The defense kicks in against the *next* attack to which it could apply. (So if you decide to block as a defensive action, the block won't count against the shot fired at you, but will count against the next punch or kick.) Good news is you can still take a defensive action even after your normal turn is over, but any active defensive actions count against your number of actions for the following turn.

Example: Zoe finds herself in the middle of yet another barroom brawl. (Funny how that always happens when she's with the Captain in an Alliance bar on Unification Day!) At the beginning of the turn, Zoe announces that she'll punch a drunk in the face and block his first attack. Her attack roll is a good one, and she gives the Alliance-loving thug a one-way ticket to a dentist's chair. On the thug's Initiative, he throws a punch her way, and her block action (announced earlier) is successful.

Bad news, though—two of the guy's buddies show up later in the same combat turn, swinging bar stools. Zoe decides to dodge both of those attacks, but since her turn is over, she's already used up two actions for the next turn, which means she's at a big disadvantage and things may start going south—fast. A strategic withdrawal is advised.

Innate Defense: Even if you're too busy bringing on the hurt to worry about actual defensive maneuvers, moving around is still better than standing flat on your feet, which makes you an Easy target (Difficulty 3) at close range. If you are aware of your attacker (even if you are otherwise occupied), you can make an unskilled Agility roll (meaning the die value counts only once) as your defense number. If you roll high enough, the *lurn shwei jah jwohn* might miss you. Using Plot Points never hurts, either. You cannot Botch on an Innate Defense roll. (Innate Defense counts as 0 actions.)

Block: Fancy folk call the action "parry"—meaning that you intercept a hand-to-hand attack. Blocking a punch with your arm, or deflecting an enemy's blade with your own—it's all handled the same. Blocking an action requires an Agility + the appropriate Skill roll, which opposes your foe's attack roll. If your roll is higher, you succeed in blocking. If your roll is equal to or lower—ouch.

Note that if you block a weapon attack while you are unarmed, your opponent automatically inflicts the weapon's listed damage on you. Probably not as bad as getting stabbed in the gut, but you're still gonna bleed.

Don't try to block firearms or energy weapons—that's the same as just standing still. Dodge those instead. (Blocking counts as 1 action.)

Dodge: The best defense against an attack is not being there in the first place! Declare a Dodge before the attack roll is made, and use an Agility + Athletics/Dodge roll, which becomes the Difficulty number to hit you. As always, higher is better. (Dodging counts as 1 action.)

All-Out Defense: When you've decided that you really, really want to live, and running isn't an option, an all-out defense might be the way to survive. If your only actions for the turn are defensive, you gain a +2 step Skill bonus to the rolls (though multiple action penalties still apply). It may even keep you alive! Note that if you have any actions carrying over from a previous turn (such as defensive maneuvers) you cannot declare All-Out Defense.

Cover: There's a reason why people start diving under tables when guns are drawn. Cover makes you harder to hit. The numbers modify whatever difficulty normally applies. For instance, if you're standing still behind medium cover, the difficulty to shoot you at close range jumps from 3 all the way to 11. (See Table 6.7.)

Table 5.8: Cover

Cover	Difficulty	Description (Example)
Light Cover	+4	Up to half the target is concealed. (A man standing behind a small overturned table that conceals the lower part of his body; someone lying down.)
Medium Cover	+8	More than half the target is concealed. (A woman is hiding behind her horse.)
Heavy Cover	+12	Most of the target is concealed. (A man is peeking out from around a corner.)
Total Cover	+16	Only a tiny portion of the target is visible. (A man is looking out through the keyhole of a door.)

Range: If you can't find cover when the bullets are about to start flying, you might want to be in the next county. Unlike cover, which affects the difficulty number, range modifies the Skill die of the attacker for ranged weapons only. (You don't get a point-blank modifier for punching someone in the face!) See Chapter Three: *Money and Gear* for the ranges involved for specific weapons.

Table 5.9: Range	
Range	Skill Modifier
Point-Blank (within 10 feet)	+1 Skill step
Short (1 increment)	–
Medium (2 increments)	–2 Skill step
Long (3 increments)	–4 Skill step

Table 5.10: Called Shots		
Type	Skill Modifier	Effect
Limb	–1 step	+2 step modifier to damage dice. Endurance test to avoid incapacitation.
Vital Area (head, groin)	–2 step	+4 step modifier to damage dice. Endurance test to avoid stun.
Miniscule (heart, kneecap)	–3 step	+6 step modifier to damage dice for critical area. Endurance test to avoid special injury.

Protective Gear: Some folk feel it's prudent to wear protective gear—anything from bullet-proof vests to full body armor, though folk decked out head to toe in such are likely to draw the wrong kind of attention. Armor doesn't make you harder to hit. In fact, if it slows your movement, you might make an easier target. Armor does block damage, based on its Armor Rating. As an example, an Armor Rating of 4W protects against the first 4 points of Wound damage on a given attack. Note that called shots to unarmored parts of your body or an attack that gains Extraordinary Success will penetrate or get past your armor protection. A protective vest isn't much help if you're shot in the head. See Chapter 3: *Money and Gear* for more details.

INFLICTING VIOLENCE

This is the part where you drill an enemy with holes, knock the teeth out of his mouth, or some similar enjoyment. A basic attack action is an Attribute + Skill roll like any other. If your roll is equal to or greater than the Difficulty needed to hit, you inflict damage. Otherwise you miss. Things change just a bit if you try something tricky.

Aim: You can aim a shot from a ranged weapon for up to three turns. As long as no other actions are taken (including movement of any kind), you gain a +1 Skill step bonus per turn aimed.

All-Out Attack: When all you care about is seeing the other fellow dead, with no regard to your own safety, you have a better chance to hit—but so do all your enemies! When you choose this option, you can make only attack actions in the turn (which means no defense or carry-over actions from previous turns), and you may not take defensive actions later in the turn. This provides a +2 Skill step modifier on your attack actions for the turn.

Called Shot: Sometimes you want to aim for the head, kick to the groin, or blow off a kneecap. Any time you are going for a specific location on a larger target, you use a called shot (unless you're trying to disarm; keep readin' for more info on that). A called shot affects your Skill roll, but can also yield gratifying results. The GM may decide that Extraordinary Success on such attacks has results that go beyond what is listed below.

• **Limb**: Damage increased by +2 die steps, and the victim must succeed at an Average Endurance roll. If the roll fails, a Stun or Basic damage weapon makes the limb immobile for d6 turns; a Wound weapon makes it immobile until repaired through surgery.

• **Vital Area**: Your damage die gains a +4 step modifier. The victim must succeed at an Average Endurance roll. Failure means the target is knocked out and cannot take any actions for d6 turns.

• **Miniscule Target**: If you are aiming for a critical area (shooting for the heart or in the eye), you gain a +6 step modifier to the damage die and the victim must succeed at an Average Endurance roll or fall dead instantly. If you've aimed for a kneecap or elbow, damage is normal, and the Endurance roll determines if the limb is immobilized until major surgery is performed; pain incapacitates the victim for d6 turns. If you succeed at a precise shot such as this, you can deliberately forego any or all of the damage bonus (if, say, you are a Shepherd willing to shoot kneecaps, but don't want to kill anyone).

Disarm: You reckon that the gun (or whatever weapon) is better off on the ground than in your enemy's hand. You make a normal attack at –2 Skill steps if you're fighting melee and –4 if you're using a ranged weapon. If your attack succeeds, the target must make a Hard Agility + Willpower roll or he drops the weapon.

Feint: You want to make a false move that tricks your opponent into expecting the attack is coming from another direction. This works only in hand-to-hand combat. Close observation of your opponent can really come in handy, and so the GM determines your roll based on the nature of your feint (often an Alertness + the hand-to-hand Skill you're using). Your opponent opposes with either an Alertness or Intelligence + Perception/Intuition roll. If your roll is higher, your target may use only Innate Defense against your next attack.

Grapple: (There can be a salacious connotation to the word "grapple" in the 'Verse, but here we're talking about combat—not sex!) Say you feel the sudden urge to snap that sadistic old man's neck.

Or maybe you want to subdue your crazy sister to keep her from smashing up the infirmary. First you have to get hold of the person, which is done with an Agility + Unarmed Combat/Specialty (several specialties work just fine—including brawling, certain martial arts styles, and wrestling).

Once you have a hold, your opponent must succeed at an Agility + Strength action against you in order to break free. (Good news—holding on does not count as an action.) Each turn you have a hold, your foe is an Easy target for unarmed attack actions—or you can choke him (see "Suffocation" in the *Damage* section). You can also use the same type of attack to push a foe (handy if he is standing at the edge of a ravine) or knock someone down. The target is Prone (more later on) until he gets back on his feet.

Sneak Attack: A target who isn't aware of your presence is usually an Easy target—unless he's moving quickly and erratically enough to warrant an Innate Defense roll.

Thrown Weapon: Some weapons are made for hurling (darts, knives, etc.). Some are not (pistols). Use this rule when you throw a weapon that wasn't designed for the purpose. The GM determines if this is feasible, and what your Skill step penalty (–1 through –4) is based on the distance of the enemy from you and the unwieldiness of your chosen weapon. This can come in handy if you find yourself in some *chwen* sword fight and want to give your foe a surprise!

SPECIAL SITUATIONS

As if things weren't chaotic enough during a fight, unusual factors may come into play that will make your life a lot more complicated.

AUTOMATIC WEAPONS

When one bullet just isn't enough, automatic weapons come in mighty handy. Most have three settings, which act in the following ways:

• **Single-shot**: The weapon fires one bullet per attack and is handled with a standard attack.

• **Burst**: The weapon fires a short burst of three rounds. A burst counts as one attack action and allows you to make three attack rolls against the target, though with a –2 step Skill penalty, since firing a burst is less accurate.

• **Autofire**: This is where you target a general area (about 5 to 10 feet wide) and spray it full of lead. You make one Easy attack action to make sure you targeted the area correctly. If your attack succeeds, all potential targets must make defense rolls (just as they would against normal attacks) against an Average difficulty. Those unaware and standing still are Easy targets, which mean they are automatically hit. Anyone who fails his roll is hit as if struck by the original attack roll against his defense. Plot Points can be used only to add a bonus die to an attack against one target.

Example: Jayne switches his submachine gun to autofire and sprays the 10-foot area where three security guards, Harry, Joe, and Burly, stand. Jayne's player rolls a 13 on the attack roll, far more than the 3 he needed to "paint" the area. The GM rolls defense for the trio. Harry dives for cover, and his Agility + Athletics/Dodge yields him a 15—saving his *pee goo* for the moment. Joe is an aware, moving target, and gets Innate Defense. His Agility-only roll yields a 5—meaning he's hit with the original 13 attack! Burly's attention was elsewhere, and he's standing still and an unaware target. He's hit and the poor bastard gets only a 3 (the Easy difficulty) as a defense.

COVERING

You might want to keep your eyes (and weapon) trained on a spot to attack the first misfortunate to walk into your sights. Doing this essentially allows you to delay your action during the turn. (You might lose the chance to act at all if the area you are covering remains empty during the course of the turn!) As long as you maintain the covering action, it will carry over to the next turn, allowing you to take attack actions the moment an enemy appears (allowing you to act out of the normal Initiative sequence).

THREATENING

Sometimes you've got someone dead to rights—be it a gun trained on his head or holding a knife at his throat. If the target you are threatening decides to take any sort of action, you have the option to take a free attack action outside the normal Initiative order at +2 step Skill bonus. You'll get to act normally on your turn in Initiative order. The free action does not count against your total number of actions for the turn.

BREAKING STUFF

Plenty of times you'll want to kick down the door, break out of a pair of handcuffs, or shoot through the rope to stop the hanging. Inanimate objects that are not moving have standard difficulties to hit based on their size and range. Moving targets (such as the tires of a sandbuggy) have a defense based on the operator's Skill or otherwise determined by the GM. Objects are immune to Stun damage and have protection identical to an Armor Rating in order to damage them at all, along with "Life Points" in order to break them. A few examples:

- **Handcuffs**: Armor 6; Life Points 2
- **Reinforced Door**: Armor 10; Life Points 8
- **Rope**: Armor 2; Life Points 2
- **Standard Door**: Armor 4; Life Points 6

Note this is for damaging such items. Dealing with them in other ways incurs standard difficulties (picking locks, untying a knot, etc.).

EXPLOSIONS

Jayne once said, "Boy, sure would be nice if we had some grenades, don'tchya think?" Some things go boom and when they do, it's best not to be standin' close by. An explosion has damage listed as multiple dice. (The first number lists the number of dice to be rolled.) Anyone within the first distance increment takes the full brunt of the explosion, while each increment reduces the damage by one die until there are no dice left. A thrown explosive requires an Average attack action to hit the correct area, otherwise it lands somewhere unintended (determined by the GM). If circumstances give a step bonus or penalty to damage, that increases or decreases the die type, not the number of dice rolled. Cover might reduce damage, as determined by the GM.

Example: Jayne isn't finished with those security guards, so he lobs a frag grenade at them. An Agility + Ranged Weapons/Grenades roll yields an 8. Not great, but good enough! The grenade does 5d6 Wound damage at a distance increment of 5 feet. Poor Harry is standing right over the pineapple. The GM rolls 5d6 to inflict 18 Wounds. Joe is about 18 feet from the center of the blast, and the GM rolls a 2d6 for 2 Wounds. Burly was over 25 feet away, so he isn't damaged by the grenade at all.

FIRING INTO A CROWD

Ranged weapons fired at a target engaged in hand-to-hand combat or fired into a crowd can be especially dangerous. You take a –2-step Skill penalty on the attack roll, and if you botch, you'll have to make a separate attack roll against an unintentional target (determined by the situation and the GM). This makes it inadvisable to try to shoot the fellow who is trading punches with one of your crew (unless you know you are a damn good shot!).

UNARMED COMBAT

Unarmed attacks are resolved normally, but inflict Stun damage only. In other words, instead of calculating basic damage, subtract it from the target's Life Points as Stun damage. The "Mean Left Hook" Trait is for those scary people who might easily kill someone with their bare hands. If you're brawling and reach for a weapon within easy reach, however, you'll need to read on.

IMPROVISED WEAPONS

Weapons of opportunity can be beautiful things, especially when a bar fight breaks out, and you didn't think to strap on your iron this morning. Brawling allows you to use appropriate improvised weapons (broken beer bottles, pool sticks, bar stools) just as you would use a weapon in which you are skilled. For example, you want to use a broken beer bottle as you would use a knife. You apply your Skill in the appropriate similar weapon, but also apply a penalty of –1 to –4 Skill steps, depending on the size and heft of the weapon as decided by the GM. (A broken-off chair leg is easier to wield than a step ladder.) The GM also determines damage, usually basing that on the weapon the object most resembles (a knife for a broken bottle, club for a pool stick, etc.).

OBSCURED VISION

Can't shoot what you can't see, and sometimes the lights go out. Such situations cause the Difficulty to shoot up, making easy pickings tricky targets.

- **Dim Light, Thin Smoke, or Fog**: Add +4 to the Difficulty of hitting any target more than 10 feet away. (An Easy target 20 feet away would now require a 7 or better to hit.)
- **Dark, Thick Smoke, or Fog**: Add +8 to the Difficulty of hitting any target more than 10 feet away. (An Easy target 20 feet away would now require an 11 or better to hit.)
- **Pitch Black or Blinded**: When you can't see anything, any type of ranged attack has only a small chance of hitting a target, and that's assuming you have a rough idea of its location. Any potential target (intentional or not) must make a normal or innate defense roll against an Easy Difficulty. Failure means they are hit, with the lowest roll getting the hit if there is more than one failure. If someone is hit, make a new attack roll against the target's original defense roll to determine damage. Note that characters with the Blind trait don't suffer this penalty, but have their own penalties.

PRONE

You got knocked on your ass. Getting up is an action. Attacking while you're down incurs a –2-step Attribute penalty. If you are lying flat, you have the benefits of light cover (see "Cover", Table 6.7). Attacking or not, you're a non-moving target.

UNSTABLE TERRAIN

Whether you're in an earthquake or a ship maneuvering in atmo (when the grav drive starts working against actual gravity, it tends to stir up the lunch), there's a whole lot of shaking going on. All actions taken on such unstable terrain suffer a –2-step penalty to all Attributes. When there is a sudden lurch, characters must succeed at an Average Agility + Alertness roll to avoid being knocked Prone.

ZERO-GRAVITY

Movement and certain actions are more difficult in zero-G conditions. (You might be "out for a walk" in a space suit or the grav drive could be fried on-board ship.) Before you take an action during the turn, you must succeed at an Average roll using the Survival/Zero-G Skill (or other Skill reflecting experience in such an environment). If you fail, you suffer a –2-step penalty for all actions during the turn. The GM determines the Attribute for the roll based on the situation and your actions during the turn. Moving to a specific spot would be Agility-based, for example, while shooting a free-floating target would be Alertness-based.

A WORLD OF HURT

Even sheltered rich folk fall down and skin their knees every now and again. Sooner or later, you're gonna wind up hurt. Each character has Life Points—a number based on Vitality, Willpower, and certain traits (explained in Chapter One: *Find a Crew* and Chapter Two: *Traits and Skills*). You can take two different kinds of damage—Stun and Wounds. When your total damage (both Stun and Wounds) equals your Life Points, you're probably out like a light. When you've taken all your Life Points in Wounds, you're most likely about to be dead.

Stun: Fortunately, some damage is just light trauma: exhaustion, bruised muscles, scratches, abrasions, shallow cuts. These are not serious and heal quickly with rest.

Wounds: This trauma is more worrisome: broken bones, punctured organs, deep lacerations, significant burns. Such injuries cause considerable pain, which means that at a certain point you're not going to function as well (see "Wound Penalties" later on). While time heals all wounds, these Wounds will require medical attention for any hope of a speedy recovery.

TAKING DAMAGE

Maybe a lug nut falls off your *lao deow ya* ship and hits you in the head, or you eat some of Jayne's cooking. Other times, a fellow gets himself bloodied as a result of an attack. When that happens, here's what you do:

1. DETERMINE BASIC DAMAGE

The better the shot, the deader the target. The higher your attack roll, the more damage you inflict. (Just remember this works against you when it's the other guy's turn!) Simple damage is determined by this formula:

Attack – Defense = Basic Damage
Divide between Stun and Wounds (favor Stun)

Subtract the defense (either a roll or a flat Difficulty number) from the attack, and you get your basic damage. Now split those evenly into Stun and Wounds, favoring Stun if you end up with an odd number. If the attack roll was much higher than the defense, that means inflicting serious pain. But we're not quite done yet…

2. DETERMINE WEAPON DAMAGE

A successful attack—even one that only equals the defense—makes a damage roll based on the weapon. Each weapon lists damage as Stun, Wound, or Basic (which is split between the two damage types, exactly as above). Once that damage is rolled and recorded, the attack has been fully resolved.

Note that if Plot Points are being used to reduce the damage done by an attack, their use is taken into account *after* both basic and weapon damage are figured. Damage reduction roll reduces all Wounds first, then Stun if there are any points left over.

3. FALLOUT

If the injury is minor, you can slap a bandage on it. But if things are more serious, Bad Stuff can happen.

Passing Out: If your total damage from both Stun and Wounds equals your Life Points, you must make an Average Endurance (Vitality + Willpower) roll or fall unconscious. For every turn thereafter (unless you somehow recover enough damage to put you back under your Life Points total), you must make the check again with a cumulative +4 to the Difficulty.

Example: Desperate to protect his sister, Simon attacks an Alliance Fed using his fists. The two exchange blows for a few turns, but the Fed has the upper hand. One final punch puts Simon's total damage equal to his total Life Points. Simon's player makes a Vitality + Willpower roll against a difficulty of 7 and scores a 9—success! He is able to function for one more turn. Simon manages to stagger away from the fight as his vision starts to blur. The next turn his roll must be an 11 or higher, otherwise the good doctor is down for the count.

Shock Points: When a character receives Stun damage after falling unconscious (or beyond his capacity if he has suffered no Wounds), the additional Stun is recorded as Shock Points. An unattended character with Shock Points is unconscious for one hour. After that, he may make an Average Endurance check once per hour to reduce the Shock Points by 1 each. Medical treatment can speed up or circumvent this process. With proper medication, 1 Shock Point is Easy to eliminate with a cumulative +4 to the Difficulty for each additional Shock Point. A botch may damage the patient even further! Once Shock Points have been reduced to zero, the character recovers Stun normally. If accumulated Shock Points equal or exceed the character's Life Points, he is in a coma and requires serious medical attention to recover.

Example: The Alliance Fed follows Simon and delivers one final haymaker. Poor Simon is knocked unconscious and gains 3 Shock Points to boot. With no one around to help, Simon is left lying on the floor. After an hour (in game time), Simon's player makes an Endurance roll and fails—leaving his Shock Point total unaffected. Fortunately he succeeds on the next three rolls (thanks to some Plot Points!). He'll wake up after four hours.

Wound Penalty: Blood is pouring out of your mouth and a Reaver harpoon is sticking through your leg. Chances are you're not performing at your best. When your Wounds are equal to or greater than half your Life Points, you are seriously wounded and suffer a –2-step penalty to all Attributes. For easy reference, here are the Wound levels that cause penalty.

Table 5.11: Wound Penalties

Total Life Points	Seriously Wounded (–2 Penalty)
8	4
10	5
12	6
14	7
16	8
18	9
20	10
22	11
24	12

Dying: When your Wound damage equals or exceeds your total Life Points, you must make an Endurance check every minute or be dead. The good news is that the check starts off Easy, but you must repeat the check for every minute of game time with a cumulative +4 to the Difficulty—so first aid is definitely advised. If your total Wounds ever equal a number that is double your total Life Points, you are dead in a most brutal fashion with no chance of salvation (at least the worldly variety). Time to work on that new character.

OTHER WAYS TO GET MANGLED

Bad enough that you might get beaten up, filled with lead, or knifed in the back. There are other, even nastier ways to get hurt. Try hard to avoid them!

Burns: Make a special note of burn damage taken as Wounds. Except with the use of expensive and sophisticated medical equipment, burn damage heals at half the normal rate and can leave you with disfiguring scars.

The Black: If you get the urge to take a swim out in space without benefit of a suit, you might want to reconsider unless you're curious to see how fast your blood can boil out of your ears. Exposure to the vacuum of the 'Verse is pretty much instant death. If a player really wants to know how much damage he'll take, the GM is encouraged to pick up all the dice at the table, roll 'em, and count the number as Wounds—an excellent reason not to turn on your crew and tempt your captain into tossing you out an airlock.

Drugs & Poisons: Alcohol, drugs, and poison are fought with a Resistance (double Vitality) roll, with difficulty and effects adjudicated by the GM. This could lead to a mild buzz, certain death, or you might start seeing little lights in front of your eyes before you collapse onto the cockpit floor in a puddle of your own drool.

Environmental Hazards: Extreme (yet still Earth-Normal) conditions of heat and cold, along with other hostile environments (high altitude or low oxygen, for example) result in 1 Stun damage every hour if the character does not have adequate protection. A character with the Survival Skill might discover a way around the problem through resourcefulness and a good roll. Conditions that are worse might increase the damage or decrease the time between rolls.

Falling: A fall from 10 feet or less is an Easy Agility + Athletics/Gymnastics (or other Skill approved by the GM) test to avoid damage. There is a cumulative +4 difficulty for each additional 10 feet. The total Difficulty becomes an "attack" and the character rolls a defense, with damage accrued just as in combat.

Example: Shepherd Book is pushed from the catwalk in *Serenity*'s cargo bay and falls 30 feet. The "attack" of the fall is 11. Book rolls Agility + Athletics for a total of 8. He takes 2 Stun and 1 Wound as damage from the fall.

Illness: When you're exposed to an illness, you must make a Resistance roll to see if your immune system fights it off. (The Difficulty varies based on the nature of the illness.) A simple cold might mean you are at a –1 step Attribute penalty for a few days, while major diseases could have dangerous or lethal consequences. Some serious illnesses can be cured or at least "stalled" by specialized medication.

Radiation: The most common form of radiation exposure in the 'Verse come from a badly-maintained (or deliberately altered) spaceship engine. Exposure to radiation requires a Resistance check for every time increment starting at Easy, by increasing by a cumulative +4 Difficulty for each roll. Failed rolls during exposure result in d2 Stun damage. After no further Stun can be taken, the character suffers both Wound and Shock damage. Proper precautions (inoculations, protective gear) can prevent any chance of damage.

Suffocation: Breathing is good. Holding your breath starts out Easy, made every other turn with a Resistance roll, with a cumulative +4 difficulty each roll. Once you fail, you must resume breathing or suffer d2 Stun every other turn. When you run out of Stun, additional damage is taken as both Shock Points and Wounds, meaning you'll be out for a long while at the very least—or dead at the very most.

PATCHING UP

Contemporary medicine in the 'Verse is capable of truly amazing things. Organs can be transplanted without fear of rejection, severed limbs can be fully re-attached and will eventually be good as new. Dead patients can sometimes be resuscitated. Of course, the best care anywhere is in a Core world hospital— but like as not you'll be on some frontier moon with only a portable medical kit.

NATURAL HEALING

Not every hurt needs a doctor around to mend. And sometimes your enemies don't have enough gorram courtesy to wait until a doc shows up before they start shooting at you. In such an instance, you're on your own, forced to trust to the miraculous healing powers of the human body.

STUN DAMAGE

Exhaustion, bumps and bruises can usually be overcome after just a little bit of rest. There are two ways to deal with Stun. (If you've accumulated Shock points, read up on them above to find out how you'll recover.)

• **Second Wind**: Once per day, a character can "shake off" some Stun damage, gathering inner reserves and strength to keep flyin' (or walking, or whatever). Roll either your Vitality or Willpower die (you pick!) to gain back that many Stun.

• **Rest**: Periods of high activity (anything where you're moving around a lot) don't allow a fellow to heal any Stun damage at all. Periods of low activity (still awake, but not doing much) let a character heal 1 point for every 2 hours. Resting (sleep is best, but just laying in bed is fine) allow for healing 1 point per hour.

WOUND DAMAGE

More serious damage takes a mite longer to recover. Sure you don't want that doctor? First off, forget any sort of recovery if you don't get sufficient rest and nourishment. After one full day, you must succeed at a Endurance test to be "on the mend" and starting to heal. The worse hurt you are, the harder it is to recover. Recovery is automatic for the first couple of Wounds (1-2), but after that, the check becomes Easy (for 3-4 Wounds); difficulty increases by 4 for every two additional Wounds suffered. Once a character is on the mend, 1 Wound is healed for every two days of rest. Note that extreme damage is very difficult to recover without medical aid (see Table 5.12).

Getting Worse: If you botch on a recovery roll for Wound damage, you're getting worse—not better. You will take d2 points of additional Wound damage every two days from infection, internal bleeding, or some other complication. Each period you suffer more damage you may make another Endurance check (based on your current number of Wounds) to halt the process. It will take another two days and another successful check to start recovering Wounds. Medical intervention can really help in this case!

MIRACLES OF MODERN MEDICINE

Information on specialized devices and wonder drugs can be found in Chapter Three: *Money and Gear*, while the Skills required to use them are covered in Chapter Two: *Traits and Skills*. The following are more general uses of medicine, with the note that Difficulties can vary based on those dang circumstances.

Table 5.12: Healing Difficulty & Wounds

Wounds	Healing Difficulty	Surgical Difficulty
1-2	No check required	–
3-4	3	15
5-6	7	35
7-8	11	55
9-10	15	75
11-12	19	95
13-14	23	115
15-16	27	135
17-18	31	155
19-20	35	175
21-22	39	195
23-24	43	215

First Aid: If someone is in immediate danger of dying, either suffering additional Wounds or from a vicious attack (see "Extraordinary Success"), you can attempt to stabilize the character and prevent the worst (that final ride into the sunset). This takes a few minutes and a Hard Alertness + Medical Expertise/Appropriate Specialty. The use of your Skill is modified by the situation.

Table 5.13: First Aid

First Aid Conditions	Skill Step Modifier
Improvised supplies, heavy distractions	-2
Limited supplies, light distractions	-1
Standard supplies, no distractions	±0
Superior supplies, ambulance conditions	+1
Cutting-edge supplies, hospital conditions	+2

Reviving the Dead: When someone has expired there is a chance to revive them. One step beyond first aid, this requires the same check and modifiers as a first aid attempt, but the check is Formidable and goes up by a cumulative +4 Difficulty for each minute the victim has been clinically dead. If the check is successful, the character is allowed another Endurance check (at the same Difficulty as his last) to "come back to life." Further first aid is required to stabilize the patient and prevent death from happening all over again!

Waking the Unconscious: Someone knocked out can sometimes be revived with a light slap, cold water, a loud shout, or other unsophisticated method. This allows for an Average Endurance check by the character to regain consciousness. The recently-awakened will be groggy and unable to engage in any but the mildest activities, but can otherwise recover damage normally. The use of stimulants can give temporary Stun back to the patient (anywhere from d2 to d12), though after the stimulants wear off (usually within a few hours) the points immediately disappear—potentially leading to unconsciousness. As a side note, sedatives work exactly the opposite way, causing a given amount of temporary Stun damage.

Painkillers: Sometimes you don't have a bullet to bite on (or you'd rather not). In this case, the right drug can ease you something wonderful. The proper medication can negate the Attribute penalty for a seriously wounded character (see above). An Easy Intelligence + Medical Expertise/Specialty check provides the proper dosage. (An overdose can have nasty side-effects, while an under dose might not help at all.)

Surgery: When you're really tore up from the latest scrape, you need someone who can cut you open, dig out a bullet, or re-attach your leg. This sort of treatment (even the most minor stuff) is considered "surgery", and is a complex action. The Difficulty depends on the level of Wounds (see Table 5.12) with a time increment of usually 10 or 30 minutes. If surgery is successful, the patient is automatically considered "on the mend" and will heal at the normal rate—though severe injuries might require rehabilitation, advanced equipment, expensive drugs, or something else to get the person back in fighting form. (A person who has had his leg sewn back on won't be jogging for a while!)

Botching twice in a surgery is *jwohn gao bu yi*, causing d2 additional Wounds to the patient and the **whole process must** be started anew.

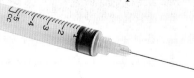

CHAPTER 6

OUT IN THE BLACK

THE DEVIL'S SHOES

Captain **Maxx**, of the ship *Aces and Eights*, lay on his belly in the crew quarters, cussing. He was not doing this by choice.

He was doing this because Devil, his medic, owned at least 4,568 pairs of shoes–give or take a pair–and she had a bad habit of kicking them off whenever she sat down and then never bothering to pick them up . Maxx was convinced that he'd tripped over at least 2,568 of Devil's shoes since she'd come on board his ship.

Which is just what had happened now.

Captain Maxx had served on board an Alliance cruiser until the loss of an arm meant the loss of his military career. He was used to barreling through a ship, never watching where he was going, because no one in the gorram Alliance military ever carelessly left his or her shoes (or anything else, for that matter) lying around on the deck.

Maxx glanced over his shoulder. Sure enough, there was a red shoe at his feet. He cussed some more, and was about to push himself up off the deck, when he stopped, stared, focused, blinked, focused again, and choked on his swear words.

In front of him was a bomb.

At least, he was 99.9% sure it was a bomb. He wasn't an expert, but he'd seen more than a few in his lifetime. The bomb was attached to one of the girders on the bulkhead. The bomb was at floor level and stuck to the shadowy side of the girder. He would have never noticed it if he hadn't been flat on his belly on the deck.

"Captain!" Devil's voice rang out. By the sound, she heading this way. "Have you seen one of my red wedgies—Oh! Never mind. There it is by your foot. Cap'n, what are you doin' on the floor—"

"Don't move!" Maxx growled.

Devil froze. She knew by the tone of his voice that something was up.

"What is it, Cap'n?" she asked in a whisper.

"I think there's a bomb in here," Maxx said as calmly as he could manage. "Go over to the comm and tell Time Bomb to get his ass up here."

"I can't, sir. You told me not to move," said Devil, still frozen.

Maxx ground his teeth. "I also told you to pick up your gorram shoes and you didn't do that—"

"Going to the comm, Cap'n," said Devil and, slipping out of her shoes, she padded slowly and cautiously over to the comm. "Time Bomb!" she whispered into the comm.

Maxx rolled his eyes. "You can talk normally!"

But he noted that he himself had not yet moved from his prone position on the deck. Thinking things over, he decided that if motion made the bomb go off, his tripping over the shoe and falling flat on his stomach with a resounding crash—he'd taken out a metal stool on his way down—would have sent him and his crew to their eternal reward by now. Slowly and cautiously, he eased himself up off the deck and went over to the bomb to take a closer look.

"Yup," said Time Bomb. Leaning over, he adjusted his wire-rim specs, and nodded. "She's a bomb." He sounded pleased. "Now, Captain, if you would step aside so that I can take a closer look—

"Now, then, little darling," he added softly, speaking to the bomb. "What are you, sweetheart? What sets you off, you pretty thing?"

"Jeez, you'd think he was in love," Devil grumbled.

"Devil!" Maxx whipped around. "What are you still doing here? Get the hell off this ship! You and Rawhide both—"

"If you say so, Captain," Devil answered with surprising meekness. She generally argued with him when he ordered her to do something. This time, she was out the door before he'd finished his sentence.

"And Devil—" he bellowed.

"Sir?" She sounded a long way off.

"Contact Jack and Hwa Ling and tell them that wherever they are, they should stay put—"

"Captain," came Rawhide's voice over the comm. He was on the bridge, and it occurred to Jack that he hadn't yet told his pilot yet what was going on. "I just heard from Jack and Hwa Ling. There's been some sort of trouble—"

CHAPTER 6

"Gorramit! Are they all right?" Maxx demanded.

"They're all right." Rawhide sounded grim. "But some other folk ain't. Apparently our friends ran into some Tong assassins. Hwa Li and Jack had to fight their way out. They're racing back, with the bad guys in pursuit. Jack wants to be able to take off the moment they're safely on board."

"That may be a problem," said Maxx grimly. "We've discovered a bomb down in the crew quarters."

"Damn," said Rawhide. Maxx waited for more, but that was it, apparently. Rawhide was never much for unnecessary talk.

"Captain, sir," said Time Bomb, rising to his feet. "She is armed. All she needs is a transmitter signal and she'll blow. She'll do a fair amount of damage, too. Likely open up a largish size hole in the bulkhead. Would be very nasty."

"How did it get here?" Maxx demanded. "I assume we haven't been trotting all over the Rim with that thing ticking its little heart out–"

Time Bomb hooked his glasses back around his ears and gazed fondly at the bomb. "No, sir, it hasn't been there very long. My guess is the cleaning crew that came through today planted it." Time Bomb blinked at Maxx. "They were Chinese . . ."

Maxx scowled and shook his head. "Last time I ever let Jack talk me into letting strangers on my ship!"

"Oh, and, sir," said Time Bomb. "There's probably more like her hidden around the ship. We should do a sweep–"

"Captain!" Devil's voice came over the comm. She sounded panicked. "The hatch controls won't work! We can't get out!"

"Rawhide!" Maxx roared.

"I'm on it, sir." Rawhide came back a moment later. "Some of the electrical systems are going *jeoh huo loo moh*, Sir. We can't do a damn thing. Can't open the hatches. Can't do a sweep. Can't take-off. Wait a moment. Someone's got somethin' to say to us . . ."

He was silent, listening. Jack could hear the crackle of voices, then Rawhide returned, "I think you better get up here, Captain. The Tong fellas want to have a little talk with you. Something about an exchange. Us for Hwa Ling. If not, they'll blow up the ship."

Maxx turned to Time Bomb, eyed the young man. "Can you disarm these things?"

"I think so, Captain. The people who planted them didn't have time to do anything really sophisticated and it's obvious from where they put this one that they wanted to hide them from us. Lucky you found her." Time Bomb crossed his arms over his chest. He shook his head, puzzled, "But, say, what were you doing crawling around on the deck anyway?"

"Never mind!" Maxx grunted. "Just disarm that blasted thing. Then take Devil and find the others."

"It's a mighty big ship, Captain," said Time Bomb.

"It'll be a mighty small one if you fail. I'll be up on the bridge. I'll do my best to stall them."

"I'll go get my tools." Time Bomb trotted off, whistling. He actually looked happy—for a change.

Maxx shook his head. "Red wedgies nearly kill me. A mechanic in love with bombs. What a crew!"

He sighed deeply, and went to have a nice little talk with the *da dwei liu tse* threatening to blow up his ship.

CHAPTER 6

ROLE OF THE GAME MASTER

Playing the *Serenity Role Playing Game* can be a lot of fun. Taking on the role of Game Master can be even more challenging and exciting. And now we're going to get a little serious. We'll try to keep things fun, but there are some important lessons to learn here.

Being a Game Master takes some work, but will bring you greater rewards than pulling off a successful train job. As a Game Master, you make up the adventures, reveal the secrets, create new dramas, imagine new places to visit, and then invite others to join in the fun. Together with your players, you bring to life the stories of folk working hard to survive in a dangerous and exciting world.

This chapter of the book will give you some ideas on how to prepare a campaign, help your players create great characters, design exciting adventures, and provide tips on running the game.

Most important tips: 1) The story is the heart of a *Serenity* adventure. 2) The rules serve the story, not the other way round. In other words, if it comes to a fight between story *vs* rules, shoot the rules.

Keep in mind that the more thought and preparation you put into the game, the richer and more rewarding the experience will be for everyone involved. You'll be providing your friends with an enjoyable game, while creating great memories.

LAUNCHING POINT

The start of any campaign should be selection of the campaign concept, creation of the characters, and determining the relationships of the characters to each other. Each one of these activities can affect the others, so they should be done around the same time. You may find it most effective to have a session where you and your players come together to discuss concepts and characters. You don't need to share everyone's secrets, but the group may come up with an interesting mix of roles, personalities, and relationships.

SERENITY BASICS

All role playing games are intended to relate to a specific genre, time period, or universe. Rules are meant to assist the role playing that brings the setting to life.

To that end, the Game Master should be aware of—and respect—some basic conventions of the 'Verse. Keep these in mind as you are selecting campaign concepts, creating characters, and designing adventures.

GAMER TERMINOLOGY

When referring to the folk playing the game and the characters inside the game, there are a few terms that help keep everything straight.

Player: A person in the real world who is playing the game.

PC: "Player Character." An individual fictional character controlled by a player.

Crew: A group of player characters.

GM: "Game Master." The person who prepares the game and presents the world and all the characters not controlled by players.

NPC: "Non-Player Character." A role in the game portrayed by the Game Master.

SCIENCE FICTION

The world of *Serenity* exists five hundred-odd years in the future. Humanity has escaped a dying Earth to seek new lives among the stars. Against popular expectation, humans found no other life forms—no emotionless aliens with pointed ears, no cutesy furry bears. The Core worlds were established, and then humanity began to spread to the rest of the available planets and moons in the system. Much of that new territory is considered the Rim.

On the Core Worlds, most people live lives of ease, assisted by the most advanced forms of technology. Mansions float in the sky. Shuttle-craft clog the airways. Advanced medical care is available to everyone. The Core worlds are "peaceful"—the peace of those who have given up independence in order to be safe. But don't kid yourself—there's a dark underside to life on the Core. You just have to know where to look to find it!

On the Rim, folks are less safe and more independent. Some might think that's a pretty good trade-off. Life isn't easy. It's rare for a piece of Core-tech to show up out there and when it does, it is undoubtedly in the hands of the local officials or gentry. That being said, you find all types on the Rim—the rich, the poor, and the in between. A shiny new ship with a well-off crew might be plying the black for reasons of their own. And they might not take kindly to questions.

Serenity is a different type of futuristic setting. Not everyone is running around with a laser blaster, nor do we transport people through space by scrambling their molecules. In the 'Verse of *Serenity*, a space ship captain might ride a horse when he's on land and tote a six gun or a Bowie knife. The blending of future and past is what makes this world unique and just plain fun. This world gives you, the Game Master, a wealth of material from which to choose.

Will you set your campaign beneath the glaring lights of a teeming Core city that glitters on the surface, but is rife with crime and corruption beneath? Or will your players adventure in the wide-open spaces of a backwater moon on the Rim? Are your heroes eating protein out of cans and worrying about where their next fuel cells are coming from? Or are they flying the black in luxury, worrying about the assassin who is hot on their trail? Doesn't matter what you choose. The world of *Serenity* offers you a wide variety of exciting possibilities.

TECHNOBABBLE

Serenity is not meant to be a "hard" science fiction game, where you have to have a degree in quantum mechanics in order to be able to describe how the spaceship functions. On the other hand, you want to make your players feel as if they are really living in a futuristic world, and it helps the reality of things if you can tell them a bit more about the engine of the spacecraft than that "the part's broke."

Anytime you need to describe technology you know nothing about, try using technobabble (words that sound plausible, but don't come with a detailed description). For problems with the ship's engines, roll on the Technobabble chart to come up with quick details about mechanical problems. (If you don't like the results you've rolled, try again, or pick the one that seems to best fit the situation.)

You might want to give some of the technobabble to the players who have Mechanic or Engineer characters so they can also use the right words when speaking in character. Remember,

mechanics in the 'Verse are familiar and common to the crew. They would talk about them in "short hand," much like we talk about a car or the dishwasher.

LANGUAGE

Folk in 'Verse use very colorful language. They cuss in Chinese, use witty turns of phrase, and speak with all types of accents. With folks coming from all cultures on Earth-That-Was, any accent or ethnicity is possible. There are also new swear words in English that can let your players indulge in earthy language without having to hustle the children out of the house.

Players schooled or fluent in secondary languages can bring them into play as tongues their characters speak. Since the Chinese are a predominate force in the 'Verse, most everyone in the 'Verse who speaks English also uses Chinese phrases and exclamations in situations where the English language just doesn't quite tell how really *gun tah ma duh* bad things are!

26TH CENTURY SLANG

Folk who curse in English stick with the basics: Gorram ("Run! It's the gorram law!"); Ruttin' ("It's gettin' too ruttin' hot in here."); or Humped ("He's got a gun on us. We're humped!").

Since most everyone's picked up some Chinese just to get along, its no shock that the curse-words are the most popular words folk learn. You can find a list of Chinese words and phrases in the Appendix at the back of the book, along with some of the 26th century slang that gets the most use.

Table 6.1: Technobabble

Die Roll	Part A (d6)	Part B (d8)	What Happened (d10)	What It Means (d12)
1	Primary	Boot	Cracked	No ability to steer or maneuver
2	Compression	Coupling	Wedged	Engine quits, part can be repaired
3	Grav	Housing	Collapsed	Engine quits, part must be replaced
4	Hydraulic	Stabilizer	Bent	Engine fire, can be repaired
5	Reg	Vent	Fell Off	Performance problem, one ship Attribute suffers –2 step penalty
6	Power	Lines	Shattered	Ship won't stop unless shut down or repaired
7	–	Converter	Seized	Fuel consumption doubles until fixed
8	–	Feed	Jammed	Major system (propulsion, navigation, communications) completely loses power
9	–	–	Burnt	Engine emits a horrible sound that can be heard throughout the ship
10	–	–	Exploded	Engine startup routine becomes erratic until repaired
11	–	–	–	Nav sats and communications equipment broadcast "noise" on all frequencies
12	–	–	–	Landing gear won't function

Knowing the lingo helps out a bit. You should know, for example, that "the black" means outer space. "On the drift" means you're stuck in the black with no way to get home. A "shindig" is a fancy party. "Shiny" means good. A "Browncoat" is someone who fought for or sympathized with the Independents.

WESTERN

What makes the 'Verse of *Serenity* unique is the mingling of futuristic technology with the distinct flavor of the post-Civil War American West. Spaceship pilots hang out with preachers, whores, and gunslingers. A spaceship might soar over a herd of galloping mustangs.

As the GM, you should provide the Old West flavor that will spice up a campaign. Folk met on the Rim should be described with a bit of a Western flair. Instead of simply saying a man is "armed," tell the players he's "strapping iron." Human settlements on the Rim will have a "wide-open spaces," agrarian feel to them. Communities might appear both boom and bust in a single glance. Inspiration for the look and personalities of the people who live on the frontier of the future can be drawn from many of the classic archetypes of the Western tradition—though with unexpected twists.

Core world cities should have a more futuristic feel to them—skyscrapers, flying cars, rampant commercialism. Everyone is always busy, always on the move. In the Core worlds, only people of money and influence seem to matter. The average working-class person is reduced to a number.

Characters from the central planets are often more educated and worldly, familiar with the latest technology. Folk who leave the Core are usually running away from something—or maybe running *to* something. Either scenario makes for interesting stories.

Players in a campaign should be constantly reminded of the flavor and mood of the campaign as they role play their characters during the adventures. This will help keep their minds immersed in the 'Verse.

IN WITH THE OLD, AND IN WITH THE NEW

A good campaign set in the 'Verse should feature a mixture of Old West sensibilities with a dash of modern or futuristic flavor. For example, folk in a Rim-world saloon might wear clothes that have an old-fashioned Western cut to them, as these same folk toss darts at a holographic target. When they are done with their beers, they may hop into an all-terrain-vehicle to go back to their spaceship.

Those on primitive planets have to make do with the most basic technologies, and can't usually rely on help or supplies from the outside. Survival issues

override most other concerns, including civilized sensibilities or old-fashioned notions of morality. Some of the folk who are on these out-of-the-way places are here for a reason. They might not be the best folk to turn your back on. Glad to say, though, that there are plenty of good-hearted people in such places as well—just trying to get by and mind their own business.

Folk making due with the basics usually only have a few high-tech trinkets to remind them of the other worlds. Social activities such as festivals and card games become the primary entertainment for those without easy Cortex access.

LIVIN' LEAN & HUNGRY

The keys to portraying life and adventure on the Rim are the principles of scarcity and necessity. Like life in the frontier towns of the West, the more recently terraformed planets have small settlements with the bare beginnings of local industries. High tech gear is pretty rare. The money required to ship expensive tech from the central planets places is outside ordinary folks' reach.

When you're scratching food out of moon rock without many credits in the bank (if there is a bank), you tend to figure out what's important pretty quick. Why waste the money on a power-driven tool when an ordinary hammer will do the job? Why worry that your fancy grav-car will break down on you and you can't get the spare parts, when you can raise your own horses?

Still, that doesn't mean that such folk won't dream of some day owning that shiny grav-car…

ALL IN THE FAMILY

Created family is a very important concept in the *Serenity* style of storytelling. The crew may have come together for various reasons—looking for work, running away from something, or just wanting to walk the world for a spell. No matter where they came from, out in the black, all they have is each other. A bond can (and should!) form among the crew, along with all sorts of interesting relationships.

This thinking allows for a diverse crew who get the job done. Even if they squawk at each other like old married couples, ultimately they may come to realize that they have somehow accidentally formed a family. Course, not every family is fully functional…

There are many kinds of ties that folk have with each other. Characters can be related by blood—the closer the relationship the stronger the tie. Parents and children or siblings such as Simon and River are good examples. Blood ties can make for excellent character development potential. And just because they're related doesn't mean they always get along!

A daughter may rebel against an overbearing father. Two brothers who are steadfastly loyal to each other during crisis situations may fight like wildcats any other time.

Characters can be tied to each other romantically. Such ties offer the potential for love triangles, jealousies, misunderstandings like those that occur between Kaylee and Simon. Even a loving, committed couple like Wash and Zoe find many things to argue about, though when the chips are down, they can count on each other more than on any one else in the 'Verse.

Some members of the crew may stick together because of a common experience or tragedy. Zoe and Mal fought in the war together, and they survived the bloody Battle of Serenity Valley. Such a bond, forged in desperation, danger, and anguish, is stronger than steel.

The best crews will show a reflection of deep bonds and affection, but there will also be plenty of room for conflict as well. Jealousy, rivalry, and even some genuine dislike might be present among one or more of the crew. Living in close quarters with other folk can be trying at times, and when flying out in the black there are not many places you can go to "get away". Arguments, feuds, and bickering among the crew will increase the "real" feel of the game.

Note we said "crew". As Game Master, you will need to help the players remember that they are acting out parts, taking on roles. It can sometimes be easy for "fake" arguments to turn into real ones. This can cause hurt feelings, make other players feel uncomfortable, and ruin the game for everyone. If a couple of players appear to be taking things a mite too seriously, you should pause the game just long enough to remind everyone that they're here to have fun. Either that or take the two aside and ask them to cool it!

THERE'S NO PLACE LIKE HOME

Most everyone needs a place where they feel safe. In a classic *Serenity* campaign, the crew live on a ship of some sort, taking work as it comes, and doing their best to keep flyin' in a 'Verse that's not always easy or fair. The ship is their home, their haven, a place they can escape to (and escape in!). Home could be a Firefly (an obvious choice) or a fancy boat like *Aces & Eights*. Home could just as easily be a giant gambling ship like the *El Dorado*, an Alliance Cruiser, or a run-down space-station out on the Rim. Home, whatever and wherever it may be, is a place for the crew to relax, for everyone to be themselves, to find solace for a spell.

Once the heroes have their home, they'll become very attached to it, and protective of it. If home is a ship, that ship becomes another character in the campaign. Each ship should have quirks and characteristics. Even luxury cruise ships break down at inopportune moments. The crew aboard an Alliance cruiser might have to contend with spies, sabotage, or potential mutiny—and that's just in one game session!

The captain of a ship will probably feel more affection for his ship than a mere passenger. However, if that passenger goes through a crisis on board the ship, and the ship is responsible for saving his life, then he may also come to love his new-found home. A good crew will be well aware of the role the ship plays in their lives, and treat her the best they can given their circumstances.

Not every campaign or character thinks of a ship as "home." Home could be a favorite watering hole (where the beer is good and cheap), the family ranch of your home planet, a religious monastery, Companion House, or the space station where your grandpappy works an Alliance postal franchise.

CAMPAIGN CONCEPTS

When the time comes for a Game Master to start a new game, he needs to roll up the mental sleeves and figure out the concept that will serve as the framework for the whole campaign. The idea should appeal to him, and work well with the style of the players.

Some groups may want to play the characters from the movie on board *Serenity*, ready to do most anything it takes to keep flyin'. The crew of *Aces & Eights* are another good choice for those who want to get started quickly. The *Aces & Eights* crew lives a bit higher on the hog, but they have their fair share of troubles and obligations. Experienced gamers may well want to jump straight into character creation and make up a new crew from scratch; a crew with a unique style and stories that will be completely different from anything yet seen in the 'Verse.

Perhaps your gaming group is fluid, attendance is irregular, people never know if they can make the game session or not. Yet, when they do come, they want to feel like they're making a contribution. In that case, you should consider designing a game setting where crew members come and go frequently.

This crew could be members of a community (a settlement on one of the outer planets or on an orbiting skyplex) who are trying to survive and make their fortunes on the frontier. Adventures come riding in on horses or landing in spaceships. They have to deal with other locals, and since they can't just zoom away from those they don't like, they have to learn to manage these relationships.

Or perhaps they are a group of bounty hunters traveling the Rim in search of criminals or enemies of the Alliance. This sort of campaign will suit players who like lots of action, who enjoy settling matters with fists and sidearms. The group could be a band of mercenaries or gunfighters looking for work. Sometimes the job might not pay well, but there's some honor in it that has appeal. Then again, a job might pay well, but it's low-down, mean, and involves hurting innocents. The crew would have to decide whether or not to accept—a hard decision, especially if their bellies are creakin' with the empties.

The group might be agents of an Alliance organization with its own agenda. Doesn't have to be sinister. Might be out to do some good, even if they have to knock some heads together to get the job done. All sorts of characters can be drawn into their plans and schemes. They might even require quick passage aboard a rust-bucket Firefly!

Concepts that allow for a varied mix of people tend to make for better play, since the differences between the characters will provide plenty of opportunity for conflict and role playing.

UNDERLYING THEMES

Some basic themes can help involve the crew in the story you're creating in your role as Game Master. Your campaign might emphasize some themes more than others, suiting them to your group's individual style. Campaign themes are important enough to warrant a moment's consideration.

Thrilling Heroics: The heroes are supposed to act heroic sometimes. Be wary of allowing players to create characters who are nasty, evil, no-good skunks. Some greedy scoundrel-types are acceptable, but there's a limit. Flawed people are interesting, but flat-out evil folk will end up locked up or—more likely—on the wrong end of a gun barrel. Let consequences in the game teach a crew member the error of his ways, and if that doesn't work, allow events to reach the natural conclusion.

Hidden Secrets: Secrets are an important concept in *Serenity*-style storytelling. Most everyone has something to hide, even if it's just a crush on a fellow member of the crew. Could be more dramatic, like a Shepherd who knows the ins and outs of the Alliance military. A Shepherd who beats up Federal Marshals. A Shepherd who can shoot out kneecaps with frightening accuracy. The secret might be the reason the character is on the move out in the black, instead of living whatever life he started once upon a time. Interesting secrets lead to interesting role play.

Outcasts & Misfits: The kind of folk who get into the scrapes likely to happen in a campaign are not the sort who settle down and raise a bunch of young 'uns. The scrapes they are in may not have been part their original life-plan (such as Simon and River), but circumstances have forced them to become misfits who can't find a place in life—but might find one with a group of other misfits.

Freedom: Try all you like—you can't take the sky from me. Freedom and what it truly means to be free is a strong underlying notion that should play a part in any *Serenity* campaign. What is the price of freedom? Should living safe be purchased at the cost of freedom? Answers aren't that simple, as the crew will likely find.

CREATING THE CREW

Whether you'll be running adapted or pre-packaged adventures, or if you plan on weaving your own tales in the 'Verse, you need to know your crew. Your stories should feature a fair bit of customization to allow the strengths and flaws of the heroes to each shine in the spotlight for a spell.

If the crew are a scruffy lot living hand-to-mouth and willing to take whatever jobs are available, your adventures will reflect that. If money and basic survival aren't an issue (due to wealth or connections), then the adventures will have a different tone (though being rich doesn't necessarily mean you can't find yourself in a pack of trouble!).

CHARACTER BUILDING

If your players want to use one of the pre-generated crews, grab 'em and move right along. But if your players want instead to create their own characters, then first you need determine what sort of characters they'd like portray. Hand out paper and pencils. Encourage the players to think of possible characters, and then discover the various aspects of those characters by brainstorming facts about them on paper. For example, Renae wants to play a dance hall girl on the run. She needs to ask herself these questions: "Why is my character on the run? Who is after her? What did she do to get herself into trouble? How does she plan to get out of trouble?"

Most important question: "What are my character's motives?"

MOTIVATION

Just about everyone's got one (or more) forces driving his life. Motivation should be one of the first things to consider when creating a character.

In the film, Simon loves his sister and will do anything to keep her safe. Not only did he give up his original life and become a criminal to save her, he pushes aside other people when he feels they might distract him from taking care of River. Jayne acts out of greed. Book follows his beliefs. Mal does whatever he can to keep his ship flying and protect his crew.

A motivation for a new character is a good foundation for layering on the complexity. Mal is trying to steer clear of Alliance trouble, yet he takes on the Tams as passengers. Jayne's ready to be a bad guy to get his reward, yet would likely tear the head off of any *uh soo* who laid a rough hand on Kaylee. Jack Leland would normally never transport livestock aboard *Aces & Eights*, but he might do so to honor a lost bet or if one of his crew was in trouble.

Coping with difficult situations that test a crew's motivations leads to great role playing and excellent stories at game's end. As GM, you'll want to note how well players follow each character's various motivations, and reward them with Plot Points for following them. (And withhold Plot Points from those who ignore their characters' motivations!)

CHARACTER ROLES

During the brainstorming session, encourage discussion between the players. Ideas in some may spark ideas in others. The players will want to have an idea of what functional roles the characters will play in the campaign. For example, everyone can't be captain! A crew on a Firefly won't be likely to need three doctors. Nor should everyone take skills that focus on engineering (who'll fly the ship?). As the players talk about the campaign concept, you might want to have them look over the various Skills that are available so they realize what roles and skills would make sense in support of the campaign concept. For example, if your group is playing Badger and his gang of thieves, you probably don't need someone with the piloting Skill.

> "I'll kill a man in a fair fight... or if I think he's gonna *start* a fair fight, or if he bothers me, or if there's a woman, or I'm gettin' paid—mostly only when I'm gettin' paid."
>
> —Jayne Cobb

Group brainstorming also allows the players to find natural relationships between the characters. Possible links can be suggested and either accepted or declined. Two players may determine that their characters will likely not get along, which is just fine for role playing.

If a player is having trouble coming up with some ideas, suggest that he try to imagine just one thing about the character. Suggestions include: what is his racial background, what type of gun does she carry (if any), how much money does he have in his pockets, how nice are her clothes, what does she look like, what is his most refined skill, what does she believe in, what does she want most in the world, what is his favorite activity, or even just what is the person's name. Once you have one detail, the next details come easier.

It is important to have a diversity of player characters, so encourage your players to consider this as they are creating their characters. Their views on life and values should vary greatly. They should come from all walks of life, be of different racial and ethnic backgrounds, and could even be of drastically different ages.

ESTABLISHING RELATIONSHIPS

Many gaming groups skip over the reasons that bring the characters together. "We're all in the same bar looking for work" is pretty lame. The players will develop stronger bonds with their characters and the characters with each other if they determine how they met, how they feel about each other, and why they should risk their lives for the party.

For those crew who already know each other, such relationships should be predetermined during character creation. For those who don't know each other, ask the question: "Why are you together?"

You and the players could start with the assumption that the crew has all known each other for years, and are already a part of a unit. While this makes things simpler, it robs the players of the chance to role play the interesting ways people meet or the reasons why they decide to join the group. Such beginnings can have profound impacts on character relationships later on. For example, Zoe and Mal get a very clear impression of Jayne's character when they first meet him, discovering right away that he can be bought for the right price.

Character relationships can be guided by the character creation process, but they will also develop organically. Two characters who are meant to fall in love may end up role playing the origin of that relationship in many different ways, giving their relationship unexpected nuances. (Zoe dislikes Wash when she first meets him.)

As a Game Master, you might want to set up the "origin events"— situations and scenes where characters meet each other, are introduced, and decide to join the group. These can be separate from adventure events, or the introduction of characters can be entwined with a first adventure.

Give a lot of thought to the origin events. For characters who are joining the group for the first time, you'll be weaving them together in ways that will affect the relationships they form with their fellows. First impressions do mean a lot. Whether someone pays for her passage or is smuggled aboard is likely to have an effect on what the captain of the ship thinks of her. An engineer looking for a job might be seen as a salvation to the crew or merely tolerated if certain aspects of his character rub folk the wrong way.

Within the crew of the *Serenity*, we have many different relationships: unconfessed love (Mal and Inara); marriage (Zoe and Wash); business arrangement (Mal and Jayne); circumstance (Simon and Mal); family (Simon and River); admiration Kaylee and her Captain); fate (Shepherd Book). Most of these relationships are even more complex, having several different layers. (Mal has a business relationship with Jayne, but doesn't trust him.) Layers of relationships bring complexity and depth to characters, making them more fun to play, and allowing the GM to design more in-depth adventures for them.

For characters who will meet for the first time during the game, give some thought as to why they would choose to join the others. These new relationships will have be worked out through role playing, so it's fine if they are unpredictable. Many of the same relationships as mentioned above could apply, but now others can be added. Some of the less tangible reasons for characters to join and stay with a group are: the need to escape, the need for freedom, the need for love, the need to belong, the need for a home, the need to make a difference in the world.

In addition to understanding the positive relationships characters have with each other, it is also important to understand the negative relationships, as well. Which characters get on each other's nerves? Who teases whom? Who suffers from a conflict of interest, forcing him to continually choose between sides? Such interesting aspects of the crew will enhance the role playing. Note that much of this will not (or even should) be determined before the game starts. Much of this will come out in the role playing, as players "grow into" their characters and learn more about them.

Here are some interesting personality aspects that can be used to create character friendships and friction: optimism *vs* pessimism, civility *vs* barbarity, piety *vs* atheism, cold-blooded killer *vs* avowed pacifist, law-abiding *vs* law-breaking, quiet *vs* boorish, high class *vs* low class, haves *vs* have-nots.

CREATING NEW TRAITS

It possible that a particular part of a character's history or a type of relationship is not well-represented by the Traits listed in the book. In that instance, the GM can create a new Trait (Asset, Complication, or situation) by following these guidelines:

• The new Trait should not significantly copy or replace an existing Trait. The current Trait might work as is.

• The benefit of an Asset should be weighed against the other Assets to determine whether it should be a Major or Minor Asset.

• The penalty of a Complication should be weighed against the other Complications to determine whether it should be a Major or Minor Complication.

• If you're unsure of the power of a new Trait, tend toward a weaker version to avoid unbalancing the system.

• The flavor and origin of the Trait should be well described and suit the flavor of the 'Verse.

TRAITS AND RELATIONSHIPS

The choice of Traits can also help in defining a character's motivations and relationships. By choosing the most fitting set of character Traits (Assets and Complications, see Chapter Two: *Traits and Skills*), a player can capture not only the major points of a character's background, but also his or her relationships within the crew. Traits encourage role playing and Plot Point rewards encourage playing Traits well.

Choosing Traits suitable for each character will take some thought and discussion among the players and GM. Here are some examples of how the right Asset or Complication can not only reinforce the character's relationship with others, but earn the player Plot Points.

Here are a few ideas about how Traits can serve as inspiration to how your character relates to others.

Allure: When you smile, people fall all over themselves to do your bidding.

Amorous: There are some right pretty women on board that ship! Think I'll join up!

Branded: The cause of your branding makes you a hero to a select few who will welcome you to their crew. Too bad the rest of the 'Verse don't see it that way.

Credo: Your beliefs have earned you many enemies, but they have also earned you friends.

Good Name: People trust you.

Highly Educated: Your medical degree allows you to save lives.

Hero Worship: I love my captain!

Leadership: You exude confidence and a sense that you know what you're about.

Loyalty: You're part of my crew and under my protection.

Math Whiz: Your reputation as a poker player has earned you the status accorded high rollers.

Remember, Traits are described in general terms. They need to be role played in very specific ways to provide a good characterization. Don't just say that the character is greedy. Show his greed in the small ways he tries to sneak a few extra credits or cheats at card games played around the dinner table. Sure, he'd consider selling out his crew mates if the money is good enough, but not all role playing of complications needs to be on that grand scale.

DESIGNING ADVENTURES

Adventures are created by outlining a plot or plots, and then enriching the plot by adding characters, complications, interesting places, and situations. Specific situations in the adventure are known as "events". You assemble events like a puzzle to enhance or carry the plot forward. You should continue to create pieces of the puzzle until you have enough so that you know how the story might go, the folk the characters are likely to meet, and how the action might flow. You will end up tossing out some pieces, while others will take on more importance than you expected. Remember: Game Master and players create the story together! Don't make the players feel like they're being herded along the story trail.

Remember to save all the pieces you've created, even if you don't use them. You might not use certain colorful characters in this adventure, but you'll have them available for use next time.

STARTING THE ADVENTURE

One of the best ways to start the game quickly is to begin with the players landing square in the middle of the action: performing a salvage job under the nose of the Alliance, delivering a dangerous cargo to a planet swept by storms, wearing a brown coat when walking into an Alliance bar on Unification Day. When you start the adventure by giving the players something to do, the group doesn't have to sit around trying to decide where to go and what action to take. The over-all adventure may be related to this job, or the opening sequence could simply serve as an introduction to what's coming next.

If you haven't run an origins event, this can also be a good way to introduce characters to each other. People naturally tend to bond in the face of imminent threat or peril. A group of strangers who find themselves in danger may run to the nearest ship just in order to escape, only to discover that they are unlikely companions for the rest of the journey.

Make sure when you start the players in the middle of the fun that they have a believable motivation for doing what they're doing. A group of law-abiding settlers will not appreciate the GM telling them they are currently engaged in robbing a bank. That same group of settlers might find themselves the victims of a robbery, however, and that could start the action.

A teaser scene gives the players plot momentum and a starting point. As the adventure and campaign continue, the players may want to be more involved in finding and selecting their jobs, or they may prefer to let you handle that as the story moves forward.

You can create a similar amount of excitement by creating a scenario that isn't necessarily action-oriented, but offers a lot of tension and forces the players to make quick decisions. For example, you might let the crew know they've been stuck on one planet for weeks, unable to get enough cash to refuel the ship so they can leave. Meanwhile, the crime boss who loaned them money is coming to collect his payment—that payment being their ship!

ADVENTURE STRUCTURE

When creating adventures, you can benefit by understanding some basic principles of story structure. While the adventures will likely stray from any defined model, the following elements have their place, and can assist you to tell the stories of the individual characters.

DESIRE

All drama is born of the desires of the characters. Understanding those desires is crucial to creating adventures that will hold the interest and excitement of your players.

We've already discussed creating interesting characters who have motivations, goals, needs, and problems. Adventures are born from the crew's attempts to address those needs, to obtain what they do not have, or to keep what they do have. Adventures should incorporate the desires developed in character creation. The players are likely to be disappointed and confused if they find they have to deal with desires that come out of nowhere for no reason.

CONFLICT

You've established the desires of your characters, and now the characters are ready to go after them. In order to create drama, there should be forces that oppose the characters' goals, or choices presented that will test their commitments to those goals. Characters should have to struggle to attain their wants and needs. The meeting of these two forces, or the presentation of difficult choices creates conflict.

The characters' response to troubles, conflicts, and difficult choices will reveal much about them. When Mal takes a job that helps others, but doesn't profit him, it proves that he values some things above his expressed goal to 'just keep flyin'.

Opposing forces can take many forms: individuals, organizations, civil authorities, criminal elements, hazardous environments, the vagaries and hardships of everyday life.

The major organization involved in a *Serenity* campaign is the Alliance; either overtly with its military and police forces, or covertly with its secret agents. The Alliance can be good or bad, depending on how the characters view it, and it is likely that they will none of them view it in the same way. Other organizations exist in the 'Verse, all with their own agendas and degrees of influence. These include Guilds, such as the Companions Guild, and corporations like Blue Sun. Any of these organizations may act in ways that indirectly affect our heroes, or the organizations may take a particular interest in the heroes.

Criminal elements exist at all levels of power within the 'Verse, from government corruption to groups of petty thieves. If the crew is known or believed to be threatening a criminal organization's reputation or solvency, the heroes will definitely be targeted for some level of interaction—whether it be a message to back off or hired guns kicking in the door.

Sometimes the world itself is out to get you. Problems with the ship may leave the crew threatened by catastrophic mechanical failure (explosion or loss of hull integrity), or the dangers of outer space (freezing, asphyxiating). On planets, all manner of weather and terrain may serve to thwart the heroes' goals.

The heroes may be their own worst enemies. Internal conflicts among the crew or situations where the clash of multiple goals forces the crew to face moral choices or decisions may significantly alter their relationships with others in the group.

Choices should be difficult to make, not obvious. The characters should not be given a choice between saving orphaned children from being evicted by a heartless landlord or robbing a bank. One option is obviously good, the other bad. The heroes could be given the choice of saving children from being evicted *by* robbing the bank (to come up with enough money to buy off the landlord). That would not be a tough call for heroes who are not above breaking the law, but a group of law-abiding settlers might have trouble making such a decision. Each choice should have consequences that make the decision interesting.

RISING ACTION

To engage players and build a compelling adventure, action should start out low-key and then rise as the stakes grow greater, and the details of the situation or predicament become known.

Rising action is not restricted to combat (going from a scuffle to an all-out gun battle), but also refers to the development of the situation, as well as the consequence of actions the characters take. At the beginning of a story, the crew doesn't much care which cargos or passengers they allow on their ship for a trip to Whitehall. As the crew becomes enmeshed in plots and conflicts, the people they've brought on board, and what they do with them and for them becomes much more important and dramatic. Getting rid of a troublemaker once you're in space has greater consequences than if you're on land where you can leave him unconscious in an alley.

As you map out your plots in an adventure, consider how situations could escalate and the crew's actions become ever more important. Keep in mind that the crew may not always succeed in their endeavors. Don't be dismayed by failure or tempted to let the heroes win every time, especially if it is obvious that there's no possible way they can. A failure can be a setback that challenges the crew to overcome their obstacles another way. A few defeats will make the final victory all the more satisfying.

CLIMAX

This is the point in the adventure where important questions are answered, and the crew may or may not overcome the obstacles in their path. The crew are tested as never before, with the most at stake should they fail. Plots are resolved and relationships may be permanently changed.

Do the characters achieve what they've set out to do? If not, they must decide if the struggle was worth it anyway. Is what they sought still important to them? If they fail, will they try again another day? The climax is the point where actions based on previous decisions occur. What's done can't be undone. Characters make choices, the dice are cast, and then it's time to live with the results.

While a climax is born out of the plots, providing a good setting for a climax is also important. Dramatic situations could include: battles in space, gunfights, daring rescues, a long-planned heist, the revelation that an ally is an enemy, the delivery of the cargo in a dangerous situation.

RESOLUTION

Once the climax of an adventure has been overcome, it's time to pause a moment to catch a breath and reflect on what has occurred, celebrate victory, mourn a loss. As Game Master, you need to consider the consequences of the crew's acts and decisions. Do others change their opinions of the crew? Does success earn them wealth, respect, friendship, or something else? Does failure rob them of something? This is also the time to deal with any deaths that have occurred.

There will likely be some cleanup to do during the resolution period as crew ties up loose ends and address issues from earlier in the adventure. Mundane decisions, deferred due to the rising action, may now be considered. Their future courses of action are discussed, and either planned or set into motion.

Resolution is the best time to take care of bookkeeping, allowing characters to improve themselves with unspent Plot Points, buy new Traits or remove old ones, and discuss the direction their characters might take. That last bit is important, so the Game Master should have input on the direction of the campaign. (Do the players like the current adventure style? Do they want to pursue a secondary clue left unresolved in this adventure in the next adventure?)

PLOTS

At its simplest level, game plots usually involve an achievable goal that is helped or hindered by NPCs, and influenced by the relationships of the characters with each other and by their needs and desires.

PLOT TYPES

The major plot line is usually the most obvious plot (the "A" plot). If you are playing the crew of *Serenity*, this could be a job the crew is hired to do. Plots can also include: goals one character wants to pursue with the aid of his friends, group goals all agree to pursue. The A Plot should appear straightforward. Its completion will indicate that one adventure has ended and the next one can begin. No matter what else goes on, the group's obvious goal should be completion of the A Plot.

Entwined with the A Plot are secondary plots. These "B" plots may directly involve either one or several members of the group. B plots are often a good way to explore a minor point unrelated to the A Plot, permit two characters to deal with friction between them (perhaps coming to some resolution), allow characters to pursue private agendas, or deal with a minor Complication. The course of a B plot can certainly interfere with the A Plot, or the two can exist without much interaction.

When characters separate for a significant amount of time, B Plots are a good way to keep those who are left out of the A Plot involved. Let's say some of the crew go into town to steal a laser gun (the A plot), leaving the others on the ship. Those who are left on the ship suddenly find out that the group going to steal the laser gun is walking into a trap (B plot that involves the A plot). Or the group on board ship might look out a window to see that they are being surrounded by lawmen who have reason to believe that a local hoodlum has sneaked aboard. (B plot has no bearing on the A plot.)

FLESHING OUT PLOTS

Once you've created a major and some minor plots, run them through your head and ask questions about them. How do the characters learn about the plot? How they will get involved? What questions will the characters ask? To what locations does the plot take them? Can you describe those locations and the NPCs that they meet there? This process should help you predict the questions that the players will ask, and predict the directions in which they might take the plots. It also gives you a guide to what material you'll need to create before the game session begins.

Determine how the plot starts. (How do the characters first become involved?) For example, you might have a man deliver a mysterious message to the crew. He dies before they can question him, and they find out he's been shot. Now the players are head-over-heels in danger and mystery. The message could be the A Plot, enticing them to travel somewhere or meet someone. The man's death and the mystery of who killed him and why could be B Plots or a twist on the A Plot. Thinking of a dramatic way to begin an adventure is a great way to get players hooked, and establish the level of danger, intrigue, and opportunity at hand.

Don't bother writing all the plots fully from beginning to end. You aren't creating this story on your own. This is a collaborative story with your players adding much of the input. To paraphrase Helmuth von Moltke, "no plot survives first contact with the players". Create general outlines, important NPCs, locations, and events, but always be prepared to change things around to suit the story as it unfolds at the table.

Here's an example. You have a simple cargo hauling job as the A Plot with a B Plot of a disruptive passenger who knows a member of the crew from the past. You expect the action to occur on the ship in this order: Event – Get the Job. Event – Meet the Passenger. Event – Passenger Gets Unruly. Event – Settle Passenger (either lock him up, knock him out, soothe him). Event – Reach Destination. Event – Get Rid of Passenger. Event – Deliver Cargo/Get Paid. It is quite possible that the way the PCs handle the passenger in the very beginning will throw the job off-schedule, incur the wrath of the person who hired the crew (the passenger was his son!), and cause them to fail to deliver the goods.

NON-PLAYER CHARACTERS

An important aspect of any plot is understanding the actions that will be taken by the Non Player Characters. Determine how different NPCs will affect the plots and the course of events. Then spend a moment reflecting on each NPC or NPC group to try to understand their motivations, which are as important as the motivations of the characters. What are the goals of the NPC? How might NPC actions, decisions, or plans be altered or affected by the heroes? The more you know about the NPCs, the richer the campaign will be for the PCs, who will need to defeat them, resolve their issues, or gain their assistance. See *Fellow Travelers* in this chapter for some ideas on NPCs.

PLOT TWIST

One aspect that can enhance the game is the plot twist—something for which *Serenity* is known! Just when things are going great, all hell breaks loose. And when things can't possibly get worse, they get worse. Coming up with plot twists takes time and thought, and you might not want to do it for every campaign. But it's often fun to spring the unexpected on the players when they're least looking for it.

It is important to remember that a plot twist must be believable and fit into the plot, or the players will have good reason to shoot the Game Master. The person who appears to be an innocent passenger has actually been hired by the bad guys to make sure the crew doesn't deliver the cargo on time. Or the cargo they've been hired to transport turns out to be hot, and the Alliance is tipped off that they're carrying it. A job, like life, is never simple.

EVENTS

Events are the building blocks for plots and adventures. An event is a scene that may include NPCs, and offers a chance to advance or alter one or more plots. Events might include: a showdown with a tenacious adversary, a negotiation for fees for a job, in-character conversations, dealing with mechanical problems on board the ship, encounters with Reavers.

Key events often signal the revelation of a secret or an important piece to a puzzle. The heroes might spot someone they thought was dead in conversation with their adversary. Recovery of a cherished possession might cause an NPC to open up to the characters and share what he or she knows. Scenes involving intimidation, bribery, or interrogation might reveal secrets and clues.

For each event you want to plan, set the scene by making some notes as to where it might likely occur, who will be involved, and how it might affect the course of a plot or the adventure. You might want to organize all the events related to a particular plot line and put them together. Keep your descriptions flexible in case player choices necessitate the event occurring in a different location or with different people.

You may also consider having some 'flavor' events close to hand. These reinforce the look and feel of the Serenity 'Verse without having a direct influence on the plot. They remind the players that they are not the center of the 'Verse, as well as reinforcing the "common man" element to their lives. Good flavor events include: resupplying the ship, visiting the local town for entertainment, a rendezvous with an old friend, encountering the Alliance in action, mechanical difficulty with their ship, stopping at a skyplex to pick up supplies, receiving messages from friends and loved ones over the Cortex.

STRANGE SCENES

You can change the pace and feel of an adventure by introducing a carefully prepared flashback or dream for a particular PC. You could also choose to present an interlude where the players are witness to something their PCs are not.

For dreams, present the scene privately to the dreamer and let that person decide if he will tell his dream to the rest of their crew. Some things are better left private. Dreams can deal with personal demons, choices confronting the character, or future events. The dream might help a PC work out her conflicts or may foreshadow trouble ahead. Dramatic or terrifying dreams may end with the dreamer waking with a scream, while other dreams may fill them with elation.

Flashbacks are extremely useful for filling in a character's background, expanding his understanding of past events, or planting information that may become useful later on. The PC generally does not have any control of a flashback, but experiences it as vivid memories. If the past event was shared among multiple characters, they can all recall the same events. Flashbacks work well when presented before the whole group, while saving any secrets or private information as a note or quick discussion with a single player in the other room.

Interludes are best used to reinforce the flavor of an adventure, the nature of a foe, or the truth about what is really at stake. You describe events to the players outside of what the PCs could be perceiving. Perhaps you will describe the villain in his place of power, showing how he speaks and to what extent he is willing to go to stop them, or they see the pain and suffering in an orphanage whose director is calling for aid. Other interludes could include crucial events which the PCs could reasonably learn about through gossip or via reports on the Cortex.

You can prepare much of these scenes ahead of time, giving you a chance to provide exceptionally inventive and rich descriptions. The right time to present one of these scenes is during a pause in the drama of the adventure.

ADVENTURE CONCEPTS

A good inspiration for *Serenity*-flavored plots are the television shows and movies of the American Old West. Such plots include elements often seen in the 'Verse: folks seeking their fortunes in the frontier, the absence of law and order, the struggles of the weak against the powerful, the individual against companies, civilization overtaking an untamed land.

Such themes are why tales of the Old West have fascinated people for years. People leaving behind an old life to start anew. People being judged for who they are, not who they were. People experiencing a sense of absolute freedom, with no laws to constrict them. Comes with a cost, though, as there are no laws to protect them. People striking it rich over night. People fleeing religious, racial, and other types of persecution. Disillusioned and embittered Civil War veterans leaving a South that is undergoing reconstruction. Countless numbers of homesteaders—men, women, children—risking all to find a better life.

Depending on the theme of your campaign, you could choose a few of these to be regular parts of your adventures.

LONG ARM OF THE LAW

If the crew are sometimes on the shady side of the law (like the crew of *Serenity*), it's important for "the Law" to play a large role in their adventures. *Serenity* doesn't have any ship's weaponry, so blasting it out in a space battle isn't an option. If the crew can't outrun the Alliance, they'll have to expect to be boarded. The presence of Alliance soldiers in a city or town (or on a train!) can certainly alter a crew's plans.

If the crew commit crimes, they should be pursued by the authorities. This might happen immediately, if a sheriff and his posse hear that they've robbed the train, or later as word of their misdeeds travels through beaurocratic channels. Fugitives and outlaws can expect to be accosted by officers of the law and bounty hunters on a regular basis, especially if their deeds and actions continue to attract attention.

SOMETIMES DANGER FINDS YOU

You can't always wait for your players to get into trouble (though some groups will have no problem finding it regularly on their own). The 'Verse is a dangerous place, and your campaign needs to remind the crew of this.

During their travels, they might come across the aftermath of a Reaver attack. A con artist might try to swindle them out of their loot. Through bad luck or poor maintenance, they may need to deal with the dangers of mechanical failure aboard their ship while in deep space.

Sometimes the crew may get swept up by major events over which they have no control. They might blunder into a major space battle between the Alliance and an Independent insurgency. The planet on which they've landed might be experiencing a bloody revolution. Perhaps a settlement leader has been assassinated, prompting a witch hunt. Strangers are always prime suspects when anything goes wrong.

BREAKING THE MOLD

Adventures in the 'Verse should be fun, fast-paced adventures, with plot twists and humor used to elevate the mood. It will be important to not let yourself fall into the rut of time-worn plots and stereotypical people and events. The game excels when twists and turns are thrown at the crew, forcing them to adjust their plans on the fly and at times explore parts of their characters they had not anticipated. The setting and mood is gritty and realistic, but open for in-character humor.

Remember that the bad guys should not be monolithic, single-minded individuals. Villains have depth too, making dealing with them more realistic and interesting. If your antagonist has several goals and things he cares about, the crew are more likely to find ways to convince him to let them live.

Don't reveal everything about PCs' or NPCs' pasts at the start. Campaigns work best when the revelation of people's pasts occurs over time, naturally, as clues appear or the people become close enough to let others into their secrets. This doesn't mean that every character will be a brooding loner that the others avoid because he isn't willing to put it all on the table. Folks on the Rim tend to take a person at his word, until its proved that word isn't good.

Another trap to avoid is casting the player characters as larger than life heroes. These aren't the people plotting to take down the tyrannical Alliance through another war. *Serenity* characters are generally working-class folk making their way in the world the best way they know how. They earn the title of heroes by the way they treat others and how they stand by their beliefs.

PLAYING THE PARTS

As Game Master, you are responsible for describing the 'Verse to the players--everything from the mountains and prairies and the stars, to the dangers around them, to the people they encounter. *Serenity* does not focus on futuristic technology or the weirdness of aliens. *Serenity* focuses on the characters and how they interact. Portraying interesting and realistic NPCs is extremely important.

You will need to portray the NPCs that your players see, meet, talk with, and possibly fight.

TELLING WHOPPERS

Everyone lies—including NPCs! An NPC may have some information the crew needs, but this doesn't mean he's going to spill his guts even if they ask politely and say the magic word. Create some lies for your NPCs to hand out along with the truth. Some good reasons for NPCs to lie include: protecting themselves, protecting others, protecting their wealth and possessions, serving masters who are opposed to the crew, a need to make friends, messing with the characters' heads, advancing the NPCs' own ambitions and goals.

Luckily, while there are millions of folks in the 'Verse, you don't need to portray them all with the same level of detail. Most will have limited interaction with the heroes and can be summed up in a sentence or two. Only the very most important NPCs will need to be defined as thoroughly as a PC. The rest fall in the middle. You should know a few things about them, find interesting ways to describe them, and have their stats so that you could run them in combat if the need arises.

"STOCK" CHARACTERS

These are the people who walk the streets of Persephone or who are patients in the hospitals of Core worlds. They farm the soil of Higgin's Moon and fill the bars and gambling dens of countless Rim settlements. You should have a list of names and professions for these NPCs within easy reach, in case a hero talks to one long enough to require more details. Such NPCs aren't usually fighters and don't have notable skills beyond whatever their job or situation requires. Their numbers can be generalized or assumed if they are ever forced to take part in the action.

Stock NPCs who are true to their stereotypes don't make much of an impression and are easily forgotten, even if you've named them. Not everyone in the 'Verse is striking or memorable. This dilutes the ones you want them to remember.

When you want a stock NPC to be remembered, consider giving him at least one aspect that will make him or her memorable: an annoying mannerism (such as spitting on the sidewalk), remarkable beauty, unbelievable klutziness, or even an Asset or Complication.

Thugs and minions of important NPCs, guards, and gang members need little more than the most basic stats in case they need to use a Skill or fight. Even "faceless" members of organizations, such as a Chinese Triad gang member, should be given cursory descriptions, Attributes, and Skills, since they may be rated better than ordinary street thugs.

IMPORTANT NPCS

Some Game Master-created characters, such as allies, bystanders, or opponents, who will have significant direct interaction with the crew, should be detailed more fully. These NPCs might have the same amount of detail as the crew, with descriptions, skills, and traits.

The crew will most likely have to interact with and test their skills against these NPCs during the course of an adventure. Such NPCs may include: con artists, criminals, officers of the law, private detectives, bounty hunters, businessmen looking to move cargo, passengers, competitors, old friends, old enemies, local celebrities, mercenaries, gunfighters, prostitutes, Companions, government agents, hijackers, renegades, outlaws, etc.

Important NPCs should have distinguishing mannerisms and descriptions, specific ways of speaking, full stats, Skills, and Traits. You should have some idea of their history, background, and their current positions. Understand their primary goals and the importance of these goals, so you know what they'll do in order to accomplish them.

Make your NPCs colorful by using flamboyant or interesting speech patterns, a memorable style of dress, imposing physical attributes, or an unusual obsession. Perhaps they have characteristics that run opposed to their profession or nature. The local school marm has the beauty, the manners, and charm of a Registered Companion. A cattle rustler is well-versed in the plays of Shakespeare and quotes them frequently.

For example, the GM is going to create a competitor for the heroes for a classic-style *Serenity* campaign. Name of Thomas Barnaby Liu. Liu is the owner of another space vessel similar to a Firefly Class ship. He is Asian in appearance, although, since he was raised by a Caucasian, Irish mother, he doesn't speak Chinese so well.

Thinking on his history a spell, the GM decides that Liu has been flyin' the black most of his life, working one menial job after another, all the while saving his credits to buy his own ship. His dream has come true, though he now has a large debt that he has difficulty paying down. The GM determines Liu's attributes and skills, giving him skills in most of the critical operations of a ship.

So what makes Liu even more interesting? The GM decides that during the war, Liu ended up as a civilian contractor on a Browncoat destroyer. The pay was good at times, but he never developed an affection for the cause. He is in constant need of money, so that is his driving factor. He is very protective of his ship and his ability to keep flying. Liu is a bit vain as well, liking to boast about his abilities as a mechanic and a pilot. That vanity could be used against him if handled the right way.

As for a physical description, Liu is a wiry man in his fifties. He has a friendly manner and a cool demeanor, unless the whisky is flowing and someone is willing to listen to his braggadocio. He wears coveralls that are generally grimy. He has surprising strength in his skinny arms and a knee-knocking case of the nerves when confronted by pretty women. He loves dogs and he has any number of mutts living on board his ship. They all accompany him when he goes to town. The dogs are extremely well-trained and protective of their master.

The GM will have to name his ship and decide what kind of ship it is, but that can come later. The key is that Liu could be a potential ally, rival, or enemy, all depending on how the heroes interact with him and how he reacts to the events in the adventure.

VILLAINS

Above and beyond stock NPCs and even important NPCs are the villains. Since these NPCs will have the greatest impact on the heroes' adventures, villains should be given the same amount of detail as an important NPC with one additional aspect—motivation. The GM must understand why this person is an enemy of the heroes or, if he is not an enemy now, what happens that will make him an enemy in the future.

When creating a villain, remember one important fact: No one wakes up in the morning and says, "Gosh darn it, today I'm going to be evil!" Good villains should be human, with flaws and foibles and maybe even some redeeming characterisstics. Good villains do what they do for logical reasons—or at least reasons that appear logical to them!

Seeds of villainy include: suffering a humiliating defeat, obsessive competitiveness, avenging a personal insult, a difference of beliefs, jealousy, greed, overweaning ambition, lust.

For example, Jack Leland defeats the settlement's championship poker player at cards. He thinks nothing of it. She, on the other hand, loses face with those whose regard she has worked hard to foster. She must pay back Jack Leland for the humiliation of her loss and she will spend every waking moment working toward Leland's defeat, humiliation, or death. Leland, of course, knows nothing of this and it will come as an unpleasant surprise to him when he finds out.

A villain may not notice the PCs at first, but if they thwart his schemes, he may take a much greater interest in them. The villain may perceive the PCs as a threat to his security. The villain might be jealous of their success or angry that they cut him out of a job.

Villains don't generally stalk about the 'Verse dressed in black capes and breathing heavily. Some of the best villains may be friendly and charming, appearing to the PCs to be their best friend, all the while smoothly manipulating the PCs toward their doom.

In general, tend to avoid running insane villains. These may seem tempting, because they are guaranteed to act irrationally and they don't require much motiviation for doing the horrible things they are doing. This lack of logical motivation can bring about a real sense of let down if and when the heroes finally catch up to the lunatic. "Oh, him? He's just crazy." Even Niska has a logical rationale for torturing people (beyond taking a sadistic pleasure

in watching them suffer). He has his reputation to uphold!

Based on how the adventures play out and the PCs act, an important or even stock NPC may naturally develop into a villain. Actions which may appear harmless or unavoidable to the PCs at the time could be viewed quite differently by those harmed or disadvantaged by it. The villain may seek to avenge a wrong the heroes honestly don't remember inflicting.

Villains are most exciting to portray when they are as real and complex as the PCs. Devote plenty of time to their creation.

FELLOW TRAVELERS

As your players explore the 'Verse, their characters will encounter many different people along the way. Some of NPCs the players encounter will be of vital importance. These NPCs might have valuable information to impart or perhaps they have been hired to kill the crew or are planning to arrest them.

But not every person the crew meets is going to have an impact on their lives. In fact, in order to give the characters the feeling that they are living in an immense 'Verse populated by millions of people, the GM should provide encounters with a wide variety of folks who may have nothing to do with the plot.

This section provides the GM with various "stock" characters that can be used either as major NPCs or minor ones, including minor characters from the movie, *Serenity*. These characters come with all the stats necessary for use in the game, as well as some hints as to how to play them in order to give each of them a unique personality. Some also come with story "hooks" that can be used by the Game Master to further the plot. Any of these characters can be altered, expanded upon, or "fleshed out" by the Game Master in order to meet the needs of a particular adventure.

Please note that although the NPCs are portrayed as either male or female in the text, the stats for most could apply to either a man or a woman. Those who are obviously male (Buddhist Monk) or obviously female (Dance Hall Girl) are listed as such.

ALLIANCE OFFICER, DISILLUSIONED VETERAN

Agi d6, Str d8, Vit d8, Ale d8, Int d8, Wil d8; Life Points 18; Initiative d6 + d8.

Traits: Tough as Nails (Minor Asset), Military Rank (Minor Asset)

Skills: Athletics d6, Covert d4, Discipline d6/Mental Resistance d10, Guns d6/Pistol d10/Assault Rifle d8, Knowledge d6/Military History d10, Perception d6/Tactics d12.

Description: He is in his middle-years. He's seen it all, done it all. He knows every trick in the book, and can size up a person in a glance. He once wanted to be a hero, but he came to his senses during the war. He's not going to rise higher in rank. He is counting the days to his retirement and his pension. He won't make trouble for folk, if they don't make trouble for him. After all, shooting someone means filling out a ton of paperwork.

ALLIANCE OFFICER, GUNG-HO

Agi d8, Str d10, Vit d8, Ale d6, Int d6, Wil d6; Life Points 14; Initiative d8 + d6.

Traits: Military Rank (Minor Asset), Prejudice (Minor Complication), Overconfident (Minor Complication).

Skills: Athletics d6, Discipline d6/Interrogation d8, Guns d6/Pistol d8/Assault Rifle d8, Knowledge d4, Perception d6.

Description: He was a bonafide hero in the war, and he has the medals to prove it. He hates Browncoats, considers them terrorists who are trying to destabilize the government. He is working hard to ingratiate himself with his superiors, and a fine show of heroics would certainly go a long way to earn him that promotion. He is looking for trouble, and if none comes his way, he'll make it up on the spot.

ALLIANCE OFFICER, YOUNG AND GREEN

Agi d6, Str d6, Vit d8, Ale d6, Int d6, Wil d4; Life Points 12; Initiative d6 + d6.

Traits: Weak Stomach (Minor Complication),

Skills: Athletics d4, Discipline d4, Guns d6/Pistol d8, Knowledge d6/Military Regulations d10.

Description: He has just graduated from the Academy. This is his first assignment. He is proud of his new uniform. You could cut a steak with the knife-edge crease in his pants. His head is filled with rules and regulations that he can cite chapter and verse. He gives an outward appearance of confidence, but secretly he knows he's in over his head, and he's scared to death. He constantly touches his gun, as though to reassure himself it's still there. He's guaranteed to lose control the moment the situation gets tense, and may start shooting at anything that moves.

ALLIANCE GRUNT

Agi d6, Str d8, Vit d8, Ale d6, Int d6, Wil d8; Life Points 16; Initiative d6 + d6.

Traits: Military Rank (Minor Asset), Loyal (Minor Complication).

Skills: Athletics d6, Discipline d6, Guns d6/Assault Rifle d8, Perception d6, Melee Weapon Combat d4.

Description: He does his duty. He obeys orders. He tries to never think for himself, since that's against regulation. He's well-trained, well-armed, efficient, and nobody's fool.

BOUNTY HUNTER, HIGH TECH

Agi d12, Str d8, Vit d6, Ale d10, Int d8, Wil d8; Life Points 14; Initiative d12 + d10.

Traits: Fightin' Type (Major Asset), Steady Calm (Minor Asset).

Skills: Athletics d6/Dodge d10, Covert d6/Stealth d10/Infiltration d10/Surveillance d8/Streetwise d8, Discipline d6/Concentration d8, Guns d6/Pistol d10/Sniper Rifle d12, Influence d6, Knowledge d6, Melee Weapon Combat d6, Perception d6/Tracking d10

Description: She works alone, because she doesn't like to share the wealth, and she doesn't trust anyone anyway. She has her own ship—top of the line, of course. She has the best weapons money can buy, the best information, the best sources. She is an expert, skilled at her job, and she will do whatever it takes to bring in her quarry. She has no feelings, no heart, no sentimental side to her nature. She once caught her man by murdering his only child, knowing that he'd come out of hiding to go to the funeral.

BOUNTY HUNTER, BORDER PLANET

Agi d6, Str d6, Vit d6, Ale d10, Int d8, Wil d6; Life Points 12; Initiative d6 + d10.

Traits: Friends in Low Places (Minor Asset), Greedy (Minor Complication).

Skills: Covert d6/Surveillance d10/Streetwise d12, Guns d6, Influence d4, Knowledge d6, Perception d6/Tracking d8/Intuition d10

Description: He is too lazy to go chasin' all over the black for his prey. He hangs around the bars and saloons in places like the Eavesdown Docks on Persephone, waiting for his prey to come to him. He keeps a record of faces, and names, and how much money they're worth in a handheld electronic database. He has a small camera hidden in a shot glass that can take a picture whenever he raises the glass to his lips. He then runs the picture through a face-recognition program on his handheld device. If it matches, he sends in his hired goons to make the capture.

BROWNCOAT ALLY

Agi d8, Str d6, Vit d6, Ale d8, Int d8, Wil d6; Life Points 12; Initiative d8 + d8.

Traits: Friends in Low Places (Minor Asset), Fightin' Type (Major Asset), Loyal (Minor Complication).

Skills: Athletics d6, Covert d2, Discipline d6, Guns d6/Assault Rifle d8, Melee Weapon Combat d4, Perception d4, Survival d6.

Description: She served in the war on the side of the Independents. Though she's a stranger, she will immediately come to the aid of anyone she recognizes as a fellow Browncoat—no questions asked.

UNIFICATION WAR VET AND PROUD OF IT

Agi d6, Str d10, Vit d8, Ale d6, Int d4, Wil d6; Life Points 14; Initiative d6 + d6.

Traits: Mean Left Hook, (Minor Asset), Prejudice (Minor Complication), Overconfident (Minor Complication).

Skills: Athletics d4, Discipline d2, Guns d6, Knowledge d4, Melee Weapon Combat d4, Unarmed Combat d6/Brawling d8.

Description: The sight of a brown coat is like a red flag to a bull. He will immediately try to pick a fight, no matter where the characters are or under what circumstances.

BARTENDER AND OWNER

Agi d8, Str d6, Vit d6, Ale d10, Int d8, Wil d6; Life Points 12; Initiative d8 + d10.

Traits: Sharp Sense—Hearing (Minor Asset).

Skills: Guns d6/Shotgun d10, Knowledge d4, Influence d6, Perception d6.

Description: The owner of the saloon doubles as the bartender. She takes a dim view of fights that break up the furniture, and she'll order everyone outside the moment there is trouble. She keeps a double-barreled shotgun behind the bar to let folk know she's serious. She will use the shotgun to insist that folk pay for any damages or blood spill clean-up that may be necessary. She's an excellent marksman.

BARTENDER, HIRED HELP

Agi d6, Str d6, Vit d8, Ale d6, Int d6, Wil d4; Life Points 12; Initiative d6 + d6.

Traits: Hooked—Alcohol (Minor Complication).

Skills: Knowledge d4, Influence d4, Perception d4.

Description: He is hired to serve drinks, and that's it. No one is paying him to be a hero. He hits the floor behind the bar at the first sign of trouble, taking a glass and the best whiskey with him "to keep it safe."

BARFLY

Agi d6, Str d8, Vit d6, Ale d6, Int d4, Wil d6; Life Points 12; Initiative d6 + d6.

Traits: Heavy Tolerance (Minor Asset).

Skills: Athletics d4, Guns d2, Melee Weapon Combat d4, Unarmed Combat d6/Brawling d8.

Description: He works all day at a boring, grubby job. He lives for the moment the whistle sounds, and he can go join his buddies for a beer. He won't throw the first punch, but he does enjoy the occasional bar fight, because it breaks up the monotony of his otherwise bleak existence. He won't much care what side he takes.

DANCE HALL GIRL

Agi d8, Str d6, Vit d6, Ale d8, Int d6, Wil d6; Life Points 12; Initiative d8 + d8.

Traits: Dead Broke (Minor Complication), Combat Paralysis (Minor Complication).

Skills: Influence d6, Performance d6/Saloon Dancing d10/Singing d8.

Description: She sought a career on the stage on Londinum. She couldn't make the big time, and ended up in a touring company that came to the Rim. The company went bust here, leaving her stranded. She took this job because it was either dance in a saloon or starve. She longs for the day she can leave this place and return to civilization.

BAR FLOOZY (FEMALE)

Agi d6, Str d6, Vit d6, Ale d8, Int d6, Wil d8; Life Points 14; Initiative d6 + d8.

Traits: Greedy (Minor Complication), Filcher (Minor Complication).

Skills: Covert d4, Influence d6/Seduction d8.

Description: She rents a room over the saloon where she entertains her clients, paying the owner a percentage of her take. She spends her time in the bar, looking for marks, and enticing men into buying her drinks. She wears a red spangled dress, limp feathers in her bright orange hair, and too much make-up. Her only love is money, and she'll do anything in order to earn it, including lacing drinks with knock-out pills or rifling through the pockets of her slumbering victims.

REGISTERED COMPANION (FEMALE)

Agi d8, Str d4, Vit d6, Ale d8, Int d8, Wil d10; Life Points 16; Initiative d8 + d8.

Traits: Allure (Minor Asset), Friends in High Places (Minor Asset), Highly Educated (Minor Asset).

Skills: Artistry d6, Covert d4, Influence d6/Seduction d10/Persuasion d10, Knowledge d6, Melee Weapon Combat d4, Perception d6, Performance d6, Ranged Weapons d4, Unarmed Combat d6.

Description: She is elegant, beautiful, refined, sophisticated, well-educated. She can intelligently discuss art and music, literature and philosophy. She is a superb dancer, and plays a wide variety of musical instruments. She knows the right thing to say at any social gathering. Gentle and gracious, she goes out of her way to make people feel at ease when they are around her. She strictly adheres to the tenants of her Order. She is highly skilled and well-trained in the art of sexual pleasure. She is widely respected and welcome anywhere, gracing important social, political, or business functions with her presence.

She is trained in the art of self-defense, and since she never goes to a client armed, most of her training is in the martial arts. She can use a variety of weapons, however. She has access to an impressive data base that she uses to screen her clients, selecting only those who meet her high standards. She protects her clients, and will never, under any circumstances, reveal their secrets to anyone.

REGISTERED COMPANION (MALE)

Agi d8, Str d4, Vit d6, Ale d8, Int d8, Wil d10; Life Points 16; Initiative d8 + d8.

Traits: Allure (Minor Asset), Friends in High Places (Minor Asset), Highly Educated (Minor Asset).

Skills: Artistry d6, Covert d4, Influence d6/Seduction d10/Persuasion d10, Knowledge d6, Melee Weapon Combat d4, Perception d6, Performance d6, Ranged Weapons d4, Unarmed Combat d6.

Description: He is suave, handsome, refined, sophisticated, well-educated. He can intelligently discuss art and music, literature and philosophy. He is muscular, in excellent physical condition. He is a good dancer, and can play a wide variety of musical instruments. He knows the right thing to say at any social gathering. Charming and witty, he goes out of his way to make people feel at ease when they are around him. He strictly adheres to the tenants of his Order. He is highly skilled and well-trained in the art of sexual pleasure. He is widely respected and welcome anywhere, including important social, political, or business functions.

He is trained in the art of self-defense, and since he never goes to a client armed, most of his training is in the martial arts. He can use a variety of weapons, however. He has access to an impressive data base that he uses to screen his clients, selecting only those who meet his high standards. He protects his clients, and will never, under any circumstances, reveal their secrets to anyone.

SHEYDRA

Agi d8, Str d4, Vit d6, Ale d8, Int d8, Wil d10; Life Points 16; Initiative d8 + d8.

Traits: Allure (Minor Asset), Friends in High Places (Minor Asset), Highly Educated (Minor Asset).

Skills: Artistry d6, Covert d4, Influence d6/Seduction d8/Persuasion d10/Administration d10, Knowledge d6, Melee Weapon Combat d4, Perception d6, Performance d6, Ranged Weapons d4, Unarmed Combat d6.

Description: A registered Companion, middle-aged, still beautiful and alluring. She is the mistress of a Companion Training House on a world far removed from the shiny lights of the Core. This is the first House the Alliance has ever established in such a remote area. She is skilled in her craft, though she is not as gifted as some—a fact that she is wise enough to recognize. She personally selects those boys and girls who are chosen to enter the House, looking for intelligence, breeding, beauty, charm, and discipline.

BUDDHIST MONK (MALE)

Agi d6, Str d4, Vit d4, Ale d8, Int d8, Wil d6; Life Points 10; Initiative d6 + d8.

Traits: Religiosity (Major Asset), Non-Fightin' Type (Minor Complication).

Skills: Craft d4, Discipline d6, Knowledge d6/Buddhism d10, Medical Expertise d4, Perception d6.

Description: He is thin and wiry. His head is shaved. He wears the traditional red robes. He is a vegetarian and a pacifist. He does not drink alcohol. He has no martial arts training or weapons training of any kind. He is strong in his faith, and will do what he can to protect the innocent and defenseless. He will spend part of every day in meditation.

WHORE WITH A HEART OF GOLD (FEMALE)

Agi d8, Str d6, Vit d6, Ale d8, Int d8, Wil d10; Life Points 16; Initiative d8 + d8.

Traits: Allure (Minor Asset), Highly Educated (Minor Asset).

Skills: Artistry d4, Covert d6, Influence d6/Seduction d10/Persuasion d10, Guns d6, Knowledge d6, Melee Weapon Combat d4, Perception d6, Performance d2, Ranged Weapons d4, Unarmed Combat d6, Survival d4

Description: A former registered Companion, she left the Order under mysterious circumstances. She runs a bawdy house on a Rim world. She cares for her people, and runs a clean and well-ordered establishment. She employs both men and women. She has worked hard to build her business, and will fight anyone who threatens it or tries to harm her people.

SETTLER FAMILY

Hard-working folk, they could be encountered anywhere—on a ship traveling to a newly terraformed planet, on their own homestead, at a town festival. The parents, father and mother, are poor and not that well-educated. Their clothes are worn and shabby, but clean. The children, boy and girl, are exuberant and rowdy, but fairly well-behaved. The parents are working hard to make a better life for the children. The parents may or may not be carrying weapons. If so, the weapons are probably old and neither parent is a very good shot.

FATHER

Agi d6, Str d8, Vit d6, Ale d6, Int d4, Wil d6; Life Points 14; Initiative d6 + d6.

Traits: Tough as Nails (Minor Asset), Superstitious (Minor Complication).

Skills: Animal Handling d6, Athletics d4, Guns d4, Survival d6.

MOTHER

Agi d6, Str d6, Vit d6, Ale d8, Int d6, Wil d6; Life Points 12; Initiative d6 + d8.

Traits: Religiosity (Minor Asset).

Skills: Animal Handling d2, Craft d6, Guns d2, Perception d4, Survival d6.

LITTLE BOY

Agi d6, Str d4, Vit d4, Ale d6, Int d4, Wil d4; Life Points 8; Initiative d6 + d6.

Traits: Allergy—Flowers (Minor Complication)

Skills: Animal Handling d2, Perception d4, Survival d2

LITTLE GIRL

Agi d6, Str d4, Vit d4, Ale d6, Int d6, Wil d4; Life Points 8; Initiative d6 + d6.

Traits: Sweet and Cheerful (Minor Asset).

Skills: Craft d2, Perception d4, Survival d2.

SALOON PIANO PLAYER

Agi d6, Str d6, Vit d6, Ale d6, Int d8, Wil d6; Life Points 12; Initiative d6 + d6.

Traits: Talented—Piano (Minor Asset).

Skills: Performance d6/Piano d10.

Description: His mother was the local piano teacher. He's classically trained and works at the saloon to make his living. He likes his work, especially the free drinks that go with it. He occasionally gets bored playing the same old tunes and will sometimes break into a fit of Chopin or Rachmaninoff. When that happens, the patrons throw beer mugs at him until he goes back to the standards. He enjoys accompanying the bar fights with exciting music. He will play requests, but only if you buy him a drink first.

ALLIANCE HOSPITAL PERSONNEL

Depending on where they are and who they are, the characters may or may not be admitted to an Alliance medical facility. If the characters come into an Emergency Room in a hospital on a Core planet, they will have to present the proper identification and proof of government-issued insurance. If they don't have insurance or if their paperwork is questionable, the hospital personnel may refuse treatment and send them to a hospital for "charity" cases.

If they are accepted, they will be triaged by a nurse first, then, depending on the severity of their injuries or illness, they may encounter a long wait before the doctor sees them.

If they come to a medical facility on a space station or an Alliance cruiser, the players will most certainly need to present the correct ID before they are even permitted on board. Such facilities have been hijacked before, and the Alliance is taking no chances.

TRAUMA SURGEON

Agi d8, Str d6, Vit d6, Ale d8, Int d10, Wil d6; Life Points 12; Initiative d8 + d8.

Traits: Highly Educated (Minor Asset).

Skills: Discipline d6/Concentration d8, Influence d4, Knowledge d6, Perception d6, Medical Expertise d6/Internal Medicine d10/Physiology d10/Surgery d12.

TRAUMA NURSE

Agi d6, Str d6, Vit d6, Ale d8, Int d8, Wil d6; Life Points 12; Initiative d6 + d8.

Traits: Steady Calm (Minor Asset).

Skills: Discipline d4, Knowledge d4, Perception d6, Medical Expertise d6/Physiology d8/Pharmaceuticals d8.

HOSPITAL ADMINISTRATOR

Agi d6, Str d6, Vit d6, Ale d8, Int d8, Wil d6; Life Points 12; Initiative d6 + d8.

Traits: Good Name (Minor Asset).

Skills: Influence d6/Administration d10, Knowledge d6, Perception d6, Medical Expertise d6.

SECURITY GUARD

Agi d6, Str d8, Vit d8, Ale d6, Int d6, Wil d6; Life Points 14; Initiative d6 + d6.

Skills: Athletics d4, Guns d4, Melee Weapon Combat d6/Clubs d8.

PARAMEDICS

Agi d8, Str d6, Vit d6, Ale d8, Int d8, Wil d6; Life Points 12; Initiative d8 + d8.

Traits: Steady Calm (Minor Asset).

Skills: Discipline d6, Knowledge d4, Perception d6, Medical Expertise d6/Physiology d8/Pharmaceuticals d8/Surgery d8/Internal Medicine d8.

SCHOOL TEACHER

Agi d6, Str d6, Vit d6, Ale d6, Int d8, Wil d6; Life Points 12; Initiative d6 + d6.

Traits: Highly Educated (Minor Asset).

Skills: Artistry d4, Influence d6/Leadership d10, Knowledge d6/Education d10, Perception d6.

Description: She is from one of the Core planets, where she received her education at one of the universities. She has been hired by the local townsfolk on this far away world to educate their children. She traveled to the Rim with high ideals that have since been shattered by the harshness and brutality of the life. She has come to respect the hard-working settlers, and she is doing what she can to bring a better life to them and their children. She is the most educated person in the town and often has to fight against ignorance, prejudice, and superstition in order to protect her charges—and herself.

HIGH FALUTIN' GENTLEMAN

Agi d6, Str d8, Vit d6, Ale d8, Int d6, Wil d8; Life Points 14; Initiative d6 + d8.

Traits: Moneyed Individual (Major Asset), Overconfident (Minor Complication).

Skills: Athletics d4, Guns d6/Pistols d10, Influence d6/Negotiation d10, Melee Weapon Combat d6/ Sword d12, Perception d4.

Description: He bought and paid for his social standing. He is pretentious and arrogant, but has a certain amount of charm that he can turn off and on when needed. He is convinced that everyone has a price. His business dealings are shady, but he never gets caught, since he has bribed all the right people. He wears fine clothes, and is sleekly handsome. He is an expert in dueling with either pistols or swords.

SOCIETY BELLE

Agi d6, Str d4, Vit d4, Ale d8, Int d6, Wil d6; Life Points 10; Initiative d6 + d8.

Traits: Moneyed Individual (Major Asset), Prejudice—'Lower Classes' (Minor Complication).

Skills: Artistry d4, Influence d6, Performance d4.

Description: Thanks to Daddy she has all the money she wants. She dresses in what she believes to be the latest fashion trends from the Core, though her clothes are, in reality, cheap knockoffs she buys because she doesn't know the difference. She is snooty and prideful, silly and vain. She despises her parents and the Border planet on which she was born. Her main goal in life is to find a rich husband

who will take her to the Core and introduce her to "people who count."

ITINERANT FRONTIER REVIVALIST

Agi d6, Str d8, Vit d6, Ale d6, Int d6, Wil d10; Life Points 16; Initiative d6 + d6.

Traits: Religiosity (Major Asset), Superstitious (Minor Complication).

Skills: Influence d6/Leadership d10, Knowledge d6/Religious Retribution d12, Melee Weapon Combat d6, Performance d6/Hell-Raising d12.

Description: He totes a Bible in one hand and an axe in the other. He travels from planet to moon holding revival meetings. He is fanatically opposed to just about everything, including demon rum, gambling, and prostitution. He is a rabble-rouser, and can move crowds to tears of repentance or acts of violence. Saloons and bawdy houses are his favorite targets, and he often leads hymn-singing, axe-wielding mobs of zealots against such institutions.

PREACHER MAN

Agi d6, Str d6, Vit d8, Ale d6, Int d6, Wil d10; Life Points 18; Initiative d6 + d6.

Traits: Religiosity (Major Asset).

Skills: Craft d4, Influence d6, Knowledge d6/Religion d10, Medical Expertise d4.

Description: He is sincere in his beliefs and humble in his nature. He is truly determined to do what he can to help people find a better life, or at least a better place to go to when they die. He doesn't have much, but what he does have he's always willing to share. He is tolerant, merciful, and forgiving.

ANGEL OF MERCY

Agi d6, Str d4, Vit d6, Ale d6, Int d8, Wil d6; Life Points 12; Initiative d6 + d6.

Traits: Trustworthy Gut (Major Asset).

Skills: Craft d6/Homeopathy d10, Influence d4, Knowledge d6/Herbalogy d12, Medical Expertise d2, Perception d6.

Description: She has no formal medical training. Her remedies are homeopathic, handed down from mother to daughter. She can treat most ordinary ailments with good results, and is an excellent mid-wife. She has a store of herbs that she uses to make poultices, potions, crude pills, tinctures, and salves. She knows her limits, and will not hesitate to summon trained medical help if such is available. If not, she'll do the best she can for her patients.

KING OF THE DUNG HEAP

Agi d6, Str d6, Vit d6, Ale d10, Int d8, Wil d8; Life Points 14; Initiative d6 + d10.

Traits: Friends in Low Places (Minor Asset), Greedy (Minor Complication)

Skills: Covert d6/Streetwise d12, Guns d6, Influence d6/Negotiation d8/Intimidation d10, Knowledge d6, Perception d6/Black-Market Trends d10

Description: The leader of a gang of thugs, pick-pockets, smugglers, and petty thieves, he is into every sort of illegal enterprise that he thinks he can safely get away with, including protection rackets, smuggling, trafficking in stolen goods, etc. He is street-wise, cocky, and smart-mouthed. He maintains control by having something on everyone who works for him. He never goes anywhere without his well-armed body guards.

BULLY BOY [MALE]

Agi d6, Str d10, Vit d10, Ale d6, Int d4, Wil d6; Life Points 20; Initiative d6 + d6.

Traits: Tough as Nails (Major Asset).

Skills: Athletics d4, Guns d4, Melee Weapon Combat d6/Knives d8/Clubs d8, Unarmed Combat d6/Brawling d10.

Description: This guy is all muscle, from the head down. He is big and brawny, tough and mean, and uses his size to intimidate. He is good at beating up people and not much else.

"TONG" LEADER

Agi d8, Str d8, Vit d8, Ale d6, Int d10, Wil d10; Life Points 18; Initiative d8 + d6.

Traits: Friends in Low Places (Minor Asset), Leadership (Major Asset)

Skills: Covert d6/Streetwise d12/Stealth d10, Discipline d6/Interrogation d12/Mental Resistance d10, Guns d6, Influence d6/Negotiation d10/ Intimidation d10, Knowledge d6, Melee Weapon Combat d6/Swords d10/Knives d10, Perception d6/Black-Market Trends d10, Unarmed Combat d6/Tai Chi d12.

Description: The Alliance has worked hard to eradicate the Chinese gangs known as "Tongs" and has been mostly successful on the Core planets, forcing the Tongs underground, or causing them to move their base of operations to the Rim. The leader is cruel, clever, resourceful. He is skilled in the martial arts, and can use most weapons. His followers are fanatically loyal. He is into various illegal enterprises. He is not a person to cross, and most people in his community know him and fear him.

FRONTIER SHERIFF

Agi d6, Str d8, Vit d8, Ale d6, Int d6, Wil d6; Life Points 14; Initiative d6 + d6.

Traits: Wears a Badge (Minor Asset).

Skills: Athletics d4, Guns d6/Rifle d10/Pistol d10, Influence d6, Perception d6, Melee Weapon Combat d4.

Description: There are mainly two types of sheriffs on the Rim. Both are skilled with weapons and fists. Their personalities are vastly different, however.

One sheriff is brutal, corrupt, and self-serving. He protects those who pay him, including outlaws. He may be hired by the mine owners, or whoever runs the town, to keep everyone in line. He enforces law and order by means of torture, intimidation, and murder. He is a bully and a coward.

The other sheriff is determined to bring justice to the frontier. He is not afraid to take on the bad guys. He does what he can to protect those who can't defend themselves. He is hard-working, honest, and courageous.

FRONTIER DEPUTY

Agi d6, Str d6, Vit d8, Ale d6, Int d6, Wil d6; Life Points 14; Initiative d6 + d6.

Traits: Wears a Badge (Minor Asset)

Skills: Athletics d4, Guns d6/Pistol d10, Influence d2, Perception d4, Melee Weapon Combat d4.

Description: As goes the sheriff, so goes his deputy.

FRONTIER DOCTOR

Agi d6, Str d6, Vit d6, Ale d8, Int d10, Wil d8; Life Points 14; Initiative d6 + d8.

Traits: Steady Calm (Minor Asset), Hooked—Alcohol (Minor Complication).

Skills: Discipline d4, Knowledge d4, Perception d6, Medical Expertise d6/Physiology d8/ Pharmaceuticals d8/Internal Medicine d8.

Description: He has formal medical training, but his work is often hampered by the fact that out here on the Rim, he lacks the proper medical supplies and equipment. He sees folk dying that he knows he could save, if only he had the right medicine, which he can't obtain due to government ineptness. He has grown callous and embittered. His bedside manner is atrocious, and he is never quite sober. But he is good at his job, and often pulls his patients through, when by rights they should have died.

RIM SHOP KEEPER

Agi d6, Str d6, Vit d6, Ale d8, Int d8, Wil d6; Life Points 12; Initiative d6 + d8.

Traits: Trustworthy Gut (Minor Asset).

Skills: Influence d6/Negotiation d8, Knowledge d6, Perception d6.

Description: She is brisk and business-like, polite to her customers, and determined to make a sale. She is knowledge about her wares, be it guns, butter, or bullet-proof corsets. She will bargain, but only up to a point. How good a deal you get depends on how good business has been for her these past few weeks. If she has a large store, she will have a security guard at the door. If not, she handles her own security. She doesn't prosecute shop-lifters. She shoots them.

FANTY AND MINGO

Agi d6, Str d4, Vit d6, Ale d8, Int d10, Wil d8; Life Points 14; Initiative d6 + d8.

Traits: Friends in Low Places (Minor Asset), Greedy (Minor Complication).

Skills: Covert d6/Streetwise d12, Influence d6/Negotiation d10, Knowledge d4, Perception d6/Black-Market Trends d12.

Description: Identical twins, they have paid informants scattered all over the 'Verse, who send word of "sweet deals"—such as the arrival of unguarded payroll in a small town bank. The twins then hire folk who aren't too picky about the kind of job they take to perform heists, smuggling operations, or whatever the deal happens to be. The twins' cut varies, depending on what they think they can get away with. Their HQ is a bar known as the Maidenhead on Beaumonde.

HIRED GUN

Agi d8, Str d8, Vit d8, Ale d6, Int d6, Wil d6; Life Points 14; Initiative d8 + d6.

Traits: Greedy (Minor Complication).

Skills: Athletics d6, Discipline d4, Guns d6/Pistol d8/SMG d8, Knowledge d4, Perception d4.

Description: He'll work for anybody, no matter what the job, so long as the money is good. He's a drifter, never stays in one place long. Most people don't know his name. Or care to know it.

CON ARTIST

Agi d6, Str d6, Vit d6, Ale d6, Int d10, Wil d8; Life Points 14; Initiative d6 + d6.

Traits: Greedy (Minor Complication).

Skills: Covert d6/Pickpocket d8/Forgery d8, Guns d4, Influence d6/Persuasion d10/Seduction d10, Knowledge d6/Poisons d8, Perception d6.

She is a swindler, a cheat, a liar. She generally has some scheme going all the time. She is a master of deception and disguise. She can be charming, ingratiating, seductive, and deadly. She is an expert in poisons and drugs, and small, easily concealable weapons. Whatever name she is using at the time is likely not her own.

FORGER

Agi d6, Str d4, Vit d6, Ale d8, Int d10, Wil d6; Life Points 12; Initiative d6 + d8.

Traits: Natural Linguist (Minor Asset).

Skills: Covert d6/Forgery d12, Influence d6, Knowledge d6, Linguistics d6, Perception d6.

Description: He can forge anything from money to documents and he will—for a price. The really good forgers are found on the Core planets, where they have access to advanced technology.

PURVEYOR OF STOLEN GOODS (THE CORE)

Agi d6, Str d6, Vit d6, Ale d6, Int d8, Wil d8; Life Points 14; Initiative d6 + d6.

Traits: Friends in Low Places (Minor Asset).

Skills: Covert d6/Streetwise d8, Influence d6/Negotiation d8, Knowledge d6, Perception d6.

Description: Her front is an antique business. Those who want to do business with her have to maintain the charade that they are dealing in antiques, or she will pretend not to know what they are talking about. Those who have guns to sell, for example, speak knowingly about "Louis XIV chairs" and "Ming vases". She screens her clients carefully, and will not accept anyone without the proper references from former clients. Her security guards are top-notch.

PAWN BROKER/ FENCE (BORDER PLANET)

Agi d6, Str d6, Vit d6, Ale d6, Int d8, Wil d8; Life Points 14; Initiative d6 + d6.

Traits: Friends in Low Places (Minor Asset).

Skills: Covert d4, Influence d6/Negotiation d8, Knowledge d4, Perception d6.

Description: His front is a pawn shop. He will buy or sell anything, no questions asked.

TOWN LEADER

Agi d6, Str d8, Vit d6, Ale d6, Int d6, Wil d10; Life Points 16; Initiative d6 + d6.

Traits: Leadership (Minor Asset)

Skills: Guns d6/Rifle d8, Influence d6/ Leadership d10, Knowledge d6, Perception d6, Survival d4

He is the leader of a small community of settlers. A charismatic individual, he is devoted to his job, and dedicated to his people. Even if he is corrupt, as some are, he will maintain that he does what he has to for the good of his people. (This may be true!) He is not very well educated, and is suspicious of outsiders, who will have to prove themselves to him in order to get on his good side—either that or provide him with something he desperately needs. He is the only law in these parts, and his followers will see to it that his law is enforced.

MR. UNIVERSE

Agi d6, Str d4, Vit d4, Ale d10, Int d12, Wil d8 Life Points 12; Initiative d6 + d10.

Traits: Cortex Spectre (Major Asset), Talented—Technical Engineering/Cortex (Major Asset), Loyal—Lenore (Minor Complication), Hooked—Cortex (Major Complication).

Skills: Covert d6/Security d12+d4, Discipline d6/Concentration d10, Knowledge d6/Truth (Specialty restricted to Mr. Universe) d12, Perception d6/Deduction d10, Technical Engineering d6/Cortex d12+d8

Description: A young man, unkempt, over-caffeinated, and sweet in a geeky kind of way. He lives in his own "mediaverse"—a satellite moon that appears to have once been a gigantic communications complex. Some of the equipment is new. Some of it is old and long-neglected.

No one knows much about Mr. Universe. There is speculation that he either bought this complex from a corporation that went out of business, or he is a squatter who moved in and performed necessary renovations.

He sits at his central control panel, day and night, surrounded by screens that each show different feeds coming from all parts of the 'Verse. He sees the truth of what is happening in the 'Verse, and at the same time, he sees the propaganda the government dispenses to an unsuspecting public.

No one knows how he makes a living. He is completely and totally absorbed in watching life flash past on his screens.

His only companion is a manikin-like LoveBot named "Lenore." She says nothing, rarely moves. He quite obviously adores her.

REAVER

Agi d8, Str d10, Vit d10, Ale d8, Int d6, Wil d10; Life Points 24; Initiative d8 + d8.

Traits: Tough as Nails (Major Asset), Fightin' Type (Major Asset), Sadistic (Major Complication).

Skills: Athletics d6, Covert d6/Stealth d8, Discipline d6, Guns d6/Pistol d8, Perception d4, Melee Weapon Combat d6/Knives d10/Club d8, Unarmed Combat d6/Brawling d10.

Special Note: If Reavers feel pain, they are not hindered by it—but rather thrive on it. Reavers ignore the effects of Stun damage, and do not suffer Wound penalties for injuries. (They will, however, suffer penalties for obvious physical problems. A Reaver whose arm has been severed can only attack with one arm!)

Description: A terrible corruption of something that was once human, a Reaver is obsessed by pain—both causing it and feeling it. The Reaver's flesh is disfigured with radiation burns, slashed by self-inflicted knife wounds, and pierced by various sharp objects—everything from nails to barbed fish hooks. His hair is sparse and falling out in clumps. His teeth are filed to sharp points and stained with blood. His clothes are ragged, held together by patches made out of human skin stripped off his victims. The cloth is stiff with the dried blood of those he butchered.

His breath is foul. He stinks of blood and death. His weapons double as implements of torture. He takes pleasure in the killing, and he wants his victim to remain alive as long as possible. He is utterly savage, without mercy or compassion of any kind. He has no fear of dying himself—he may even welcome the thought. The threat of death will not deter him from his bestial, brutal acts.

DR. MATHIAS

Agi d8, Str d6, Vit d4, Ale d8, Int d12, Wil d6; Life Points 10; Initiative d8 + d8.

Traits: Steady Calm (Minor Asset).

Skills: Discipline d6, Knowledge d4, Perception d6, Medical Expertise d6/Physiology d10/Pharmaceuticals d10/Surgery d10/Internal Medicine d8/Neurology d12.

Description: Coldly analytical, he views his patients as mere scientific experiments, indistinguishable from lab rats. He works on an unnamed project for the Alliance at a lab in a secret location. The project is shadowy, but rumor has it that the government is performing brain surgery on people who have psychic powers in order to train them as spies and assassins.

THE OPERATIVE OF THE PARLIAMENT

Agi d12, Str d10, Vit d10, Ale d10, Int d8, Wil d12; Life Points 22; Initiative d12+d2+d10.

Traits: Fightin' Type (Major Asset), Steady Calm (Minor Asset), Lightnin' Reflexes (Major Reflexes).

Skills: Athletics d6/Dodge d10/Climb d8, Covert d6/Stealth d10/Infiltration d12/Surveillance d8/Streetwise d8/Disable Device d8, Discipline d6/Concentration d10/Interrogation d12, Guns d6/Pistol d8/Sniper Rifle d8, Influence d6, Knowledge d6, Melee Weapon Combat d6/Swords d12+d6, Perception d6/Tracking d10/Intuition d8, Unarmed Combat d6.

Description: Known only as the Operative, he is obsessed with his mission. He does the work of the Parliament, though he has no name, rank, or title. The public knows nothing of his existence. He receives government funding, and has high-level security clearance. He is granted anything he wants or needs in order to fulfill his assignment.

He is thoroughly convinced that the ends justify the means. He believes that he is working to bring about a better future for humanity. He has a certain amount of regret for the terrible acts he commits, but he is able to justify them by the belief that even though he is forced to commit monstrous acts to gain his goal, the end result will be a better world.

His favored weapon is a sword that he uses for ritualistic, ceremonial killings. A death for his cause is a "good death," particularly one that is met bravely at the end of his sword. He sometimes admires his victims for their work or resourcefulness, but he does not waver in his belief.

JACK LELAND

Agi d8, Str d4, Vit d6, Ale d10, Int d8, Wil d6; Life Points 12; Initiative d8+d10.

Traits: Deadly Enemy (Minor Complication), Dull Sense—Taste (Minor Complication), Friends in High Places (Minor Asset), Moneyed Individual (Major Asset), Talented—Covert/Gambling (Major Asset).

Skills: Artistry d6, Covert d6/Gambling d12 + d8*/Sleight of Hand d10, Discipline d4, Guns d6/Pistol d8, Influence d6/Etiquette d10/Persuasion d10, Knowledge d6, Perception d6, Scientific Expertise d4. (Gambling skill is modified by the Talented trait.)

Description: Jacob Leland was born to poker—literally. His untimely arrival caused his mother to have to abruptly leave a high stakes game.

The Lelands owned a casino on Osiris. Jacob was raised in a world of fast money, high rollers, roulette wheels, and glitzy dancers. He could deal blackjack by age nine and his father often sent the boy onto the casino floor to help spot card counters.

When the casino went bust through poor business practices, Jack saw where his father had gone wrong. Jack went to college to further his education, using poker to fund his schooling. He gained degrees in accounting and business. He often says the smart gambler knows how to hang onto his winnings.

Jack did quite well for himself. He is in his early forties and his skill at poker and his smart investments have already made him a very wealthy man. Handsome, with black skin, melting brown eyes, and a disarming smile, he is suave and debonair and is at home in all the fine casinos on all the Core planets.

Jack is a high roller. Limo-shuttles pick him up. He is given penthouse suites, and provided with whatever his heart desires, including a generous line of credit. He is always seen in the company of beautiful women, though rarely the same woman twice (with the exception of his female bodyguard, Hwa Ling). This is Jack's life six months out of the year.

The other six months, Jack travels the black in his own ship, that he named *Aces and Eights*, taking his high stakes poker game to the Border planets. More than few wonder why Jack would leave a life of glamour and luxury to endure the hardships and danger of life on the frontier. Some sneer that he does so in order to bilk the "yokels" out of their hard-earned cash.

The truth is, Jack rarely breaks even on these trips. He has grown bored with the easy, over-regulated life of the Core planets. He is a gambler. He enjoys risk-taking. He likes the unpredictability of life on the Border. He also likes the people, who may be crude by Core standards, but are to him far more real than the "plastic" people of the Core. Jack also enjoys the unpretentious living conditions on board *Aces and Eights*—a marked contrast to his life on the Core.

Jack's poker games are much anticipated by people on the Border planets, where they are the social event of the season. The games are by invitation only. Jack carefully screens all players in advance, though he will take walk-ins if they have the cash. He looks not only for those with stakes, but also those who might provide him a challenge, and he has been known to bankroll players who are low on funds.

Jack is an expert at cheating and spotting cheaters, though he never cheats at cards himself. As he says, cheating is the hallmark of a bad poker player. He is remarkably observant of other people. He can tell by the twitch of a man's eyebrow if he's holding that third queen (or if he's about to go for his gun).

Jack is aware that the ship's crew does their own business on the side during his travels—this is part of the deal he made with the captain. Jack makes it his business to find out all he can about what's brewing. He will help, if called upon. Otherwise, he won't interfere—unless the odds are against them.

Jack carries a small, silver and gold-plated derringer in an inside pocket of his expensive and finely tailored dress jacket. He is an expert shot with this weapon.

Jack has friends in high places in the Alliance. He has enemies, too, though he doesn't know it. Before leaving the Core, Jack played a game of high-stakes poker with a high-ranking government official. Jack won big that night and, rather than embarrass Cabinet Minister, Ferdinand Vita, who could not cover his bets, Jack accepted his I.O.U.

The Cabinet Minister is on the verge of financial ruin and he cannot cover the I.O.U. Knowing that such a scandal would finish him politically, Vita has put a private government arrest flag for Jack, claiming that he is a "reader." Government agents hunt him, ready to secret him to an installation to do a surgical examination of the gambler's brain. Jack knows nothing of any of this.

Jack Leland is a loner who trusts only one person implicitly and that is his bodyguard, Hwa Ling.

HWA LING

Agi d10, Str d8, Vit d6, Ale d6, Int d6, Wil d6; Life Points 12; Initiative d10+d6.

Traits: Deadly Enemy (Minor Complication), Friends in Low Places (Minor Asset), Steady Calm (Major Asset), Talented—Unarmed Combat/Kung Fu (Minor Asset).

Skills: Athletics d6/Dodge d10, Covert d6, Guns d6, Influence d2, Knowledge d4, Medical Expertise d4, Melee Weapon Combat d6, Perception d6, Ranged Weapon Combat d6/Throwing Star d8, Technical Engineering d4, Unarmed Combat d6/ Kung Fu d12+d2*. (Kung Fu skill is modified by the Talented trait.)

Equipment: Pistol, Throwing Star (d2W, 10 ft. range), Small Knife, Hidden explosive, "flash bang" hair barrettes.

Description: Hwa Ling was born to violence as Jack was born to poker. Her father and mother were both members of the 14K Triad, a Chinese "Tong" that has been around since 17th century China on Earth-That-Was. Her brother was killed in a gang fight and Hwa Ling might well have met the same fate but that she was, oddly enough, saved by the draft board.

When the Unification War started, the Alliance was forced to draft young men and women into the military. The twenty-year-old Hwa Ling was called up. Taking note of her exceptional skills as a martial artist, the military sent her to commando training. Hwa Ling participated in numerous secret and dangerous missions during the war.

After the war ended, Hwa Ling was planning on making the military her career when she received word from her mother that her father had been brutally tortured and killed by a rival Tong. Hwa Ling took leave to attend to "family matters". She and her mother avenged her father's death, with the result that both were arrested for murder. Nothing could be proven against them, for no one dared come forward to testify. She was freed, but the military didn't like the scandal and handed her discharge papers.

Hwa Ling went to work as a security guard for one of the large casinos on Osiris and this was where she met Jack Leland. He admired her martial abilities, but what particularly caught his notice was her professional demeanor, her aloof detachment.

Hwa Ling saw and did a lot that was ugly and brutal during the war. She was particularly close to her father and his death and her experiences in the war combined to leave a deep gash in her soul. She reasons that if she doesn't want to get hurt like that anymore, she can never come to care for anyone. This includes her boss, Jack Leland. She works hard at not caring about him.

Hwa Ling is thirty years old. She is tall and slender with the hard-muscled body of the martial artist. She is expert in just about every weapon, including Oriental weapons, as well as standard military issue. She wears her blue-black hair in a bob with straight cut bangs over arching eyebrows. She has large, almond-shaped dark eyes that can, as Maxx once remarked, "skewer a man at twenty paces." She wears fatigues and combat boots when on board ship. When she accompanies Jack to his high-stake games, she wears a simple, elegant, long-sleeved, ankle-length black sheathe that is slit to the thigh, in case she needs to use her feet or legs in a fight.

On such occasions, she is a walking armory. Her star-shaped diamond necklace is really a lethal throwing star. Her long gloves hide a knife strapped to her arm. The knife is made of hard plastic and will not be picked up by metal detectors. She can draw and hurl this knife with deadly accuracy as fast as a man can draw and fire a gun. Her jeweled hair barrettes are "flash-bangs". When tossed into a room, the bright flash and loud noise will temporarily blind and stun anyone inside.

It is well Hwa Ling has this training, for a Tong known as the Hip-Sing—the same gang that killed her father—has vowed vengeance and they are actively searching for her. The Hip-Sing are known to have a large presence on several of more populous border planets. Her own Tong also has people on these planets and they will provide Hwa Ling with information, support, and assistance should she require it.

Hwa Ling told Jack the truth about her past when he hired her, for Hwa Ling has her own code of honor. None of the crew of the *Aces and Eights* knows anything about her, however, except that she was in the military. She likes and admires Captain Williams and the one time Hwa Ling ever seems to relax is when the two swap "war" stories. Captain Williams did some private investigating on his own about her past. He keeps what he found out to himself.

"MAXX" WILLIAMS

Agi d6, Str d8, Vit d8, Ale d8, Int d6, Wil d6; Life Points 14; Initiative d6+d8.

Traits: Friends in Low Places (Minor Asset), Leadership (Minor Asset), Loyal—Family (Minor Complication), Two-Fisted (Major Asset).

Skills: Athletics d6, Discipline d6, Guns d6/Pistol d8/Assault Rifle d8/Sniper Rifle d12, Influence d6, Knowledge d4, Melee Weapon Combat d6, Perception d6/Tactics d10, Pilot d2, Ranged Weapon Combat d2, Technical Engineering d4, Unarmed Combat d6.

Equipment: Pistol, Assault Rifle, "Good" Prosthetic Arm (Strength bonus of +2 steps when using this arm, plus the benefits of the "Mean Left Hook" trait; Armor 4, Life 10), Spare Prosthetic Arm (Strength/Agility penalty of –1 step with the arm; Armor 2, Life 6).

Description: Career military, as was his father and grandfather before him, Maxx Williams was a member of an elite commando squad in the Alliance during the War of Unification. Trained as a sniper, he did his job well, was wounded several times, and was decorated for his bravery in battle. He was looking forward to a brilliant career when an enemy missile brought down his troop carrier. Maxx lost his right arm at the shoulder in the crash and, although he was fitted with a prosthetic arm that functions as well or better than his real arm, the Alliance relegated him to a desk job.

After the war, Maxx resigned the military and went into business for himself. He now earns his living selling his services to anyone who has the means to pay. Maxx knows what he is worth—and that is considerable.

Maxx has done extremely well for himself and now, in his early forties, he owns several ships of various types, suitable for a variety of purposes. He has put together a good team of men and women, all expert in their fields.

Maxx has made an arrangement with Jack Leland to ferry him around the border planets for his high stakes poker games. Under this arrangement, Maxx serves as captain of Jack's ship (which Maxx helped him buy and outfit). He takes Jack where he wants to go and sees to it that he gets there safely and leaves safely. Aside from that, Maxx is free to pursue his own business on the side.

Maxx and Jack have come to respect each other. The two maintain a distant, politely cool relationship. Each knows that the other has lines that are not to be crossed. During the few times that they have found themselves caught in a tight spot, they have learned that they can rely on each other. Maxx is not above asking Jack to help on occasion and Jack, who always enjoys an adventure, generally agrees.

Maxx runs his ship with military discipline. Square-jawed, well-built, with buzz-cut gray hair, he keeps himself in top physical condition. He is an expert in all types of weapons, a crack shot with any sort of gun. He buys only the best.

His prosthetic right arm and hand are indistinguishable from the real deal and will even "bleed" if cut. He has above normal strength in his prosthetic arm. His right fist packs quite a punch. He is ambidextrous, having trained himself to use his left hand while his right was healing. His prosthetic arm is extremely expensive, specially made to his design by a company on Sihnon. Maxx carries a "spare" for emergencies, but the spare arm is of cheaper quality and he doesn't like it. One of the few things that will cause him to lose his temper (and his cool) is someone damaging his "good" right arm.

Maxx knows the military and not much else. He is an expert in military tactics, strategy, and history. He is bitter at the Alliance for sidelining him when he lost his arm, but he carefully maintains his connections in the military, figuring that this is good for business. He will hire out for any type of work—legal or illegal (the lines are blurred on the Border), except bounty hunting and fighting Reavers. He considers the first demeaning and the second suicidal. He will battle bandits, assist in range wars, or launch an assault on a neighboring moon. He can put together a small army, if called for, or handle the job with his team.

Maxx's only soft spot is for his wife, Irene, and baby daughter, Elizabeth, who live on Sihnon. He sets aside time every day to communicates with them and only a dire emergency will cause him to miss this. His people have learned that at such times, he is interrupted only at their peril. They also know to flee when he takes out the baby pictures.

TIME BOMB

Agi d8, Str d6, Vit d6, Ale d8, Int d12, Wil d6; Life Points 12; Initiative d8+d8.

Traits: Dull Sense—Sight (Minor Complication), Talented—Heavy Weapons/Demolitions (Major Asset).

Skills: Athletics d2, Discipline d6, Heavy Weapons d6/Demolitions d12+d4, Knowledge d6/Explosives d10, Mechanical Engineering d6/Construct Device d10/Repair d10, Melee Weapon Combat d2, Perception d6, Survival d6, Technical Engineering d6, Unarmed Combat d4.

Equipment: Concussion Grenades (3), Flash-bang Grenades (3), Tool Kit.

Description: Joe Henderson (a.k.a. "Time Bomb"), is the ship's mechanic of *Aces and Eights* and demolitions expert. A short, meek-looking young man, Time Bomb is often mistaken for an accountant. He wears wire-rim glasses, for he is quite near-sighted. He is very neat and tidy and precise in everything he does—borderline obsessive/compulsive. He always cuts his food—any food—into one inch squares before he will eat it.

The twenty-five year old Time Bomb was born and raised on a mining colony. His father was the owner of the mine and Time Bomb could have lived a life of relative ease, but he was fascinated with explosives and spent as much time with the miners as possible. After an accident in which he nearly blew up himself and the family home, his father took the boy to the mine foreman and told him to teach him all he knew.

Having learned all he could about blasting rock, Time Bomb went to college to learn more. He studied chemical, mechanical, and civil engineering and accumulated a lot of hours, but never bothered to take the courses necessary for gaining a degree.

The commercial flights from his home planet to the college being long and boring (with nothing to blow up), Time Bomb became friends with the ship's mechanic and spent his time studying the ship's engines, which he found almost as interesting as explosives. Maxx met Time Bomb on one of these voyages. Bored himself and always interested in ships, Maxx wandered down to the engine room. Before the end of the trip, he'd hired Time Bomb on as ship's mechanic.

Guns make Time Bomb nervous and he is a hopeless shot. He is shy around women, has trouble even looking at one. He generally stares at their shoes and there is speculation among the crew that he's never seen Hwa Ling from the waist up. The only woman he's really comfortable around is Devil.

His engine room is so clean that one could eat off the compression coil. His quarters are neatly organized with everything in its proper place. He freaks out if the smallest object has been moved. He blushes easily and giggles at jokes. Yet, when Time Bomb is dealing with any sort of explosive device, he becomes another person—cool-headed, steady of hand and eye, completely and totally in command of himself and the situation.

He can dismantle bombs, as well as build them. When he does this, he has the unnerving habit of talking to the bomb lovingly, as if it was a woman.

RAMONA CORTEZ

Agi d8, Str d4, Vit d6, Ale d8, Int d10, Wil d10; Life Points 14; Initiative d6+d6.

Traits: Allure (Minor Asset), Greedy (Minor Complication), Talent—Covert/Disguise (Minor Asset).

Skills: Artistry d2, Athletics d4, Covert d6/ Disguise d10*/Forgery d8, Guns d4, Influence d6/Negotiation d8/Seduction d8, Knowledge d6, Medical Expertise d6, Perception d6, Perform d6/ Acting d10, Pilot d4, Planetary Vehicles d2, Scientific Expertise d4, Technical Engineering d4, Unarmed Combat d4. (Disguise skill is modified by the Talented trait.)

Equipment: Pistol, Pocket Knife.

Description: The ship's doctor, "Devil-Take-Me" Cortez, or Devil, as she's known for short, was a medic in an army field hospital during the war. This is where she met Maxx, who was there recovering from the loss of his arm. They became good friends and, when Maxx left the army, Devil went with him to be his ship's medic. Unfortunately, Devil "forgot" to tell the army she was leaving.

Devil is officially AWOL, something Maxx does not know. Since Devil didn't give the army her real name when she joined, the military is having a difficult time tracking her down.

Devil gained her nickname from her habit of using the oath, "devil take me if I'm not telling the truth!" Due to the fact that she never tells the truth and generally has no idea what the truth even is, she figures that she is safe in this, for the devil undoubtedly laid claim to her long ago.

Devil is a good medic. She can also be a good university professor, a good lawyer, a good dance-hall girl, a good pilot, a good corporate executive. In other words, she can take on the role and occupation of any person and be good (not great) at it. Devil is a con woman, a scam artist, an expert forger. She has dabbled in blackmail. She can disguise herself as anyone—male or female. She can pass for a cowpoke down on his luck or play the part of a registered Companion. She is fast-talking and glib, with a vast store of knowledge about all sorts of things. She is utterly convincing in all she says and does. Devil is not particularly good with weapons and relies instead on her wits and charm to get her out of difficulty.

Devil is twenty-eight, slender and graceful, with a boyish figure and a highly mobile face that she can mold like putty. She has a shaved head because she almost always wears wigs from her large wig collection, changing them on a daily basis. She has dark eyes and an irresistible smile. She is witty, likeable, and never loses her temper.

Devil has an immense wardrobe of costumes that she and the team often find useful. She adds to this

wardrobe on a regular basis, picking up pieces from each planet they visit. She has uniforms for every branch of the military on every planet and for every branch of government. She has ladies' ball gowns, gentlemen's fancy dress clothes, frontier chaps and dusters, kimonos, homespun shirts and dresses, lawmen gear, executive suits, shepherd's wear, Buddhist monk's robes, and so on. She also has a wide selection of rubber masks, false noses, ears, eyebrows, eyelashes, etc. Devil can pass for a twelve-year-old boy one day and an eighty-year-old matriarch the next. Devil has extensive connections on all the major Border planets. If she doesn't have what's needed, she knows where to find it.

Devil is so charming that half the time her own associates don't know when they're being scammed, including Maxx, who has no idea that Devil has never received any formal medical training. Thus far, she's managed to keep the crew alive and has patched up a good many serious wounds and injuries with a combination of skill and luck.

Devil has made a lot of enemies in her time and if any of them should ever chance to recognize her, she could be in a world of trouble.

CHAPTER 6

RAWHIDE

Agi d10, Str d8, Vit d10, Ale d8, Int d4, Wil d6; Life Points 16; Initiative d10+d8.

Traits: Religiosity (Minor Asset), Steady Calm (Minor Asset), Straight Shooter (Minor Complication).

Skills: Animal Handling d6/Riding d8, Athletics d6/Dodge d8, Discipline d4, Guns d6, Knowledge d4, Mechanical Engineering d6, Perception d4, Pilot d6/Mid-Bulk Transports d10, Planetary Vehicles d6, Technical Engineering d4, Unarmed Combat d6/Brawling d8.

Equipment: Pistol, Bible.

Description: The pilot of *Aces and Eights* is Ross Macintosh, known to all as Rawhide. One of eight children of a struggling rancher, he never went to school, but had to work on the ranch to help support his family, as did all his brothers and sisters. When his parents died—worn down by their hard life—he and his siblings sold the ranch and split the proceeds. Rawhide used his share to put himself through flight school, figuring this was the only way off the moon that had killed his parents.

He had a tough time in school, for at age twenty-three the only book he'd ever even read was his mother's tattered Bible. Learning doesn't come easy for Rawhide. By working twice as hard as anyone else, he managed to graduate, though at the bottom of the class.

When the war broke out, Rawhide joined the Independents as a bomber pilot. He was wounded several times and taken prisoner once. He never talks about his experiences during the war.

Rawhide is a tall man, lanky and bony. He is all muscle, no gristle. He is thirty years old, but his leathery skin and a perpetually sad look in his blue eyes make him appear older. He is generally solemn, for he takes life seriously, and rarely smiles. When he does, his smile is wide and generous and seems to warm even the cold black of space.

Rawhide wears denim jeans, cowboy boots, serviceable shirts, and a leather vest. His most treasured possession is his mother's Bible. If he has religious beliefs, he never shares them.

Maxx found Rawhide from an employment agency on Persephone. Maxx was in desperate need of a pilot, his own having been shot through the head in a bar fight. The agency sent over various candidates and, after interviewing several pilots, Maxx chose Rawhide. He didn't have the best references or credentials, but there was something about the tall, quiet man that Maxx liked.

Rawhide is a better pilot than he gives himself credit for, as the captain is always telling him. Rawhide is a slow learner, but once he learns something, he never forgets it. His most valuable asset is his

unflappable calm. Nothing ever gets him riled or excited. He never panics. He keeps a cool head in any emergency. If he's in a barroom brawl, he'll sit in his chair unless someone hits him, then he'll calmly stand up, calmly slug the guy, and then calmly resume his seat. If someone brings up the war, Rawhide says nothing. He will simply get up and leave the room.

Rawhide can handle a gun and is a good shot when he needs to be. He wears a sidearm in a holster whenever he leaves the ship.

Rawhide admires and respects Captain Williams and would do anything for him. Rawhide is in awe of Jack Leland, considering him to be the most brilliant man in the 'Verse. Rawhide has fallen quietly in love with Hwa Ling. He knows quite well that she cares nothing for him. He suffers in silence, as is his way, so that no one except the sharp-eyed Devil suspects.

Devil is Rawhide's best friend. They make a truly odd couple. As the Captain describes them, "they run together like a rat terrier and a sheep dog." If Devil has a tender spot in her heart, Rawhide has managed to touch it. She looks out for him and he is protective of her, though he is often bewildered by her schemes and intrigues.

The only thing in the 'Verse that Rawhide truly hates are Reavers, who killed his favorite sister and her family in a raid. Rawhide had the misfortune to be the one who found what was left of their bodies—a horrible sight that he's never forgotten. Once, when an Alliance officer was on board their ship, making a routine inspection, he made the mistake of claiming that Reavers are nothing more than figments of overwrought imaginations. Rawhide coolly and calmly slammed the officer into a bulkhead, breaking the man's neck. Maxx's quick talking and Jack's influence kept Rawhide out of an Alliance prison, but now, whenever any Alliance officials board the ship, Maxx sees to it that Rawhide is confined to his room.

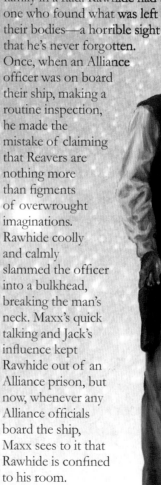

CHAPTER 7

A BRIEF GUIDE TO THE 'VERSE

I think we can safely say that *bei bi shiou ren* won't be blackmailing any more young women for some time to come," Mal stated, emerging from a store room in the back of the dance club.

Zoe nodded agreement. "That was a clever scheme of yours, Inara."

"I'm like Jayne," said Inara, smiling. "I graduated high school."

Mal grunted. "Most likely the only time Jayne came near a school was to part the kiddies from their lunch money at gun point. You got the incriminating evidence?"

"Right here," said Inara, placing her hand on her breast. "Next to my heart. No one will find it."

"Not 'less they pay for privilege," Mal remarked.

He stepped out among the tables. Pink spotlights glared on the crowd on the dance floor or shone on scantily clad women in pink cat costumes jiggling in cages suspended from the ceiling. The bar was lit with neon lights, as were the tables, as were the waitresses, who wore glowing pink body paint and little else.

Mal halted in the swirling shadows, reached down to his boot, drew his pistol, checked to see that it was loaded, then slipped it back into the boot. "I'm thinking we best make ourselves scarce. Uncle won't be too pleased when he finds out what we've done to his nephew. Just walk onto the dance floor like nothin's happened. Don't make ourselves conspicuous. Zoe, you see that husband of yours?"

"Yes, sir," said Zoe, pointing. "He's over there by the bar."

"No, he's not," said Inara. "He's by the cage watching the dancer."

"You've both gone gorram blind," said Mal impatiently. "He's sitting at that table—"

"I think I should know my own husband, sir," Zoe began. She stopped, blinked.

"*Wo bu shin wo dah yan jing!*" Inara exclaimed. She stared into the room. "'Don't make ourselves conspicuous', you said . . ."

"I'm gonna have to kill him," said Mal. He put out his hand to collar the Wash that was sitting at the table. His hand passed right through Wash's shirt, came back with nothing. "Soon as I figure out which one he is."

For there were Washes everywhere. Wash was leaning against the bar. Wash was dancing. Wash was telling a bawdy joke. Wash was strolling across the floor. Wash was perusing the menu.

Then Wash—the real Wash—was right in front of them, grinning like a pink Cheshire pussycat. "Isn't it great, honey?" he asked Zoe. He waved his hand at himself. "You always said you wanted more of me to love! Well, now you have twenty! They're holograms! Half the people in this place are holograms! You see, they have this machine and you go behind the curtain and for only one credit—"

"I have dibs on the killing him, sir," said Zoe.

"Wife's rights should always come first," Mal said gravely, nodding. He reached down to his boot, surreptitiously slipped out his gun. "Though you might get some argument with those folk as just walked through the door. They don't appear right friendly and I think they may be lookin' for us."

Six men, big and husky, with guns drawn, walked into the dance club and began shoving their way through the crowd.

"How do they even know what we look like?" Wash demanded.

Inara glanced over her shoulder, saw a half-naked and thoroughly irate young man standing in the door of the storeroom. He was pointing them out to an older man who was saying something into a headpiece.

"I wonder how he got out of those handcuffs? I must be losing my touch." Inara shook her head. Sighing, she tugged on Mal's sleeve and pointed. He glanced over his shoulder.

"'Cause Junior is giving the old man a complete description," Mal said grimly.

"We could go out the back," suggested Inara.

"Like as not the goon boys got their goon twins posted in the alley," said Mal. He paused a moment, thoughtful, then said, "They want us, they'll get us—about twenty of us apiece. Wash, I may let you live after all. Take me to that gorram holo machine . . ."

> "Half of history is hiding the truth."
>
> —Malcolm Reynolds

If you're going to make your way in the 'Verse, best to understand a bit about its planets and moons. Don't expect to learn everything here—just enough to keep flyin'. For now. The black holds its secrets close. 'Fore you go out, take a little knowledge with you.

THE YEAR 2518

Life in the 'Verse depends a lot on where you live and into what circumstances you were born. The central planets, those as formed the Alliance, are flush with the newest technologies. Folk live in large cities and travel in style on highways of air. Advanced medical care is free to all. There are no slums in those huge cities, but there are many who don't live quite as comfortable as other folk. There are some dark parts to those cities of light, too.

On the Core, those born suckin' on the proverbial silver spoon lead lives of comparative luxury. They are well educated in good schools. They live in a world full of technological marvels. Their lives are safe and secure. Least for the most part. The biggest threats folk face in the Core cities is that business and dealings are more socially oriented than physical, though there is the occasional duel (despite the laws against dueling). Men and women and children are expected to behave with dignity and grace at all times. Honor and position are just as important as the credits in the family account. Losing face can be as hurtful as a bullet to the belly.

There are some wealthy folk who dwell on the outer planets—often called "the Rim." These folk do their best to copy the lives of the rich on the Core, though truth be told, their Core cousins look down their noses at them. The ordinary folk on the Rim don't much worry about social sparring or high-and-mighty matters of honor. They tend to concern themselves with basic notions, such as where they're going to find their next meal. Survival is at the forefront of their lives. The newly terraformed planets don't have the infrastructure to support many of the luxuries that Core folk take for granted—supermarkets, telephonic communications, and advanced medical care are just a few of the many things in short supply outside the Core. Hard work and the kind of smarts that don't come from books make life work on the Rim.

Some folk tend to lump the worlds in the 'Verse into two categories: civilized and primitive. You've either got the diamond sky elevators of Londinum or the sod huts of Whitefall. Truth is, things just ain't that simple. Most worlds fall somewhere in between. On certain planets and moons, you may fly over miles and miles of desolate landscape, then suddenly see the glittering lights of an enormous city rise up before you.

'Course, life in the 'Verse extends far beyond the planets and moons. Space stations, such as skyplexes and refueling stations, are strung about the system. Such stations offer a wide variety of goods and services and play host to a wide variety of folk, from honest business people to wanted criminals.

When you're flyin' the black, just keep this in mind: not all Core people are good-for-nothing snobs and not all those who dwell on the Rim are good-old-boys. Don't matter where you travel. Folks is folk. Might be a good idea to watch your back no matter where you are.

HISTORY IS PROGRAMMED BY THE VICTORS

The history of the 'Verse, as far as most folk are concerned, begins with the terraforming of the central planets. People don't have a real sense of the history of Earth-That-Was, nor do they much care. Not with the pressing concerns of the present weighing them down.

Some cynical folk don't believe much of what is written about the past, thinking it to be the propaganda of an oppressive government. Others are moon-brained enough to swallow every campfire tale. The wise know that if you don't learn from history, you're doomed to repeat it, which it seems we keep doin' again and again and again . . . .

The following text comes courtesy of Andrew Falcon, Professor of History and Planetary Studies, now living on Persephone, retired.

EXODUS

The original cradle of humanity, Earth, has long since faded into legend. Dreamers and tale spinners glamorize Earth-That-Was. It's become a sort of Garden of Eden, where mankind was always happy. Its relics are now priceless. Truth is, mankind sucked Earth dry.

The story goes that depleted resources, overpopulation, and a compromised ecosystem forced mankind to abandon Earth-That-Was.

Some do speculate, however, that the planet wasn't completely abandoned, that folk still survive on mankind's original home, though there is no proof to back the notion and no easy way to conjure the truth. It is possible that Earth is not quite as drained as the old legends suggest and has been quietly regenerating ever since man left. One day, mankind may find the lost keys to Eden and return to their old home once again. That day is a long way off, though. If it even comes at all.

The wise searched the heavens and found a star system with planets and moons that could, with a little help, support human life. Mankind began the great exodus. They set out in enormous ships they called "arks," after the tale of Noah and his crew. Lacking "faster-than-light" drives, folk found the journey to their new home long and taxing. At least one full generation was born, lived, and died without ever leaving the huge, contained ships that crawled through the black. The initial excitement of the voyage quickly faded into the monotony of keeping the ships moving, keeping the life-support systems intact, and perfecting the technologies that would give future generations good lives on new worlds. Naturally, some folk expected to encounter alien life, but the only signals on the scanner were the natural static of the stars. So far as we know, mankind is alone in the 'Verse.

With so many different folk of all nationalities and races packed inside small ships, the old ethnic and political barriers began to blur. People learned the native tongues of their fellow ship dwellers. Subsequent generations would come to speak fluently the two dominant languages, English and Chinese, and phrases from other cultures.

Not surprising, some folk lost hope along the way. There were accidents, malfunctions. If an ark lost life support, thousands died. The arks became their coffins, forever drifting in the cold. But for every person that lost hope, hundreds were there to keep it alive. Each day brought mankind closer to home.

And then, one day, there it was.

THE AGE OF THE TERRAFORMERS

Even after continued refinement, the process of terraforming a moon or a planet takes decades. Terraforming requires atmospheric processing plants, the regulation of gravity, environmental adaptation and the introduction of creatures great and small brought from Earth-That-Was—everything from algae and bacteria to insects, birds, and mammals. The power to make such *jing chai* changes is astonishing, but is not without its limits. While most all terraformed worlds are suitable for human life, each has its own quirks.

The first two planets terraformed and settled were Londinum and Sihnon, and they became the center of culture and business throughout the system. The governments of these two planets took an enlightened view of civilization. They worked to maintain order, but also encouraged diversity of language, ethnicity, religion, and expression of thought.

Despite all the best efforts and intentions of the original founders, the problems of the common folk did not go away with the formation of new worlds. Mankind is restless, always looking to find greener pastures somewhere else. Pioneers left the crowded cities and traveled out to the most newly terraformed worlds, hoping to build a better life for themselves.

As mankind spread out, he brought with him his usual miseries: greed, corruption, crime. Disagreement over resources, trade, and political

"Earth-That-Was could no longer sustain our numbers, we were so many. We found a new solar system with dozens of planets and hundreds of moons. Each one terraformed—a process taking decades—to support human life. To be new Earths.

"The Central Planets were the first settled and are the most advanced, epitomizing civilization at its peak. Life on the outer planets is much more primitive and difficult. That's why the Central Planets formed the Alliance, so everyone can enjoy the comfort and enlightenment of true civilization. That's why we fought the War for Unification."

—Primary School Lesson, Osiris

Zoe: "In the time of war, we woulda never left a man behind."
Mal: "Maybe that's why we lost."

influence led to general unrest among the planets. A movement began in the oldest, most stable planets to form a unified parliamentary system of government that would work to regulate such matters and keep the peace. The popular idea was quickly ratified and the Alliance was formed.

The Alliance was started out of an idealistic belief that a strong central government that controlled every aspect of a person's life, from cradle to grave, could provide that person a better, safer, and more secure life. Some folk in the Alliance truly believed this and they dedicated their lives to bringing this about. Other folk saw this as a chance to grab power for themselves.

The Parliament formed a military council that acted quickly to quell any unrest among the Core planets and their neighbors. Maintaining order meant keeping tight control over the populace, and that led to the creation of many secret programs. Their hope was to make people obedient, complacent, compliant— "better" by the government's definition.

The Alliance was the protective parent. The Core worlds were model children. But the Alliance had another problem. They feared their "good children" were going to be corrupted by the bad seeds who lived on the wrong side of the 'Verse. The worlds on the Border and the Rim were self-governing, outside the limits of Alliance control. Each world had its own set of laws and rules that suited its own particular needs. Folk living on these frontier planets had been forced to be self-reliant in order to survive, and they had come to be free-thinkers who saw no need for a lot of government meddling. The Alliance considered such independence a threat to civilization. (They also considered that a lot of valuable resources and real estate were outside their control!) For the benefit of all people in the 'Verse, the Alliance decided that every planet in the system should come under Alliance rule, whether its people wanted it or not.

Idealistic folk of the Core planets thought this was a great idea. Doesn't everyone want to live on a safe, comfortable, and civilized world where folk are cared for by their betters? The movement for Unification spread like wildfire through dry brush. The leaders on the Core thought they had only to open their arms in a wide embrace and those poor benighted souls on the Rim would come running home to their mothers.

Those on the Border did come running. Only one problem—they carried guns.

UNIFICATION WAR

The War for Unification was the most devastating war in human history. All those who lived through it are marked, like a scar left behind by an old wound. (Just that some happen to have big scars traced all 'cross their faces while others have tiny ones hidden away.) Outer planets, including Shadow, Persephone, and Hera, mustered forces and formed an alliance of their own—the Independent Faction (known as "Browncoats," thanks to the brown dusters their soldiers took to wearing). The Parliament of the Alliance instituted a draft to build its forces. They were considerably astonished to learn that more than half of the Independent forces were composed of volunteers. The Alliance (known as the "Purple Bellies" for their style of dress) had the manpower, the ships, and technology to make the result of the war a forgone conclusion—but no one anticipated that freedom would be something so many folk would be willing to die to protect.

The war raged for just over five years, taking place on land, sea, and in the dark of space. The largest space battle in terms of scale and human cost was the Battle of Sturges, one in which countless ships were destroyed, creating a massive graveyard preserved in the vacuum of the black. The largest land battle, the one that brought about the end of the war, was fought on the planet Hera in Serenity Valley. This battle raged on for seven weeks before the Independent High Command surrendered. Even then, some of the Browncoats continued to fight on for two weeks after that. Those soldiers who continued to fight even after being ordered to lay down arms were captured and tried for war crimes. Ultimately, the Alliance released the soldiers and officers as a peaceful gesture to those outer planets now under its rule. Some look upon those who fought in the Battle of Serenity as criminals. Others see them as big, damn heroes.

Since the battles were mostly fought on the Border and the Rim, the Core planets escaped unscathed. To this day, many outer planets still bear terrible scars. Shadow was effectively destroyed, and it remains uninhabitable seven years later. Major cities on Athens were bombed. Several key land battles were fought on Persephone. Moons that had no strategic value, such as Whitefall and Jiangyin, were untouched, but they still suffered as a result of the disruption of trade. Supplies had been hard to get as it was, and the war made it harder. Almost every person living on those planets saw their homes leveled, their businesses fall into ruin, their loved ones killed or maimed—all in the name of making their lives better.

Small wonder folk are still bitter.

THE HERE AND NOW

Life in the 'Verse has returned to normal—leastways on the surface. In truth, no one has forgotten and few have forgiven. The Alliance now has jurisdiction over every inhabited planet in the system. The Alliances does not fully control everything within its far-flung territory,. In reality, the Alliance only has full control over the Core planets. On these worlds, the eyes of the Alliance are everywhere. Federal police can be called at a moment's notice, and cameras record every citizen's every move. The Core worlds have the best comforts that money can buy. 'Course, every citizen pays for such security and comfort with more than a bit of his freedom.

The outer planets were meant to be kept under the same level of strict control, but the Alliance is short on manpower and ships. They just don't have enough folk to keep a proper eye on things. Yes, it's true that they hire security firms to help enforce their laws and maintain order. And they send their hulking patrol ships out into the black to remind everyone who is in charge. Still, the cracks in the system are large enough for folk to fly a Firefly through.

Take slavery, for example. Slavery is outlawed by the Alliance government, but it's an open secret that terraforming companies, mine owners and the wealthy on the Rim regularly use slave labor in their operations, and pay big sums for human cargo. Every so often, the Alliance will bust one of these owners and free the slaves—always looks good on the nightly news. But then it's back to business as usual. Same with indentured servants. That's not legal, either, but most folk on the Border planets accept indentured servitude as a way of life. If you're desperate for the credits and you got nothing to offer up as collateral except yourself, then that's what you do. *Dohn ma?*

GOVERNMENTS

These days, there is only one central government in the 'Verse. Leastways, that's what the Alliance wants you to believe. It's hard work to rule over a whole star system of bazillions of people and hundreds of worlds, especially when so many of those worlds are so very far away from the Core. Some in the Alliance might be starting to wonder if maybe they bit off more protein than they can chew by trying to extend their control over the outer planets. Some might be thinking they made a mistake. If they do, they're keeping mighty quiet about it. These days, the Alliance is all about keeping things quiet.

There are local governments on the Border and Rim planets. Cities have mayors. Planets have governors. Moons have magistrates. All these answer to the Alliance. At least, that's the way it's supposed to work. Local officials on the outer worlds tend to wield heaps more power then their counterparts on the Core, just because no one's close enough by to tell them they can't.

The Independent Faction is gone, but that isn't to say there are no more Independents. Some are still fighting the war, though now they do it more by being an annoyance than a major threat. But over the last few years, some of these folk have left off fighting guerrilla actions and are now fighting on the political front. Be right interesting to see what happens when someone from the inside starts prying open secret doors.

Then of course, there are the corporations. Large corporations control powerful lobbies that have considerable influence inside the government. Favors are traded and eyes stay blind and the wheels of commerce and politics keep turning. We're going take a brief look at all this, just so you know where you stand.

THE ANGLO-SINO ALLIANCE

The Anglo-Sino Alliance is the governing body for the entire system. Originally formed between the two first-settled planets, Londinum and Sihnon (where the "Anglo" and "Sino" come from), the Alliance is rich and powerful, with resources that most folk can't begin to imagine—manpower, intelligence-gathering, military might, and technological innovation. And, like an overprotective parent, it thinks it knows what's best for its "children"—all those who live and work under its rule. The Alliance government believes that by controlling information, technologies and even people's lives, they can forge a better 'Verse, one where people live in peace and no one ever goes hungry. Some call this Utopia. Others call it hell.

Londinum is the formal seat of government, home to Parliament and the Prime Minister. While every planet (at least within the Core) is allowed to organize its own affairs on a planetary level, system-wide policy is set by legislation. The planet of Sihnon is home to the headquarters of the trade associations and guilds in the system. The most powerful of these have their academies here. Trade tariffs for all manner of goods are established in Sihnon's bureaucratic halls.

Most people of the Alliance are allowed a say in their government. Anyone can stand for a seat in the Parliament and be voted in by the home folk. But the money required to run a campaign generally prevents the common man from ever winning a governmental position. To raise the necessary funds, one must make deals with businesses, guilds, and private interest groups. As to voting, only those who are "full citizens of the Alliance" actually get a vote. Folk who fought in or supported the Independents are not considered "full citizens." (After all, if they couldn't be trusted to fight for the right side, how could they be trusted to vote for the right candidate?) Thus only candidates who support the Alliance are ever elected. That law is due to expire after ten years, though there are some on the Core worlds who are pushing for it to be extended.

Since the Alliance can't be everywhere at once (not for lack of trying!), it has to trust the local governors to do the right thing. Each Core world under Alliance control has a governor who holds a vast amount of power. The Alliance has given guidelines on how such a person is elected, but out of respect for the sovereignty of each world policies vary from place to place. Some Core worlds are fairly ruled by honest folk. On others, local political machines or long-standing family dynasties rule.

THE INDEPENDENT PLANETS

The confederacy of planets and moons that formed the Independent Faction was doomed from the start. Each of the outer worlds had its own form of government. They'd never really worked together except to do one thing—deliver the mail. Out on the frontier, folk liked to keep themselves to themselves, dealing with their own trouble in their own way. On the Border planets, it could be dangerous to stick a gun in someone's face because often as not three more could be pointing back at you.

While leaders among the scattered outer worlds expressed concern over the formation of the Sino-Anglo Alliance, most folk didn't much care, figuring it wouldn't affect them. They were concerned with far more mundane troubles: food shortages, low medical supplies, and the "quirks" of recently terraformed planets. It wasn't until the Alliance's proclamation that it intended to extend control over the entire system that the folk on the outer worlds woke up and smelled the tea leaves. They came together to present a unified front of resistance. And resist they did—far more than the Alliance had anticipated. Folk fightin' for their homes, freedom,

and way of life fight a hell of a lot harder than those drafted into the army or who carry arms in exchange for credits. What the Independents lacked in training and equipment, they made up for in spirit.

Sad to say, spirit wasn't enough. The Independents couldn't combat the massive Alliance forces. Outgunned, outmanned, and outmaneuvered, they were forced to surrender. The Independent governments of every planet that had resisted Alliance control were removed and replaced with an Alliance Governor. Very little actually changed for the people who lived on these planets, as the new Governors usually kept much of the political infrastructure intact. The people still paid their taxes to the local tax collector. Except now the money went to the Alliance, not to those who needed it at home.

The Alliance promised they would send the manpower, money, and supplies needed to rebuild the bombed and burned-out cities. To give them credit, they did send some. Just not near enough. You see, some folk on the Core think the former Independent supporters should be punished for their rebellion. So when government folk start bringing up measures to help those on the outer worlds, such measures usually find themselves voted down.

Each planet outside the Core is ruled by an Alliance-appointed Governor (or Magistrate, in the case of a moon). These individuals wield tremendous power, and though some wield it with an iron fist, others take a more hands-off approach and allow the smaller communities to deal with their own problems.

When a Border planet or moon requires the assistance of the Alliance government, the governor has to wade through an immense amount of bureaucratic red tape. Instead of going through the hassle, they'll hand over problems to Alliance-contracted private security firms. While these firms are tightly regulated in theory, in practice they are generally poorly managed, if not downright corrupt. The cure is worse than the ailment.

Tough times for some mean good times for others. The unrest has been a boon to the mercenary trade. Former soldiers from both sides now hire out their guns to communities, security firms and businesses who pay them to clean up their towns, fight range wars, or put down slave revolts.

THE MILITARY

The strength of the Alliance military ensures that the Alliance stays in control. Though currently stretched quite thin, the military is still impressive. Massive cruisers the size of small cities patrol space, keeping a watch for smugglers, illegal salvage operations and pirates. No one in the system is willing to take on an Alliance cruiser, which has enough firepower to atomize most other spacecraft.

The men and women who serve in the military are well-trained, disciplined, and carry state-of-the-art firearms and body armor. On the upside, like any other immense organization, the military has its share of blackguards, idiots, and scoundrels who can be bribed, bluffed, or fooled. And, yes, the occasional soldier might fall asleep on guard duty. But don't count on it. Most troopers in the Alliance military are dedicated, smart, and know every trick in the book.

THE LAW

The Alliance military tends to ride to the rescue only when the big guns are needed. For the more mundane crimes, the local sheriffs, Interpol, and the Feds are the folk to call.

Just about every town on every planet and moon has some form of local law. In many cases, the law is a man with a tin star looking to keep everyone in town honest. In others, the law is a bunch of brigands who go around breaking kneecaps on orders from the local governor or magistrate. Whatever form the local law takes, they tend to deal with petty theft and hooligans. When something major comes along—such as the assassination of a governor or the kidnapping of a powerful Guild leader —the locals call in either Interpol or the Federal Marshals.

Interpol (Interplanetary Police) deals with criminals who have fled the jurisdiction of local law enforcement, as well as crimes committed in areas that are outside local control, though still under Alliance control. (In other words, just about everywhere.) Interpol generally deals more with tracking suspects and investigating interplanetary crime than direct enforcement. The enforcement of federal law and the pursuit of criminals across interplanetary borders falls under the jurisdiction of Federal Marshals.

Federal Marshals (or simply, "Feds") track down wanted criminals and/or bring to trial those who fail to answer a summons. Some Feds are righteous enforcers of the peace, but there are a few who are more bounty hunter than law enforcer and will go after anyone if the money's good enough. Since they have to travel a far piece to do their jobs, the Feds have a great deal of autonomy. Feds work alone or in teams. They are provided with excellent ships and equipment, though some choose to work undercover if they are on the trail of particularly dangerous (or lucrative) fugitives.

CORPORATIONS

Some wit said: "The Alliance runs the system; the corporations own the system." The wheels of government turn smooth due to the liberal amount of corporate grease spread on them. Some folk have a tough time trying to figure where business ends and politics begins. The war was bad for business on the whole (though arms dealers and manufacturers did right well for themselves). Stability and predictability make the surest money, and the largest companies are the least likely to take major gambles.

BLUE SUN CORPORATION

Without doubt, the ubiquitous Blue Sun is the richest and most politically connected corporation in the system. Blue Sun is on every planet, in every home—rich and not so rich alike. For all its fame, it is one of the most shadowy institutions in the 'Verse.

The Blue Sun logo is everywhere: on T-shirts, billboards, posters, food cans, etc. The logo has become so much a part of daily life that people don't even notice it anymore. Blue Sun products are considered essential to a person—like water and breathing. Just look for the Blue Sun label. It's never difficult to find. The company doesn't operate retail outlets, but every shop stocks its products. While not the best on the market, Blue Sun products are the most reliable. If you buy Blue Sun, you always know what you're going to get. There are never any surprises—good, bad, or otherwise.

Blue Sun produces a lot of different things, but the company concentrates mainly on the basics of life. Folk will always need food and drink, and Blue Sun is there to sell it. They hold the monopoly on packaged foodstuffs, and their products have become essential to people on the newly terraformed worlds. Many new settlers wouldn't have made it through their first year without Blue Sun packaged food.

Like all corporations, Blue Sun didn't get into business out of love for their fellow man. They started the company to make a profit. No one begrudged them that. Profit pays the bills and folk's salaries. But then, as the company grew bigger and bigger, and became more and more powerful, greed and corruption took over. Profit was the only thing those running Blue Sun could think about. They set out to make more and more money by extending their power as far as they could mange.

It's an open secret that Blue Sun engages in deadly corporate espionage and then calls in favors from powerful government officials to cover their tracks. Its subsidiaries and shell corporations have branched out far from food and service industries, going into computer systems, communication technology, and even spaceship design, along with the biotech industry—even going so far (some whisper) as to conduct experiments involving living humans. Only top executives have a good grasp on what the "big picture" is when it comes to this mega-corporation. Its research and development division is a mysterious place guarded by security equal to top secret Alliance military projects.

THE CORONE MINING CONSORTIUM

The Corone Mining Consortium, formed just before the war, is made up of several of the most powerful mining corporations in the system. Those corporations were having a problem with prospectors mining claims of their own. Individually, the corporations couldn't muster the resources to put the small fry out of business. By combining, they could afford the best lawyers, pay off the right politicians, and acquire the technology needed to buy up claims, drive people off their land or simply make it unprofitable for the lone miner to keep operating.

Corone will first try to buy any claim that appears to be worth a full mining operation. If that fails, they buy a piece of land nearby, and then encroach on other folk's claims by digging tunnels underneath them. When the locals complain, they are told it was an unfortunate accident that caused the company to strip their assets. Few locals can afford to take the company to court to get back what was stolen.

Corone keeps costs down by making use of indentured workers. Some even claim they use slaves, going so far as to pay well for human cargo and never mind where it came from. On the flip side, they've been known to employ the locals they put out of business, promoting them to positions of authority and paying good salaries. They recognize the skills these people have, and hope that loyalty can be purchased with platinum or credits.

Corone does not operate every mine in the 'Verse. Not every claim is worth bringing in the expensive technology. Most locals have learned to keep real quiet about any major finds on their land, though Corone agents always seem to be in every two-bit mining town, poking around in the hope that they can loosen a few tongues with bribes, trickery, or threats.

In some areas, the Miners' Guild has taken on the Corone Consortium and won, bringing about improved condition for workers and justice for those who lost property.

ISKELLIAN TECHNOLOGY SOLUTIONS

There are many tech companies throughout the system, producing everything from computers to lasers, and Iskellian is the largest. Iskellian holds the Alliance contracts to produce arms, spacecraft, and weapons for their troops. The products it sells are the best money can buy, and what Iskellian charges for its wares more than makes that point. Given that the Alliance buys arms from Iskellian, the Alliance has laid down the law that none of these weapons can be sold to anyone else.

However, Iskellian does manufacture weapons for civilian use. These are not the same weapons that the military buys, of course, but they are of the same high quality and have the price tags to prove it. Such weapons are rarely seen on the outer worlds and few are on the black market. If you can get hold of an Iskellian weapon, you count yourself lucky.

UNIFIED RECLAMATION

There is a lot of trash in the 'Verse, and Unified Reclamation owns it.

The company began small with a few garbage-scows, but its founders were wise enough to see the potential of trash hauling and, by taking out huge and risky loans, they were able to secure an exclusive contract with the Alliance government to haul off folk's refuse.

At Unified Reclamation, they consider garbage a growth industry. Picking up dirty diapers isn't a very glamorous job, but someone has to do it and it makes for a very good living. Where Unified Reclamation struck gold wasn't in diaper pails, however. Real money comes from issuing licenses for legal salvage. Currently Unified is the only system-wide operator allowed to claim salvage rights. Due to the sheer magnitude of a system-wide salvage collection operation, Unified Reclamation also issues licenses for small operators to collect salvage on their behalf. The small operator can go through the local government to obtain a salvage license, but that involves mounds of paperwork and fees. Such licenses are more quickly obtained by going through United Reclamation, though they see to it that you pay for the convenience.

Small operators make more money if they run unlicensed, illegal salvage operations. Best to be careful, though, as things can get right ugly if Unified catches you poaching on their territory. You'd better hope the Alliance catches you doing illegal salvage before Unified Reclamation gets its hands on you.

GUILDS

Guilds have been around for centuries, starting way back in history on Earth-That-Was. Then came the union movement and guilds died out. Now, in the face of ever-expanding corporate wealth and power, the guilds are back, stronger than ever. These days, guilds wield great power and influence. In an area the guild controls, you cannot find work unless you are a member of the guild. This can often impose real hardships on people, yet the guild is also in place to protect its members. Guilds negotiate with employers and fight for the rights of workers. Many guilds, such as the Companion's Guild, provide a member with a recognized qualification that is respected and honored throughout the 'Verse.

COMPANIONS' GUILD

The oldest profession in the 'Verse has one of the oldest and most respected guilds in the Core. Prostitution as it had existed on Earth-That-Was was abolished long ago, replaced by a government-approved profession officially titled "Companion." The Companion's Guild established Guild Houses throughout the system to train its members, though, due to the war, there are few Houses currently on the outer worlds. The Guild establishes its own laws and rules. For example, Guild law states that no House may ever be run by a man. The law also states that a Companion is free to choose her clients. Originally a female organization, the Guild has since allowed males to enter. The men undergo the same training as the women and, like the women, they service both sexes. The Houses exist to provide training to the Companions. No work is ever done inside a House.

Girls and boys as young as twelve may begin training, which includes a well-rounded education and years of physical discipline, religious study, and the arts. Girls and boys are taught dance, martial arts, calligraphy, how to play musical instruments, and singing. The children undergo rigorous testing on all subjects, and those who fail are sent back to their homes. They are taught the art of love play only upon successful completion of their schooling.

> "On Sihnon we started training at twelve. Years of discipline and preparation before the physical act of pleasure was even mentioned. Control was the first lesson. And the last."
>
> —Inara Serra

Companions must pass a test in order to gain their registration. To maintain that registration, they must also pass a yearly physical examination conducted at a licensed hospital.

Clients must pay a subscription fee to earn a place in the client registry. The Guild and the Companion must approve of the client. If a client ever mistreats a Companion, that client will earn a black mark in the client registry, preventing him or her from ever securing such services again.

A Companion House is run much like a monastery, protecting its inhabitants and sheltering them from the outside as they undergo their training. The services a Companion performs for the client are steeped in tradition and ritual. A Companion greets a client and bids that client farewell with ceremony, and the act of lovemaking is designed to make each client feel that he or she is special and valued—only one of the reasons an evening with a Companion is so highly sought after.

Contracting with a Companion earns the client "an evening of pleasure" that goes far beyond the sexual encounter. A Companion is trained to listen, to entertain, to soothe, and even to offer advice, for they are well-versed on any variety of subjects from politics to the economy. A Companion knows traditional and contemporary dance. They are skilled musicians, schooled in literature and stay current with all significant newsworthy events. They have a high degree of empathy and are trained in psychology, so they can understand their client's needs.

The beauty, elegance, and skills of the Companions have earned them the highest respect in social circles. There is no stigma to bringing a Companion to a party, as doing so proves you have both money and the ability to impress the Guild, whose members set very high standards. However, few Companion marry the wealthy prince and go off to live in the glittering castle. While of the social elite, Companions still exist outside society. Though a Companion is welcomed as an escort at party, a Companion would not be so well-received as husband or wife. A Companion might commit to an exclusive, long-term contract, but that would still be a business arrangement. A Companion is encouraged to enjoy the work, but is taught to stay emotionally detached from the clientele.

Most Companions work on the Core planets, entertaining clients in their own suites or meeting them elsewhere. Some choose to travel and may contract with a luxury liner—servicing clients on a cruise or flying the ship's shuttles to visit clients on nearby worlds. Few Companions choose to travel on their own or ally themselves with a small ship, and even fewer visit the outer worlds. Those who travel off the beaten path can pick and choose their clients, though they may not make as much money as working on the wealthy Core worlds. One has to wonder, though, what secrets would cause a beautiful Companion to leave a life of privilege and security for the dangers and uncertainties of the black?

THE SYNDICATE

While not a guild in the official sense, the Syndicate styles itself as such and has many of the same trappings. The Syndicate controls most of the organized crime in the system. Only a few people are aware the Syndicate even exists, and they know better than to start mouthing off.

If a crime boss manages to claim a territory for himself, or comes to monopolize a certain area of illegal trade, he may be offered membership in the Syndicate. Those who receive such an offer are fools to refuse. While the position brings responsibility, it also brings benefits. (Plus those who say "no" have a tendency to become very dead very quick.)

When a *Ser Toh* joins the Syndicate, he is in hog heaven. The Syndicate makes it clear to the rest of the underworld that their boy is now in charge and no one better try to muscle in. It is the crime boss's responsibility to maintain his position, since his assets are effectively considered Syndicate property. Members of the Syndicate help each other expand their businesses into other areas not currently controlled by Syndicate members. The Syndicate can also provide muscle and loans to help keep business running smooth.

The Syndicate does not demand money from its members, but they do expect to be paid in other ways: receiving preferential treatment, getting cut-in on sweet deals, warned of any potential problems with the law, doing favors for the board or other members.

When the boss joins the Syndicate, he is presented via wave to the entire Syndicate board (the current board numbers fifteen people). They see him, but he does not see them. He communicates with them through go-betweens, never meeting them in person. Who they are or where they reside, no one knows, though there is speculation that they all live on the Core worlds under the guise of honest business men and women.

THE TONGS

The Tongs come from ancient China on Earth-That-Was. The word "tong" is innocent enough, meaning "hall," or a place to meet and talk. The original tongs began as business or social organizations for Chinese men. When the Chinese immigrated into the West, the tongs provided an extra measure of security for the immigrant, giving

> "Sermons make me sleepy, Shepherd. I ain't looking for help from on high. That's a long wait for a train don't come."
>
> —Malcolm Reynolds

him a "family" that would protect his interests in a strange land and unfamiliar culture.

Problem is, this meant that rival tongs would often clash—a business deal gone sour, a dispute between families—and they would settle the matter with bloodshed. Traditional rivalries also caused wars to break out between the tongs, some of whom have been enemies for centuries. Many tongs got wrapped up in lawless activities—running illegal gambling concerns, brothels, and opium dens—gaining for themselves a criminal-minded reputation.

The tongs continue to operate in a not-so-different way to this day. To their credit, tongs help their own members, whether they are rich or poor; speaking up for them when they are in trouble with the community or helping out if they get into disputes with rival tongs. Still, human nature being what it is, the traditional hatreds and feuds carry on, and have even grown stronger. Some of the tongs are mightily involved in various illegal dealings throughout the system. Tongs have a strong presence on the outer worlds, where they can operate openly, as opposed to the Core worlds, where they tend to keep a low profile. It is said, though (however quietly), that their influence can be felt even in the Halls of Parliament.

TRADERS' GUILD

One of the newest guilds, the Traders' Guild, came about to help small and independent traders compete against the mighty corporations. This Guild offers legal advice to its members, allows them to work together to gain large contracts, and provides contacts. Anyone who lives by trade can join the Guild, be he store-owner, cargo ship captain or supplier.

Despite the small size of the organization, the Alliance has taken a keen interest in it. Businesses and officials on Sihnon are alarmed at the rise of the Guild, fearing that it may cut in on their profits. If the Traders' Guild becomes a power in the system, it could seriously damage the economic power of Sihnon. Sihnon does everything it can to discourage membership and works against the organization. The Guild has support from important members of Parliament, though that has raised suspicion as to the motives of those involved.

THE MINERS' GUILD

The Miners' Guild is one of the largest guilds in the system, and probably the most controversial. Though it has successfully fought for the rights of exploited miners and gained a great many concessions from the large corporations, some human rights groups have accused it of turning a blind eye to slavery.

When it comes to the rights of the individual prospector on the frontier, the guild has been of great help. It provides lawyers and money for individuals to take on corporations such as the Corone Mining Consortium. It was the Miners Guild that forced the Alliance to send much needed medical supplies to the Georgia system to help the miners who had contracted a rare disease in the mines.

The Miners' Guild is very large. It is slow moving and like any other organization has its share of heroes and goats. The guild claims that it is trying to fight the practice of using indentured servants and slaves to work in the mines and, to give credit where it so happens to be due, the Miner's Guild has done some good in some places. In others, however, guild members have taken bribes from the corporations to look the other way. The guild is under immense pressure to clean up its act, and corrupt members are finding that things are getting a little too hot for comfort.

FAITH IN THE 'VERSE

Despite (or maybe because of) man's technological achievements, a majority of folk in the 'Verse still follow the tenets of one religion or another to some degree.

Buddhism—usually of the Mahayana tradition—is the dominant religion throughout the system, particularly on the Core planets. Christianity ranks second, with larger concentrations on the outer worlds, as Christians migrated away from the centers of Buddhism. Most Christians in the 'Verse follow a Protestant tradition hailing back to Earth-That-Was. Catholicism still exists, though the exodus of long ago ended its original structure.

One group of Christian missionaries, the Order of Shepherds, still follows the monastic tradition. These men and woman take vows of poverty and chastity similar to those of a priest or monk of old. They may live and work in an abbey or travel the

Black to find a flock in need of a Shepherd. Their peaceful order is generally respected throughout the system. Shepherds look to Christian scripture as their faith's grounding. They do not claim to have all the answers, but are here to help spread the word to those that need it told to.

There are many other religious groups in the 'Verse, including Muslims, Jews, and Hindus, who tend to form their own communities where they can worship in a body, follow their own traditions, and bring up their children in their own culture.

Out on the Rim, one can find any number of faith healers and wandering preachers who have founded their own churches or, in some instances, established entire communities. Some of these people are well-meaning and do lots of good, but others are swindlers, who use what they call religion to bilk the innocent out of their hard earned.

REAVERS

Some folk scoff at the campfire stories about men gone mad on the edge of space, saying they are too fanciful to be true. Unfortunately, the stories are generally a tame version of a truth so horrible that it has been kept from the knowledge of even the most powerful.

How Reavers came to be, no one really knows, and no one is about to ask them. Leastways anyone looking to not have their insides yanked out and gnawed on. It is said that they are the travelers who went too far from humanity. Out there on the edge of space, cut off from their own kind, they looked into the great void beyond and went mad. Another theory about the Reavers' descent into madness says it wasn't random, but deliberate. That some shady dealer tried experimenting with folk's brains and

dumped their failures on a far away planet. Or that the experiments found a way to escape their tormentors and ran as far as they could.

All that's truly known is that the Reavers have carved out a territory on the outer reaches of the Burnham quadrant (and no one has a guess of just how many are out there). They keep their ships going by cannibalizing other ships and machinery. Reaver ships run "hot," operating without engine core containment, leaking enough radiation to kill normal folk twice over. Their ships are often cobbled together from other craft and look like nothing ever seen in the 'Verse. The ships are crudely painted in garish colors, and often sport gruesome totems, such as the skeletal remains of victims strapped onto the bow. Reavers themselves suffer from horrible radiation burns and practice self-mutilation, marking their skin with primitive tattoos, body piercings, and by cutting on their own flesh.

Reavers send raiding parties out to steal ships, technology, and supplies. Unfortunate folk who get in the Reavers' way are captured, raped to death, eaten and skinned—in no particular order. The savages seem to feel no pain themselves. They derive pleasure only in inflicting pain on others. Sometimes they force one victim to watch their reavings, then they leave him behind to go mad. Ships that venture into Reaver territory are never seen again.

Those folk living their safe comfortable lives on the Core planets don't believe in Reavers, thinking them tales dreamed up by illiterate hicks. Those on the outer worlds know better. Ships, farms, and entire communities have been lost to the Reavers' savage appetites. Reavers do not discriminate in their choice of victims and will attack, torture, and kill men, women, and even little children without so much as a glimmer of mercy.

> "He didn't lie down. They never lie down."
> —River Tam, *regarding Reavers*

MIRANDA

BURNHAM QUADRANT 2B12Q7
MEAN DISTANCE X TO SUN 7 NMS
MEAN DIAMETER 19,910 KM
RE/NO/CORIO
H2O ATMOSPHERE

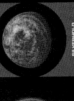

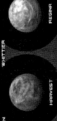

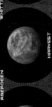
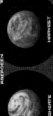
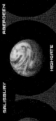

Reaver space should be avoided at all costs. If by some mischance you bump into them flying the black (and every year they seem to be venturing farther and farther out), don't try to run from them. Reavers have a wolf's instinct to chase their prey. If you are lucky and stay put, they may not notice you, or they could decide you're not worth the trouble. If you come across a ship that has been attacked by Reavers, be mindful that they often leave booby traps for the unsuspecting.

Only a fool thinks of Reavers as mindless savages. They're insane, not stupid. They are cunning and capable of using modern technology. They're not monsters. They're humans. And that's what makes them terrifying.

THE 'VERSE

Now, if you've turned to this section to find out all there is to know about the planets and moons that make up the 'Verse—how much each planet weighs, what the percentage of oxygen is compared to hydrogen, how many continents each planet has, that's *bai lih mohn*. Truth is, we just plain don't have room for all that in this book. Someday we might come out with a book that does have room. But this ain't that day. We're going to give you the information on each world you might need to land, do the job, then pack up and leave.

After all, no one gets paid for sight-seeing.

CENTRAL PLANETS

The central planets are a wonderland of peace and technology. All citizens have enough to eat. They work in glistening skyscrapers and live in high-rise apartment buildings. The grass is green and the skies are clear and no one wants for anything. That's if you believe the Alliance propaganda.

To be fair, the propaganda is mostly true. Even the poor who live on the Core worlds rarely want for shelter or food. Still, contrary to what the Alliance might want everyone to think, not everyone on the Core worlds is well-to-do. Those who aren't wealthy don't find life much better than those living out on the Rim. They may be better schooled, and their work might not involve dirt collecting beneath their fingernails, but there are plenty of folk who don't much like their lot in life.

Trapped in repetitive, unimaginative jobs, viewing nothing but the four low walls of a cube all day, they have the watchful eye of the Alliance on them at every turn. There is so much surveillance on a Core world "to prevent crime and ensure the safety of citizens" that almost everything a person does is recorded on a monitor somewhere.

The authorities will tell you that crime is almost non-existent on the Central Planets, since their scanners are almost everywhere. Still, folk being folk, there are some who manage to find a way to poke the Alliance in its electronic eye now and then.

Most folk on the Core worlds are content. They lead comfortable lives, with time and leisure to spend with their families. Their children all have access to the best quality education and health care. They have found the peaceful, prosperous existence that mankind has been seeking since he left the Garden of Eden. If they have to trade away some of their freedom to get this, they would tell you it was worth it.

These are the same folk who can't understand why other folk on the outer worlds fought so hard against it.

ARIEL

Like the rest of the Core worlds, Ariel is a paradise of technology. Tall buildings constructed of gleaming glass and steel reach into the sky. Holographic billboards advertise all manner of wonders. The night is filled with light. The day with the hustle and bustle of business.

Ariel is known among the central planets for its excellent medical facilities. The technology in Ariel's hospitals is the very latest, featuring such fancifications as holographic scanners and lots of machines that you gotta shout "clear!" to use.

The restaurants on Ariel are so good that folk travel here from other worlds just to have dinner. All the famous chefs come from Ariel or go to Ariel to open their own restaurants. It is said that even the hot dog vendors on Ariel are gourmet.

As with most planets in the Core, Ariel is a restricted landing zone. Only those with legitimate business (such as bringing in a Companion for a yearly check-up) are allowed to land. (Though, in most cases, if you look like you belong on a Core world, no one asks many questions.)

BERNADETTE

After the initial colonization of Londinum and Sihnon, Bernadette was the first planet to be terraformed and settled by humanity. The only remaining ship that brought the folk who made the Exodus stands in the capital city of New Paris as a monument to their courage. The ark is a monstrous starship, at least five times the size of an Alliance cruiser. The sheer sight of the ark inspires all manner of awe and jaw-dropping. The inside of the ark is a museum containing information about the journey, and also information on the cultures and history of Earth-That-Was. The great ark is named Prometheus, after the legendary god who gave man fire.

Bernadette is a traditional launching point for those leaving to settle on other worlds. Settlers arrive here from other planets on the Core and make preparations to set off for a new life on the Rim. Many businesses cater to these settlers, selling tools and supplies.

Best watch your step here. There is an underground slave-trade on Bernadette. Settlers are captured and hauled off to work on terraforming stations. The slavers are smart enough to leave locals alone. They figure outsiders won't be missed.

Bernadette is also home to many churches and religious groups. Buddhists and Christians rub shoulders with Islamic clerics and Hindu fakirs. In addition, the planet is home to a number of fringe cults and fanatical devotees.

Bernadette is a restricted landing zone. However, if you claim to be a settler or you have a group of kiddies on board for a field trip to see the ark, you're usually welcome.

LONDINUM

Of all the planets, Londinum is the most like Earth-That-Was and was therefore one of the first two planets to be settled, since it needed little work to make it ready for human habitation. Most of the original colonists from the European and American continents came to Londinum, where they honored their roots by combining old tradition with new technology. All the buildings are constructed of the most modern material, but they look as if they were built of stone and are of archaic design. The general look of the cities is what book-smart folk call the "imperial gothic" style of London from Earth-That-Was. May not look so shiny to those from the Rim, but it still makes the place popular with looky-loos and picture-snappers.

The Parliament building and government complex that surrounds it are the most impressive sights on the planet. As big as a small city, the Parliament building contains the great debating chamber ("The House"), while the surrounding building complex provides offices for all the ministers and civil servants. It also features a huge clock tower that has become the planet's symbol. Seems like almost everyone on Londinum works for the government or for businesses who deal with the government.

Government is not the only business of Londinum, however. The planet is also home to some of the greatest collections of western art in the system. The Londinum Museum, which contains the Museum of History and the Museum of Art, is a splendid building that holds all manner of treasures. Most come from the early days of colonization, but the most valuable pieces are the ancient artifacts from Earth-That-Was.

As the center of Alliance control, Londinum has a strong military presence. The Alliance flagship, *Victoria*, patrols its space. The planet is home to the elite SAS (Special Alliance Support) troops. The Ministry of Intelligence also has its headquarters here.

Londinum is heavily restricted with "no fly" zones above and around government buildings. Any ship venturing near these areas is shot down, no warning given. Tourists arrive on Londinum via authorized shuttles that travel to and from the other Core worlds. Tourists may visit only those areas that are approved. Anyone caught venturing outside the approved areas without proper ID is immediately arrested.

OSIRIS

Osiris is the heart of the Alliance's judicial branch. Here the High Court hears important cases. Their decisions affect the interpretation of parliamentary law with repercussions throughout the system. The Court is housed in a large pyramid-shaped building (honoring the Egyptian god of the dead for whom the world was named) in Capital City. The most important law firms are also based here, linked to their branch offices on other worlds by the Cortex. The University of Osiris boasts the most prestigious law school in the Core, as well as a fine medical school.

The corporate offices of the Blue Sun Corporation are also on Osiris. Originally on Sihnon, they were recently moved into a massive structure that is attached to a combined manufacturing plant, distribution center, and spacedock. The Corporation complex is off-limits to everyone except employees. No one enters, even on business, without first undergoing a thorough background check. The very latest in security systems makes this complex nigh impossible to break into.

Landing on Osiris is restricted, though not as heavily as some planets (just so long as you don't go near Blue Sun). If you claim you need to see your lawyer, you'll usually be permitted to set down. University students and their parents are always welcome.

SIHNON

The world of Sihnon is known for its beauty. Words alone won't do the great city itself justice. At night, it is said to be an ocean of light.

Sihnon is the heart of the Buddhist religion, a fact made obvious by the many monasteries and temples located here. Those seeking to learn more about Buddhism travel here to study.

Sihnon is also the central hub for the guild system. The Companion's Guild is based here, with multiple houses in the large cities, and a massive temple dedicated to the schooling of young girls and boys.

All other guilds have headquarters on Sihnon or maintain a large presence here. Guild business takes place behind closed doors. Disputes are handled by registered arbitration houses. The city of Chang'Pei is given over completely to trade administration, making it the largest civil bureaucracy in the 'Verse.

The penalties for bribes, taking or giving, are harsh, but that doesn't stop some folk. Officers of the Sihnon Trade Commission work undercover to root out the worst offenders. The officers know that they cannot stop the corruption completely, but they work tirelessly to see that it doesn't get out of hand. These folk take their jobs seriously. They are well trained in combat and interrogation procedures, as well as espionage and accounting.

The capital of Sihnon is Lu'Weng. Local legend maintains that Lu'Weng was once a fire-breathing dragon that fell from the sky and was bound to the planet with silken ribbons. The numbers of hot springs here seem to bear this theory out, and every home traditionally has a silken awning or a curtain across the door to keep the dragon bound. Lu'Weng (the city) is one of the largest producers of silk in the system. Raw silk is farmed all over the planet and then sent to Lu'Weng, where it is refined and bolted or made into beautiful clothing that never falls out of favor with the rich throughout the system.

Landing on Sihnon is restricted, though there is so much traffic coming and going on this busy world that the government issues passes to those who come here on a frequent basis. Such passes aren't hard to get, nor are they hard to forge.

BORDER PLANETS

The Border planets are near enough to the central planets that they have business dealings with those on the Core. However, the Border planets are far enough away from the Core that the eyes of the Alliance can't always make out what's going on.

Thus, these planets are excellent locales for certain unscrupulous folk from the Core to conduct business dealings "in private." They don't have to move to these planets, thank God! (Though there are those eccentrics who travel here from the Core to "get away from it all"—the kind of people who build strong fortresses to keep out the riffraff and would never dream of socializing with the local yokels.) The irony is that these same folk are all in favor of the rules and regulations that govern business dealings throughout the system—just as long as those rules and regulations don't affect them.

To give the folk on these planets credit where credits are due, there are plenty on the Border worlds who are eager to do business with those on the Core. And there are always countless numbers without a silver in their pocket here looking for work.

Landing on Beaumonde and Persephone is supposedly regulated, but the traffic is so heavy that the harried Alliance officials who try to police it have mostly thrown up their hands in frustration and sometimes don't even bother to ask what your business is. (Perhaps they figure it's best they don't know!) Landing on Bellerophon is more difficult, since the world is basically off limits to all who don't own one of its elegant estates. Still, there are ways...

The Border planets are the best and worst of all possible worlds. Tall, elegant skyscrapers and magnificent mansions stare down their steel noses at cardboard hovels and crowded slums. You can buy anything on the Border planets, from someone to pick off your worst enemy to a pink ruffled dress that looks like a layer cake. (Just don't buy the "Good Dogs" from the vendor in the Eavesdown Docks. Not if you care that the sausage inside the bun was once actually a good little dog.)

BEAUMONDE

The heavily industrialized planet of Beaumonde is the manufacturing hub of the system. Its cities are surrounded by factories that produce everything from computer parts to ceramic coffee mugs. Some of the factories are owned by Blue Sun, though there are rumors that a few of these are not really factories at all or, if they are, that they're turning out something other than canned beans. Security is tight at all Blue Sun plants, so no one has ever been able to get inside one of these buildings to find out. Or

CHAPTER 7

least if they did, they never got back out to tell the tale.

Due to the high industrial output, pollution is a problem. Beaumonde's cities are covered in a perpetual haze. Weather control systems process the worst of the pollution, but the science-minded reckon the long-term effects may not be quite so simple to take care of. Every year more pollutants find their way into the water and the soil, causing all manner of difficulty for those who live off the land. Some people have moved their homes and businesses underground to escape the air pollution.

Once you get away from the cities and out into the countryside, the air quality improves a mite. Farmers and ranchers manage to make a good living. There is also a thriving spaceport on Beaumonde, much like the more famous port on Persephone.

New Dunsmuir is the capital of Beaumonde. The city is the only one on the planet that has no factories. Located on an ocean, New Dunsmuir is a popular tourist destination. Many wealthy factory owners make their homes here, as do those who work in the tourist industry. New Dunsmuir is a beautiful city with avenues of trees and carefully maintained flower gardens.

BELLEROPHON

Bellerophon is a world home to the private estates of the system's wealthiest folk. Anything they want is shipped in from off-world, so they have no need for shops or local color.

The estates themselves are each the size of a small town and float gracefully a mile above the clear waters of Bellerophon's oceans. Each estate is a self-contained world of its own. They all share a similar basic design and standardized amenities—such as a rubbish collection system.

The wealthy pay well for their privacy and the skies above Bellerophon are patrolled by both the Feds and private security companies. Visiting the estates is by invitation only. Those who come to work on the estates have to provide a damn good reason why they're here. (Fresh flowers anyone?) However, there is a lot of empty desert on this planet—a nice, quiet place to meet someone if you can sneak past the Feds.

BOROS

Ares, one of Boros' moons, is home to Iskellkian's primary military shipyards. It's no wonder then, that the planet is crawling with all manner of government agents and bureaucrats and military folk. Ares is restricted to Alliance personnel and Iskellian technicians. However, anyone who travels near to Boros can lay eyes on the Alliance cruisers being built in orbit around Ares. There are usually five cruisers in production at any one time,

since it takes roughly six years to complete one. A full battalion of Alliance troops is barracked here, as the moon is a target for terrorist attacks and corporate raiders seeking the newest technology. Few ever manage to penetrate this perimeter, as the Alliance is more vigilant here than anywhere outside the Core.

The planet Boros is not as industrialized as Beaumonde. It has a lot of prairie land where you find sprawling ranches and farms. Boros' cities have some factories that manufacture goods, though the products are meant mostly to be used on the planet. The major industry of Boros is scrap metal. Parts that didn't meet the Alliance's rigorous standards, castoffs, damaged parts, and plain old junk find their way from Ares to Boros. Smaller and less reputable tech-companies hoping to pick up the scraps of Alliance contracts keep outlets on Boros. Small wonder that folk see Boros as a good place to find parts for almost anything, often at a good price.

Better still, the planet has few landing restrictions. Ares is, of course, off-limits unless you can prove that you have a damn good reason to be there. Assuming the patrolling Alliance doesn't just shoot you first to be on the safe side.

HERA

Hera is a largely agricultural world, considered the breadbasket for the entire system. Food is grown, processed and packaged on Hera.

The planet is also the home of the infamous Serenity Valley, where the bloodiest battle of the war was fought. Lying midway between the Core and the outer planets on a major shipping lane, Hera was of great strategic importance during the war, making it an important staging ground for both sides. Taking Hera was a key to winning the war, and Serenity Valley became the turning point for the conflict.

The war devastated Serenity Valley. Seven years past, the valley is still blackened and charred by the fire storm that swept through it. The only landmark is a graveyard on the hills next to the valley. Over half a million men and women—Alliance and Independent alike—are buried here, each with his or her own small identical headstone. Some have names. Most don't.

The graveyard is located on the opposite side of the valley from the town of Serenity View. Families and friends of the fallen come to Hera to visit the graves, which bloom with flowers, photos and mementos. Even the unmarked graves have their share. Plenty of families never saw their children return, and many have picked an unnamed grave and honor it, hoping someone else is doing the same for their son or daughter.

Serenity graveyard is one of the most hallowed and sacred pieces of ground in all the 'Verse.

NEWHALL

Newhall is a newly-terraformed planet with large oceans. Stands to reason that water is the planet's primary commodity. Newhall's people live on small island chains or on floating stations on the oceans.

Newhall's water plants are always in need of workers, hence the Alliance's generous incentives for settlers who move here. Terraforming new worlds requires a lot of fresh water, and Newhall has water to spare. Processing the water and preparing it for shipping isn't an unproblematic job, though. The water needs to be collected, desalinated, purified, packaged, then loaded for transport.

Those of Newhall don't want to work the water plants can make a good living fishing. And there's always the tourist centers, for those who like to swim and cavort—or who want to tend to those who do.

PAQUIN

Known far and wide as the "gypsy planet," Paquin is home to more carnivals and sideshows, galleries and theatres than you could shake a cruiser-sized stick at. It also seems to be home to every con-artist and swindler in the system.

When it was being terraformed, Paquin was chosen to host a grand opera house. Paquin's unique atmosphere produces sunrises and sunsets the likes of which would lift even the burden of death, with colors ranging from purple to blue to red to orange. This stunning display provides a wonderful natural backdrop for the opera house, which is located on the shore overlooking a vast ocean.

As the new opera house brought theater lovers to the planet, more theatres were built to take advantage of the new trade. Paquin is the place to see all manner of entertainment from Noh theatre to experimental dance. Many new plays debut here, and those that become popular travel to the Core where they play for the elite. Artists and writers make Paquin their home to be "closer to the muse." Paquin is the artistic center of the Border worlds and rivals Sihnon in terms of culture (though the people of Sihnon will get all manner of indignant denying this!).

Like other worlds, Paquin has a dark side. Countless carnivals and sideshows dot the world, providing good honest entertainment for the prairie folk, featuring circus acts and magic shows, freaks and jugglers. But there are those carnies who exist purely to fleece their patrons of all their cash or use their bright lights as cover for even darker activities.

PERSEPHONE

Persephone is an interesting mix of people and cultures. The world's environment is much like Earth-That-Was: desert, rainforest, plains, tundra, and such. While not as heavily populated as the worlds of the Core, Persephone still seems a very big place to those from the Rim. Persephone has a tradition-oriented aristocracy, a small but thriving middle class, a fair share of the poor and desperate, and a shadowy underworld.

The Eavesdown Docks is the largest spaceport on Persephone. Even folk who think themselves hotshot pilots are confused now and again by its chaotic layout. (And woe to the new pilot trying to make his way to a dock for the first time!) Ships often touch down only a few yards from street vendors selling cheap goods to the crews and potential passengers. The docks are situated in the poor section of town (the nobles and other rich folk have their own private airfields), but it's just a short drive or a long walk to the business district—in which just about anything in the 'Verse can be bought for the right price.

The docks are home to several criminal "lords," who collect illegal salvage, move contraband off-world and have hundreds of other ways to make quick, if not Alliance-approved, easy cash. A good crew with a flyable ship could make good coin here, so long as their morals aren't overly high and they don't mind avoiding the Feds. Not far away is a famous racetrack that is home to a famous derby that brings in folk from throughout the system (not to mention the throngs of Cortex-viewers), offering a huge cash prizes to the winning horse.

Like the horses, the aristocracy of Persephone all lay claim to a pedigree. Then again, anyone with the right stack of coin can purchase his own lordship, what with its fancy sash and all. Noble families live on large estates, attending to business, dancing at opulent balls, playing golf or tennis, and settling matters of honor in formal duels.

Persephone is an impressive cross-section of humanity, which is just another way to say that it's a world with an over abundance of opportunity and danger.

SANTO

One of the great triumphs of terraforming is the planet Santo. The planet is picture-perfect, with clear blue seas, azure skies and ideal weather. Though it has a thriving agricultural base, Santo was once known for the tourists who thought it a paradise. The rich flocked to the planet as an exclusive vacation spot, and resort communities commanded every good view to be had.

The war ended Santo's glorious days as a destination for the rich and beautiful. Though the planet escaped destruction, no one from the Core worlds dared travel here while the fighting was about. Hotels and casinos were abandoned. Those that stayed open did so by finding other ways to attract customers. Brothels, strip clubs, and other ventures catering to less savory appetites opened up. Santos has become known as a "fun" place, no matter what pleasures you're into. After the war, casino owners found that they could avoid Alliance restrictions by operating in this out of the way place. The world became a Mecca for high rollers (and those who were not so high).

Santo's resorts are now beginning to recover. No longer a playground exclusively for the rich, Santos attracts a more middle-class crowd. Its resorts are still beautiful, its small towns picturesque, its casinos open twenty-four seven.

You'll have a good time here, but you might not want to bring the kiddies.

VERBENA

Verbana is a lush world of thick forests., making the land difficult to clear and farm, though several fruit-producers have done well with large orchards. The world was largely underdeveloped until the Alliance made it a centerpiece of its "rejuvenation after Unification" campaign. Government incentives funded new construction, including a factory to supply parts for military vehicles.

The factory seemed a promising start for Verbena, but that ended when a former Independent soldier-turned-terrorist bombed the factory, killing hundreds of people and destroying the structure. The bombing sent the world into an economic depression and—far worse—created an atmosphere of paranoia, fear, and hatred for Browncoats and the Independence movement. There were riots, lootings, burnings, as both sides lost their heads.

The Alliance has pledged to help the people of Verbena, but the appropriate legislation and resolutions are trapped in parliamentary committees. The world is low on the government's list of priorities. Some folk have fled, hoping to find a better life elsewhere. Many more would like to leave, but don't have the means, and so remain trapped.

A small security force is more or less permanently stationed on Verbena. While ostensibly there to guard against more terrorist action, it is really there to watch a restless population.

RIM PLANETS

Out on the farthest edges of the system, life can be quite challenging. The Rim worlds are the latest results of terraforming technology, only recently settled, and raw and untamed. The comforts of civilization common to the Core Worlds just aren't so here. Technology and power are far more expensive out on the outer worlds and moons, so folk have to make do without. People

ride horseback, farm with archaic tools, and resort to entertainment that doesn't require electricity or batteries to operate. While some folk dream of the luxuries available on the central planets, others enjoy the freedom of open air and hard toil. In their own way, they're as stuck-up as the Core-Worlders, looking down their noses at soft folk who've never dug a ditch or mucked a horse stall.

While the Alliance government has a presence on the Rim, its grip is more than a mite looser here than elsewhere. Folk can't count on help coming right away (or at all), so they are accustomed to taking care of themselves and their own. Frontier-folk are usually armed, ready to draw at a moment's notice. Children learn to aim by shooting cans off a fence post. The lack of government interference and monitoring has made the Rim a haven for outlaws, outcasts and shady business folk, as well as a middle class who started to feel like their own planets were getting too crowded for comfort. There is money to be made on the outer worlds, something plenty are just now figuring out.

Each world has a Governor, each moon a magistrate. As long as the general peace is kept and the proper reports are filed, such powerful figures may pretty much do as they please, least as far as the Alliance is concerned. Some government officials are good. Some not. Same here as most everywhere else in the 'Verse.

A citizen of the central planets who wakes up on a Rim world might think he's traveled backwards in time: people riding horses and shooting six guns. Yet, here and there, you can still find the technology of the 26th century, from Cortex access terminals to high-security bank vaults.

ATHENS

Located in the Burnham quadrant, Athens is a world known for rapidly changing weather and winds that blow constantly. Aside from that, the climate is relatively mild. Certain crops thrive here, and there's plenty of beautiful marble to be quarried and shipped off-world.

One of the few outer planets to fully support Unification, Athens was captured by the Independents. "Ownership" of the world changed hands several times during the course of the war. Finally, running low on manpower and weary of ground battles on this otherwise minor rock, the Alliance took to bombing the world's major cities to drive out the Browncoats. 'Cept for the piles of dead civilians and heaps more hurt and homeless that lost everything, the strategy worked.

Recently, the Alliance opened up the bombed-out cities for legal salvage operations. Licenses for these operations can be obtained from United Reclamation or (more slowly) from the Alliance.

Then again, these cities are so chaotic that it's not so hard for the unlicensed to sneak in and out.

The world's farmers were more fortunate than the city dwellers. Those dwelling in rural areas found it easier to scratch by during the war. It's taken time, but they're slowly reconnecting their ties to the rest of the 'Verse.

Athens has four moons, all terraformed and a lot nicer to live on than the planet they circle. Folk on the moons live by farming and ranching. Everyone keeps an eye out for Reavers, since undefended moons are easy prey for the nearby marauders. On Whitefall, the fourth moon, the threat of Reaver raiding parties has made the settlers over-protective and perhaps a bit paranoid.

There is also a rumor currently circulating that the Blue Sun corporation has a hidden factory or complex located in the mountains on one of the moons, though what they manufacture or why they would come here is anyone's guess.

BEYLIX

While the planet has many large farming communities, Beylix has the distinction of being the system's garbage dump (make that "reclamation and recycling center").

The scrap yards and refuse centers are managed by United Reclamation, which owns property all over Beylix. Soon after the company began to dump trash here, its agents reported that scavengers were coming to pick over the remains, since there was little to no security. It turned out that what was trash to people on the Core was treasure to the folk out on the Rim.

United responded by licensing junk dealers. Some entrepreneurs began selling rebuilt ships—everything from old Starfinders to out-of-service Fireflies. Others devised creative uses for scrap, either jury-rigging old technology into something useful or turning it into art and selling it back to the Core where it decorates office lobbies.

Beylix is a place to start a new life, as you can often find some old ship and the parts to get her flyin'. Beylix is also a good place to drop off smuggled goods. It's not as if the Alliance or the corporations want to pay any attention to this gorram heap of *feh wu*.

EZRA

A planet in the Georgia system, Ezra is currently in transition. Once Ezra was a relatively peaceful world known for farmers and ranchers. Then, near the end of the war, its governor died unexpectedly, throwing the planet in chaos. (Conspiracy theorists alternately blame either Alliance or Independent

assassins, but in truth the man choked on a piece of chicken.) The lieutenant governor was ill-equipped for the job. To make matters worse, thousands of war refugees and former soldiers from both sides were pouring into Ezra. Jobs got real scarce, the ranks of unemployed swelled, and the economy went belly up. Criminals flocked to Ezra as word spread of overwhelmed law enforcement and the potential to hide under the larger problems.

It was during this chaotic time that a crime lord, one Adelei Niska, moved his skyplex into Ezra's orbit and set himself up as the local power. Using some legitimate businesses as a front, he manages to avoid prosecution through the use of bribes, assassination, and the threat of his torture chambers.

The Alliance Parliament is currently considering what to do about the "Ezra situation." A new governor is needed, but he or she would have to confront Niska, and thus far there have been no candidates willing to take on that task.

Farming and ranching are still common pursuits. Ezra's business enterprises have at least provided jobs for some folk. The law of the gun is absolute on Ezra: if you can't defend yourself or what you've got, someone will take it from you. That rule applies to people as well as property, since many slavers come here to pick up a little extra cargo. Despite the risks, there is now work to be found on Ezra, though it may not be to everyone's liking.

GREENLEAF

The world has a large tropical belt, creating massive jungles and rainforests. Tropical plants provide a variety of life-saving drugs that cannot easily be synthesized in a laboratory. Major drug companies set up shop on Greenleaf, providing the bulk of work for the locals.

Some of Greenleaf's residents, seeing the enormous profits that were being made, began to make "clippings" of pharmaceutical plants and grow them privately to sell on the black market. The problem became so great that the drug companies began engineering new plant strains with traceable genetic tags, so that confiscated merchandise could be traced back to the origin point. The technique has not yet led to any major arrests, mostly because there are dozens of small cartels, and they are difficult to track down in the jungle.

The Alliance is aware of the drug-smuggling problem out of Greenleaf, and they are clamping down on enforcement. Landing is more restricted on Greenleaf than on other Rim worlds, though smugglers who know the jungle can always find ways to sneak through.

HAVEN

A small mining moon, Haven is home to an independent group of miners who laid claim to this rock and are not about to be shoved off it. The miners of Haven have not yet struck it rich, but they have seen enough signs to believe that they are close to a major haul (just what, they're not saying!).

Others in the 'Verse apparently think that Haven has something worthwhile beneath the surface. The Corone Consortium recently sent in spies to try to dig up information. The spies were caught and, after revealing the name of their employer, they were sent back—a little the worse for wear—carrying a message for the Consortium to stay the hell out of Haven.

Since then, the mining communities of Haven have pooled their resources to buy a large surface-to-air cannon which they have mounted near the edge of the largest mining town to discourage visitors.

HIGGINS' MOON

A man named Higgins was appointed magistrate of a small, unnamed moon. (There were rumors that he won his appointment in a card game.) At the time the moon was founded, it did not appear to have useful resources or much potential for agriculture. A few years later, it was discovered that some areas have a mineral-rich clay that can be harvested, chemically treated and kiln-fired into a ceramic that is ten times stronger than steel at half the weight. It formed a new industry: mud.

The company town of Canton was founded near the largest mud pits. Over two thousand workers, known as "Mudders," live in Canton and work for Magistrate Higgins. Many of these are slaves and indentured laborers (who probably will never be able to purchase their way out of debt). Higgins rules through intimidation and the use of force, and is hated by virtually everyone. The foreman and his prods enforce the company rules, either with long-term hard-labor, imprisonment, or hacking folk up and rolling them into the bog.

The Mudders of Canton sing songs of a hero who has twice defied the magistrate and sailed away: Jayne Cobb. The Hero of Canton, they say, will one day return to Higgins Moon and free them from oppression. The more likely way for conditions to improve will be the magistrate's son, Fess, who is quietly working to reverse some of his father's harshest policies.

JIANGYIN

Jiangyin is a small planet suitable for cattle ranching and foresting and little else. Jiangyin is dotted with small towns, where folk generally go about their business without much interference from the outside. Those who do come here from off-world usually have goods to sell to the ranchers and foresters.

Since the planet really has nothing of value, it is ignored by the Alliance, which doesn't even bother to patrol it. Jiangyin has no central government. Each town or village is left to govern itself. It is one of the most primitive and backward planets, its people in such desperate need that they are forced to steal what they can't acquire by lawful means—such as doctors to treat their sick.

The people of Jiangyin are a simple lot, especially those who live apart from what little civilization there is. These "hill folk" are superstitious and mostly uneducated, easy prey for unscrupulous leaders. A strong show of force is usually enough to intimidate them.

LILAC

Lilac was named by someone gullible enough to believe what the terraformers promised—a planet of perpetual springtime. As it turned out, Lilac is more like a planet of *ri shao gou shi bing*. A small crop moon, Lilac is plagued with heat and a serious lack of water. Most of the farmers wage a continual battle against the elements, and what crops they do bring in are generally self-sustaining. There are some locations on Lilac where the rain falls on a regular basis and the sun nurtures the crops, not fries them. Farmers lucky enough to have land here do very well for themselves.

To add insult to injury, Lilac is located on the edge of what has now become Reaver territory. The people of Lilac fear that it's just a matter of time before they're attacked. Several of the major land-holders have joined together to contract with a private security firm to protect their property and lives in case of Reaver attack. That private security firm has its payroll delivered to one of the local banks. Just in case you're interested in making a withdrawal.

MIRANDA

The planet Miranda is not listed in the Cortex nor is it found any history database. Miranda is rumored to be a Blackrock, a planet where a terraforming "event" killed the settlers and left the planet forever uninhabitable. Some folk might still be curious enough to pay Miranda a visit, maybe see if there might something left to salvage, were it not for the fact that it lies in the heart of Reaver territory.

REGINA

The mineral-rich planet of Regina is known for its massive mining operations. Over three-quarters of the population work in one part of mining industry or another. Most of the mines are run by the Corone Mining Consortium, although there are still a few local owners hanging on. Corone's workers are underpaid and their working conditions can be extremely dangerous. The miners of Regina take a stoic pride in their work and the suffering they endure. As if things were not hard enough, the ore-processors and atmospheric conditions of Regina have created conditions for a disease called Bowden's Malady, a degenerative affliction of the bone and muscles that leaves victims weak and in constant pain. While there is no cure, regular treatment with Pasceline-D halts the progression of the disease and makes life tolerable.

The Alliance sponsors regular shipments of the expensive drug to Regina. The drug is drop-shipped to central location and delivered by train to the individual mining towns. The people of the world are dependent on this government handout, though shipments are not as frequent as they should be.

SHADOW

Once it was said that the prairies of Shadow stretched out so far under such a clear sky that a man could see from here to God's plan. These days, all that is left is charred and blackened rock.

Shadow was known for its grain farms and cattle ranches. The planet was almost entirely rural, with small towns dotting the countryside. While it had a few impressive towns, there were no actual cities. Its people were hard workers and independent-minded. Shadow was one of the first worlds to stand against the aggression of the Alliance. Most of its young people volunteered to fight for Independence.

The aggressive bombing of Shadow during the war was meant to teach the Browncoats a lesson about the might of the Alliance. Instead, the bombing only hardened the resolve of those who fought and increased the Browncoats' hatred of their enemy. Those few from Shadow who survived this difficult time lost loved ones, their lives forever changed.

Shadow today is a ghost planet. No one lives there. No one can.

TRIUMPH

Triumph is a tiny moon in orbit around the Heinlein gas giant near edges of the system. With little to offer other than small areas suitable for farming, the moon became a refuge for folk who wanted nothing to do with modern life. The Triumph settlers live like the Amish of Earth-That-Was, using little in the way of advanced technology (though they do have the ability to contact the outside world if they are in need of aid).

The people follow their own customs. For example, in one town, the young girls are raised in a convent called the Maiden House. Trained to be subservient and to respond to a man's needs, girls are married off in trade—a form of currency for settlers who have little else to offer.

Thugs and bandits find the settlements easy pickings, since the people are pacifists. The thieves steal goods and rough up the locals. The people of Triumph sometimes arrange with bands of mercenaries to protect them.

ST. ALBANS

One of the coldest planets in the 'Verse, St Albans' terrain is almost entirely mountainous. What really makes St Albans a whole lot of unpleasant is the gorram weather, for it snows almost continually. The entire planet is covered in drifts, even during what some laughingly call summer.

The people here are a hardy folk. The principal work is mining the world's rich mineral deposits. The Consortium's not interested due to the harsh climate. The planet is divided into claims that the inhabitants prospect for whatever they can find. Theirs is a tough and lonely life, so the folk have developed a very strong community. If you offend one of them, you have offended all of them. The reverse is true, however: if you make one friend on St. Albans, the entire community will look out for you.

APPENDIX: GORRAM CHINESE

The movement to leave Earth-that-Was stands out as a remarkable event in human history, one in which cross-cultural cooperation helped to achieve what some thought was impossible. In the effort to find a new home for humanity, the primary powers of the era—the United States of America and China—worked together to create the necessary technology, manpower, and logistics for the largest migration of people ever known.

Once the exodus of mankind had begun, the close quarters and difficult survival conditions in space broke down traditional barriers of language and culture. After a full generation had lived and died in the massive convoy of ships slowly trudging from star to star, the average person was at least bi-lingual and had a very multicultural outlook. A person's ethnicity became far less importance than competence and character.

Thus many generations later, the children of Earth-That-Was don't think much back to the days of colonization, but continue the legacy by their almost universal fluency in both English and Chinese. Culture and language have both continued to evolve, with economics becoming a primary dividing line. It is easy to distinguish a person from the central planets from one born and raised out on the Rim. Slang and linguistic shortcuts are used on the frontier, though some have filtered back into the refined speech usually found on worlds of the Core.

ENGLISH AND CHINESE

Folks in the 'Verse speak English or Chinese, one or the other being the dominant tongues most everywhere. It pays to know at least a little of both if you plan to get very far. Of the central planets, Londinium is primarily English-speaking, while Sihnon stands out as a center of Chinese influence.

MUTT TONGUES

Hundreds of languages made the great leap from Earth-That-Was and most of them survive in pockets and ghettos on most worlds. Only rarely, however, will anyone encounter a community that speaks a non-dominant language exclusively.

CUSSIN'

Human beings have happily fouled the gift of language with whatever inventive, vindictive, and insulting expressions they can imagine. While the traditional English swear words have survived intact, a few additional crude cuss words have been added to the common man's vocabulary.

The basics include **Gorram** ("Run! It's the gorram law!"), **Ruttin'** ("It's gettin' too ruttin' hot in here."), and **Humped** ("He's got a gun on us. We're humped!"). Cursing in Chinese is considered more imaginative and expressive, and most everyone does it—at least when his mother has left the room.

FIGHTIN' WORDS

Some speech isn't cursing by traditional definition, but it will cause fists and bullets to fly just the same. Religion, politics, social class, and wealth are touchy subjects—as is mention of the Unification War.

Browncoat: Member of the Independent Factions, Independent veteran. Adopted early in the war by the Independent Factions, a brown coat has become indelibly linked to supporters of the Independents' cause. After the war's end, clothiers made good money dying brown coats blue or gray as folks wanted to forget the past and let the past forget them. Those that still "wear the brown" do it on purpose.

FRONTIER SLANG

In English, there are two predominant speech patterns. "Core Speech" is carefully used and grammatically correct. "Frontier Slang" sounds sloppy and quaint to Core speakers, who judge the speaker as poorly educated and low class. Those born outside the Core are more likely to have at least a little of the Frontier in their speech.

BASIC RIM WORLD SPEECH

• Truncate the "g" for "ing" words ("Schoolin'")
• Pepper with slang adjectives.
• Double negatives. ("It don't mean nothin' out here.")
• Using odd words and word forms in phrases.
• Use "don't" instead of "doesn't."
• Ain't.
• Odd Words: druther, yonder, dang, plumb, right smart.
• Prefixing on "-ing" ("a-runnin'").
• No –*ly* on adverbs. ("She described the plan real simple. That job's awful hard to do.")
• Subject and Verb don't match. ("We was goin' there. He got none of that.")

• Malformed verbs. ("He growed up real good. He come by here last night. I seen it with my own eyes. He done run off again.")

A FEW EXAMPLES

—"Looks like we got us some imminent violence."

—"We got no short of ugly ridin' in on us."

—"I'm just feeling kind of truthsome right now."

—"We're in some peril here."

—"We just need a small crew, them as feel the need to be free."

—"This here's a recipe for unpleasantness."

—"I'm shocked my own self."

—"We'll be there directly."

—"But she does have an oddness to her."

SLANG: FRONTIER LIFE

• **All-fired** — completely. ("Where'd she go gettin' all-fired jealous 'bout this?")

• **Awful, Dreadful, Mighty, Plumb, Powerful** – adjectives for emphasis. ("Gettin' awful crowded in my sky.")

• **Bang-up** – great. ("They did a bang-up job.")

• **Bughouse** – mental hospital.

• **Git** – go away.

• **Ornery** – Stubborn, not passive.

• **Peck** – a large amount.

• **Preacher** – anyone religious.

• **Shindig** – A party, usually with dancing.

• **Shiny** – good or valuable.

• **Size someone up** – judge how tough they are or what their intentions might be.

• **Tetchy** – sensitive or complaining.

• **Run afoul** – to get into trouble with.

SLANG: SPACEFARING

• **Atmo** – atmosphere, as in to "leave atmo."

• **The black** – space.

• **Clean your housing** – to give a thorough beating (as in a spaceship's engine housing).

• **Feds, Federals** – Members of the Alliance, its military, law enforcement, or functionaries.

• **Go to blackout** – shut down power on the ship to avoid detection.

• **On the drift** – in space without fuel unable to travel.

• **Reavers** – madmen who live on the edges of civilized space, flying dangerous ships and preying on other space vessels.

• **The Rim** – frontier planets, not the core.

• **The 'Verse** – inhabited space or the universe.

• **Being buzzed** – Sensors from another ship are actively sweeping you.

SLANG: UNDERWORLD

• **Doxy** – prostitute.

• **Drops** – illegal, addictive, narcotic drugs.

• **Second story job** – breaking and entering robbery.

• **Scratch** – valuables.

• **The goods** – loot.

• **Went south** – problems appeared, the plan fell apart.

• **Tonic** – amateur or illegal alcoholic drink.

• **Bushwhack** – ambush.

• **Footpad** – pickpocket thief in a town.

• **Hornswoggle** – to trick someone.

• **On the dodge** – wanted by the police.

SLANG: TECHNICAL

• **Advocate** – a lawyer.

• **Cortex** – wide-spread information network

• **Genseed** – Genetically engineered crop seeds used on freshly terraformed worlds.

• **Skyplex** – orbital city or space station.

• **Wave** – a communication: text, audio, video, or holographic.

CHINESE PHRASES

The Chinese that became one of the two primary tongues of the 'Verse was originally known as Mandarin—China's official language. Mandarin, or Pekingese, is a dialect once spoken in that country's northern part, primarily around the Beijing city. The other major Chinese dialect was Cantonese, spoken down south in the Canton Province. Way back in the Earth-That-Was days, the Chinese folk actually went through a bruhaha as to which of the two tongues to make official. Though no blood was shed far as we know, it was a verbal civil war. North *vs.* South fought with volleys of dead-waking hollers over the virtues of their respective cant.

Obviously in the end Mandarin won out. So instead of *yat zeu*, people shout *chui se* to tell folks to go to hell.

Chinese is a very different tongue than English, and is difficult to learn for those who don't pick it up in the earliest years. Traditional Chinese has four inflections, five if you count the fifth, "soft" one. You best enunciate each just right or you might have folk scratching their head, wondering why you're so upset about losing a shoe when you're really trying to alarm them of a man overboard.

We said traditional, because in the 26th century we go by New Chinese. Like English where new words constantly replace the old and nobody utters the Earth-That-Was slang, Chinese got a makeover too. The progression of humans into a bilingual community evolved the original language into a strip-downed version. The main languages, Chinese and English, each have certain subjects and ideas it can express more efficiently. Over time, folks figured out what they are and started replacing different parts of speech with whichever language that related their thoughts the best. A doctor in the 26th century wouldn't hope to explain *chi* flow in English, for instance, any more than a control station would give docking instructions in Chinese.

Words and phrases became further streamlined—curmudgeon sticklers would say "corrupted." But only those reared in true Old Chinese-speaking households would complain, and the accessibility made it much easier for lower-class folk of English-speaking heritage.

JUNG J'WOHN GUO HUA LIKE A TRUE SPACER

The above would read "Speaking Chinese Like a True Spacer" in English. In humanity's new home, a collective of humans is all able to swear in a 5,000+ year-old language — with a cowboy twang.

The following phrases can be tossed into whatever situation seems most appropriate—or not. These just scratch the surface of Chinese cursing possibilities. While even educated, refined folk swear every now and then, you're more likely to hear most of these phrases out of a free-boosting fringe rat.

A switch to those girls' backsides is just good enough: *Byen Dah Tah Muhn Dug Bay Jo Go Lai.*

Abracadabra-alakazam: *Tian-Ling-Ling, Di-Ling-Ling.*

Accusing someone of lying, a ridiculous notion, or talking out of the posterior: *Fuhn Pi*, literally "farting."

Agitate someone out of hiding: *Da Chow Jing Ser*, literally "beating the grass to startle the snake."

Alas, not good, what a mess, too bad: *Jao Gao*, literally "spoiled cake."

Alliance: *Nien Mohn.*

Are we clear?: *Dohn luh mah.*

Attributing an unfortunate longshot occurrence: *Yeh Lu Jwo Duo Luh Jwohn Whei Jian Guay*, literally "do enough nighttime travels and one will eventually see a ghost"; also a warning of future retribution.

Awesome or extraordinarily clever: *Gao Guhn*, literally "high pole."

Baboon's ass crack: *Feh Feh Pi Goh.*

Bastard, jerk: *Huen Dahn*, literally "rotten egg."

Big boss or operator of a business: *Lao Buhn*; *Lao Buhn Ni'un* for female boss or proprietor's wife. Also informal appellation for acquaintants.

Big brother: *Ghuh* or *Ghuh-Ghuh*, the former is more intimate and connotes blood relation.

Big stupid pile of stinking meat: *Yi Dwei Da Buen Chuo Roh.*

Big sister: *Jei* or *Jei-Jei.*

Blindside or conspire against someone secretly: *Fahn Leong Jian*, literally "shoot a cold arrow."

Bottoms up: *Gon Beh*, literally "dry cup."

Brilliant: *Jing Chai.*

Browncoat (slang for soldiers of Independent): *Jone Yee.*

Cheap floozy: *Jien Huo.*

Check at once: *Ma Shong Jien Cha.*

Cheering or urging someone on: *Jah Yoh*, literally "add fuel," equivalent of "go (name)!" in English.

Chinese/Mandarin language: *Jwohn Guo Hua.*

Cool: *Ku.*

Commit blunder of great magnitude: *Bie Woo Lohng.*

Complete disarray or sheer pandemonium: *Tian Fuhn Di Fu*, literally "sky tumbles while earth turns over."

Completely useless: *Tian Di Wu Yohn.*

Congratulations: *Gohn Shi.*

Conniving or scheming person: *Guay Toh Guay Nown*, literally "ghost head and ghost brain."

Crazy dog in love with its own feces: *Ai Chr Jze Se Duh Fohn Diang Gho.*

Cursing: *Ma Jung Hwa*, literally "chastise with dirty words."

Cute: *Kuh Ai.*

Damn or damn it: *Ta Ma Duh*, literally "his mother's..."

Dangerous person or animal: *Wei Shian Dohn Woo.*

Daydream or wishful thinking: *Bai Lih Mohn.*

Deserving of bad consequence or fate: *Hwo Gai.*

Despicable: *Kuh Wu.*

Do something for nothing in return, or wasted endeavor without a payoff: *Yee Yan*, literally "a charity show."

Done for or imminent doom: *Wong Dahn*, literally "finished (cooked) egg."

Dumbass: *Chwen*, descriptive, literally "retarded"

Earthshaking: *Jing Tian Dwohn Di*, literally "startle the sky and shake the earth."

Engage a monkey in feces-hurling contest: *G'en Ho Tze Bi Dio se.*

Enough of this nonsense: *Go Hwong Tong.*

Everything under the sky: *Tian Shia*, can be used to allude to the world or universe.

Excrement: *Mi Tian Gohn*, slang, derives from the fact that when you stack the three characters — "mi" (rice), "tian" (paddy), and "gohn" (public or mutual) — from top to bottom in that order, they form the ideograph for excrement.

Explosive diarrhea of an elephant: *Da Shiong La Se La Ch'wohn Tian.*

Fear nothing but (fill in the blank): *Tian Bu Pa, Di Bu Pa, Tze Pa. . .*

Fellow: *Ja Hwo,* also slang for weapon.

Female companion or girlfriend: *Ma Tze,* a somewhat derogatory slang; add *Dow* in front for "looking to get a girlfriend."

Filthy fornicators of livestock: *Ung Jeong Jia Ching Jien Soh.*

Fire!: *Kai Huo* (as in shooting), *Fuhn Huo* (as in starting).

Fire at will or terminate with extreme prejudice: *Da Kai Sa Jeh,* meaning "breaking the Buddhist vow against killing."

Flat-chested: Hur Bao Duhn, slang, literally "eggs cooked sunny side-up."

Foiled or ruined at the last moment: *Soh Ya Feh Tian,* expression, literally, "a cooked duck flies away."

Fool: *Sah Gwa,* literally "stupid melonhead."

Friend, pal, buddy: *Puhn Yoh.*

Gang, crew, or confederate of diehards: *Se Duhng.*

Gang or faction leader: *Da Gher Da* for male, *Da Jeh Da* for female, slang.

Garbage: *Luh Suh.*

Get bold or audacious: *Fahn Dahn,* literally "release courage."

Get lost: *Kwai Jio Kai.*

Go all out, hold nothing back: *Ping Ming,* literally "fight for one's life."

Go to hell: *Chui Se,* literally "go die."

Good or okay: *How.*

Good journey or bon voyage: *Yi Lu Shwen Fohn.*

Good luck: *Joo How Rin.*

Greetings: *Ni How.*

Handsome: *Shwie.*

Happy development or fortuitous turn of event: *How Shi Sung Chung,* literally "a good show's about to start," can be used sarcastically.

Have desires above one's social/financial position, or beyond one's ability to realize: *Lai Huh Moh Sheong Tze Tian Uh Zoh,* literally "for a toad to think of eating a swan."

He or she: *Tah, tah-duh* for his or hers, *tah-muhn* for them, *tah-muhn-duh* for theirs.

Homewrecking tramp: *Hu Li Jing,* literally "fox spirit."

Hump: *Gun.*

Hurry, speed up: *Guhn Kwai.*

I or me: *Wuo, wuo-duh* for mine.

I don't believe my eyes!: *Wo Bu Shin Wo Dah Yan Jing.*

I neither see nor hear you: *Wuo Dwei Nee Boo Ting Boo Jen.*

Idiot, moron: *Buhn Dahn,* literally "stupid egg," or *Chwen Joo,* literally "retarded pig."

Impossible: *Bu Kuh Nuhn.*

Impressive display or visage but no substance: *Da Chung Wu Dahn,* literally "big gun, no bullet."

In someone's doghouse: *Luhn Gohn,* literally "a cold palace," which is where an emperor confines those concubines who have fallen out of favor.

In that case, never mind: *Nah Mei Guan Shee.*

Junk: *Feh Wu.*

Leader of a criminal operation: *Ser Toh,* literally "snakehead," derogatory.

Leave one to his own fate: *Tze Sh'un Tze Mieh.*

Let me repeat myself: *Wuo Jai Jeong Yi Chi.*

Life support failure: *Shuhn Ming Shi T'wohn Gu Jong.*

Like hell: *Jien Ta Duh Guay,* literally "see his ghost."

Little brother: *Di* or *Di-Di.*

Little sister: *Mei* or *Mei-Mei.*

Long time no see: *How Joh Bu Jian.*

Male companion or boyfriend: *Kai Tze,* also a somewhat derogatory slang.

Manipulate, or playing somebody for a fool: *Swa.*

Merciful Buddha protect us: *Rung Tse Fwo Tzoo Bao Yo Wuo Muhn.*

Merciful God, please take me away: *Rung Tse Song Di Ching Dai Wuo Tzo.*

Merciless bastard: *Lurn Shwei Jah Jwohn,* literally "cold-blooded mixed breed."

Merciless hell: *Ai Yah Tien Ah.*

Mind your own business: *Gwon Ni Tze Jee Duh Shr.*

Miss: *Shao Jeh,* literally "little lady." Follows a name when addressing a known person, so River would be addressed as Tam River *shao jeh,* or simply Tam *shao jeh.*

Mister: *Shian Shen,* literally "born before me," also follows a person's name.

Monkey raping: *Cheong Bao Ho Tze.*

Motherless goat of all motherless goats: *Mei Yong Ma Duh Tse Gu Yong.*

Muddled, mixed-up, confused: *Wu Toh Wu Now,* literally "without a head or a brain."

No problem: *Mei Wen Ti.*

Not advised: *Jwohn Gao Bu Yi.*

Not enough: *Bu Goh,* or *Hai Bu Goh* for "not enough yet."

Not keeping a rendezvous: *Fahn Gher Tze,* literally "release a pigeon" but insinuating not picking up the bird at the destination.

Now, immediately: *Ma Shong.*

Nuts: *Shiang Jing Ping* or just *Shiang Jing, Fah Shiang Jing* for "going nuts."

Oddball or a goof: *Chai Neow.*

Of course: *Duhn Ruhn*.

Oh my God: *Wuo Duh Tian Ah*.

Old: *Lao*.

Old man/husband: *Lao Gohn*.

Old lady/wife: *Lao Puo*.

One must be ruthless to be a great: *Wu Du Bu Juhn Fu*, literally "a person without poison is not a great man."

Outdo someone or doing one better: *Dao-Gao-Yee-Chi Moh-Gao-Yee-Juhn*, expression, literally "the solution advances a yard, the problem advances a mile."

Pal: *Lao Sheong* if addree's older, *Lao Di* if younger; used for men only. *P'n Yoh* for "friend."

Pathetic wretch: *Bei Bi Shiou Ren*, literally "shameless dirty little person"

Peon, small fry, a nobody: *Wu Ming Shao Jwu*, literally "nameless little foot soldier."

Prehistoric: *Lao Deow Ya*, literally "so old as to lose all teeth"

Pig's Sty: *Joo Fuen Chse*.

Pile of sun-baked dog poo: *Ri shao gou shi bing*.

Plain, bland, bare: *Yong Chwen Mien*, slang taken from the namesake generic, flavorless noodle dish.

Please be quiet: *Ching Ahn Jing Yi Dien*.

Pool of excrement: *F'n Zse*, can be used in an expression for "deep crap."

Pool of pig droppings: *Joo Fuen Chse*.

Posterior: *Pi Gu*.

Precious, darling, sweetheart: *Bao Bei*.

Real man: *Nuhn Tze Huhn*.

Really dangerous: *Wei Shan*, more poetic, *Wo Hu Chung Long*, which is "crouching tiger, hidden dragon," an expression for something dangerous.

Redundant, unnecessary complicating something: *Wua Ser Tian Jwoo*, literally "draw a snake and add feet to it."

Retreat, run away: *Jio Weh Sung Chiuh*, phrase summarizing the last of the Chinese "36 Stratagems," which extols the virtue of fleeing to fight another day.

Ridiculously stange, illogical or nonsensical: *Mo Min Chi Meow*, literally "not understanding the pecularity."

Ruined, finished: *Wan Duhn Luh*.

Ruthless or savage beast of a person: *Ching Soh*.

Screw him/her running: *Gun Ta Jwo Lu*.

Screw you: *Chwee Ni Duh*.

Shameless Hussy: *Meh Lien Duh Jyah Jee*, literally "faceless bastard prostitute."

Shiny, awesome, fantastic: *Jahn*!

Shut up: *Bi Jweh*.

Shut up and make us wealthy: *Bi Jweh, Lung Wuo Mun fah tsai*.

Sir: *Da Yeh*. When used as a nobility, *Nuhn Jwei*, following the name.

So guilty as to deserve a thousand deaths: *Jwei Gai Won Se*.

Son of a bitch: *Wong Ba Duhn*, or *Go Neong Yung Duh* for a more literal and vicious translation.

Speak now and quickly: *Yo Hua Kwai Suo*.

Speaking without a clue: *Shiah Hwa*, literally "blind talk."

Stop talking: *Joo Koh*.

Stupid son of a drooling whore and monkey: *Lio Coh Jwei Ji Neong Hur Ho Deh Yung Duh Buhn Jah J'wohn*.

Swindle: *Gwai*.

Suicidal idea: *Tze sah ju yi*.

Surrender, give up: *Toh Shung*.

Take care, stay healthy: *Bao Jone*, literally "maintain weight."

Talk nonsense: *Shia Suo*.

Thanks: *Sheh Sheh*.

There's nothing in this plan that isn't horrific: *Juh Guh Jee Hua Juhn Kuh Pah*!

Things never go smooth: *How W'rin Bu Lai*, *Whai W'rin Bu Jwo*, literally "good luck don't come, bad luck don't leave."

To throw in a monkeywrench: *Gwai Ma Jeow*, literally "twist a horse's legs (while it's galloping)."

Trouble, problem, complication: *Ma Fuhn*.

Tyrant, iron-fisted ruler: *Ba Wong*.

Ugly or perverted person: *Joo Bah Jeh*, insult taken from the name of the hoggish, lecherous character in the popular Chinese folktale, "Journey to the West."

Understand: *Dohn*, *dohn-ma* for "understand?" *dohn-luh-mah* for "are we clear here?"

Very: *Feh Chun*.

Wait/hold on a second: *D'un Yi Shia*.

Warning someone against doing things "the hard way": *Jin Joh Bu Chi Chi Fah Joh*, literally "choosing to sip the wine of penalty over that of respect."

We, us: *Wuo Mun*, *Wuo Mun Duh* for ours.

We will enjoy your silence now: *Bai Tuo, Uhn Jin Yee Dien*.

What: *Shuh Muh*?

What the hell is this crap: *Juh Shi Suh Mo Go Dohng Shee*?

You: *Ni*, *ni-duh* for yours, *ni-muhn* for plural, *ni-muhn-duh* for plural possessive.

You don't deserve it: *Ni Bu Ying Duh Jur Guh*.

You wanna bullet right in your throat?: *Nee Yow Wuo Kai Chiung*?

You wanna die?: *Nee Tzao Se Mah*?

Young one: *Nyen Ching Duh*, or *Yo Chr*, slang for underaged (literally "infant teeth.)

Water: *Swei*.

角色大名 CHARACTER NAME: _____
绰號 NICKNAME:
玩家名稱 PLAYER NAME: _____
家界 HOME WORLD: _____
角色概念 CONCEPT:

特質 ATTRIBUTES

- STRENGTH
- AGILITY
- VITALITY
- ALERTNESS
- INTELLIGENCE
- WILLPOWER

轉特徵 DERIVED TRAITS

- LIFE POINTS
- INITIATIVE
- ENDURANCE
- RESISTANCE

規則援助 RULE HELPER

MOVEMENT [feet]:

ACTIONS 0 = 15 • ACTIONS 1 = 30
ACTIONS 2 = 30 + [Agl+Athletics/Running]

ACTION DIFFICULTY

Action	Diff	Extraordinary
EASY	3	10
AVERAGE	7	14
HARD	11	18
FORMIDABLE	15	22
HEROIC	19	26
INCREDIBLE	23	30
RIDICULOUS	27	34
IMPOSSIBLE	31	38

SKILL COMPETENCY

D2	INCOMPETENT
D4	NOVICE
D6	COMPETENT
D8	EXPERT
D10	PROFESSIONAL
D12	MASTER
D12+	SUPREME

提進 ADVANCEMENT

- PLOT POINTS
- CHAR GEN PT.
- UNUSED ADV PT.
- TOTAL ADV PT.

命分 LIFE POINTS

技能 SKILLS AND SPECIALTIES

ANIMAL HANDLING	MEDICAL EXPERTISE
ARTISTRY	MELEE WEAPON CMBT.
ATHLETICS	PERCEPTION
COVERT	PERFORMANCE
CRAFT	PILOT*
DISCIPLINE	PLANETARY VEHICLES
GUNS	RANGED WEAPONS
HEAVY WEAPONS	SCIENTIFIC EXPERTISE*
INFLUENCE	SURVIVAL
KNOWLEDGE	TECHNICAL ENG.*
MECHANICAL ENG.*	UNARMED COMBAT
LINGUIST*	

SERENITY ROLE PLAYING GAME

裝備 EQUIPMENT

盔甲 ARMOR

TYPE _____
AR _____
COVERS _____
PENALTY _____

武器 WEAPONRY

TYPE _____
DMG _____ RANGE _____
ROF _____ AMMO _____

TYPE _____
DMG _____ RANGE _____
ROF _____ AMMO _____

TYPE _____
DMG _____ RANGE _____
ROF _____ AMMO _____

麻煩 COMPLICATIONS

☐ MINOR ☐ MAJOR

☐ MINOR ☐ MAJOR

☐ MINOR ☐ MAJOR

☐ MINOR ☐ MAJOR

☐ MINOR ☐ MAJOR

☐ MINOR ☐ MAJOR

☐ MINOR ☐ MAJOR

☐ MINOR ☐ MAJOR

長處 ASSETS

☐ MINOR ☐ MAJOR

☐ MINOR ☐ MAJOR

☐ MINOR ☐ MAJOR

☐ MINOR ☐ MAJOR

☐ MINOR ☐ MAJOR

☐ MINOR ☐ MAJOR

☐ MINOR ☐ MAJOR

☐ MINOR ☐ MAJOR

劇分 DICE STEPS AND PLOT POINTS

1	2	3	4	5	6	7	8	9	10	11	12
D2	D4	D6	D8	D10	D12	D12 +D2	D12 +D4	D12 +D6	D12 +D8	D12 +D10	D12 +D12

INDEX